URBANIZATION, POLICING, and SECURITY

GLOBAL PERSPECTIVES

International Police Executive Symposium Co-Publications

Dilip K. Das, *Founding President-IPES*

**Global Trafficking in Women
and Children**
By Obi N.I. Ebbe and Dilip K. Das
ISBN: 978-1-4200-5943-4

**Contemporary Issues in Law
Enforcement and Policing**
By Andrew Millie and Dilip K. Das
ISBN: 978-1-4200-7215-0

**Trends in Policing: Interviews with
Police Leaders Across the Globe,
Volume Two**
By Dilip K. Das and Otwin Marenin
ISBN: 978-1-4200-7520-5

**Criminal Abuse of Women
and Children:
An International Perspective**
By Obi N.I. Ebbe and Dilip K. Das
ISBN: 978-1-4200-8803-8

**Urbanization, Policing,
and Security:
Global Perspectives**
By Gary Cordner,
AnnMarie Cordner and Dilip K. Das,
ISBN: 978-1-4200-8557-0

Global Environment of Policing
By Dilip K. Das, Darren Palmer,
and Anthony L. Sciarabba
ISBN: 978-1-4200-6590-9

**Trends in Policing: Interviews with
Police Leaders Across the Globe,
Volume Three**
By Dilip K. Das and Otwin Marenin
ISBN: 978-1-4398-1924-1

**Police Without Borders:
The Fading Distinction between
Local and Global**
By Cliff Roberson and Dilip K. Das
ISBN: 978-1-4398-0501-5

**Terrorism, Counterterrorism,
and Internal Wars:
Examining International
Political Violence**
By Austin Turk, Dilip K. Das,
and James Ross
ISBN: 978-1-4398-2104-6

**Effective Crime
Reduction Strategies:
International Perspectives**
By James F. Albrecht and Dilip K. Das
ISBN: 978-1-4200-7838-1

**Strategies and
Responses to Crime:
Thinking Locally,
Acting Globally**
By Dilip K. Das, Mintie Das,
and Larry French
ISBN: 978-1-4200-7669-1

**Justices of the World:
Their Views, Opinions
and Perspectives**
by Cliff Roberson and Dilip K. Das
ISBN: 978-1-4200-9978-2

**Cross Cultural Profiles
of Policing**
By Dilip K. Das and Osman Dolu
ISBN: 978-1-4200-7014-9

URBANIZATION, POLICING, and SECURITY

GLOBAL PERSPECTIVES

Edited by
Gary Cordner
AnnMarie Cordner
Dilip K. Das

CRC Press is an imprint of the
Taylor & Francis Group, an **informa** business

CRC Press
Taylor & Francis Group
6000 Broken Sound Parkway NW, Suite 300
Boca Raton, FL 33487-2742

© 2010 by Taylor and Francis Group, LLC
CRC Press is an imprint of Taylor & Francis Group, an Informa business

No claim to original U.S. Government works

Printed in the United States of America on acid-free paper
10 9 8 7 6 5 4 3 2 1

International Standard Book Number: 978-1-4200-8557-0 (Hardback)

Library of Congress Cataloging-in-Publication Data

Urbanization, policing, and security : global perspectives / edited by Gary Cordner, AnnMarie Cordner, Dilip K. Das.
    p. cm.
Includes bibliographical references and index.
ISBN-13: 978-1-4200-8557-0
ISBN-10: 1-4200-8557-3
    1. Urbanization. 2. Community policing. 3. Security, International. I. Cordner, Gary W. II. Cordner, AnnMarie. III. Das, Dilip K., 1941- IV. Title.

HT361.U727 2010
363.209173'2--dc22   2009018491

Visit the Taylor & Francis Web site at
http://www.taylorandfrancis.com

and the CRC Press Web site at
http://www.crcpress.com

To Dubai Police

Contents

SECTION III: PRIVATE SECURITY RESPONSES

Editors

Gary Cordner is professor of criminal justice at Kutztown University of Pennsylvania and commissioner with the Commission on Accreditation for Law Enforcement Agencies. Previously he served as professor and dean at Eastern Kentucky University, director of the Kentucky Regional Community Policing Institute, president of the Academy of Criminal Justice Sciences, and editor of the *American Journal of Police* and *Police Quarterly*. He worked as a police officer and police chief in Maryland and received his PhD from Michigan State University. He served as the program coordinator for the 2007 International Police Executive Symposium conference in Dubai, where most of the chapters in this book were presented.

AnnMarie Cordner is assistant professor of criminal justice at Kutztown University of Pennsylvania. She previously taught full-time at Temple and Niagara Universities, as well as part time at Eastern Kentucky University. She worked as a criminal justice planner for the Kentucky Criminal Justice Council and was research director for the Kentucky Statistical Analysis Center. She has published works on various topics, including capital punishment, comparative criminal justice education, and law-enforcement technology, and is currently researching hate crime and rural criminal justice. She received her PhD in criminology and criminal justice from the University of Maryland.

Dilip K. Das is the founding president of the International Police Executive Symposium and founding editor of *Police Practice and Research: An International Journal*. After obtaining his master's degree in English literature, he joined the Indian Police Service, an elite national service with a glorious tradition. After 14 years in the service as a police executive including Chief of Police, he moved to the United States where he achieved another master's degree and a doctorate in criminal justice. Dr. Das has authored, edited, and coedited more than 30 books and numerous articles, extensively traveled throughout the world conducting comparative police research, served as a visiting professor in various universities; organized annual conferences of the International Police Executive Symposium, and served as a human rights consultant to the United Nations.

Contributors

Amos Oyesoji Aremu
University of Ibadan
Ibadan, Nigeria

David K. Chiabi
New Jersey City University
Jersey City, New Jersey

AnnMarie Cordner
Kutztown University of Pennsylvania
Kutztown, Pennsylvania

Gary Cordner
Department of Criminal Justice
Kutztown University of Pennsylvania
Kutztown, Pennsylvania

Orkhan Dadashov
Executive Administration of the
    President of the Azerbaijan
    Republic
Baku, Azerbaijan

Dilip K. Das
International Police
    Executive Symposium
Guilderland, New York

Julia Davidson
Kingston University
London, United Kingdom

Michael Doyle
Cleveland Police Division
Cleveland, Ohio

Fasihuddin
Northwest Frontier Province
Police Service of Pakistan
Peshawar, Pakistan

Patricia L. Gatling
New York City Commission on
    Human Rights
New York, New York

Yakov Gilinskiy
St. Petersburg Juridical Institute of the
    Academy of the General Prosecutor's
    Office of the Russian Federation
St. Petersburg, Russia

Fazil Guliyev
Ministry of Internal Affairs of Azerbaijan
Baku, Azerbaijan

Želimir Kešetović
Faculty of Security Studies
Belgrade, Serbia

Ines Klinkon
University of Ljubljana
Ljubljana, Slovenia

Velibor Lalić
Defendology Center for Security,
    Sociology and Criminological Research
Banja Luka, Bosnia and Herzegovina

Elena Martellozzo
University of Kingston and
    University of Westminster
London, United Kingdom

Darko Maver
University of Maribor
Maribor, Slovenia

Elizabeth H. McConnell
University of Houston–Clear Lake
Houston, Texas

Gorazd Meško
University of Maribor
Maribor, Slovenia

Benjamin Namanya
Uganda Police Force
Kampala, Uganda

Christine Nixon
Victoria Police
Melbourne, Victoria, Australia

Uros Pena
Republic of Srpska Police
Banja Luka, Bosnia and
    Herzegovina

Chantal Perras
University of Montreal
Montreal, Canada

Emil W. Pływaczewski
University of Bialystok
Bialystok, Poland

Wiesław Pływaczewski
University of Warmia and Mazury
Olsztyn, Poland
and
Higher School of Police Training
Szczytno, Poland

P. J. Potgieter
University of Zululand
KwaDlangezwa, South Africa

Johan Ras
University of Zululand
KwaDlangezwa, South Africa

C. J. Roelofse
University of Venda
Thohoyandou, South Africa

Gary R. Scheibe
Houston Police Department
Houston, Texas

Mile Šikman
University of Banja Luka
Banja Luka, Bosnia and Herzegovina

Branislav Simonovic
University of Kragujevac
Kragujevac, Republic of Serbia

Carmen Lee Solis
John Jay College of Criminal Justice
City University of New York
New York, New York

Adki Surender
Department of Public Administration
Osmania University
Hyderabad, India

Kathleen M. Sweet
Risk Management Security Group
Lafayette, Indiana

Duško Vejnović
University of Banja Luka
Bosnia and Herzegovina

Alex S. Vitale
Brooklyn College
Brooklyn, New York

Margaret York
Los Angeles County Police
Los Angeles, California

Introduction: Policing and Urbanization

1

GARY CORDNER, ANNMARIE CORDNER,
and DILIP K. DAS

Contents

The origin of this book was during the 14th annual International Police Executive Symposium (IPES) held in Dubai on April 8–12, 2007 with the theme "Urbanization and Security." This theme was especially significant for Dubai, which is one of the United Arab Emirates. Dubai had a largely rural population of less than 200,000 people as recently as 1970, but has become a modern city-state with a population of well over 1 million people in the twenty-first century. Moreover, Dubai is still growing and has attracted a substantial expatriate and foreign worker population. Rapid growth and the changing nature of the population naturally give rise to security concerns, although it seems that Dubai has remained remarkably safe thus far (Abdullah, 2007).

The IPES Dubai conference was generously and graciously hosted by the Dubai Police. The conference was attended by 175 police executives and police researchers from 40 countries. The conference program included two featured sessions and 17 panels, for a total of 68 papers and presentations. From that wealth of knowledge and experience, a subset of the papers that most closely coincided with the "Urbanization and Security" theme was selected for this book. The authors of those papers then had the opportunity to polish and update their manuscripts for inclusion herein.

IPES has held conferences around the world, bringing together police practitioners and police scholars, since 1994. Many of the IPES conferences have produced books like this one, helping to develop the international

1

literature and knowledge base about world policing. More information about the remarkable (and continuing) IPES story can be found at the back of this volume.

Urbanization

Our world is becoming more urbanized. According to estimates developed by the United Nations (2008, pp. 3–4), the proportion of the world's population living in urban areas increased from 29% in 1950 to 49% in 2007, with a projection to 57% in 2025. In raw numbers, world urban dwellers have increased from 740 million in 1950 to almost 3.3 billion in 2007, a more than fourfold increase. During the period 2007–2025, the world's urban population is expected to increase by almost 2% per year, while world rural population will be nearly flat.

Table 1.1 looks at urbanization by country, focusing on a sample of countries (those represented in this book). The table shows the percentage of

Table 1.1   Urbanization in 1950 and 2005 in 17 Countries (Percentage of Population Living in Urban Areas)

Country	1950 (%)	2005 (%)	Relative Change (%)
Uganda	2.8	12.5	+346
Cameroon	9.3	54.3	+484
Nigeria	10.2	46.2	+353
Bosnia and Herzegovina	13.7	45.7	+234
India	17.0	28.7	+69
Pakistan	17.5	34.9	+99
Slovenia	19.9	49.5	+149
Serbia	20.3	51.5	+154
Poland	38.3	61.5	+61
South Africa	42.2	59.3	+41
Azerbaijan	42.5	51.5	+21
Russia	44.2	72.9	+65
United Arab Emirates	54.5	77.7	+43
Canada	60.9	80.1	+32
United States	64.2	80.8	+26
Australia	77.0	88.2	+15
United Kingdom	79.0	89.7	+14

Source: United Nations. (2008). *World Urbanization Prospects: The 2007 Revision.* New York: United Nations Department of Economic and Social Affairs, pp. 74–83. On-line at http://www.un.org/esa/population/publications/wup2007/2007WUP_Highlights_web.pdf

each country's population that was living in urban areas back in 1950, and then more recently in 2005. The urban proportion of the population increased in every single country in the table. The greatest relative increases were in Cameroon, Nigeria, Uganda, Bosnia and Herzegovina, Serbia, and Slovenia—countries that had relatively low levels of urban population in 1950. As of 2005, the least urban countries (with the lowest proportions of urban population) were Uganda, India, and Pakistan, while the most urban were the United Kingdom, Australia, the United States, and Canada.

Urbanization is related to population density, but it is not the same thing when examined country by country. Australia provides a good example. As noted in Table 1.1, it is highly urbanized, with 88% of its population residing in urban areas. However, Australia is also a very large country in land mass. Consequently, even with 20 million people, it has one of the lowest population densities of all countries, ranking 187 out of 192 (World Atlas, 2006). Table 1.2 presents the population densities of the countries reported on in this book: India, the United Kingdom, and Pakistan have the highest population densities, while Australia, Canada, and Russia have the lowest.

Another way to look at changes in urbanization over time is to focus on major world cities. Table 1.3 shows the world's ten largest "urban agglomerations" in 1950 and then again in 2005. One thing to notice is that cities are

Table 1.2   Population Density in 2006 in 17 Countries (Per Square Mile)

Country	Population (Thousands)	Land Area (Thousand Square Miles)	Population Density
Australia	20,090	2,968	7.0
Canada	32,805	3,852	9.0
Russia	143,420	6,593	21.8
United States	295,734	3,718	79.6
United Arab Emirates	2,563	32	80.1
Cameroon	16,380	184	89.2
South Africa	44,344	471	94.2
Bosnia and Herzegovina	4,026	20	203.9
Azerbaijan	7,912	33	236.6
Slovenia	2,011	8	256.9
Serbia	10,829	40	274.0
Uganda	27,270	91	299.2
Poland	38,635	121	320.0
Nigeria	128,772	357	361.0
Pakistan	162,420	310	523.3
United Kingdom	60,441	95	639.4
India	1,080,264	1,269	851.0

Source: World Atlas. (2006). Countries of the World by Highest Population Density. On-line at http://www.worldatlas.com/aatlas/populations/ctydensityh.htm

Table 1.3 World's 10 Largest Urban Agglomerations in 1950 and 2005 (Population in Millions)

1950		2005	
City	Population	City	Population
New York, U.S.	12,338	Tokyo, Japan	35,327
Tokyo, Japan	11,275	Mexico City, Mexico	18,735
London, U.K.	8,361	New York, U.S.	18,732
Paris, France	6,522	Sao Paulo, Brazil	18,333
Shanghai, China	6,066	Mumbai, India	18,202
Moscow, Russia	5,356	Delhi, India	15,053
Buenos Aires, Argentina	5,098	Shanghai, China	14,503
Chicago, U.S.	4,999	Calcutta, India	14,282
Calcutta, India	4,513	Dhaka, Bangladesh	12,576
Beijing, China	4,331	Buenos Aires, Argentina	12,553

Source: United Nations. (2008). *World Urbanization Prospects: The 2007 Revision.* New York: United Nations Department of Economic and Social Affairs, pp. 164, 166. On-line at http://www.un.org/esa/population/publications/wup2007/2007WUP_Highlights_web.pdf

getting bigger—the 10th largest city in 2005 (Buenos Aires) had more residents than did the largest city in 1950 (New York). Back in 1950, there were only two urban agglomerations with over 10 million population (New York and Tokyo); in 1975 there were 3, in 2005 there were 19, and in 2025 there will be 27 (United Nations, 2008, p. 10; also see BBC, 2008). In addition, the list of largest cities has changed—by 2005, London, Paris, Moscow, Chicago, and Beijing had dropped out of the top 10, replaced by Mexico City, Sao Paulo, Mumbai, Delhi, and Dhaka.

What are the consequences of urbanization? When people move from the countryside to towns and cities, they generally leave an agrarian or nomadic lifestyle in return for employment in commerce, industry, or service. Often they are separated from family, clan, or tribal relationships and they enter a social setting that offers more variety, personal freedom, and anonymity. The results are perhaps predictable—greater creativity, productivity, and personal fulfillment, but also alienation, social disorganization, disorder, and crime.

Each urban area has its own particular history, dynamics, and setting. It should be expected that cities will vary in their levels and types of crime, disorder, and associated problems. Still, it is generally found that urban areas have more crime than rural areas (United Nations, 2007a, p. 5; also see Ellis & Walsh, 2005; Shelley, 1981).

Urban crime is universal, but research suggests that patterns of urban crime are affected by the nature of cities and the social, economic and geographical environments in which they exist. For example, property crime tends to be higher in cities in developed countries, while violent crime is higher in cities in the developing world. Regardless of social or economic development, the larger the population of a city, the greater the level of crime and victimization, a relationship often most clearly manifest in homicide rates.

The foregoing description of urbanization and its attendant complications identifies general trends, but it is a bit simplistic. It should be noted that, for many people, moving from a rural to an urban setting means not just personal opportunity and higher wages, but significantly better education, health care, water, sanitation, electrical service, and other necessities. Cities might seem like magnets or engines of crime and other social problems, but they also are the places where standards of living tend to be the highest. In many parts of the world, rural people are drawn to cities for these kinds of practical and understandable reasons.

Recognizing the pros and cons of urbanization, one of the biggest challenges is *rapid* urbanization. While Australia and the United Kingdom certainly have their own challenges arising from the situation that 88–90% of their people live in urban areas, Cameroon, Nigeria, and Uganda are faced with much more rapidly increasing urbanization. In fact, for the period 1975–2007, the highest rates of increasing urbanization among the regions of the world were in Asia and Africa (United Nations, 2008, p. 5). Looking just at 2005–2010, the least developed countries of the world were expected to see an annual urban population increase of 4.1%, compared to 2.5% for less developed countries and only 0.5% for more developed countries (United Nations, 2008, p. 115).

Clearly, rapid urbanization, today and in the years to come, is most likely to be a significant problem in the least developed regions of the world (although some more developed countries, like Dubai, may also experience rapid urbanization). Rapid urbanization can overwhelm basic infrastructure (utilities, transportation, and housing) as well as government services, including public safety and police. Thus, while urbanization creates economic, social, and governmental challenges (and opportunities) in nearly all countries of the world, *rapid* urbanization presents even greater challenges—challenges currently being confronted most often in the least developed parts of the world.

Urban Security Problems

The chapters in the first section of the book primarily focus on the sorts of police and security problems often associated with urbanization. In the initial selection, Professor David Chiabi describes the situation in Cameroon, where violent crime and traffic crashes seem to be of little interest to the police, who are largely content to man roadblocks in order to extract bribes from motorists and other travelers. Also, the police and military seem largely unchecked in the use of their power and authority for personal and political benefit. Cameroon is clearly still engaged in postcolonial transition, exacerbated by rapid urbanization. Neither the rule of law nor basic government services are effectively established, making life difficult for much of the population.

Ugandan Commissioner of Police Benjamin Namanya describes conditions in his country, particularly in the capital city of Kampala. Although Uganda is still a predominantly rural country, Kampala has experienced 3–4% annual population growth since 1970, following 9% annual growth in the 1960s (United Nations, 2008, p. 194). The city now has an official population of about 1.5 million (local officials estimate the real population at 2.5 million). Statistics cited by Commissioner Namanya show a more than three-fold increase in reported crime cases in Kampala from 2002 to 2006. A complicating factor in Uganda, and other countries located in war-torn regions, is the easy availability of small arms (rifles and handguns) abandoned or sold by soldiers and rebels. Besides urbanization, postcolonial transition, and the proliferation of small arms, the Commissioner also cites poor city planning, internally displaced people, HIV/AIDS, and inadequate police staffing among the challenges to providing adequate security in Uganda, and especially in Kampala.

Another kind of transition, of the post-Soviet and postconflict variety, is illustrated by the situation in Serbia. Professor Zelimir Kesetovic explains how the break-up of the former Yugoslavia, along with subsequent Balkan conflicts, caused many people to flee Serbia, while at the same time many people immigrated to the country from other parts of the Balkans, plus there was substantial within-country movement and displacement. All this churning of the population, added to the underlying trend of ongoing urbanization, created serious challenges, especially in the capital city:

> Belgrade experienced the most pressure, multiplying the problems that already existed: the level and structure of crime, social pathology (drug abuse, prostitution etc.), traffic jams, unemployment, limited capacities of critical infrastructures, air pollution and other environmental and housing problems.

Extreme income inequality, state-sponsored crime, and organized crime are among the serious challenges now facing Serbia. The public police are still adjusting to democracy and rule of law, while new private police are largely unregulated.

Another country engaged in a major transition is Russia. Professor Yakov Gilinskiy describes the situation in Russia regarding crime, corruption, and terrorism. Russia is a huge country with a substantial population (currently about 140 million), although its population has been decreasing since 1995 (United Nations, 2007b). Russia has seen a significant increase in urbanization over the last 50 years, but still it has low population density since it is such a large country. The situation in Russia is quite difficult, with power and money heavily concentrated in a few hands and democratization proceeding slowly. As described by Professor Gilinskiy, crime rates have increased in Russia, the homicide rate is very high, citizens are reluctant to call the police, and when called, the police response is inadequate. Corruption is endemic, organized crime and human trafficking are commonplace, and the police routinely abuse their authority. These problems make life difficult for Russians living in Moscow (which grew from 9.2 million to 10.4 million residents between 1995 and 2005), Saint Petersburg (decreased from 4.8 million to 4.6 million during 1995–2005) (United Nations, 2008, p. 177), and elsewhere in the country.

The next selection looks specifically at the effects of housing arrangements on crime and disorder. Professors Emil and Wieslaw Plywaczewski draw on research conducted in Poland and elsewhere that shows that "ill-considered urbanization leads to various negative consequences such as lack or inefficiency of public facilities and destructive influence on the community." They discuss some key features of urban design, including natural surveillance, natural access control, territorial reinforcement, and maintenance. Factors that seem to help housing estates become communal rather than antisocial include reasonable size and scale, circular rather than linear designs, provision of shopping and services, good design of streets and parking, and access to public transportation. A big challenge is designing urban housing communities that achieve safety and security without building fortresses.

Drug abuse is a problem often associated with urban areas. Director Fasihuddin of the Northwest Frontier Police in Pakistan provides a detailed analysis of drug abuse and drug enforcement in and around the city of Peshawar. This is a city that has grown eightfold since 1950, from 153,000 to over 1.2 million in 2005; it has nearly doubled in size just since 1985 (United Nations, 2008, p. 176). Besides rapid urbanization, it is significant that Peshawar is located close to the border with Afghanistan, plus it is adjacent to the semiautonomous Northern areas of Pakistan. This means that major drug cultivation (opium/heroin) occurs nearby and the city is surrounded by territories that are lightly governed, if not lawless. As Fasihuddin explains, the situation is further complicated by lack of coordination between the national Anti-Narcotics Force, Customs, the Frontier Constabulary, and the Northwest Frontier Police (NWFP), as well as corruption and investigative shortcomings. He makes the point that it is very difficult for local police, or even national police, to manage what is really a huge transnational crime problem.

South Africa is a country undergoing yet another form of transition, from apartheid to an open and free society. Professor Neels Roelofse focuses on organized crime in his country, explaining that it has flourished during the transitional period since 1990 as the government and the police have been consumed by the process of postapartheid reform and reconciliation. He notes that foreign and transnational organized crime groups have become more active in South Africa, especially Chinese, Russian, and Nigerian groups engaged in a variety of rackets, frauds, trafficking, smuggling, thefts, and kidnappings. South Africa participates in various regional, African, and United Nations conventions and collaborations aimed at controlling organized crime, but its efforts are hampered by the ongoing police reform, by corruption, and by high levels of "ordinary" violent crime that necessarily demand the majority of police attention.

One country that seems to have experienced relatively modest urbanization is Azerbaijan. From 1950 to 2005, the percentage of population living in urban areas increased modestly, from 42.5% to 51.5%. The population of the capital city of Baku doubled during that period, from 897,000 to almost 1.9 million (United Nations, 2008, p. 168). Major General Fazil Guliyev of the Ministry of Internal Affairs and Senior Advisor Orkhan Dadashov of the Presidential Administration describe Azerbaijan's post-Soviet transition, which has included a serious border dispute with Armenia, drug smuggling through the country toward the West, and growing traffic safety problems. The latter are occasioned by significantly increased traffic volume associated with modernization and economic development. The authors point out that police attention to traffic safety serves an additional purpose beyond protecting vehicle occupants and pedestrians, since transportation systems are a likely target of terrorist activity aimed at disrupting oil production and distribution.

Traffic safety and traffic administration are the focus of Professor Adki Surender's chapter on Hyderabad, India. India is the second-most populous country in the world, it has three of the world's 10 largest cities; it has the highest level of population density among the countries included in this book, and yet it also has a relatively low level of urbanization. What this means is that India has big cities but it also has a lot of people living in nonurban areas, compared to other countries. Hyderabad is one of the big cities, with a population over 6 million in 2005, compared to just 1 million in 1950 (United Nations, 2008, p. 173). Dr. Surender explains that traffic problems are intense in Hyderabad for several reasons, including inadequate streets and roads, a huge and fast increasing volume of vehicles, poorly trained and regulated drivers, and demoralized traffic police. A particular challenge is the diversity of vehicles on the road, including two-wheelers, three-wheelers, cars, minibuses, trucks, and more. Mixing all these types of vehicles, some moving fast and others slow, on an outdated network of narrow streets has created a mess of congestion, disruption, and mayhem.

Michael Doyle, a police captain in Cleveland, Ohio (USA) discusses another traffic-related phenomenon particular to cities—the challenge of evacuating an urban area in the event of some type of major disaster. The need for urban mass evacuation has arisen several times in the United States in recent years, most often in anticipation of a hurricane. Other circumstances could also trigger the need to evacuate a city, including a flood, tsunami, fire, earthquake, nuclear accident, terrorist attack involving a weapon of mass destruction, or military attack. If a mass evacuation occurs spontaneously or proceeds without direction and coordination, it is likely to result in mass frustration and mass congestion. In that case, people may not successfully avoid the disaster, and the evacuation itself may cause injuries and deaths. Captain Doyle provides lessons learned from recent U.S. cases and outlines procedures that police and others should follow in order to carry out mass urban evacuations as safely and effectively as possible.

Police Responses

The first set of 10 chapters, introduced above, primarily focused on security problems frequently experienced in urban areas—crime, disorder, corruption, drugs, traffic, and so on. In the middle section of the book, eight chapters focus somewhat less on the nature of urban problems themselves, and more on police responses to those problems.

The first chapter in this section takes a careful look at the process of changing and managing a modern urban police force. The author, Police Commissioner Christine Nixon of the Victoria Police in Australia, was appointed to head her force after serving 29 years with the New South Wales Police. She provides a personal and thoughtful account of the approach she took in Victoria, which was a troubled force at the time of her appointment. Her approach incorporates both inspired leadership and good management, both anchored to a clear conception of her role and responsibility in the community and broader government. A key ingredient is what she calls her "conversational model," which emphasizes talking with and listening to colleagues and clients in order to identify and solve problems, much more than relying on higher authority, experience, or claimed expertise. To be sure, she combined this model with a strong dose of results measurement and accountability. Whether her methods represent some form of "feminist" police administration or just good leadership and management will be left up to the reader to decide.

Professor Oyesoji Aremu discusses community policing as a response to urban problems in Nigeria, which has undergone the second-most dramatic increase in urbanization over the past 55 years of the countries covered in this book (after Cameroon). Community policing is an important topic, inasmuch as it has been heavily promoted worldwide over the past decade or two as a means of democratization, as a roadmap for transitional societies, and as a police reform in both highly developed and less developed countries (Bayley, 2005; Brogden & Nijhar, 2005). Professor Aremu argues that community policing is needed to help the police in Nigeria overcome public distrust, a precondition for effective control of crime and disorder. He particularly recommends an emphasis on developing the emotional intelligence of police officers—this puts relatively more emphasis on building self-awareness, self-regulation, motivation, empathy, and social skills in young police officers in contrast to the traditional emphasis on knowledge building and technical skills.

Professor Branislav Simonovic and Police Director Uros Pena (Republic of Serpska) similarly discuss community policing as a response to the challenges of policing in multiethnic Bosnia and Herzegovina. Policing in the Balkan countries is made very difficult by suspicions and animosities between different national groups, and it is further complicated by the roles that the police played in the Soviet era and then in the Balkan conflicts of the 1990s. Rebuilding, or more accurately building, public trust in the police is a huge challenge, as is staffing each police force with a representative number of officers from different groups, especially national minorities. Professor Simonovic and Director Pena review the progress that has been made so far, as well as remaining obstacles. They also point out European and international standards and conventions that have assisted police and reformers in the design and implementation of improvements.

The next chapter also addresses the challenge of policing a diverse society while honoring and protecting human rights. Professor Carmen Solis and New York City Human Rights Commissioner Patricia Gatling describe an approach to police training designed to help participants "develop self-awareness by recognizing how their own behavior and attitudes impact public and political perceptions" and to "help participants develop a plan to implement strategies in their respective organizations and communities that demonstrates how respect for human dignity, human rights and the rule of law would be strengthened and reinforced to promote improved methods of security in urban areas." The authors focus on the fundamental tension that pervades policing, that between collective security and individual freedoms. This tension is greatly heightened when the people in a community are diverse and when the police are suspected of engaging in discriminatory, unethical, abusive, and/or illegal behavior. Somehow police need to develop self-awareness and self-control that enable them to overcome their own biases and misperceptions in order to police fairly in a diverse community. Similar to the emotional intelligence focus suggested by Professor Aremu, the human rights/human dignity training model aims to change police officers' thinking and behavior.

One kind of urban challenge not heretofore mentioned is protest. Certainly nonurban protests occur too, but mass protests are more often experienced by cities, and therefore city police must develop techniques for handling demonstrations and riots. Professor Alex Vitale describes how the New York City Police Department handled protests surrounding the 2004 Republican National Convention, at which the Republican Party renominated George W. Bush as their candidate for a second term as U.S. President. Various groups wanted to stage protests outside the convention facility; the police challenge was to control the protests without unduly interfering with the protestors' rights of free speech and assembly. As Professor Vitale explains, protest groups have become more sophisticated in the last 10–20 years, and so have the police. He also points out that the police have to operate in a complex legal and political environment—that is, they have constraints as they plan and implement their tactics for regulating and controlling protests. Interestingly, how police handled each different protest during the convention varied, and could not be explained simply on the basis of the protestors' behavior.

Shifting gears slightly, Professors Gorazd Mesko and Darko Maver, along with researcher Ines Klinkon, take a look at criminal investigation in Slovenia, focusing particularly on its four largest cities. They document a period of decreasing clearance rates (rates of solving crimes) until a recent upswing in 2007. As they indicate, changes in crime recording practices may be at the root of some of the apparent decrease in investigative effectiveness during 1996–2006—basically, police began recording all reported crimes, which swelled the denominator of the crime clearance rate, causing the overall fraction to decline. The police may have been solving just as many crimes as before (the numerator of the fraction), although that too may have become more difficult in the post-Soviet era when coercive police powers were curtailed. In any event, the police in Slovenia are now using more modern techniques including crime analysis and crime mapping, as illustrated in the chapter. Focusing on specific "hot spots" where robberies, burglaries, and thefts are concentrated should help police patrols be more effective in prevention, and also help investigators target their finite resources on the most active and serious offenders.

Chantal Perras, a doctoral student at the University of Montreal in Canada, also looks at criminal investigation, but her focus is on drug investigations at the international level. Specifically, she explores how law enforcement agencies of different countries in North America manage the process of cooperation and collaboration. Among other things, she finds that personal relationships between investigators and informal agreements play a big part, in comparison to formal agreements, conventions, and treaties. Issues of trust, mistrust, and perceived corruption strongly affect cooperation versus conflict; also, police agencies of different countries

adhere to certain philosophies and styles that condition how they participate within international coalitions. In addition, she points out that international police cooperation takes place (or fails to take place) within a
geo-political context:

> Certain countries have much more influence than others. The fact is that some
> countries may not want to take part in the war against drugs with the most
> powerful countries. But it is equally possible that they undergo often serious
> economic consequences if they refuse to cooperate. These countries do not
> really have the choice to cooperate. It is probably why the network is main-
> tained. It is also possible that there is a true hidden resistance.

Staying with the theme of cooperation, Kathleen Sweet, a professor, consultant, and former military intelligence officer, reviews and analyzes efforts
in the United States since 2001 to improve information and intelligence sharing among law enforcement agencies, as well as between law enforcement
and intelligence agencies. This is a key topic in the United States, which has
some 18,000 separate local and state police agencies, plus a dozen or so major
federal law enforcement agencies, along with a separate contingent of civilian
and military intelligence agencies. Since 9/11, the overriding objective has
been to "connect the dots" before the next major terrorist attack, with the
principal impediment being lack of information sharing within the fragmented U.S. police and intelligence system. Professor Sweet discusses the
progress that has been made so far, including the USA PATRIOT Act passed
by Congress in 2001, the National Criminal Intelligence Sharing Plan, and
other reforms and initiatives. She cautions, however, that in the years since
2001 "those responsible for quality intelligence and quality law enforcement
have not come far enough. Better training and more support at the upper
levels of management is needed to improve communication, commitment
and deterrence."

Private Security Responses

Crime, disorder, and other urban security problems might seem to be the
natural and exclusive domain of the public police, but increasingly around
the world, private police and private security are playing a growing role. The
proliferation of privatized policing is probably greater in urban areas than
elsewhere, for several reasons: (1) wealthy individuals who can afford their
own protection tend to live in cities, (2) major financial institutions, and other
multinational corporations, tend to be headquartered in cities, (3) cities have
higher crime rates, increasing the risk to wealthy people and companies, and
(4) urban police are often overwhelmed and unable to provide the level of
protection desired by those who have the most to lose. As a result, those who

can afford to hire extra protection for themselves, their families, and their companies have increasingly turned to the private sector in recent years.

In the first selection in this section, Margaret York, Chief of the Los Angeles County Police Department, provides a completely different rationale for the use of private security. Her agency is responsible for the protection of hospitals, parks, and other public facilities in Los Angeles County, California. The threats, risks, vulnerabilities, and other needs of each facility are carefully studied in order to determine what level of public police protection is required and, just as importantly, which tasks and services could be provided by private security. Why? The answer is simple—private security costs less. Chief York's responsibility is to protect the county's 200+ facilities, and the millions of people who use them, as efficiently as possible. Her agency calculates that it saves the taxpayers of Los Angeles County about $70 million per year by utilizing private security whenever possible. The chief describes the contracting and accountability systems that are used to ensure that, when private security is utilized in place of public police, their performance meets the standards that are set and provides the level of protection that is expected.

The next chapter, authored by Police Lieutenant Gary Scheibe and Professor Beth McConnell, examines changes in security and protection for the Port of Houston in Texas (USA). The City of Houston qualifies as an example of rapid urbanization, having grown in population from 700,000 in 1950 to 4.3 million in 2005 (United Nations, 2008, p. 178). The Port of Houston is a major enterprise: According to the authors, it is "first in the United States in foreign waterborne commerce, second in total tonnage, and sixth in the world." The occasion for looking at changes in port security was the post-9/11 period—the events of September 11, 2001 in the United States caused many government and private sector institutions to re-evaluate their security and preparedness. Seaports are particularly challenging from a security perspective, because of the volume of people and material that passes through them, the pressure to process cargo quickly, their complex physical structure (the Port of Houston is 25 miles long), and the fact that they typically include both public and private property. Scheibe and McConnell find in their study that private security providers in the Port of Houston have made improvements in almost every aspect of access control, emergency planning, technology, training, and target hardening since 9/11.

Professors Dusko Vejnovic, Velibor Lalic, and Mile Sikman next provide a description and analysis of the development of private security in Bosnia and Herzegovina. Of course, private security is a relatively new, and novel, concept in post-Soviet societies. Private security seems to grow somewhat naturally in conjunction with the introduction of private enterprise and capitalism. In Bosnia and Herzegovina (BiH), the situation is further complicated because it is "a postconflict area and transitional society, where the whole security sector is going through a transformation from authoritarian and war to democratic model." Regulation of the private security sector has been delegated by the national government to the regions. The authors find that performance and accountability of private security in their country is improving but that it still falls short of European standards. They conclude that "the current situation in the private security sector is not satisfying and that this sector can play a much more important role in public safety than has been the case so far. Particularly, it is necessary to devote a lot of effort to building partnerships with the police—what has been largely ignored so far."

The final two chapters in this section focus on aspects of private security in South Africa. Professor P. J. Potgieter looks at the big picture of urbanization, crime, and the government's lack of success in crime prevention and crime control over the past 15 years in the postapartheid era. This has inexorably led to growth in the private security sector. He explains that businesses and citizens have little choice but to seek private protection. Unfortunately, private security providers have their own problems, including crimes committed by private security officers, labor unrest in the private security industry, violence committed against private security officers by armed criminals, and general weaknesses in training and regulation. Professor Potgieter concludes:

> Whether the private security industry will be able to cope with the criminal onslaught in the new millennium, shall, to a large extent, depend on the sustainability of that industry. Residential burglary, theft and robbery, cash-in-transit heists, destruction of Automated Transmission Machines (ATMs) with commercial explosives and the hijacking of large carriers on highways are only a few of the major risks facing both policing and private security in the new millennium.

Professor Johan Ras describes and analyzes a particular form of private security that may be more prevalent in South Africa than in most other countries—body guarding. He notes that "wealthy and prominent business people, celebrities and those with high status who normally can afford private security bodyguards, are normally most of the time urban based—whether at home or at work, busy with their business transactions, holidays or enjoying the high life." It can also be noted that South Africa has more than its share of violent crime, helping create the demand for private security (reportedly outnumbering police 5–1), including bodyguards. Professor Ras makes a strong case for the need to professionalize the business of body guarding, and describes steps already underway in South Africa to accomplish that. He even sees a connection to tourism, noting that his country has many attractions and enhanced worldwide appeal postapartheid, but its reputation for crime and violence keeps visitors away or limits them to only a few safe havens. If he has his way, your next tour guide in Cape Town, Johannesburg, or Kruger National Park may also be a trained body guard.

Conclusion

Professors Julia Davidson and Elena Martellozzo from the United Kingdom served as the official reporters for the IPES Dubai conference. In their concluding chapter in this book, they identify some of the key themes and issues arising out of the conference papers and presentations regarding the theme "Urbanization and Security." It is quite clear from the contributions in this book, and from their conclusion, that ongoing urbanization will continue to create major security challenges in most countries of the world, making it an extremely important topic at the international level as well. It is hoped that groups like the United Nations, the International Association of Chiefs of Police, and the security association ASIS International will devote more attention and resources to the challenges created by worldwide urbanization.

In the spirit of IPES, it is also strongly recommended that police leaders take every opportunity to learn from the experiences of other countries, and collaborate as closely as possible with police researchers, in order to continue building the knowledge base of policing and the professionalism of police forces everywhere. We hope that this volume is a good representative of the IPES philosophy and that it makes some small contribution to global understanding of policing and security.

References

Abdullah, M. M. (2007). *Dubai: A Nonviolent Emirate*. Paper presented to the International Police Executive Symposium, April 8–12, Dubai.

Bayley, D. (2005). *Changing the Guard: Developing Democratic Police Abroad*. Oxford, UK: Oxford University Press.

BBC. (2008). Interactive Map: Urban Growth. London: BBC News. On-line at http://news.bbc.co.uk/2/shared/spl/hi/world/06/urbanisation/html/urbanisation.stm

Brogden, M., & Nijhar, P. (2005). *Community Policing: National and International Models and Approaches*. Devon, UK: Willan Publishing.

Ellis, L., & Walsh, A. (2005). *Criminology: A Global Perspective*. Boston: Pearson-Longman.

Shelley, L. I. (1981). *Crime and Modernization: The Impact of Industrialization and Urbanization on Crime*. Carbondale, IL: Southern Illinois University Press.

United Nations. (2007a). *Crime Prevention and Criminal Justice Responses to Urban Crime*. New York: United Nations Commission on Crime Prevention and Criminal Justice. On-line at http://www.unodc.org/pdf/crime/session16th/E_CN15_2007_CRP3_E.pdf

United Nations. (2007b). *World Population Prospects: The 2006 Revision*. New York: United Nations Department of Economic and Social Affairs. On-line at http://esa.un.org/unpp/

United Nations. (2008). *World Urbanization Prospects: The 2007 Revision.* New York: United Nations Department of Economic and Social Affairs. On-line at http://www.un.org/esa/population/publications/wup2007/2007WUP_Highlights_web.pdf

World Atlas. (2006). Countries of the World by Highest Population Density. On-line at http://www.worldatlas.com/aatlas/populations/ctydensityh.htm

Urban Security Problems

I

Urbanization and Crime in Cameroon

2

DAVID K. CHIABI

Contents

Since the 1920s most criminologists are of the opinion that urbanization and industrialization bring about social changes. Industrialization, modernization, and urbanization are said to cause the breakdown of traditional patterns of the social fabric of society. The breakdown results in all forms of changes that may lead to personal alienation and instability, which may lead to anomic conditions that lead to increases in crime. Social disorganization theories link crime rates to neighborhood ecological characteristics, urban decay, and breakdown in social life (Shaw, 1929). Drawing upon Shaw and McKay's (1942) theoretical roots, many researchers have continued to study how and why neighborhoods affect the social dynamics and characteristics of changing environments. One of the most studied effects is the crime rate and its patterns (e.g., Cohen & Felson, 1979; Sherman, Gartin, & Buerger,

1989; Stark, 1987). Recent criminological research has focused on the impact of social characteristics on the patterns of crime and victimization (Morenoff & Sampson, 1997; Sampson & Groves, 1989; Taylor, 1997).

While some attention has been given to the physical ecology, or layout/ composition, of neighborhoods, social scientists have primarily measured the effects of neighborhood social ecological context. Characteristics studied have included economic/poverty rates, racial heterogeneity, age composition, and gender composition, among others. The importance of individual characteristics and other social ecological phenomena has been demonstrated when studying the rates of crime and deviance. However, differences in a neighborhood's physical characteristics, such as land use patterns, are also important when studying neighborhood crime rates. Other researchers have examined the importance of physical ecology when studying various social phenomena (Newman & Franck, 1980; Sampson & Raudenbush, 1999; Shaw & McKay, 1942; Stark, 1987; Taylor & Gottfredson, 1986), yet these same researchers have faced many challenges and difficulties when attempting to measure and define physical characteristics of neighborhoods.

Urbanization brings about environmental, as well as varied social changes, for inhabitants of urban areas. Social change is inevitable and sometimes results in disharmony, conflict, and cultural dichotomy. These effects are more serious if change occurs at a fast pace (Warner, Wilcox, & Rountree, 1997) and are exacerbated in transitional societies. Social disorganization leads to the decrease of the influence of existing social rules upon different sectors of society leading to the most noted effect of urbanization—crime.

Crime in urban societies can be attributed to cultural conflicts between diverse values of different sectors of society, between old and new values, between local and imported values, between traditional and imposed values, or may be simply due to a cultural lag. Since 1910, Shaw and McKay and other criminologists see crime as a product of development in society, with change and conflict which affects the behavior of those within it (Bursik, 1984). Urban areas are often characterized by poverty, unemployment, poor housing conditions, and other factors, which as indicated above, are magnets for crime. The United Nations has indicated that one-tenth of urban populations in transition economies live under such conditions (Tibaijuka, 2005).

Developing nations are by nature transitional. Research suggests that developing countries, particularly those undergoing rapid social changes, usually experience rising crime rates (Tibaijuka, 2005; Wolfgang, 2004). They face multiple problems, most commonly crime and general disorder, mostly in urban areas. Developing and transitional societies have no stable institutions with the capacity to combat crime and other problems. In these societies, national institutions and judicial institutions, in particular, lack legitimacy, legal structure, and established law enforcement mechanisms.

This chapter explores the effect of urbanization in Cameroon and the resultant crime wave that flows from it. It examines crime as a complex social, economic, and political problem that requires prevention strategies integrated throughout the affected system. It addresses how crime problems experienced by transitional societies can be avoided by those currently undergoing rapid changes often experienced during transition. Because transitional societies are to a large extent lawless, the adoption of the rule of law is explored as a meaningful first step in any crime prevention measure. Thus, the rule of law is viewed as a *sine qua non* for dealing with crime in transitional societies.

Developing Societies and Crime

Most developing countries are transitional in nature. Because they are undergoing transition they are inherently weak. They lack structure and regularity. Almost all institutions in such countries, both public and private, are undergoing transition. All of a developing country's systems—political, economic, social as well as institutions of justice and crime control—are subject to restructuring (Spuy, 2000). Social and political institutions are determinant factors for individual and group behavior that are also necessary for survival. They control and may even shape individual lives and actions in the society (Dukes, 1999). Unfortunately, in transitional societies, these social institutions are characterized by exploitation, political exclusion, and unequal access to resources.

The breakdown of social and state controls is one of the leading factors that contributes to the growth of crime in diverse transitional societies (Cavallaro & Ould Mohamedou, 2005). During transition, old forms of control that kept society together are weakened. Community control structures are weakened and informal institutions such as churches are less effective than they usually are during normal periods. Family, neighborhood groups, social groups, and even nongovernmental organizations are equally weakened. Often, the whole society is politically, socially, and culturally disintegrated (Koci, 1996). The disorganized and malfunctioning nature of transitional societies produces a myriad of social and other problems. One of the main consequences of such disorganization is rising crime and the creation of new avenues for crime. Moreover, the social problems are accompanied by instability and violence, with an increase in crime as a prominent feature (Zsuzsa, 1997).

There are transitional systems across the globe. Carothers (2002) identified transition trends in seven different regions of the world: (1) the fall of right-wing authoritarian regimes in Southern Europe in the mid-1970s; (2) the replacement of military dictatorships by elected civilian governments across Latin America from the late 1970s through the late 1980s; (3) the decline of authoritarian rule in parts of East and South Asia starting in the mid-1980s; (4) the collapse of communist regimes in Eastern Europe at the end of the 1980s; (5) the breakup of the Soviet Union and the establishment of 15 post-Soviet republics in 1991; (6) the decline of one-party regimes in many parts of sub-Saharan Africa in the first half of the 1990s; and (7) a weak but recognizable liberalizing trend in some Middle Eastern countries in the 1990s.

With the breakdown of the former Soviet Union, changes in Eastern and Central Europe created several transitional systems/countries and since the late 1980s, there is a shift from centrally controlled communist governments to some form of pluralism (Sztompka, 1993). It is a rapid revolution involving all societal sectors: political, social, and cultural. Moreover it involves a total ideological change (Calder, 1996).

Currently, many African countries are undergoing different forms of transition. After achieving independence in the 1960s, most of these countries turned into dictatorships or military regimes. The last decade was marked by several attempts at some form of democratic rule and willingness by some to experiment with pluralistic rule.

Studies indicate that crime increases during political transformation in many countries around the world. Similar patterns are found in transitional societies evolving from civilian rule to military rule in Latin America, nations evolving from communist regimes in Eastern Europe, and in African countries evolving from authoritarian rule or civil wars to attempts at democracy. Common elements fueling crime have been identified in these societies and they are related to political, social, and economic trends that existed before and during transition (Cavallaro & Ould Mohamedou, 2005; Spuy, 2000). The various forms of crime are transnational organized crime, violent crime, corruption, trafficking in firearms, terrorism, human trafficking, money laundering, and cyber crime.

Spuy (2000) described the problem of crime in African countries that are transitioning from their previous forms of government to some forms of democracy. She stated that "the explosion of armed crime in Africa underlines the shortcomings of the security apparatus just when it is most desperately needed." She cites United Nations surveys showing that three Africans out of every four in cities were victims of crime during the latter half of the 1990s. As she noted, "opportunities for illicit enterprise and profit multiply in changing societies. For example, in South Africa crime peaked in 1990, the year transition began (Shaw, 1995). New avenues for criminals and criminal activity grew in the newly found freedom of the former Soviet block and criminals took advantage of 'lawless regimes and with minimally controlled borders to enhance their criminal activity' (Koci, 1996)."

Apart from the lack of permanent institutions and instability, some of the other reasons advanced as to why changing governmental systems witness rising crime rates include conflict; economic deprivation and opportunity for crime; and, sometimes, the existence of arms. The following sections address each of these reasons.

Institutional Instability

Weak governmental institutions and weak law enforcement regimes provide new opportunities for criminals. As Gray (1997) noted, laws may exist only on paper and may not be known to the public, respected or enforced. Transition is a time for redefinition of the roles of the state in all areas of government. Changes caused by the dramatic impact of political transition are exacerbated by long-term processes of industrialization and urbanization, which by themselves have considerable impact on changing the nature of community and social controls. Sometimes there are changes in ownership structure. Additionally, an abundance of structural and other motivational factors for the involvement of people in alternative opportunities is created and some of these alternatives provide ample access to criminal endeavors.

Conflict

Improvements in economic and social conditions of developing societies are contingent upon the maintenance of peace. Many developing societies, however, and particularly those of Africa consistently suffer from various forms of conflict. For example, just as Mozambique and Rwanda are showing some signs of peace and stability, the Republic of Congo and Sudan are making sure that Africa cannot completely enjoy peace. Conflict is usually accompanied by violence leading to crimes, such as looting, rape, homicide, and trafficking in human and other goods (Masamba, 2004).

Economic Deprivation and Opportunity for Crime

The levels of deprivation and crime are stronger in transitional societies (Hannon, 2002) and the relationship between inequality and crime is apparent considering the chaotic state of affairs (Fergusson, Swain-Campbell, & Horwood, 2004). Poverty, or stratification by social class, is the first sociological variable ever examined as a possible cause of crime. Research on the relationship between crime and economic factors generally supports the proposition that relative economic deprivation produces higher crime rates. Weatherburn, Snowball, and Hunter (2006) examined the different effects that economic forces may have on participation in crime and the rate of offending. Higher rates of crime found among young people from socioeconomically disadvantaged families reflect a life course process in which adverse family, individual, school, and peer factors combine to increase individual susceptibility to crime (Fergusson et al., 2004). Criminal opportunity theory suggests that community economic deprivation causes strain and disorganization, which may encourage some individuals to turn to crime.

Most countries enmeshed in transition are weak, creating opportunities for growth in criminal activity. Developing countries, attempting to make the transition, have limited resources for combatting crime. Systems of criminal justice (law enforcement and security, justice, and corrections) are in crisis and are unable to perform policing functions as the ability to prevent, process, and deter crime in any meaningful manner is greatly reduced. Moreover, the links between them are weak and as Shaw (1997) realized in South Africa, "the involvement of departments such as Welfare, Education and Health, who have key roles to play in the prevention of crime is minimal."

Availability of Arms

The existence of any form of arms facilitates the commission of crime. One of the realities of conflict is that most weapons cannot be accounted for after armed conflicts end. Societies that have gone through such conflict during the past few decades abound around the world. Available arms, when left unchecked, filter through into civilian hands. Often, they contribute to increased crime, particularly in vulnerable societies in transition. In some cases, forces of law and order are directly or indirectly the main suppliers of the weapons. When transitional countries cannot control such weapons, criminals are provided an added incentive and assistance to commit crime.

Law and Order in Transitional Societies

There is an obvious need for effective law enforcement in transitional societies. Unfortunately, as is often the case in developing transitional societies, formal institutions including law enforcement and legal systems are in a state of transition and extremely weakened, making it virtually impossible to carry out meaningful law enforcement. Moreover, changing societies often find that changing laws are equally difficult to enforce. As Gray (1997) noted "in developing countries and countries in transition some form of central planning laws may exist only on paper, and may not be known or respected by the public or enforced by the state." Legal systems are a reflection of societal traditions and cannot be separated from legal processes or from the broader historical, political, cultural, and economic settings in which they function. Strong legal systems such as the American and English common law were built on historic and traditional values (Dammer & Fairchild, 2006).

A major problem of transition is that changing governmental systems include those responsible for maintaining the peace (Shaw, 1995). Law enforcement agencies in transition are undergoing changes as to their mandate and organization. They are restructuring at the time they are needed the most (Spuy, 2000) and affected by a sense of political displacement. Compounding the problem is the fact that transitional governments often pay more attention to politics, forgetting other sectors of the society. The lack of attention to the economic, social, and other sectors of the society produces instability. Crime prevention institutions understandably follow government priorities and would not be particularly driven to fight crime, if the government has other priorities. Moreover, law enforcement agencies are like other institutions in the process of establishing an identity and often have priorities other than security and crime.

Preventing Crime in Transitional Societies

Crime is a multifaceted problem with different causes and requires different strategies for controlling it (Spuy, 2000). As stated above, during transition, formal and informal institutions responsible for preventing crime are rendered incapable of effectively preventing crime. The re-establishment of formal and informal means of social and community control is the key to easing the crime problem in transition systems. Law enforcement alone cannot stem long-term crime problems of states emerging from a period of transition. Tested methods in developed systems may also be inappropriate or are not well implemented. The best formal legal systems operate only at the margin, leaving most standards in a society to be internalized and "self-enforced" by society itself. As Gray (2005) noted, legislators and administrators are the main actors in the crafting of responses to crime. Their role, therefore, is crucial to change and needs careful planning and design. Clear government policies for crime prevention are necessary, and the government needs to always be cognizant of practical implications of its policies.

Training police to understand their new role in democratic systems is essential for any success. The main idea is how countries undergoing transition could successfully do so and, at the same time, prevent crime from becoming a hindrance. The development of a new police and security system that embraces the country's social, cultural, and political values—while at the same time adopting fair and effective methods—is the challenge to be overcome in any changing system (Koci, 1996).

Often police have allegiances to the old systems they are used to protecting and are thus reluctant to accept change. They carry over habits from previous regimes that are difficult to change. Moreover, the conservative nature of police makes them tend to protect their institutions without question. The reluctance to change creates problems when old methods are applied in changed circumstances (Carothers, 2002). For example, Cohen (1979) found that Soviet police, who were a highly centralized force owing total allegiance to the communist party whose structure and functions were determined by party ideology, were extremely reluctant to change after the collapse of the Soviet Union.

Identifying and dealing with resistance to change is required for any successful approach to crime prevention. Police in transition systems need to be informed through a strategic structure, while at the same time be flexible to adapt to new changes. Additionally, they need to be constantly evaluated and scrutinized (Beck, 2002; Kertész, 2000; Rauch, 2000).

Many developing countries of Africa tend to accept assistance from other countries, and most accept assistance from their former colonial masters. Seeking assistance in the form of know-how is helpful. Criminal justice and criminological expertise to inform governmental strategies and police in particular can be beneficial. Targeted assistance tailored to the needs of transitioning countries may be useful. The problem with such assistance is that many assistance programs are designed without the specifics of any particular country and are not based on the specific needs of the transitional society. Some even distort local agencies because of priorities of providing political power (Carothers, 1998).

Police in transition need to establish a *raison d'etre* for their existence as speedily as possible. Legitimacy and acceptance of police by the public is necessary, because it facilitates the introduction of new policies and programs. Fogel (1994) stated that change in a country's circumstances is reflected in the legitimization of police and in its structures and functions. New systems demand different methods and tactics of policing, making law enforcement agencies prove their legitimacy all over again for the new policies to be regarded as legitimate (Carothers, 2002; Rauch, 2000).

Additionally, public perception of police is a major factor to consider when introducing police reforms. The success or failure of police is evidenced by public perception. The perception of police in many transitional societies of Africa and Latin America is already extremely low. The populace has little or no confidence in police protection. Moreover, as stated above, when protecting citizens is not a priority of the government, police are not provided with the resources needed for performing their functions. The key to building police legitimacy is to ensure effective forms of local control and accountability. It requires making citizens believe that the police are responsive to their needs and are willing to assist them (Carothers, 2002).

Urban societies across the globe, particularly those undergoing transition, are struggling with the problems outlined above. During the last few decades the world has witnessed growing threats to the safety and security of cities. Some have come in the form of catastrophic events, while others have been manifestations of poverty and inequality or of rapid and chaotic urbanization processes. The portrayal of Cameroon's crime problems below illustrates how developing countries are struggling with crime and other urban problems.

Brief History of Cameroon

The Portuguese were the first Europeans to arrive Cameroon in the 1500s, and it was not until around 1870 that many more Europeans started arriving on the West Coast of Africa. By 1884, present-day Cameroon became the German colony of Kamerun. After the First World War, the former East Cameroon became French Cameroon, while the former West Cameroon became British Cameroon under the United Nations Trusteeship agreement. The two European powers ruled Cameroon until 1960–1961.

Cameroon is in West Africa, situated north of the equator on the Gulf of Guinea. It encompasses 185,569 square miles, roughly the size of California. It borders Nigeria to the West; Chad and Central African Republic to the East; and Congo, Gabon, and Equatorial Guinea to the South. Cameroon has a population of approximately 15 million people. The French occupied three-fourth of Cameroon and the French speaking Cameroonians are known as Francophones. This explains the bilingual nature of Cameroon with the Anglophone Cameroonians in the minority. There are 10 provinces and only two are Anglophone: Northwest Province and Southwest Province (see Njeuma, 1990 for more details).

Like other African nations, the struggle for independence started in the middle of the 1900s. In 1955, the outlawed Union of the Peoples of Cameroon (UPC) began an armed struggle for independence in French Cameroon (U.S. Department of State). This rebellion continued until 1960 when French Cameroon became independent.* The following year, British Cameroon, which was at the time part of Nigeria,† rejoined the Republic of Cameroon to become the Federal Republic of Cameroon following a United Nations sponsored referendum. Amadou Ahidjo‡ became the first President of the Federated Republic. Cameroon began its independence with a bloody insurrection which was suppressed only with the help of French forces.§ This was followed by 20 years of repressive government under President Ahidjo.

---

* These events influenced the type of police system adopted by the French in Cameroon. The French had to suppress the bloody insurrection and needed a force that could handle the situation. Similarly, Ahidjo, the first president was facing similar problems and needed French Assistance. He maintained the police system the French had created to deal with similar problems.
† Under the League of Nations mandate of June 28, 1919, this part of Cameroon was given to the British as a trust territory and the British ruled it from Nigeria, the capital of Nigeria.
‡ Ahidjo ruled Cameroon till 1982 when he ceded the presidency to the Prime Minister, Paul Biya, the current President.
§ See U.S. Department of State: Bureau of African Affairs. Background Note. (2003). Ahidjo, relying on a pervasive internal security apparatus, outlawed all political parties but his own in 1966. He successfully suppressed the UPC rebellion, capturing the last important rebel leader in 1970. In 1972, a new constitution replaced the federation with a unitary state.

Over 200 ethnic groups make up the diverse population within the country. Since independence, Cameroon was ruled by former President Ahamadou Ahidjo, until November 4, 1982, when he unexpectedly resigned and handed over his powers (the presidency) to the Prime Minister, Paul Biya. Since 1982, Paul Biya has continued to govern in his capacity as President of Cameroon, Chairman of the Cameroon Peoples Democratic Movement (CPDM), and Supreme Commander of the Armed Forces.

Police Performance

In Cameroon, internal security responsibilities are controlled largely by the Presidency of the Republic. This function is shared by the General Delegation of National Security, the National Intelligence Service, the "Gendarmerie Nationale," the Ministry of Territorial Administration, Military Intelligence, the army, and, to a lesser extent, the Presidential Guard. The police and the Gendarmerie have dominant roles in enforcing internal security laws. The civilian Minister of Defense and the civilian Head of Police are, also, responsible for internal security (U.S. Department of State, Country Reports on Human Rights Practices, 2002).

The organization of Cameroon police and the functions performed reflect the political, social, and economic past of the evolution of Cameroon. As stated above, Cameroon inherited a system of police introduced during the colonial period to fight forces that were struggling for independence and to protect colonial administrations and their objectives. They used unconventional tactics including the "kale-Kale,"* *laissez passez,*† administrative detention,‡ collective punishment,§ burning of villages, arrest for challenging governmental authority, detention in underground jails,⁑ curfews, and summary executions. Additionally, roadblocks were introduced very early in the history of Cameroon to control citizen movement, particularly in

---

* The process was used to round up citizens for no specific crime or violations. Those rounded up would be checked for identification and suspects for insurrection. Those without proper identification or suspected of insurrection were often detained for extensive periods without charge.
† The *laissez passéz* was a form of permit issued by police that allowed citizens to go from one section of the country to another.
‡ It is often used by high level government officials, to detain those who challenged their authority. These detentions often had no legal basis.
§ Collective punishment included arresting and detaining groups of people on the assumption that suspects for various violations would be among them. Often, some would lie about others criminal activities to be released.
⁑ A form of maximum security prison used mainly for political prisoners (e.g., members of the UPC and other groups that used violent insurrection against the government) located primarily in noninhabited areas.

major cities like Douala. Thus, the French and early Cameroon indigenous governments legitimized the use of these tactics (brute force, roadblocks, etc.) under the pretext of combatting guerilla groups such as "marquisards" and other freedom fighters that were violent to colonial governments and even to their citizens.

There is ample evidence indicating that Cameroon police continue to apply practices and tactics used prior to independence and in the years following independence. Unwarranted torture and other forms of abuse by the police and by the gendarmerie are still widespread (Mentan, 2001). As late as two years ago, antigang units—using a mix of army personnel, police, and gendarmerie—created under the direct authority of the Ministry of Defense (not subject to legal rules and operating outside the normal chain of command of law and order) were accused of carrying out extrajudicial executions (Mentan, 2001). Amnesty International reports of recent years have maintained that torture and brutality by the unitary forces remain routine. Critics of the government including supporters of opposition parties, journalists, and human rights activists are often harassed, arrested, and imprisoned (Amnesty International Country Report, 2000, 2001, 2002, 2003).

As noted earlier, the Ahidjo government had to quell rebellion after coming to power.* He needed French assistance and upon receiving it allowed for the police to employ the same tactics used by the French prior to independence. Long after the rebellion ended, Ahidjo and subsequent governments have maintained the same police structures, policies, and practices. This system does not serve any public need, but rather serves only the government's political agenda and the personal economic interests of the police.

The government's primary interest in controlling the people is apparent. As Mentan (2002) states, to achieve this goal the government continues to operate repressive machinery through its armed forces to impose constraints, terror, and coercion on its citizens. The systematic use of armed intimidation is achieved through the pretext of maintaining law and order. Police (including the gendarmerie) and the military are used regularly to arrest, torture, or kill those suspected of violating the laws of the state. A corrupt judiciary directly under the control of the president† is used to pass judgment and determine punishment (Mentan, 2001).

---

* When Ahidjo, the first president of Cameroon assumed the presidency after Cameroon's independence, the Union des populations du Cameroun continued to fight the government which was installed by the French. They claimed the government was illegitimate.
† In Cameroon, members of the judiciary are appointed by the president and are directly answerable to the presidency.

The desire of the government to exercise total control over police is obvious. Though complicated by attempts to project to the public and the rest of the world that it expects its police to respect the public and law, the government has permitted police use of unacceptable practices in its attempt to eliminate opposition and to fight rising crime (Mentan, 2002). These police practices are well documented. In a special United Nations report, Nigel Rodley* describes the practice of torture in Cameroon as widespread and systematic. Reports of the country's hard-handed paramilitary police troops committing extrajudicial killings of alleged criminals are very common (Africa, 2001). For example, an Operational Command of the forces[†] established to combat banditry, especially in Douala, the economic capital of the country, has often been accused of carrying out human rights abuses, arbitrary detentions and other abuses.

According to U.S. government sources, arbitrary arrest and prolonged detention remain "a serious problem" in Cameroon. Government officials and security forces also "use arbitrary arrest tactics to harass and intimidate critics and opposition party members" (Guichi, 2001). Often, security forces subject prisoners and detainees to degrading treatment including stripping, confinement in severely overcrowded cells, and denial of access to toilets or other sanitation facilities. Police and gendarmes often beat detainees to extract confessions, as well as the names and whereabouts of alleged criminals. While the law provides for a judicial review of an arrest within 24 hours, the courts do not convene sessions on the weekend, so the detainees remain in detention until at least Monday (U.S. Department of State, Country Reports on Human Rights Practices, 2002).

The government, under the pretext of maintaining law and order and providing security to its citizens, has granted police wide discretion in the use of police powers. Regrettably, these powers are largely abused to the disadvantage of citizens. The real purposes of tolerating such misconduct are political. For example, the present government—threatened by mounting opposition to its misrule; armed robbery, due largely to wide unemployment and attendant poverty; and attempts at cleansing political opposition (Mentan, 2001)—has allowed law enforcement elements to continue to use such tactics. Consequently, different groups of armed militia torture and even kill at will because they are rarely ever brought to justice.

---

* Sir Nigel Rodley is the United Nations Special Rapporteur on torture. See United Nations Convention against Torture and other Cruel, Inhuman, or degrading Treatment or Punishment. 04/12/2000.

† These commands usually are combined units of the army, police, gendarmes, and sometimes other units of law of the state.

Effects of Lack of Performance on the Part of Police

As stated above, police are the most visible component of government in most countries (Opolot, 2001) and represent the authority of the state (Wrobleski & Hess, 2000). Their actions have consequences for the societies they police. An examination of Cameroon police leads to the conclusion that inadequate police performance or the lack of performance thereof has resulted in three main consequences: uncontrolled rising crime, economic cost, and social costs. Each must be examined.

High Crime Rate

The crime rate in Cameroon has increased consistently since independence. This is expected given the increase in the country's population from about 3 million at independence to a present population of approximately 16 million. The population of the major centers is increasing on average by 5% each year (Tetchiada, 2002). The growth of urban centers is partly due to the natural increase in the population associated with major cities, but it is also due to the loss of land resulting from land erosion, poverty, and unemployment. The working population moving to the cities in search of economic and social opportunities is often met with frustration and contempt. Because of the economy's recession and government abuse, employment is virtually unavailable. Generally, it is believed that urban problems in Cameroon were worsened by the government's economic policies in the 1980s and the 1990s, policies mostly dictated by the World Bank and the International Monetary Fund (Nguekeng, 2003).

Urban problems have resulted in horrid consequences for the country. Social unrest is evident everywhere: "A high crime rate; lack of security; corruption; the authorities' inefficiency; disparity in salaries; and, especially, omnipresent poverty" (Nguekeng, 2003). The government is faced with economic volatility, cultural strife, and particularly rising crime. In 2002, Operation Harmattan (a name in reference to the hot, dry wind that blows southward from the Sahara each year, sweeping northern Cameroon and other parts of the Sahel) was created. This was a response to the wave of killings, armed attacks against senior state officials, and break-ins at public offices in the main cities of Yaounde and Douala. Major incidents of violent crime against governmental officials: the killing of the commander of the mobile police unit in Bamenda in 2001, the killing of a magistrate in Yaounde in 2000, and, of a diplomat in Douala in the same year, often provoke some form of government response (UN Office for the Coordination of Humanitarian Affairs, 2004). But, other crimes do not often provoke a similar response. Crime has also become a political issue, with opposition leaders often issuing public calls to the government to find solutions to the ever increasing problem.

An apparent consequence of police failure is the steady rise in the crime rate. Many recent sources confirm the increasing problem of crime in Cameroon (U.S. Department of State, Bureau of Consular Affairs, 2004; Amnesty International, 2003; United Nations Office of Humanitarian Affairs, 2002). Reasons for the incidence of crime in Cameroon, according to observers, include the incoherent law enforcement effort to fight crime, lack of resources, unchecked circulation of weapons, revenge killings, poverty, and unemployment (UN Office for Humanitarian Affairs, 2004). The crime problem is so severe that in March 2003, the U.S. State Department issued a warning to its citizens traveling to Cameroon. It stated that all foreigners were potential targets for theft with possible violence. Petty crimes, crimes against persons, and thefts from vehicles are the most common criminal activities. Armed banditry is a growing problem throughout all 10 provinces in Cameroon. The risk of street and residential crime is high, and incidents of violent crime are on the rise throughout the country. Carjackings have also been reported on rural highways (U.S. Department of State, 2002). As late as February of 2004, the British Foreign Service issued a similar warning to its citizens. It warned them to avoid carrying valuables or wearing jewelry in public. Petty theft is common on trains, coaches, and in taxis (UK Foreign & Commonwealth Office, 2004).

Economic Cost

Police as civil servants are supposed to perform police duties. The contrary seems to be the norm in many developing countries of Africa such as Cameroon. There is sufficient evidence indicating that Cameroon police are not interested in performing the police duty of deviance control. As illustrated above, most Cameroon police are deployed on state roads or highways as opposed to crime fighting functions. The old tactic of mounting multiple blockades, used in colonial and postcolonial periods to control the movement of rebellious groups, continues to be the norm. It is common to have police, gendarmes, and sometimes military blockades at main entrances and exits of cities and towns. Similar blockades are common on the few state highways. The blockades mounted under the pretext of checking criminals and transportation of contraband are mostly used to shake down motorists for bribes. The average Cameroon motorist knows the standard price for a police or gendarmes stop.

The proliferation of roadblocks and checkpoints manned by the forces make travel very time consuming and costly. Though not official, many of the roadblocks are manned by military guards. They are used as a corrupt way to gather money or to intimidate those passing through (Whalen, 2003). Moreover, the difficulties of travel are exacerbated by the extortion of bribes at these checkpoints. As Peace Corps volunteer Scott Lyons (2003) remarked, "Unfortunately, travel in Cameroon is anything but easy. The roads are terrible, the police constantly harass, and public transportation is infrequent and unreliable." A common sight on the state routes is uniformed officers haggling with a motorist over the amount of bribe (Mills & Cohen, 2002). Roadblocks are frequent and will usually include identity verification of documents, vehicle registrations, and tax receipts as security and immigration control measures. Sometimes citizens are injured by police if they are thought to evade checkpoints (U.S. Department of State, Country Reports on Human Rights Practices, 2002). Security forces also use roadblocks to disrupt opposition political activities.

These police practices are very costly for the country. Most societies pay police to perform traditional police functions. But because the police force in Cameroon hardly perform police functions, but rather collect bribes from motorist for self-enrichment, the cost of maintaining the force is apparently not justifiable. The force is costly to the country in terms of time and money. It is a force that is paid for doing very little. Moreover, the countless stops of motorists cost the citizens greatly in terms of travel time. The law provides for freedom of movement within the Country. However, in practice, security forces routinely impede domestic travel. One article concludes, "... the governments of poor countries ought to pay more attention to their roads. A good first step in Cameroon would be to lift those roadblocks and put the police to work repairing potholes" (The Economist, 2002).

Social Cost

Although the social cost has never been estimated, the nature of police practices is an apparent barometer of the social costs of police performance or lack thereof. Loss of life, injuries, human rights abuses, and loss of public support are just a few examples of the high social cost of the police failure to perform their functions. Only a small percentage of police are engaged in crime prevention. Judging from police and government attitudes, crime prevention seems to be secondary to other government policies and individual police objectives (Mentan, 2001).

Like the economic cost, the social cost to the country is alarming. The failure to perform proper law enforcement duties leads to increased crime and unnecessary intrusion into individual rights. Police are more concerned with mounting roadblocks to collect money from motorists, thus little or no time is left to fight crime. Moreover, because criminals can bribe police, they are able to operate freely all over the country. The need for money and other forms of bribes also blinds the police to traffic violations. Because there is little or no interest in controlling drivers for traffic violations, accidents are therefore common, some resulting in the loss of lives.

The legitimacy of Cameroon police, as well as police in many developing countries of Africa, has never been linked to public need. As noted above, these countries inherited their police systems from European powers (Mentan, 2002; Opolot, 2001). As Koci (1996) notes, how police acquire legitimacy is of fundamental importance to understanding the relationship between law enforcement and the state and society in general. Mawby (1990) specifies that legitimacy is "granted" to the police by "the elite within society, an occupying power or the community as a whole" (Koci, 1996, p. 3). Cameroon inherited its police from an occupying power and its resulting lack of legitimacy has resulted in Cameroonians' lose of faith in their police. As Mentan (2001) states, public perception is that contacts between the police authorities and the population have grown worse. Because of the way police treat members of the public, the relationship between the public and the police is that of disrespect. A Cameroon journalist described the relationship in these words: "Bogged down by corruption, racketeering, torture and lack of discipline, Cameroon's police force does not have good press. The police pay a high price for its failings, so some kind of shock tactics are needed to set matters right" (Mihamle, 1998).

The chaotic situation in transition systems, such as Cameroon, indicates that the task of preventing crime is also hampered by confusion and the absence of proper law and order maintenance. A critical and first step in re-establishing order and consequently beginning to fight crime is the establishment of the rule of law.

The Rule of Law

The rule of law is important to all aspects of life in any country, providing countries with a safe political and social environment. The law is the primary legitimate means for solving social problems, including crime. It instills in people of all societies a sense of hope, confidence, and safety. When people lose hope or faith in the law or see it as unjust, they have no place to turn for redress. They are then more likely to resort to illegal means or worse, violence. "Violence begins when law ends."* The rule of law brings about law and order because it prevents citizens from being exposed to the uncontrolled decisions of others in conflict with them and preempts the more powerful in society from using self-help against the weaker of society. With the rule of law, states cannot act arbitrarily and thus discretionary power is restricted (Heydon, 2003).

---

* Carter warns of "uncontrollable violence." In his Nobel Peace Prize acceptance speech, former President Jimmy Carter blasts the idea of a preemptive war with Iraq.

Carothers (1998) defined the rule of law as "a system in which laws are public knowledge, are clear in meaning and apply equally to everyone." It makes societal institutions more competent and accountable and increases government's compliance with the law (Li, 2000). As a regulator of governmental power, it limits government arbitrariness and power abuse. In this instance, the rule of law is a constraint on the government and enhances rationality by limiting arbitrariness and making government more prudent. In addition, the rule of law tries to ensure equality before the law and provides means to procedural and formal justice with fair regulations and processes.

People, agencies, and governments worldwide from different regional, cultural, and legal backgrounds acknowledge the rule of law as an essential foundation of a just society (Bouloukos & Dakin, 2001). The rule of law greatly supports liberal democracy and brings about economic growth and social security (Carothers, 1998). It also aids in deterring corruption and crime. The rule of law and confidence in its application can bring societies in conflict together. Also, it is said to be the best foundation for resolving prolonged conflicts (Annan, 2004).

According to Brooks (2003), there is a current surge in the need to protect the rule of law. This is especially the case in postcrisis transitional societies. American and international efforts in this area have been prominent. The 1990s witnessed the United States and many international organizations spend vast resources assisting developing countries institute the rule of law. This effort has included rewriting constitutions, establishing comprehensive legal codes, and training legal and justice personnel. The Commonwealth Secretariat and the American Bar Association (ABA) have introduced several programs to enhance the rule of law and strengthen justice systems of developing common law countries. In the Middle East and North Africa, the ABA administers regional and bilateral programs focusing on judicial development, women's rights, role of women in the legal and judicial profession, legal education reform, and legal profession reform.* These organizations have made the judgment that institutions of justice need the rule of law to function properly in any society (Hills, 1994).

Globalization, the decline of state structures in many developing countries, intrastate group conflicts such as those in Kosovo and Rwanda, and the rise of organized terrorist groups make it more likely that the United States, other countries, and the above-mentioned organizations will continue to be

---

* The ABA's technical legal assistance programs are funded by the U.S. Department of State's Office of the Middle East Partnership Initiative, the Bureau of Democracy, Human Rights and Labor, and the Bureau of International Narcotics and Law Enforcement. The ABA also receives significant funding from the U.S. Agency for International Development.

involved and interested in the promotion of the rule of law. Also, failed states, civil wars, and human rights crises in developing societies provide an added incentive for pushing with enthusiasm for the introduction of the rule of law in transitional systems (Brooks, 2003).

Most of the developing world is undergoing some type of legal reform. Many countries of Eastern Europe (from the former Soviet block), most countries in Africa, Asia, the Middle East, and Latin America are in the process of reforming their legal systems. Many of them have been struggling to adopt democratic forms of government in the past few decades. But, unfortunately, the institutions, and particularly the judicial systems, of developing countries do not measure up to those of the West or meet the necessary standards of democratic western societies. As Carothers (1998) stated, some are stagnating or drifting backward as in Sub-Saharan Africa and Asia. According to Carothers, only 30 sub-Saharan African countries have attempted political and economic transitions since 1990, with South Africa as the most promising, with far reaching programs of transformation.

The problem in many developing countries is not mainly the lack of laws or the incapacity of legal personnel, but the unwillingness of powerful state rulers to abide by the rule of law. The willingness of the executive branches to be controlled by laws is often the main obstacle. Corrupt autocrats in developing societies who benefit from not being under the rule of law often do not see why they need to adopt it. As Fagelson (2003) noted, initial international efforts at improving the technical aspects and infrastructure of many legal systems did not enhance the rule of law in countries such as Cambodia and Haiti. Dudziak (2004) found that instituting the rule of law requires the political will of those in power in the case of Tanzania. For example, the Chief Justice of the country, Nyalali, generated a political constituency that was willing to adopt the rule of law. The result was the passage of a Bill of Rights for the country in 1984.

One of the factors required to guarantee the effectiveness of legal protections is judicial independence, but unfortunately, judicial independence does not exist in most developing countries. Judicial independence is crucial to the rule of law, because judicial independence makes judges aware that courts are forums of last resort for citizens and governments alike to resolve disputes. The absence of firmly institutionalized judicial independence usually results in executive interference and, at times, outright control of the judiciary (Glazebrook, 1999).

In democratic societies, the objective of law enforcement is to maximize both the effectiveness of deterrence and conformity to the rule of law. These goals are not in conflict, but supplement each other. Even when the rule of law exists, as Bayley (2002) argued, police in many countries see it as a hindrance to effective law enforcement. When they violate the rule of law in the name of enforcing the law, they do more harm than good to themselves and the societies they serve. Another major impediment is that some systems that have opposing beliefs to the rule of law may regard the rule of law and formal processes as inferior for resolving problems.

One of the difficulties in legal and judicial reform is finding the right balance between indigenous social, economic, and cultural values that can lead to resistance of reform and even failure (Toope, 2003). As Glazebrook (1999) suggested, laws that fulfill what the rule of law seeks to accomplish and that also fit the traditions of the society in question are most commendable.

Respect for human rights and the rule of law is considered essential for dealing with the crime problem in any society (Albright, 1998).* To face and effectively prevent crime and other crime-related problems in transition societies, governments and civil society must act together. The rule of law enables the tackling of problems without the use of force. In places where the rule of law is elusive, hatred, corruption, violence, and exclusion thrives (Annan, 2004), while the powerful manipulate the system to remain in power and accumulate wealth. The vulnerable lack effective means of recourse. For the rule of law to be effective, constitutional safeguards that protect victims against arbitrary governmental interference with individual lives are necessary (Glazebrook, 1999).

Moreover, the rule of law could alleviate several problems of developing societies. It can help reduce vulnerability to criminal exploitation and promote the integrity of justice and the security of governmental officials. Strengthening the rule of law builds a foundation for democratic governments. Without the integrity of justice personnel, crime prevention initiatives may be marginalized and even rendered fruitless through governmental intervention and corruption. One of the consequences of the adoption of democratic regimes is that the public is released from their previously held traditional norms and beliefs, factors that may have been informal constraints to crime. The vacuum created must be filled to avoid the chaos that may ensue. The rule of law usually fills that gap.

Conclusion

The world is urbanizing at a rapid rate. In just within a half century the world urban population grew from about 30% to about 50% (Trzyna, 2007). If the trends continue, humans will continue to flock to existing cities until they are overflowing. Along with the growth of huge new cities comes the rapid increase of problems caused by lifestyle changes and other contributory factors.

---

* Remarks of U.S. Secretary of State Madeleine K. Albright at Remarks at 1998 Asia Society Dinner in New York on June 17, 1998. Remarks which were supported in a letter to the 106th U.S. Congress by the International section of the ABA.

One of the consequences of change is the level of crime which continues to grow at historic highs. Underlying causes of crime include (among others) weakened transitory state institutions and the breakdown of informal controls. The cause of violence, delinquency, drug use, and the emergence of gangs can be attributed to the weakened influence of the family, schools, and churches on values and behavior. Solutions to crime and other problems of transitional societies will depend to a large degree on the ability and willingness of the governments of these states to face the problems and learn from past examples of similar situations in countries that have witnessed similar problems. Unfortunately some of these governments, as stated above, often have political priorities other than crime and the common good.

References

ABA. (2003). Available at http://www.sociology.ohio-state.edu/mlw/soc209/functions.html

Albright, M. K. (1998). Remarks at 1998 Asia Society Dinner in New York.

Amnesty International: Country Report—Cameroon (2000, 2001, 2002, 2003). On-line at http://www.amnestyusa.org/all-countries/cameroon/page.do?id=1011129

Annan, K. (2004). Today the rule of law is at risk around the world. *New African*, 1434, p. 36(4).

Anonymous. (2002). Trucking in Cameroon: The road to hell is unpaved. *The Economist*, December 19.

Bayley, D. (2002). Law enforcement and the rule of law: Is there a tradeoff? *Criminology and Public Policy*, 2(1), 133.

Beck, A. (2002). Crime and policing in post-Soviet societies: Bridging the police/public divide. *Policing and Society*, 12(2).

Bouloukos, A., & Dakin, B. (2001). Toward a universal declaration of the rule of law: Implications for criminal justice and sustainable development. *International Journal of Comparative Sociology*, 145.

Brooks, R. (2003). The new imperialism: Violence, norms, and the "rule of law." *Michigan Law Review*, 101(7), 2275.

Bursik, R. J. (1984). Urban dynamics and ecological studies of delinquency. *Social Forces*, 63, 393–413.

Calder, P. (1996). Ideologies, policies and practices in East Berlin before and after the fall of the wall. *International Journal of Early Years Education*, 4(3).

Carothers, T. (1998). The rule of law revival. *Foreign Affairs*, 77(2), 95.

Carothers, T. (2002). The end of the transition paradigm. *Journal of Democracy*, 13(1).

Cavallaro, J., & Ould Mohamedou, M. (2005). Public enemy number two? Rising crime and human rights advocacy in transitional societies. *Harvard Human Rights Journal*, 18.

Cohen, L., & Felson, M. (1979). Social change and crime rates. *American Sociological Review*, 44, 588–508.

Cohen, S. F. (1979). The friends and foes of change: Reformism and conservatism in the Soviet Union. *Slavic Review*, 38(2).

Dammer, H., & Fairchild, E. (2006). *Comparative Criminal Justice Systems*. Belmont, CA: Wadsworth/Thompson.

Dudziak, M. (2004). Who cares about courts? Creating a constituency for judicial independence in Africa. *Michigan Law Review, 101,* 1622.

Dukes, F. (1999). Structural forces in conflict and conflict resolution in democratic society. In H.-W. Jeong (Ed.), *Conflict Resolution: Dynamics, Process, and Structure*. Vermont: Ashgate Publishing Company.

Fagelson, D. (2003). Building democracy and rule of law: From Moses the law giver to World Bank conditionality? Book Review, *Polity, 36*(1).

Fergusson, D. M., Swain-Campbell, N. R., & Horwood, L. J. (2004). How does childhood economic disadvantage lead to crime? *Journal of Child Psychology and Psychiatry, 45*(5), 956–966.

Fogel, D. (1994). *Policing in Central and Eastern Europe: Report on a Study Tour*. Helsinki: European Institute for Crime Prevention and Control.

Glazebrook, S. (1999). The role of the rule of law in the Asian economic crisis. Paper presented at the Plenary session of the Inter-Pacific bar Association in Bangkok.

Gray, C. (1997). Reforming legal systems in developing and transition countries. *Finance & Development*, September, *34*(3).

Gray, D. C. (2005). *An Excuse-Centered Approach to Transitional Justice*. Duke Law School Working Paper Series.

Guichi, M.N. (2001). Rights-Cameroon: Elite army unit suspected in death of 9 youths. *Inter Press Service (IPS)*. 20 March (LEXIS/NEXIS).

Hannon, L. (2002). Criminal opportunity theory and the relationship between poverty and property crime. *Sociological Spectrum, 22*(3), 363.

Heydon, D. (2003). Judicial activism and the death of the rule of law. *Quadrant, 47*(1).

Hills, M. (1994). The rule of law and democracy in Hong Kong: Comparative analysis of British liberalism and Chinese socialism. *Socialism China, 1*(2).

IRWIN; UN Office for Coordination of Humanitarian Affairs. (2002).

Kertész, I. (2000). Changing patterns of culture and its organisation of the police in a society of transition: Case Study, Hungary. *European Journal on Criminal Policy and Research, 8*(3).

Koci, A. (1996). Legitimization and culturalism: Towards policing change in the European post-socialist countries. In M. Pagon (Ed.), *Policing in Central and Eastern Europe: Comparing First Hand Knowledge with Experience from the West*. Ljubljana, Slovenia: College of Police and Security Studies.

Li, B. (2000). What is rule of law? *Perspectives, 1*(5).

Lyons, S. (2003). Two years in Cameroon: A Cameroon travel page. On-line at http://members.virtualtourist.com/m/5e7f1/d53/

Masamba, S. (2004). Crime and development in Africa. UNAFRI. Paper Presented at the Programme Network of Institutes (PNI) Workshop on Rule of law and Developmemt, 13th Session of the Commission, Vienna.

Mawby, R. I. (1990). *Comparative Policing Issues: The British and American Experience in International Perspective*. London: Unwin Hyman Ltd.

Mentan, T. (2001). Torture as state policy. Talk delivered to group 37, Amnesty Internal USA.

Mentan, T. (2002). *Democratization and Ethnic Rivalries in Cameroon: Colonial Legacies, Democratization and Ethnic Questions in Cameroon*. Ethno-Net Africa: UNESCO.

Mihamle, J. (1998). Cameroon's police dishonored. *AND-BIA Supplement*, Issue/Edition 355.

Mills, M., & Cohen, C. (2002). Birding Cameroon: A Budget Guide for Independent Travelers. Birdlife International. Available at http://www.birdlife.org

Morenoff, J., & Sampson, R. J. (1997). Violent crime and the spatial dynamics of neighborhood transition: Chicago, 1970–1990. *Social Forces, 76*, 31–64.

Newman, O., & Franck, K. (1980). *Factors Influencing Crime and Instability in Urban Housing Developments*. Washington, DC: U.S. Government Printing Office.

Nguekeng, G. (2003). Cameroon urban deterioration: Various projects are afoot to improve home, public services, security and administration. *ANB-BIA Supplement*. Issue/edition 465, 01/11/2003.

Njeuma, M. (1990). *Introduction to the History of Cameroon: Nineteenth and Twentieth Centuries*. New York: Palgrave Macmillan.

Opolot, J. (2001). *Police Administration in Africa: Toward Theory and Practice in the English-Speaking Countries*. Lanham, MD: Rowman & Littlefield.

Rauch, J. (2000). Police reform and South Africa's transition. In M. Shaw (Ed.), *Crime and Policing in Transitional Societies, Conference Summary and Overview*. South Africa: SAIIA (South African Institute).

Sampson, R., Raudenbusch, S., & Earls, F. (1997). Neighborhoods and violent crime: A multilevel study of collective efficacy. *Science, 227*, 918–924.

Sampson, R. J., & Groves, B. (1989). Community structure and crime: Testing social-disorganization theory. *American Journal of Sociology, 94*, 774–802.

Sampson, R. J., & Raudenbush, S. W. (1999). Systematic social observation of public spaces: A new look at disorder in urban neighborhoods. *American Journal of Sociology, 105*(3), 603–651.

Shaw, C. R. (1929). *Delinquency Areas*. Chicago: University of Chicago Press.

Shaw, C., & McKay, H. (1942). *Juvenile Delinquency and Urban Areas*. Chicago: University Press.

Shaw, M. (1995). *Partners in Crime? Crime, Political Transition and Changing Forms of Policing Control*. Johannesburg: Centre for Policy Studies.

Shaw, M. (1997). South Africa: Crime in transition. Occasional Paper No. 17. Crime and Policing Project, Institute for Security Studies.

Sherman, L. W., Gartin, P. R., & Buerger, M. E. (1989). Hot spots of predatory crime: Routine activities and the criminology of place. *Criminology, 17*, 69–100.

Spuy, E. V. (2000). Crime and its discontents: Recent South African responses and policies. In M. Shaw (Ed.), *Crime and Policing in Transitional Societies, Conference Summary and Overview*. South Africa: SAIIA (South African Institute).

Stark, R. (1987). Deviant places: A theory of the ecology of crime. *Criminology, 25*, 893–909.

Sztompka, P. (1993). Civilizational incompetence: The trap of postcommunist societies. *Zeitschrift für Soziologie, 22*(2), 85–95.

Taylor, B. M. (1997). *Changes in Criminal Victimization 1994–95*. Department of Justice, Bureau of Justice Statistics. NCJ 162032.

Taylor, R. B., & Gottfredson, S. D. (1986). Environmental design, crime, and prevention: An examination of community dynamics. In A. J. Reiss & M. Tonry (Eds), *Crime and Justice: A Review of Research, Communities and Crime* (pp. 387–416). Chicago: University of Chicago Press.

Tetchiada, S. (2000). Cameroon faced with social inequalities: Despite progress already made, there's still a long way to go. *ANB-BIA Supplement*, Issue/edition 430.

Tibaijuka, A. (2005). *Poverty, Crime and Migration are Acute Issues as Eastern European Cities Continue to Grow.* UN-Habitat.

Toope, S. (2003). Legal and judicial reform through development assistance: Some lessons. *McGill Law Journal, 48*(3), 357.

Trzyna, T. (2007). *Global Urbanization and Protected Areas. Challenges and Opportunities Posed by a Major Factor of Global Change and Creative Ways of Responding.* IUCN—The World Conservation Union and the California Institute of Public Affairs.

UK Foreign and Commonwealth Office. (2004). *2003 Country Profile, Cameroon.*

UN Office for the Coordination of Humanitarian Affairs. (2004). Cameroon: Crime-fighters arrest hundreds amid complaints of rights abuse. IRWINnews.org

U.S. Department of State, Background Notes. (2003).

U.S. Department of State, Bureau of Consular Affairs. (2004).

U.S. Department of State, Bureau of Democracy, Human Rights, and Labor. (2002). Country Reports on Human Rights Practices.

Warner, B. D., Wilcox, P., & Rountree, P. W. (1997). Local social ties in a community and crime model: Questioning the systemic nature of informal social control. *Social Problems, 44*(4), 520–536.

Weatherburn, D., Snowball, L., & Hunter, B. (2006). The economic and social factors: Underpinning indigenous contact with the justice system: Results from the 2002 NATSISS survey. *Contemporary Issues in Crime and Justice,* 104.

Whalen, S. (2003). *Welcomed Like Heroes.* Professor, Loyalist College, Rotary Club International.

Wolfgang, R. (2004). Countries in transition: Effects of political, social and economic change on crime and criminal justice—sanctions and their implementation. *European Journal of Crime, Criminal Law and Criminal Justice, 7*(4).

Wrobleski, M., & Hess, K. (2000). *An Introduction to Law Enforcement and Criminal Justice.* Belmont, CA: Wadsworth.

Zsuzsa, F. (1997). Major problems and crisis phenomena of five transitional economies in Central Europe. *Regional Development Dialogue, 18*(1), 154–174.

Zveki, U. (1996). Policing and attitudes towards private police in countries in transition: Preliminary results of the International Crime (Victim) Survey. In M. Pagon (Ed.), *Policing in Central and Eastern Europe: Comparing First Hand Knowledge with Experience from the West.* Ljubljana, Slovenia: College of Police and Security Studies.

Urbanization and Security in Kampala City, Uganda

3

BENJAMIN NAMANYA

Contents

This chapter examines critical security issues facing the government of Uganda in view of rapid urban growth, with specific reference to Kampala city. The chapter also examines the strategies in place to address security concerns, as well as the challenges facing the effective implementation of strategies to improve security. Finally, suggestions and recommendations are given on how the security situation in Kampala City could be improved.

Working Definitions

Security can be defined as freedom from risk or danger; safety; freedom from doubt, anxiety, or fear; confidence; as well as something that gives or assures safety. This would include measures adopted by a government to prevent crime and improve the safety of the person.

Urbanization is the increase over time in the population of cities in relation to the rural population. This process could occur as a natural expansion of the existing population (usually not a major factor since urban reproduction tends to be lower than rural), the transformation of peripheral populations from rural to urban, incoming migration, or a combination of the three.

Background

Kampala is the capital city of the Republic of Uganda in East Africa. Since Uganda gained her independence in 1962, Kampala has grown from its original seven legendary hills (Mengo, Lubaga, Kibuli, Nakasero, Kololo, Old Kampala, and Mulago) to a sprawling metropolis covering over 20 rolling hills and suburbs. But Kampala dates further back than independence. In 1890, Captain Frederick Lugard, the British Imperial Administrator, constructed a fort for the British East Africa Company. Kampala grew around that fort. The city first sprouted as a commercial center for mainly Asian traders from as far as India and the East African coast. At the time, the seat of the colonial administration was situated in Entebbe about 32 km away. The population of Kampala then was a mere 4,000 people. It was in 1962 that Kampala replaced Entebbe as the national capital. The last population census of 2002 put the total population of Kampala City at 1,189,100 up from 774,000 in the previous census of 1991. At a growth rate of about 4% per year, Kampala's current population is estimated to be at 2,500,000 people (city authorities' statistics).

The volume of commercial, business, and administrative activities has also grown at a corresponding rate, occasionally experiencing interruptions from wars and civil strife during most regime changes. The infrastructure, particularly the planned road network had been largely static with little or no standard on other roads emerging in the city suburbs. As a result, it is now clearly overwhelmed by population explosion and expansion of the city. However, the commercial and residential structures continue to grow steadily, having peaked during the last decade or so when there has been relative security to guarantee real estate development, albeit without proper planning.

Policing of the city has fundamentally changed, having been executed by the colonial police during the preindependence era, before handing it over to the Ugandan Police. It is also worth noting that the political, economic, and social disruptions that have characterized Uganda as a nation have had a significant impact on all government security institutions, including the police. Today, the police/population ratio in Kampala stands at 1:2,500, a far cry from the internationally accepted standard of 1:500. Suffice it to note that the national police/population ratio is currently at 1:1,500 (Table 3.1).

Table 3.1   Kampala Facts

Water and swamps	13 km^2
Altitude	118 m above sea level
Total population	2.5 million
Annual population growth rate	3.88%

Source: Kampala City Handbook. (2000). Kampala, Uganda: Gava Associated Services Company and Kampala City Council.

With the aforementioned rapid growth of the city, coupled with an increasing population, critical security issues arise that cannot be underestimated. These issues range from crime, idleness, drug abuse and trafficking, congestion, traffic, population growth, and urban planning.

Critical Security Issues

The most common critical security issues were identified based on the annual crime returns of the Ugandan Police; a survey of the public, business community, and security agencies; as well as document review.

Crime: According to police crime returns based on reported cases in the past five years, crime has been increasing steadily—from 15,066 cases in 2002 to 52,988 cases in 2006 (see Figure 3.1 on crime trends in Kampala).

The crime statistics in Figure 3.1 corroborate the findings of the public survey which indicated that the most critical issues included violent crimes such as robbery, murder, and terrorism. Robbery was ranked as the most notorious crime rampant in the city, sometimes involving the use of firearms.

Proliferation of small arms in the region: Uganda's tumultuous political history, the wars, and the insecurity in parts of the country, as well as the volatile situation in the Great Lakes Region (conflict in Rwanda, southern Sudan, Democratic Republic of Congo, Somalia), have contributed to the proliferation of small arms. Many of these arms have found their way into the hands of criminals, compounding the crime management challenge.

Idleness: This is a common scenario in the city mainly caused by unemployment, poverty, lack of sustainable incomes, and rural–urban

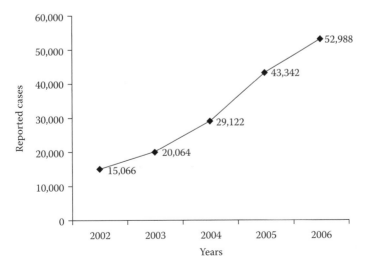

Figure 3.1 Crime trend for Kampala for the past five years.

migration involving school dropouts who flock into the city in the hope of earning a living.

Drug abuse and trafficking: The problems of drug abuse and trafficking are an escalating issue. According to the police crime returns (Table 3.2), such cases have shot up from 239 in 2000 to 656 in 2006. This is facilitated by weak controls at entry points into the city, as well as border points including Entebbe International Airport about 32 km from the city. The problem is propagated by peer pressure and worsened by weak laws against offenders.

Congestion: The city is affected by both human and traffic congestion. The crowded streets pose a challenge to policing of the city. For example, chasing a suspect in crowds can be a nightmare for police. At times the crowd descends upon a suspect to administer mob justice, occasionally overwhelming the police.

Urban planning: There is evidence of poor city planning, leading to a mushrooming in the number of unapproved structures. Some of these structures have collapsed, causing loss of life and property. Poor street lighting has facilitated dark spots and hideouts for criminals.

Other critical security issues of concern: The survey pointed to other issues such as street children, pickpockets, white-collar crime, unlawful demonstrations and riots, traffic congestion, land wrangles, inadequate police personnel, theft, illegal immigrants, and an unregulated public transport system, among others.

Table 3.2   Most Prevalent Crime (Reported Cases) in Kampala for the Last Seven Years

	2000	2001	2002	2003	2004	2005	2006
Murder other than shooting	260	230	227	176	200	255	259
Murder by shooting				22	23	25	31
Rape	50	37	48	59	86	132	98
Defilement	614	642	649	978	1,484	1,745	1,687
Aggravated robbery	681	694	592	353	382	448	392
Simple robbery	537	479	461	607	1,120	2,261	2,357
Burglary and theft	826	716	679	532	845	1,495	1,475
Theft of motor vehicles	517	370	296	311	515	441	450
Theft of all kinds	3,406	3,477	3,504	5,261	9,078	17,601	19,704
False pretences	664	576	664	786	1,567	2,858	3,113
Common assaults	3,306	2,696	2,892	4,120	4,532	4,942	7,624
Malicious damage				481	974	1,499	1,566
Drug cases	239	229	430	394	517	478	656

Source: Kampala Extra Region.

Note: Statistics for murder by shooting were until 2003 categorized under murder. Data were not available on malicious damage cases before 2003.

Contributing Factors

Some of the factors contributing to the critical security issues identified above include the following.

Unemployment: Like most developing countries and preindustrial societies, the rate of unemployment in Uganda is still high. This means that the majority of people are employed in the informal sector in jobs such as hawking, touting, or small trade. The situation is worsened by technological advancement that utilizes less labor, thus rendering many unskilled people unemployed. There are many unemployed people, some of whom have resorted to crime as a means of livelihood.

Poverty: Recent national statistics indicate that 30% of the population of Uganda is living below the poverty line. Although this is an improvement from the 38% previously posted, it still points to a grim situation. The majority of the poorest are in the rural areas. This factor has been instrumental in the increase in rural–urban migration as people run away from poverty in the rural areas, expecting a better life in the city. The level of poverty has also contributed to the gullibility of the people as they easily fall prey to con artists and get-rich-quick tricksters.

Displacement: The insecurity in parts of the country, particularly the north and north-east, has caused unprecedented internal displacement. A significant number of people have fled from such areas into the peaceful city of Kampala to live with relatives. Kampala has been host to many internally displaced people. This is another form of rural–urban migration. In addition, Uganda is host to refugees in the region, some of whom are living in the city. This has contributed to the city's population explosion.

Urban planning: The growth of Kampala has not been in tandem with the growth of the infrastructure to respond to the growing population and traffic. For example, the road network constructed decades ago can no longer cope with the increased traffic demands of today. This, coupled with the poor state of the roads, has caused heavy traffic congestion. The dark streets provide spots where criminals operate; while the mushrooming slums provide cheap alternative accommodation for jobless, idle persons and thugs, most of whom are potential criminals.

New political system: The new multiparty system, coming after 20 years of movement governance, is creating challenges for the tolerance of political differences and appreciation of opposition. This is because the population is only just coming to grips with the recently adopted political system. This has sometimes resulted in unlawful demonstrations, thus attracting police action, in addition to clashes between the different political players.

Weak laws: Some laws are weak and cannot deter criminals from committing crime. Some laws provide for penalties that do not match the gravity of the crimes, so criminals do not fear. For example, the National drug

Authority Act provides options regarding fines and bail conditions, which can easily be met by the offenders.

Power shortage: There is a persistent power shortage that can partly be attributed to increased consumption from the increased population. This has led to load shedding, which keeps part of the city in darkness at any given time. The cover of darkness is conducive for crime, as it hampers appropriate police and community response.

Force strength: The strength of the Ugandan Police Force in Kampala is at 2,500. These officers are expected to police a population of 2,500,000 people (city authorities' statistics). This is way below the international standard of police/population ratio of 1:500.

Public awareness of the law: There is a general lack of awareness among the public of the law and human rights. This affects their ability to appreciate enforcement of law and order, and to participate in crime prevention and management.

Public attitude towards crime: There have been some tendencies among sections of the city communities to ignore their moral obligation to respect the law. Some people do not regard crime as the wrong that it is, but are only restrained by the fact that someone is watching. At the extreme, crime has even been glorified, particularly where it has resulted in the quick amassing of wealth. Such attitudes negatively affect the opportunity for self-policing.

Technology advancement: Technology has led to sophistication in crime, particularly international and cross-border crime. Cyber crime is on the increase.

Strategies to Address Security Issues

The Ugandan Police Force has put in place the following strategies to address the critical security issues raised:

Community policing: (1) *Police/community partnerships* have been instituted in policing public transport, that is, Uganda Taxi Operators and Drivers' Association (UTODA) traffic wardens; as well as managing security at village level together with the local council leaders, that is, *Usalaama* Crime prevention Committees. (2) *Sensitization and involvement of the public in crime prevention and management.* Some of these activities have been community-initiated, in which police were requested to participate.

Media and public information: Crime-watch columns in newspapers, media talk shows, weekly press conferences, and so on are used to facilitate the exchange of information.

Membership on critical government initiatives: (1) National Road Safety Council. (2) National Disaster Management Committee under the Office of the Prime Minister.

Partnerships with development partners: (1) Financial and capacity support to the force. (2) Sharing of best practices.

Establishment of crack unit to manage violent crime: Operation Wembley that was transformed into the violent crime crack unit of the police force.

Joint police/security agencies coordination: (1) Joint Antiterrorism Unit (JAT). (2) Joint Security Coordination Committees for national elections.

Use of auxiliary forces: (1) Special police constabularies. (2) Local defense units.

Regional cooperation on security: (1) Eastern Africa Police Chiefs Cooperation (EAPCO). (2) Interpol (East African sub regional bureau).

National Security Coordination Committee to manage security during the Commonwealth Heads of Government Meeting: Security measures have been enhanced in preparation for the forthcoming Commonwealth Heads of Government Meeting (CHOGM) due in Kampala in November 2007.

Sector-wide approach in law and order and administration of justice: A sector-wide approach code named The Justice Law and Order Sector (JLOS) is in place to plan, coordinate, and support the justice system.

Police/private security partnerships: Private security companies play a big role in managing aspects of security under the supervision of the police.

Elevation of Kampala Extra Police Region: In recognition of the unique challenges of policing the city compared to other areas, the Uganda Police Force has recently elevated the status of the Kampala Extra Police Region, now under the command of a Commissioner of Police.

Other National Policies

Some of the national policies that have a significant impact on addressing the contributing factors to critical security issues in Kampala city include

- Universal education [Universal Primary Education (UPE) and Universal Secondary Education (USE)].
- Poverty alleviation programs.
- Investment policies.
- Fast tracking of the East African Federation.
- Peace initiatives and processes in the Great Lakes region.
- Good governance and anticorruption policies.
- Human rights promotion and protection.

Challenges to Implementation of the Strategies

Pace of technology: The level of technology advancement in the Ugandan Police Force has not kept pace with up-to-date developments. This poses a challenge regarding the management of cyber crime. As a result, it is still not possible to create databases to electronically store crime management information, including biodata of individuals. Records management is still largely manual, which affects the efficiency and effectiveness of police.

Impact of HIV/AIDS: This disease has devastated communities, leaving several orphans in its wake. This has perpetuated the dependency factor, as those affected seek out their extended families in the city, thus aggravating the rate of rural–urban migration. It has also perpetuated the cycle of poverty.

Police facilitation: There is inadequate budgetary support that results in inadequate logistics, equipment, and so on.

Police capacity: Sections of the police force, particularly the special police constables and local administration police, require comprehensive training in law enforcement to bring them up to par with the rest of the force.

Individual weaknesses: Some incidents of corruption, abuse of office, and other forms of indiscipline affect the effectiveness of the force.

Public perception of the police: The hangover of suspicion and mistrust in the police, dating to the colonial period as well as the notorious past regimes, still persists among the public.

Social–economic factors: In some instances, administration of justice has been seen to favor the rich and powerful, leaving the poor disadvantaged.

Recommendations

Some of the ways in which the identified critical security issues in Kampala city can be addressed include the following:

- Enhancing community policing.
- Enhancing public relations.
- Improving police/population ratio.
- Rights-based approach to policing.
- Training.
- Capacity building in terms of equipment, facilitation, and welfare.
- Introduction and upgrading of Information and Communication Technologies (ICTs).
- Enhancing regional cooperation and collaboration.
- Enhancing sustainable partnerships with other security agencies with the police taking a lead role in law enforcement.
- Integrated planning to enhance interagency coordination.
- Law reform and harmonization of laws in the region.
- Study tours and exchange programs.

- Participation in regional and international conferences for information exchange and best practices.
- Continuous research to keep abreast with developments in security management.

Conclusion

Urbanization has no doubt had a significant impact on the security situation in the city of Kampala. The Ugandan Police Force, which is mandated to ensure security and safety in the city, has demonstrated awareness of the demands of policing in a continuously expanding city. Where it has been possible, responsive action—both proactive and reactive—has been taken to address the challenges. However, the budgetary constraints that have persisted over the years have negatively affected the ability of the Ugandan Police Force to effectively ensure 100% security. Nevertheless, Kampala is secure and safe and proudly ranks high on the security scale in the continent.

Urbanization, Policing, and Safety in Serbia

4

ŽELIMIR KEŠETOVIĆ

Contents

A number of authors point at the significant increase of different forms of anomie* in modern towns, as well as people with strange behavior. The most frequent and typical forms of urban anomie are: suicides, violence, professional offenses, vagrancy, drug addiction, sexual pathology, psychosis, neurosis, and mass mental epidemics.

Studies of environmental influences on suicide have shown the differences between rural and urban areas. As the towns grow, the number of suicides increases proportionately. People are members of a "lonely crowd," living isolated in urban neighborhoods, without social relations. An important factor is density of population, so there are considerable differences between particular parts of the town.

Different kinds of violence are present in towns, so the residents of towns are more likely to become victims of violence than inhabitants of rural areas. Type and size of settlement do have an impact on the dimensions and kind of violence. Donald Lunde (1975, p. 98) reports that murder rate is almost twice as high in big towns than in rural areas. In addition to this are the data from

---

* Emile Durkheim in his works *Social Division of Labour* and *Le Suicide* introduced the concept of anomie in sociology, having in mind the absence of any norm in society, and absence of any self control, when an individual rejects all common rules, especially in the time of social crisis. This concept was accepted, worked out, and complemented with findings of psychoanalysis in American Sociology.

Table 4.1   Murder Rates in the United States in 1973

Area	Rate of Murders on 100,000 Residents	Percentage of Population in the Areas (%)
Urban	10.0	62
Suburban	5.5	28
Rural	6.3	10
Total	9.3	100

Source: FBI. (1973). *FBI Uniform Crime Reports.* Washington, DC: FBI.

the FBI report about the ratio between the rate of murders and density of population as can be seen in Table 4.1.

Ramsey Clark (1970, pp. 49–50) stated that the murder rate in big towns is as much as four times higher than in suburbs, and 50% higher than in rural areas. However, these high rates are result of a number of murders in a few small parts of the town. Thus, Lunde (1975, p. 7) notes that two-third of the murders in Cleveland occur in three of a total 42 town areas, in which only 12% of the residents live. He adds that the murder rate is highest in overpopulated areas with the highest percentage of unemployment, where undereducated residents live in poor conditions.

Other forms of violence, including robbery as a typical urban crime, are also more frequent in urban agglomerations. In towns with more than 250,000 inhabitants, the frequency of robbery is 10 times higher than in the suburbs and 35 times higher than in rural areas.* There is a certain regularity in the distribution of violence in particular urban areas as a result of specific human and institutional communication, given different levels and natures of the integration of human relations, as well as a specific subculture of violence as the cultural pattern of the members of similar groups (races, classes, etc.) concentrated in these neighborhoods.

Because the size of the town influences the appearance of certain kinds of violence, some authors think that the town is *per se* a criminogenic factor, while others believe that the conditions favorable to crime condition are more likely to be present in towns. Chevalier suggests that crime is more a function of the rate of town growth, and that the town is not, itself, inherently pathological. According to him, crime rates in towns do not have to be higher than in rural areas, but the demographic characteristics and behavior of urban populations are different. On the other hand, the FBI statistical report for 1966 shows correlation between the size of the town, murders, robberies, and nervous physical attacks (Table 4.2).

---

* Here there are also variations between certain urban areas. See Gudović (1996, p. 148).

Table 4.2   Violent Crime Rates by City Size in the United States in 1966

Size of the Town (Number of Residents)	Murder	Robbery	Nervous Physical Attacks
>250,000	9.9	242.5	228.1
100,000–250,000	6.9	83.5	157.3
50,000–100,000	3.6	55.1	92.3
25,000–50,000	3.4	36.4	81.1
10,000–25,000	2.8	20.6	72.4
<10,000	2.1	11.9	68.2
Rural areas	4.7	10.0	60.9

Source: FBI. (1966). *FBI Uniform Crime Reports.* Washington, DC: FBI.

The growth of crime in towns is influenced by population density, the concentration of power and wealth in certain areas and poverty in others, the inability of the urban community to integrate its members and to control the ones who resist integration, more opportunities for criminals to hide, and many other factors. In small towns, where social control is still strong and moral standards are high, crime rates are lower.

Vagrancy, squatting and the phenomenon of beggary are also among the anomies of the towns. Vagrants and beggars are usually persons from the margins of society, who have no profession, are runaways, or have been rejected by society. Among them also are lazy, asocial, invalid, or mentally disabled individuals. However, vagrancy can also be a form of protest against the values of consumer society.* Vagrants, beggars, and similar categories of people establish a network of hierarchical relations, having some towns as their particular areas (hobohemia).

Town is often connected with vices like alcoholism, gambling, drug addiction, and prostitution—but only the last two are typical urban phenomena. Drug addiction is increasing in modern towns as a certain form of urban disorientation, as a result of some objective factors. Drug dealers have to remain common-looking and anonymous. His appearance in a rural area would be soon noticed, leading to his arrest. Besides that, drug addicts dispersed in a wide territory would be a problem for dealers. In urban areas, drug addicts are concentrated, thus dealers are more anonymous and better protected.

The anonymity of the urban way of life is a convenient ground for spreading different forms of sexual pathology like voyeurism, exhibitionism,

---

* According to some typologies in France there are 14 categories of beggars, in Germany and Switzerland 28, Spain 23, and in Chicago 24 (Anderson, 1923, p. 71).

fetishism, and particularly prostitution.* Different psychoses and neuroses are widespread in modern towns. Sometimes, particularly during serious social crisis and disturbances, mass mental epidemics (hallucinations, etc.) can occur in towns, leading to mass robberies and violent riots (Kostić, 1982, pp. 211–212). Towns are also the stage for manifesting the racial prejudice and discrimination that can lead to interracial conflicts and clashes, and hate crimes as well.

Finally, the formation of social aggregates—such as public, mass, and crowd—is easier in towns. Consequently, the potential for different forms of collective violence, from clashes between fans at sporting matches to different forms of manifestation of the social and political discontent of citizens—especially in the capitals as administrative and political centers—is higher. As a result of the aforementioned factors, numerous sociologists talk about tyranopolis, a town ruled by the underground and total anomie.

Because of the specific features of towns, city police forces are often rather autonomous, while their size, organization, equipment, and methods of work are adjusted to the specifics of the urban environment and its particular parts. In police systems of some countries, the size of settlement is the criterion that determines whether a separate police organization will be established.†

Urban Safety Issues in Serbia

Serbia is situated in south-eastern Europe, occupying an area of 88.361 km², with a total of 7,498,001 inhabitants.‡ Until the end of the twentieth century, Serbia was a predominantly rural and rather safe society. For the first time in the mid-1990s more than 50% of the total population lived in towns. According to the Bureau for Statistics, in 2002 the urban population was 4,225,896 and 3,272,105 people lived in rural areas.§ The population of four

---

* Prostitution follows urbanization from the very beginning. Thus, in excavations in the Sumerian town Uruk, traces of bordellos were found. The Greek statesman Solon created, among other institutions in Athens, a bordello in 594 BC.

† For example, in France the National Gendarmerie performs police tasks for settlements with less than 10,000 inhabitants, while in the towns city police organizations that are in the structure of National police are responsible for security. In England city police are formed in towns with more than 75,000 inhabitants, while in London there are even two police forces: Metropolitan Police Force—Scotland Yard, and the City of London Police. See Milosavljević (1997).

‡ Data are taken from last census (2002) for Serbia without the autonomous provinces Kosovo and Metohija, which have been under the administration of the United Nations (UNMIK) since 1999.

§ http://webrzs.statserb.sr.gov.yu/

major towns—Belgrade, the capital (1,576,124),* Novi Sad (299,294), Niš (250,518), and Kragujevac (175,802)—comprised almost one-third of the total population of the Republic of Serbia.

As a result of wars in neighboring countries, an autocratic regime, and international isolation, the social and demographic structure of Serbia changed significantly in the last two decades. Thousands of members of national minorities, as well as young and talented people, left the country. On the other hand, more than half a million refugees came to Serbia from Croatia, Bosnia, Kosovo, and Metohija. There were also migrations from rural to urban areas as a result of devastated agriculture, and from some towns to larger urban centers due to unemployment. These processes affected major Serbian towns, slowly changing the class and ethnic structure, the ways and habits, the system of values, and the character of social control. Belgrade experienced the most pressure, multiplying the problems that already existed: the level and structure of crime, social pathology (drug abuse, prostitution, etc.), traffic jams, unemployment, limited capacities of critical infrastructures, air pollution, and other environmental and housing problems. The situation culminated with the 1998–1999 Kosovo crises and the subsequent NATO military intervention. Milošević was defeated in elections held in September 2000, and Serbia stepped into transition.

In the last decade of the twentieth century, there were several factors leading to the criminalization of Serbian society: the dissolution of federal state, war in neighboring countries, migrations, political isolation, and the sanctions of the United Nations against Serbia. These factors led to state sponsored smuggling of tobacco and other excise goods, erosion of the system of values, a number of economic problems (e.g., highest inflation in the history of mankind), the disappearance of the middle class as an element of social stability, the Kosovo crisis, and so on. Illegal actions by the state, business enterprises, and ordinary citizens in the isolated country were widespread and tolerated, leading to overall anomie. All of these factors led to rise of crime rates and the genesis of organized crime.

The concentration of business and wealth on one side and poverty on the other, together with the aforementioned features of Serbian cities, places a number of challenges before the public and private police and urban communities. This refers to the level and structure of crime; organized and high-tech crime; traffic control, regulation, and the number of traffic accidents; fires and technological accidents; demonstrations, riots, and street blockades (especially in Belgrade where are the government buildings); clashes of sport fans during football matches; protection of foreign embassies and consulates; prostitution; and homeless people, beggars, and so on.

---

* It has to be noted that the city of Belgrade consists of 16 municipalities. Six of them are mainly rural, four are pure urban, while six are mixture of rural and urban elements.

We will give just a brief overview of the main indicators of the security situation in four major Serbian towns for the last five years (Table 4.3).

The population of four major Serbian towns (Belgrade, Novi Sad, Niš, and Kragujevac) constitutes 32% of the total population of the Republic of Serbia. Around one-half of the total number of crimes and traffic accidents and around two-third of the total number of fires and explosions occurred in these towns. As one can see, almost 35% of all crimes in Serbia are committed in Belgrade, while the population of the capital city comprises only 20% of the total population (Table 4.4).

On average, around 20% of homicides and rapes,* and 68% of all robberies occur in Belgrade. As in many towns, the capital city crimes are commonly armed clashes between criminal gangs competing for dominance, which often result in murders. Comparing the number of homicides per 100,000 inhabitants in Belgrade with some other capitals in countries in transition (Table 4.5), it can be seen that the homicide rate is lower than in Tallinn and Vilnius, similar to Warsaw, and higher than in Prague, Bratislava, and Budapest. The Slovenian capital, Ljubljana, with 1.69 is very close to the rate in the Austrian capital, Vienna, with 1.64.†

If we compare the number of homicides per 100,000 inhabitants for the four largest cities in Serbia, we can see that it is highest in Novi Sad (7.66), followed by Kragujevac (6.1), Belgrade (5.86), and Niš (5.2) (Table 4.6).

Organized crime takes place in cities. All the major organized crime groups are situated in major Serbian towns. Most frequent are crimes against property. Banks, post offices, exchange offices, petrol stations, and similar objects with considerable amounts of cash are targets of robbers. Sometimes they are very creative, dressing as Santa Clause or Serbian orthodox priests.

Vehicle thefts are also a problem of Serbian towns. These crimes are committed by well-organized and specialized mobile groups. They transport stolen vehicles with forged documents in Albania via Kosovo, in Bosnia and Herzegovina, or in Russia and Ukraine. As Serbia is located on Balkan drug route, drug trafficking and drug abuse is one of the major security problems in Serbian towns. Around 60% of the organized crime groups are in this business, trying to put illegal profit into legal money flows (money laundering) (Table 4.7).

While on average around one-third of all traffic accidents in Serbia occur in Belgrade, the number of killed and injured people in these events is around one-fifth. This can be explained by the concentration of vehicles and heavy

---

* In year 2006 around 30%.
† Data for other capitals are an average number of homicides per year and refers to the years 1996–2000. Data for the western capital Vienna are given just as a report. Barclay and Tavares (2002) "International comparisons of criminal justice statistics 2000," taken from Home Office Web site www.homeoffice.gov.uk.

Table 4.3 Main Security Indicators in Serbia and Four Serbian Towns

	Crimes					Traffic Accidents					Fires and Explosions				
	2002	2003	2004	2005	2006	2002	2003	2004	2005	2006	2002	2003	2004	2005	2006
Serbia	92,804	90,365	96,791	95,603	96,952	52,177	55,660	62,434	62,036	63,913	4,895	5,393	5,147	5,259	5,709
Belgrade	30,828	31,434	34,782	34,073	34,139	17,841	19,056	21,294	22,139	23,311	2,795	3,161	3,094	3,218	3,561
Novi Sad	7,744	6,480	6,789	7,455	6,989	4,534	5,523	6,561	6,561	6,512	147	132	137	140	131
Niš	3,412	3,308	4,076	4,730	4,808	1,852	1,627	1,805	1,649	1,842	17	30	65	69	65
Kragujevac	2,714	2,273	2,351	2,431	2,148	955	946	1115	982	947	75	131	124	103	60

Table 4.4 Violent Crimes in Serbia and Four Serbian Towns

	Homicide					Rape					Robbery				
	2002	2003	2004	2005	2006	2002	2003	2004	2005	2006	2002	2003	2004	2005	2006
Serbia	395	378	315	311	350	187	158	148	121	152	3,241	2,854	2,892	2,985	3,775
Belgrade	85	82	62	84	105	55	41	29	33	35	2,266	1,940	1,734	1,986	2,457
Novi Sad	22	29	23	14	27	8	8	4	5	6	169	149	307	180	251
Niš	9	12	20	11	13	2	2	1	2	4	55	88	133	99	148
Kragujevac	14	10	14	8	8	2	4	9	2	2	54	60	51	39	54

Table 4.5   Belgrade Homicides Compared to Eight Other Cities

	Number of Homicides	Homicides per 100,000
Tallinn	137	11.14
Vilnius	169	9.73
Belgrade	88	5.86
Warsaw	257	5.29
Prague	164	4.28
Bratislava	47	3.49
Budapest	143	2.59
Ljubljana	15	1.69
Vienna	78	1.64

Table 4.6   Five-Year Averages for Homicide in Serbia and Four Serbian Towns

2002–2006 Average	Number of Homicides	Homicides per 100,000
Serbia	350	4.67
Belgrade	88	5.86
Novi Sad	23	7.66
Niš	13	5.2
Kragujevac	10.8	6.1

traffic in the capital, while at the same time driving speed is lower than in other areas. It is perhaps worth mentioning a very dangerous game known as "Serbian roulette," popular among children of the Serbian *nouveaux riches*. After midnight they drive their expensive cars very fast, running through the crossroads when the traffic light is red (Table 4.8).

Response Capacities

We can distinguish three major subjects that represent response capacities to deal with the complex security situation in four major Serbian towns. There are: public (state) police, private security sector, and citizens and their organizations. While the security situation has been aggravated over time, response capacities have weakened. The police came through the process of deprofessionalization. Private security agencies that emerged in the meantime were not regulated. Meanwhile, the citizens and local communities were factually excluded from making policy and reduced to a pure object.

Table 4.7 Traffic Accidents, Deaths, and Injuries in Serbia and Four Serbian Towns

	Total Number					Killed					Injured				
	2002	2003	2004	2005	2006	2002	2003	2004	2005	2006	2002	2003	2004	2005	2006
Serbia	52,177	55,660	62,434	62,036	63,913	854	868	960	843	900	14,760	15,953	17,573	16,890	18,405
Belgrade	17,841	19,056	21,294	22,139	23,311	156	165	162	145	174	3,056	3,049	3,225	3,343	3,517
Novi Sad	4,534	5,523	6,561	6,561	6,512	36	28	35	36	50	866	959	1,152	1,051	1,185
Niš	1,852	1,627	1,805	1,649	1,842	29	18	25	16	18	478	454	553	497	606
Kragujevac	955	946	1,115	982	947	14	25	12	19	14	415	470	469	380	418

Table 4.8 Fires and Explosions, Deaths, and Injuries in Serbia and Four Serbian Towns

	Total Number					Killed					Injured				
	2002	2003	2004	2005	2006	2002	2003	2004	2005	2006	2002	2003	2004	2005	2006
Serbia	4,895	5,393	5,147	5,259	5,709	84	94	89	95	88	165	200	223	236	257
Belgrade	2,795	3,161	3,094	3,218	3,561	15	9	18	15	18	55	59	65	84	78
Novi Sad	147	132	137	140	131	13	13	7	11	8	18	11	23	14	17
Niš	17	30	65	69	65	—	6	1	4	5	4	1	11	8	11
Kragujevac	75	131	124	103	60	1	2	3	2	3	2	9	8	8	4

Public Policing

After the dissolution of the former Yugoslavia and the establishment the personal rule of Slobodan Milošević in Serbia, police become the pillar of the regime. Their main task was not to serve and protect the people, but the ruling elite. The main purpose of law enforcement was the fierce suppression of democratic movements and participation in the Yugoslav War, while crime fighting and community policing were largely neglected. Many serious crimes remained unsolved, and the fear of crime among citizens was high. Some criminals were even protected, due to their "credit" in war ("patriotism"), and their role in smuggling operations for the state. Besides that, a number of high-ranking police officers and managers were involved in, or very closely aligned with organized criminal groups. Police were very rough in interventions against political opponents of the regime, especially during street demonstrations. The police model become very centralized and militarized, including the introduction of a military ranking system for police in 1995. Loyalty was ensured by direct appointments of politically obedient people to top positions. This all led to serious deprofessionalization of the police.

After democratic changes in October 2000, one of the first priorities for the new government was reforming of the security sector, first of all Ministry of Interior (MoI). The cornerstone challenges of this reform were marked as the four "D"s—depoliticization, decentralization, decriminalization, and demilitarization (Bakić & Gajić, 2006; Kešetović & Davidović, 2007). Police reform was slow, as neither of the post-Milošević administrations had political will and an overall reform strategy, which led to a lack of internal capacity and precise time frames. The Serbian concept of security is still state-centered, relying on MoI with around 40,000 employees. Six and a half years after democratic changes, Serbia still has a very centralized police model, a paramilitary police culture, and strong political influence over the organization and the performance of police tasks. The level of criminalization can be estimated only indirectly. Other major issues that might have influence on urban policing are a lack of police accountability, parliamentary oversight, and personal management system. Due to this, the level of public trust in the police, as well as the readiness of the citizens to cooperate and help the police, is still rather low.

The centralized police model in which heads of all city and regional police organizations, which are organizational units of the MoI, are appointed directly by the Minister of Interior, while local community has no influence at all, is not adequate for adjusting the organization and local politics of the police to the needs of local community. Police culture has not changed significantly, so policemen tend to think of themselves as state employees, not as public servants.

Due to these faults in the system, the success of implementing community policing initiatives supported by Organization for Security and

Cooperation in Europe (OSCE) and the international community in several pilot sites (including Kragujevac, and Zvezdara—Belgrade municipality) was limited. On the other hand, due to the efforts of open-minded and modern police managers, in some Serbian towns (e.g., Niš, Zaječar) cooperation between police and citizens, media, other government agencies, and NGOs has improved. In addition, a specific local network of individuals and institutions has been established, resulting in increased public confidence in police, on the one hand, and a decrease in fear of crime among residents, on the other. However, leaving the initiative for improving local security in Serbian cities, through partnership and sharing responsibility for a number of issues in the local community, solely to the local police managers and their courage and capability to creatively interpret (or even avoid) existing rules are not sustainable solutions. Also, it has to be mentioned that the operating methods and equipment of Serbian police are rather outdated. This refers to obtaining and using intelligence, the area of forensic science, Geographical Information System (GIS), crime mapping, and so on.

Besides this, it is worth mentioning that there is lack of interest in the urban population for joining the police. This is especially the case in Belgrade, where more than one-half of the policemen live up to 100 km from the town. They do not share the urban mentality and system of values, and they do not look upon the city in which they work as their own.

As in the Law on Police (2005), possibilities for the creation of local police organizations in Serbian cities that would be tailored to the specific features and needs of their residents are very limited. Some cities sought a solution in establishing city police organizations that would be outside the MoI, responsible to the local authorities, to deal with local problems (petty crime, public order, traffic, environmental issues, etc.). For example, in order to upgrade the level of security in Belgrade there were proposals for creating city police whose main tasks would be in the sphere of prevention. Creation of local law enforcement agencies is possible according to the provisions of the new Constitution (2006), but a necessary precondition is adopting the Law in the capital city. Local police would be organized in accordance with the standards of the EU and on the basis of the best practice of large European cities.*

Private Policing

Private policing is a relatively new phenomenon in the Serbian internal security system. A sudden growth in the number of private security companies at the end of 1992, and particularly after the abolition of the Law on social

---

* Vienna is the best example of how introducing city police is useful. The crime rate decreased by 8% and drug trafficking by 79%. Only three months after installing a CCTV system on city squares, crime decreased by 37%.

self-protection system 1993, is marked as the beginning of establishing the private security sector in Serbia. From the beginning, the development of private security sector has moved in two directions: (1) toward establishing private agencies that were engaged in protecting "new businessmen," politicians, and show business stars, but also criminals and both former or current members of the secret services and (2) toward establishing private security companies that inherited the role and jobs of former security services in public and/or public companies that were engaged in classic jobs of securing property, people, or business. The agencies, as a rule, worked in a frequently unlawful manner, while private security companies, which could have even a larger number of employees, were slowly developing their field of activity and the private security sector in general.

In a period of only one decade, the number of employees in the private security sector grew to around 30,000. Companies and enterprises engaged in private security are situated in Serbian towns. The qualitative jump in the offerings of the private security sector has been recorded after the change of regime following October 5, 2000. The process of privatization, and therefore the arrival of foreign companies in the Serbian market too, have also conditioned a rise in the quality and an expansion of the range of supply in the private security market in Serbia. The rise in the industry of private security in Serbia is confirmed by the data that a yearly turnover of private security companies increased from €10 million in 2001 to close to €26 million in 2003 (according to official data of the National Bank of Serbia (NBS) Solvency Centre). The investments made by the owners of private security companies were particularly aimed at new security technologies and equipment, rather than for employee training and education.

The main problems facing the private security sector are

- The absence of a contemporary categorical apparatus in the field of internal security, which emerges from the fact that there is not clearly formulated national security concept in Serbia that should be primarily focused on prevention (not repression) and adjusted to the character/course of historical changes of the social corpus that is moving toward the private as its fundamental feature.
- In connection with that, the absence of a conceptual apparatus, with which current occurrences in the sphere of internal security, especially in the private arena, would be determined adequately and that way become adaptable to critical opinion, projecting, conceptualization, and strategic planning.
- A lack of laws that would rationalize the number of negative, or at least undefined, occurrences and relations that are already present in the reality of the private security sector—for example, private investigators/detectives, private surveillance systems, abuse of private

securities, especially in situations involving the taking control of a private facility or premises; the lack of standards regulating the manner of offering private security services; the lack of systematic training and education of employees in the private security sector; licensing of the companies and employees in the sector, protection of employees' rights, and disloyal competition in the market of security services.

- A lack of partnership between the private and state security sectors, as the key precondition for achieving the security and safety of citizens, local community, and society in general. This tells us something about at least two factors: (1) the governing model of internal security in Serbia, which is always state-centralized; and, in relation to this (2) the ever present stereotype of the police as the only provider of security in the society.
- The lack of any conception of crime prevention at the national level, and therefore lack of any vision about the place and the role of private police in prevention.

The last problem directly takes us to the discussion about how much we can talk about private policing in Serbia at all. If we strictly adhere to the definition of policing* as a social concept that involves a wider circle of social factors that in both direct and indirect ways influence the realization and maintenance of security in society, whereas private security represents operationalization of the concept in manpower and technique, then we can say that we are at the very beginning of creating conditions for establishing the concept of private policing in any location at all, and consequently in Serbia as well (Kešetović & Davidović, 2007).

In the context of improving security in Serbian cities a very important factor is communication between the public/state sector and the private security sector, and their cooperation on the general concepts of crime prevention, elimination of threats by crime, helping the nation to eliminate the fear of crime that citizens suffered for the whole decade. However, at the same

---

* In essence, *policing* represents a social function that contributes to the maintenance of individual social order (and peace), which is carried out by numerous, various institutions, establishments, and bodies. It understands those activities whose goal is to provide security of social order in a certain environment, and this by way of measures and activities that are appropriate for such an objective. In that sense, policing differs from the much wider concept of social control, which includes almost everything that indirectly and directly contributes to maintenance, that is, production of social order (and peace)—of schools, parent boards, churches, youth clubs and centers, and media and public workers. In other words, policing is one aspect of social control that brings together monitoring systems with the threat of sanctions for violating social order, with its primary goal being to keep this social order safe from internal and external threats. This social order can be founded on consensus, or conflict and oppression, or a combination of the two, which occurs more frequently in modern societies.

time, the private security sector represents a real, existing force that with the expansion of activity gradually also acquires the characteristics of power. This then also conditions negotiations, although from a different negotiating position. By contrast, the measure of ceding traditional jobs and authority that have been the exclusive monopoly of the state for centuries also represents a measure of the democratization of a society. Judging from the present situation, speaking of the activities carried out by the security sector and the authority they have, the monopoly of the state power embodied in the MoI still exists.

Citizens

During the socialist regime in Serbia (1945–1989), providing security was the task of the party-state. An attempt to socialize the security function by including the widest circle of subjects involved in security ("system of defense and social self-protection") in practice was based on socialist ideology and was rather dysfunctional and dissipated (Milosavljević, 1997, p. 71). The pressure of ideology, on the one hand, and the awareness that its influence on politics is minimal, on the other, made the citizens rather passive.* They were reduced to the pure object of the socialist party and controlled mass media. This is not changing during the transition, due to the fact that democratic institutions are still weak. The power of the citizens is delegated to the members of parliament (MP) who takes into account only the interests of their political parties. Public opinion and the independent media are still not very important to the political elites. To the police it is still more important to have legitimacy in the eyes of the political leadership than to gain public trust. The state remains very centralized, and security is the function of central government. Local authorities have almost no influence. The ethnic and social structure of Serbian towns changed significantly due to wars, migrations, and refugees. Civil activism is not very high, nor is an interest in the quality of life in the community. Civil society is still weak, and NGOs are sometimes more interested in obtaining foreign donations than in solving everyday problems. Crime levels are higher, unlike trust in police and other institutions of criminal justice. In this framework, citizens are not very willing to participate in different projects designed to improve security.

Conclusion

Serbia, similar to other countries in transition, is faced with new security threats and challenges, organized crime (drug trafficking, human trafficking,

---

* In accordance with the saying in USSR that the citizens blamed the government for everything, even for bad weather, as they have known that they have no influence at all.

etc.) being the most serious among them. The security situation is endangered, especially in towns and cities. Looking at the main security parameters, one can see that around one-half of the total number of crimes and traffic accidents and around two-third of the total number of fires and explosions occurred in four major Serbian cities: Belgrade, Novi Sad, Niš, and Kragujevac, which compose one-third of total population of Serbia.

Achieving a high level of security in Serbian towns appears to be a difficult task that can be fulfilled only through partnership between police and the private security sector, when both are efficient and have high professional standards of performance and, of course, motivated citizens who are fully aware that they are also responsible for the security of their communities. Serbian police are still overburdened with the legacy from the past (authoritarian regime). The growing private security sector is not regulated, while citizens are still passive, waiting for the police to deliver a favorable state of security. In the absence of an overall strategy of national security (including the strategy of prevention) and the continuing understanding of security from state-centered perspective, it is very hard to achieve these objectives.

References

Anderson, A. A. (1923). *The Hobo*. Chicago: University of Chicago Press.

Bakić B., & Gajić, N. (2006). *Police Reform in Serbia: Five Years Later*. Belgrade: OSCE.

Clark, R. (1970). *Crime in America*. New York: Simon and Schuster.

FBI. (1966, 1973). *FBI Uniform Crime Reports*. Washington, DC: FBI.

Gudović, Z. (1996). *Socio-Anthropological Basis of Violence*, Belgrade: Edition of the author.

Kešetović, Ž., & Davidović, D. (2007). Policing in Serbia—challenges and developments. In G. Meško & B. Dobovšek (Eds), *Policing in Emerging Democracies— Critical Reflections* (pp. 79–100). Ljubljana: Faculty of Criminal Justice and Security.

Kostić, C. (1982). *Town and Time—Basic of Sociology of City*. Belgrade: Vuk Karadžić.

Lunde, D. T. (1975). *Murder and Madness*. Stanford, CA: Stanford Alumni Association.

Milosavljević, B. (1997). *Police Science*. Belgrade: Police Academy.

http://webrzs.statserb.sr.gov.yu/

www.homeoffice.gov.uk

www.mup.sr.gov.yu

Urbanization and Security in Russia

5

YAKOV GILINSKIY

Contents

Russia, or the Russian Federation (RF), came into existence in 1991 after the breakdown of the Union of Soviet Socialist Republics (USSR). The RF is over 17 million km^2 in size (> 6.5 million square miles). Depopulation is taking place: the population of Russia decreased from 148.7 million people in 1992 to 141.8 million people in 2008. Seventy-eight percent of the population live in the European part of the country, and 22% live in the Asiatic sector (west Siberia, east Siberia, and the Russian Far East). The population is comprised of 47% men and 53% women. Seventy-three percent of the people live in urban areas and 27% in rural areas (Vishnevski, 2006, pp. 10, 18).

The process of urbanization came to an end in Russia in the middle 1980s. In 1939, the urban population was 33.5% of the total population. In 1959 the urban population grew to 52.4%; in 1979 to 69.3%; in 1989 to 73.4%; and in 1991 to 73.8% of the total population. "Deurbanization" began in 1992, when the urban population decreased to 73.6%. The urban population reached its lowest point (72.9%) in 1995, 1996, 2000, and 2001.

It is clear that the communist regime was absolutely terrible. As a result of the unique experiment to establish a social utopia, the country was thrown off the path of development. Gorbachev's "Perestroika" was a necessary attempt to save the power structures by way of reform. A similar attempt made by Khrushchev is known as the "Thaw." However, every attempt at reform finished with the political death of its propagators and was followed by "Stagnation" or "Reaction." Credit is due to Gorbachev for instituting the most radical reforms (e.g., freedom of speech, freedom of the press, the multiparty system, the right to hold private property, the lifting of the Iron Curtain, the release of those states occupied by Stalin–Latvia, Lithuania, Estonia, etc.). However these reforms did not bring an end to the problems inherent in the system. It is possible that this failure may not have been a result of an attempt to maintain the communist power structures, but simply Gorbachev's misfortune.

The disintegration of production continues. Power is still retained by the ruling class (with new "oligarchs" and "*siloviki*"*). Corruption, which is common in Russia, has grown to monumental proportions, affecting all organs of power, establishment, and law-enforcement bodies. There is a crisis in health, education, transport, and other social services. Crises of spirituality and morality continue. In addition, the militarization of economics and politics continues, especially in the twenty-first century. The importance of the so-called "power structures" has grown: particularly the Federal Service of Security (FSB—Federal'naja Slugba Bezopasnosti) [former Committee of State Security (KGB—Komitet Gosudarstvennoi Bezopasnosti)], Ministry of Internal Affairs (MVD—Ministerstvo Vnutrennich Del), and other agencies. The country also permits human rights abuses on a massive scale. Tyranny and torture are especially dominant in the army and penal institutions (Abramkin, 1998; Christie, 2000, pp. 79–90; Gilinskiy, 1998; Index on Censorship, 1999; Walmsley, 1996, pp. 358–386; Walmsley, 2003). Nationalist, anti-Semitic, neofascist, and skinhead groups are active and meet with no resistance. Attacks against mass media expressing viewpoints in opposition to the government began in 1999–2000 and continue in the present. "Spy mania" began after 1999.

The ever-growing economic polarization of the population—visible in the stark contrast between the poor majority and the nouveau rich minority (the "New Russian")—is a guaranteed source of continuing social conflict. The Gini Index (index of economic inequality) showed that in 2001 Russia was far behind European countries and ranked much more closely to less developed nations in Africa and South America.

The death rate per 1,000 population rose dramatically from 10.4 in 1986 to 16.4 in 2005. This rate is well above the world average (9.0) and the death rate in Western Europe (9.0), and ranked closely to that in Africa (15.0). In 2005, Russian life expectancy was 58.9 years for men and 72.0 years for women. In comparison, Western Europe life expectancy in 2005 was 76.0 years for men and 82.0 years for women. In Japan, the life expectancy was 78.0 and 85.0 years for men and women, respectively. This is a national catastrophe for Russia.

---

* "*Silovik*" (slang from "sila"—force)—representatives of national security, defense, and law enforcement agencies, especially from FSB (former KGB).

Technological backwardness and the incompetence of the domestic production and service sectors have manifested themselves in the course of the reforms. A consequence of this is the inferiority complex of employees, their dequalification, marginalization, and lumpenization. The exclusion of workers (Finer & Nellis, 1998; Kanfler, 1965; Lenoir, 1974; Paugam, 1996; Young, 1999) is the social basis for different forms of deviance including crime, organized crime, drug abuse, alcoholism, suicide, prostitution, and so on. About 30% of the Russian population has an income lower than the official living wage (World Development Report, 2005). More than 50% of the Russian population is excluded from the workforce (Borodkin, 2000).

Security in Contemporary Russia

Personal security is a very active topic of discussion in contemporary Russia. It is a problem of "To be or not to be" for many Russian people. There is special literature about this problem (see, e.g., Tambovtsev, 2006). It is a pity, but the security of Russian people, including the urban population, is very poor. This thesis is examined in the following section.

Crime and Victims

Many people are victims of crime (for details, see Gilinskiy, 2006). The analyses reported here utilize only official data. The rate (per 100,000 inhabitants) of registered crime decreased from 1986 to 1988 (during Gorbachev's Perestroika), increased from 817 in 1987 to 1,863 in 1995, and—after a short period of decrease in 1996–1997—increased to 2,051.4 in 1999. The crime rate was 2,499.8 in 2005*. The homicide rate decreased in 1986–1988, increased from 6.3 in 1987 to 21.8 by 1994, and—after a short period of decrease in 1995–1997—increased to 23.2 in 2001. It was 21.7 in 2005. It is the third highest homicide rate in world, after Columbia and South Africa. For comparison, the average rate of homicide in 1999–2001 was < 2.0 in Australia, Austria, Canada, Denmark, France, Germany, Italy, Japan, Norway, Spain, Sweden, and Switzerland; < 3.0 in Finland, Hungary, and Poland; and only 5.6 in the United States (Barclay, Tavares, 2003, p. 10). The pattern followed by the rates of other types of crime in Russia is analogous—a minimum during Gorbachev's period, an increase from 1994 to 1995, a transitory decrease followed by an increase from 1999 to 2005. For example, the rate of robbery was 21.0 in 1987 and 242.2 in 2005; the rate of robbery with violence was 3.9 in 1987 and 44.8 in 2005.

---

* The data of Russian official statistics of crime see Annual "Crime and Delinquency. Statistical Review" Moscow.

However, we must keep in mind that the true crime rate (in any country) is significantly higher than what is shown in official statistics. In Russia, a substantial number of crimes have not appeared in the crime registration since 1993–1994 (Gilinskiy, 2000, pp. 146–148; Luneev, 1997, p. 145; and others). The homicide data in medical statistics (Questions of Statistic, 2004, p. 33; World Health Statistics, 1996) are more exact than police data (1992—22.9 and 15.5; 1994—32.3 and 21.8; and 2003—29.5 and 22.1).

Interestingly, the rate of violence crime in rural area is higher than in urban areas. For example, 68.5% of the murders took place in urban areas in 2004 where the urban population is 73% of the total population, and 31.5% of the murders took place in rural areas where the rural population comprises 27% of the total. The murder rate in 2004 was 30.3 in the Leningrad region (a rural area) and 19.7 in the city of St. Petersburg. This index was 24.5 in the Moscow region (a rural area) and 11.9 in the city of Moscow.

The number of victims in contemporary Russia is huge. As can be seen in Table 5.1, the death-toll in Russia climbed steadily from 1987 to 1992, peaked in 1992, and leveled off somewhat from 1993 to 2006. The total death-toll is 1,392,601 persons in the period of 1987–2006. In addition, 25,000 people are declared missing every year and are never found. In the military, between 5,000 and 6,000 of those who *do not participate in wars* die every year. Most of them die due to violent "uncommissioned relationships" ("*dedovshina*,"* the abuse of power by older soldiers that often takes sadistic forms and has a lethal outcome), accidents related to military service, and suicide.

Latent criminality is significant. No national victimology survey is conducted, but studies do exist. For example, our studies in St. Petersburg show (for details, see Gilinskiy, 2005, Tables 5.2 through 5.4) that the percentage of respondents reporting victimization is stable over time (1999–2002: 26.5%; 27.0%; 25.9%; 26.1%, respectively). Between 28% and 36% respondents reporting, at least one victimization were victims two or more times in a year. Between 53% and 56% respondents reported instances of theft. The number of victims who do not report crimes to the police is stable over time, averaging around 75%. Reasons for refusing to report include "police would do nothing" (34–38%); "police could not do anything" (17–19%); "did not want to have contact with police" (7–8%); and "injury was insignificant or there was no injury" (26–32%). Victims who did report a crime to the police indicated that the reaction of law enforcement took one of the following forms: "did not react at all" (12–18%); "a long time afterward" (5–8%); and "do not know anything about actions of police" (11–15%). Police reaction was immediate for only 29–38% of victims.

---

* "Dedovshina" from "ded"—old man.

Table 5.1   Number of Crime-Related Deaths in Russia, 1987–2006

1987	25,706
1988	30,403
1989	39,102
1990	41,634
1991	44,365
1992	213,590[a]
1993	75,365
1994	75,034
1995	75,510
1996	65,368
1997	65,598
1998	64,545
1999	65,060
2000	76,651
2001	78,697
2002	76,803
2003	76,921
2004	72,317
2005	68,554
2006	61,378
Total	1,392,601

[a] This figure for 1992 is most likely a statistical error, but it has been repeated in the annual official *Crime and Delinquency* statistical reports.

These results suggest that Russian people are not defended against crimes and police activity is low.

Corruption

Corruption has been defined as "the abuse of public power for private profit" (/Joseph Senturia/ see Wewer, 1994, p. 481). The UNO offers a similar definition (Resolution 34/169 of the General Assembly UNO, 12.17.1979).

There are many forms of corruption: bribery, favoritism, nepotism, protectionism, lobbying, illegal distribution and redistribution of public resources and funds, theft of treasury, illegal privatization, illegal financing of political structures, extortion, allowance of favorable credit (contracts), buying of votes, the famous Russian "*blat*" (different services for relatives, friends, acquaintances /Ledeneva, 1998/), and so on.

Table 5.2   St. Petersburg Crime Victims' Reports to Police (Percentages)

	Year of Survey			
	1999	2000	2001	2002
A. Fact of Reporting to Police				
Did not report	70.3	69.2	73.7	73.5
Reported	29.7	30.8	26.3	26.5
Proportion of victims out of the number of people surveyed (%)	26.5	27.0	25.9	26.1
B. Police Response to Report				
No response	13.8	11.9	15.4	18.8
A long time afterward	5.0	5.1	8.7	6.5
Some time afterward	30.0	33.6	33.6	29.8
Immediately	36.2	38.2	29.0	31.5
Do not know anything about actions of police	15.0	11.2	13.3	13.4
C. Reasons for Refusing to Report				
Nothing would be done	38.3	34.2	34.5	35.2
The suspect is unknown	26.1	22.7	22.4	23.4
The police could not do anything	19.5	18.8	17.2	18.3
Injury was insignificant	16.6	14.1	17.3	12.3
There was no injury	10.5	16.8	15.4	14.8
There was no proof	10.6	9.8	9.4	9.9
Did not want to contact police	8.2	7.8	7.5	7.0
It was possible to manage without the police	5.5	7.7	6.8	6.9
They were themselves to blame for what happened	5.3	4	4.7	4.5
There was no chance to contact the police	4.5	3.3	3.8	3.8
The police were not pleased with the report	3.1	3.4	3.5	3.4
They detained the guilty person themselves	1.8	2.3	2.8	2.4
They were afraid of revenge by the criminal	2.6	1.7	2.6	1.8
Felt sorry for the one who did it	0.6	0.8	2.4	0.6
Applied to other agencies	0.8	1.9	0.5	0.8
Afraid of publicity about what happened	0	0.8	0.8	1.0
Cannot precisely say what the reason was	0.8	2.4	0.9	1.8
Cannot answer the question	1.3	1.8	1.6	1.5

Corruption, common in Russia, is found on a large scale in all organs of power, establishments, and law-enforcement bodies. In 2005, the Index of Perception Corruption (from Transparency International) for Russia is 2.4, the same as Albania, Niger, and Sierra Leone. Russia placed 126th of 159 countries. In 2007, the Index of Perception Corruption for Russia was 2.3, the same as Gambia, Indonesia, and Togo.

Table 5.3   Number of Incidents (% of the Number of Victims in St. Petersburg)

	Year of Research			
	1999	2000	2001	2002
One	63.5	69.4	72.0	68.5
Two–three	31.0	25.0	24.6	27.6
Four and more	5.6	5.6	3.4	3.9
Proportion of victims among people surveyed in this year	26.0	27.0	25.9	26.1

Table 5.4   Types of Criminal Activity in St. Petersburg (% Out of the Number Victims)

	Year of Research			
	1999	2000	2001	2002
Theft	56.4	53.0	54.4	50.8
Fraud	20.2	20.6	19.8	20.8
Assault	9.1	10.5	12.6	13.6
Robbery	8.1	7.0	8.0	9.6
Extortion	5.2	6.7	4.7	6.4
Sexual violence	1.1	2.2	1.4	1.6
Proportion of victims among people surveyed in this year	26.0	26.7	25.5	26.1

Every day the Russian and foreign mass media produce reports of Russian corruption and corrupt activity. Every day different Russian newspapers and journals publish who (name and position), when, how much money or "service" received as a bribe, with no reaction from those in power. There are certain fixed prices ("tariffs"). Some of these fixed prices were published in the Russian press. The newspaper "Signal" (1996, N1) published tariffs for different illegal services of the GAI—State Auto-inspection (Gosudarstvennaja Avtobobil'naja Inspektcija). The newspaper "Vash Tain'y Sovetnik" ("Your Secret Counselor") published illegal tariffs for "free" training in different universities of St. Petersburg (including juridical faculties of the State University and Police Academy). Perhaps the most interesting data were published in the book *Corruption and Combat Corruption* (2000, pp. 62–63), which reported that there are fixed bribes for obstructing an investigation in a criminal case ($1,000–$10,000); for commutation of arrest for pledge or engagement ($20,000–$25,000); for a decrease of punishment ($5,000–$15,000); and for "ignorance" of customs infringement ($10,000–$20,000 or 20–25% of customs duty). Moreover, there are data about tariffs for the highest government position: the head of the Duma's (the Russian parliament) committee ($30,000), assistant of the deputy ($4,000–$5,000), a presentation of law project ($250,000; Sungurov, 2000, p. 41). Certainly, these prices increase at the same rate of inflation. On December 2002 (N93), "New newspaper" published data about a booklet of the Duma's deputy, Professor G. Kostin. The booklet contained published prices for buying the highest government positions: head of department of the Supreme Court of Justice ($400,000); deputy of head of Moscow's Arbitration Tribunal ($1.3 million); deputy of Ministry of Power Engineering ($10 million). The newspaper expected some reaction of officials (excuse, refutation, and inquiry), but no reaction was proffered. A Russian proverb says, "Silence is sign of conformity." Most of the highest officials have inviolability *de jure* (deputies, judgers, and other) or *de facto*.

There are complex corruption networks that include ministries, police, and FSB (Satarov, 2002; Sungurov, 2000, pp. 72–82). Corruption in contemporary Russia is an element of the political system, a mechanism of the political regime. There are two levels of corruption forms: "lower" ("face of face") and "upper," the great corruption networks. A study of INDEM Foundation (Information Science for Democracy, headed by Dr. G. Satarov, former assistant of former president Boris Eltzin) shows that the great corruption networks exist in the Ministry of Internal Affairs, Federal Service of Security, and State Committee of Customs Service.

There is a system of "*otkat*" ("recoil," "delivery," and "return"). It is 3–10% (Satarov, 2002, p. 8) or 40–60% of the sum of agreement for official (*New Newspaper*, 2003, p. 12). Corruption of police, the prosecutor's office, and judges is particularly dangerous. "Corruption of judges is one of the most powerful corruption markets in Russia … Corruption of judges penetrates different corruption networks on different levels of power" (Satarov, 2002). Arbitration courts are particularly corrupted.

Human Trafficking

Human trafficking is a global problem (Glonti, 2004; Kangaspunta, 2003). The definition of "trafficking in persons" includes three main elements: (1) recruitment, transportation, transfer, harboring, or receipt of persons; (2) the threat or the use of improper means, such as force, abduction, fraud, or deception; and (3) the objective of exploitation, such as sexual exploitation, forced labor, servitude, or slavery (*Protocol to Prevent, Suppress, and Punish Trafficking in Persons, Especially Women and Children*, supplementing the UN Convention against Transnational Organized Crime, November 2000). There are several kinds of human trafficking: trafficking of women ("white slavery"), trafficking of children (for prostitution, for pornography, and for illegal adoption), slavery, trafficking of internals, and so on. In addition, there is smuggling of migrants.

All kinds of trafficking exist in Russia. Moreover, Russia takes first place in the list of the world trafficking (Erokhina & Buryak, 2003, p. 36).

"Considering the global inequalities in affluence, it is not surprising that Africa, Asia, and the CIS member states were the main regions where victims of trafficking were recruited" (Kangaspunta, 2003, p. 91). Russia is a country with a great number of the victims of trafficking, as well as offenders, who were suspected of being involved in or had been found guilty of trafficking (Kangaspunta, 2003, pp. 94, 99).

This is no surprise, because there are very many poor and unemployed people in Russia, especially women and youth. For example, only 65.2% of men and 52.3% of women were fully employed in the Irkutsk region (Eastern Siberia) in 2000. At the same time, 60% of the population has an income below the living wage (Repetskaya, 2003, p. 31).

Unfortunately, no official data pertaining to the different forms of trafficking in Russia exist; consequently, the information presented here is based on local information and examples. Trafficking of women ("white slavery") is the prevalent form of trafficking. The International Organization for Migration names four "waves" of trafficking. The first wave is white slavery comes from Thailand and Philippines. The second wave comes from the Dominican Republic and Columbia. The third wave comes from Ghana and Niger; and the fourth wave comes from countries of Central and East Europe, including Russia (Stoecker, 2000, p. 58). According to selected data, more than 5,000 prostitutes from the Russian Far East "work" in Thailand. Slavic women are "symbol of social prestige" for Asiatic businessmen from Japan, China, and Thailand (Stoecker, 2000, p. 59). Many Russian women prostitute in Europe and the United States.

Criminal organizations operate the export of prostitutes for the border (Europe, United States, Asia, some countries of Latin America, Israel, and some other countries). Below are some fragments from interviews with scientist Dr. Yakov Kostjukovsky (the Center of Deviantology of the Sociological Institute of the Russian Academy of Sciences) with representatives of the criminal organizations about their activity.

I. (*Interviewer*): What about organization of prostitution?
R. (*Respondent*): Prostitution in St. Petersburg is already industry. And it happened not yesterday. There are hundreds "*kontor.*"* There is more developed in Moscow ... In our city the most expensive women are in pubs, hotels, and casinos. Then are "call girls," girls in saunas, girls in "centers of leisure." So ... massage salons, make-up salons. Street girls are the cheaper ...
I.: And what about children's prostitution?
R.: Sure. This is very much dearly. But there are too many drunkards, who are selling their own children. Then it is possible for the bottle

* "Kontora" is office; in this context it is the illegal agency of sex service.

I.:   of vodka literally too. I speak of prostitution in general, certainly, there is male prostitution and gay prostitution too. And males are higher in cost.

I.:   What you can say about "business trips"?

R.:   Yes, it happens. Moreover girls are not always whores. It can be the team of girls for the striptease work, or in the scope of service in general. But they are exported to, for example, Turkey and they forced to work as whores. This is their happiness if they can escape. There are usually many bad ends . . .

Trafficking of children. This is a terrible and widespread phenomenon in the world and in Russia. Trafficking of children is realized for prostitution (male and female), pornography, and illegal adoption. The social bases for child prostitution include the following: more than 2 million children are homeless or in orphanages; children of alcoholic parents; and children who desire money for the "sweet life."

The Center of Deviantology of the Sociological Institute of the Russian Academy of Sciences studies of the commercial sexual exploitation of children in St. Petersburg and Northwest Russia, including Vyborg, Petrozavodsk, and others (see Gurvich, Rusakova, Pyshkina, & Yakovleva, 2002). The main users of children for sex are the "new Russian," city "authorities," and foreign visitors (particularly from Finland and also from Sweden, Germany, Norway, and England). Oral sex, which is the service most widely offered by minors, costs 100–150 rubles ($3–5). Sexual intercourse costs 200–250 rubles ($7–8). Spending the night with a client costs from 500–600 rubles to 1,000 rubles (from $17–20 to $30–35). However, if the child's parents are alcoholics, then the payment is often a bottle of vodka (about $3). Boys are more expensive, costing 3,000–7,000 rubles ($100–250) for spending the evening with a client.

Child pornography is the least studied and most highly profitable sphere of the commercial sex trade. "The street children are the most vulnerable to exploitation as models in pornographic video and other materials. The individuals involved in the production of pornography seek out such children in the streets, marketplaces, and near metro and railway stations, and other places of the city. After feeding them, they ask the children whether they would like to 'make good money.' The minors, who are in an extremely hard economic situation, believe that it will be an easy way to make money, get food, clothes, or sometimes drugs, alcohol, cigarettes and so on. Cadets of military boarding schools of St. Petersburg are often used for the shooting of homosexual porno materials" (Gurvich et al., 2002, p. 27).

Forced labor or slavery. Strange as it may seem, forced labor has a wide distribution at the close of the twentieth century and in the twenty-first century. Contemporary Russian slaves work in Caucasian region of Russia and even in the central regions. Moreover, Russia is a "consumer" of "slaves" from the members of the Commonwealth of Independent States (CIS), especially from Tajikistan, Uzbekistan, Kazakhstan, and Moldova. Slaves are also obtained from China, Vietnam, Afghanistan, North Korea, and some African and Latin American countries. Russian and international criminal groups operate the transit of illegal immigrants. The forced labor endured by the slaves is very hard and dangerous. Many slaves of the twenty-first century see "life-saving" in suicide (Repetskaya, 2003, p. 34).

Moreover there is selling of slaves in the Russian army. There are many cases of selling soldiers to different businessmen. The last case was in September 2006 in the city of Chita, where an officer sold a soldier to a businessman for 35,000 rubles (about $1,300). This soldier is now in the hospital, having lost a leg and an eye as result of slave exploitation.

Torture in Russia

Police violence exists in different countries in different times. But there are sharp distinctions of the scale of this phenomenon and official reaction on this. It is very important.

Torture by Russian police in prisons takes place every day, too. Many newspapers, journals, and special books have written on this subject: the "News Newspaper," former "Common Newspaper," journals "Bondage," "Index: Dossier on Censorship," collected articles "Police Violence" (1998), informational bulletin "To Right," bulletins of "Amnesty International," and so on.

There are different manifestations of police violence: "simple," stab in the back (kidneys), beating, and so on. There are special tortures: "swallow," "elephant calf," "envelope," "crucifixion," "extension," and others. There are descriptions and illustrations of the different kind of tortures in the books and journals. The Russian mass media informs the citizenry about some cases of police torture. But it is very important to know about the scale of this shameful occurrence.

With the goal of uncovering the scale of this problem our Center of Deviantology of the Russian Academy of Sciences is conducting one project. The initiator of project was the "Committee Against Torture" from Nizhni Novgorod, with financial support of the John D. and Catherine T. MacArthur Foundation. We used the definition of "torture" from Art. 1 "Convention against tortures ..." (December 10, 1984). Mass representational interrogation was conducted in five Russian regions: St. Petersburg (examined more than 2,000 people), Pskov (North-West region, examined 600 people), Nizhni Novgorod (South region of European part of Russia, examined 1,000 people), Komi Republic (North region, examined more than 1,100 people), and Chita

(East-Siberian region, examined more than 850 people). Moreover, prisoners in two prisons and some experts were examined. Below are some of the results of the mass interrogation in these five regions.

Our study shows that 3.4% of the adult population experienced police torture in 2004 in St. Petersburg and Nizhni Novgorod, 4.3% in Pskov, 2.8% in Komi Republic, and 3.6% in Chita. Moreover, 5.9% of the adult population were victims of police torture in St. Petersburg in 2005 and 21.3% over the course of a life time. Between 40% and 60% of prisoners were victims of police torture as part of the investigation. Of course, the situation in Chechnya is much worse. However, that is a special topic.

Our respondents believe that police torture exists. In all five regions, more than 50% of the respondents indicated that torture was present and/or systematic. Between 68% and 85% respondents supported a proposal to bring special action against the practice of torture. Between 46.5% and 62.6% respondents believe that they need real defense against police torture.

Our respondents reported many different kinds of torture (beating, hanging, covering of atmospheric oxygen, by current, etc.), and perpetrators (policemen, police officers, and investigators). What are the causes of mass police torture in Russia? I think these are the following factors:

- Old Russian tradition from police and gendarmerie of the tsarist Russia to Soviet regime.
- Lack of qualification in contemporary Russian policemen and investigators, who have not received the necessary training to conduct impartial legal investigations without torture, lies, and falsification.
- Absolute impunity, as very few perpetrators of torture are ever charged, convicted, or sentenced.
- An immorality in society, including police and other "power structures."
- Most importantly, an absence of the so-called "political will" of those in power with higher authority.

Professor Nils Christie wrote, "Torture and death were once seen as obvious forms of punishment. Today, they are out in most countries close to our culture. The non-existence of torture and capital punishment can be seen as the Crown Jewels *in absentia* of our penal system. Their absence is our pride (Christie, 2004, p. 103)." Unfortunately, it is not a pride that Russia can share.

Hate Crimes

Hate crime is a social construct (Hall, 2005; Jacobs & Potter, 1998). There are many different definitions of hate crimes. There are many manifestations of hate crimes (from round oath and vandalism to murder and genocide). The term "hate crime" is used in the large sense of the word and in the narrow sense of the word. In the *wide* sense, it is all crimes committed with the motive of hate. For example, the murder of a hated husband or wife would constitute a hate crime in the wide sense of the term. Similarly, actions against gays or lesbians would also fit this definition. In the *narrow* sense, hate crimes are those committed with the motive of national, racial, religious hate, or enmity or feud. This definition is included in some articles of the Criminal Code of the RF. For example, one article states that hate crime is "Murder ... by motive of national, racial, religious hate or enmity or blood feud" (Art. 105, part 2 "l" Criminal Code of Russian Federation). Moreover there is special *corpus delicti* "Stimulation of national, racial or religious enmity" (Art. 282 Criminal Code).

It is a Russian paradox. On the one hand, there are too many laws and rules, but on the other hand, very bad practice. There are many hate crimes and few of these incidents are registered as crimes. For example, between 2002 and 2004, fewer than 11 violations of Art. 105, part 2 "l" were registered—nine cases in 2001, 10 in 2002, 11 in 2003, and 10 in 2004 (Babichenko, 2005, p. 128). Police and other authorities prefer to qualify these cases as "hooliganism," because it is more "genteel."

There are too many crimes with the motive of national and racial hate in Russia. Neo-Nazi skinheads butcher people with black and yellow skin, Caucasians, almost every day in contemporary Russia and almost every week in St. Petersburg. But Russian authorities—government, police, and criminal justice—do not adequately react to this terrible situation.

Who are the perpetrators of hate crimes in Russia? There are men at the age of 14–21, unemployed, or schoolboys and students, sometimes from "good families." Usually there are skinheads or Nazis, and fascists. What is the "ideology" of Russian contemporary Nazis, fascists, and skinheads? It is "Russia for Russians!," "Migrants go home!," and "Fight the blacks!"

Who are victims of hate crimes? There are citizenry of China and India, Egypt and Cameroon, Uganda and Mali, Israel and Lebanon, Ghana and Senegal, and also so-called "persons of Caucasian nations," Asians and Gipsy. Most often, they are students at Russian universities or migrants, legal and illegal. Most hate crimes are committed in St. Petersburg, Moscow, Voronezh (a city in the European part of Russia), and Krasnodar region (a region in the southern part of European Russia).

What are the means of hate crimes? Most often there is an unexpected armed attack by a group of skinheads or fascists with knives, bats, or metal rods. They try to kill "foreigners" by a stab to the throat. It is a "trademark" or "signature" of Russian Nazis.

Why? What are the causes? There are following objective causes. From our point of view, social and economic inequality is one of the biggest criminogenic factors. People have real opportunities to satisfy their needs depending on social class, stratum, or group or depending on their social and economic status. Inequality of opportunity generates social conflict, dissatisfaction, envy, and finally various forms of deviance, including hate crimes.

There are many young people who do not have secondary and professional education, work, or funds. At the same time, they see foreign cars, rich shops, restaurants, and beautiful girls with rich men. These "excluded" teenagers become spiteful and hateful of all, especially strangers.

Mass Russian xenophobia and nationalism, multiple nationalistic newspapers, journals, and nationalistic appearances of political figures (as General Makashev, Mr. V. Girinovsky and others) play a large role in the spread of hate crimes. Also, there are the historical roots of Russian fascism from 1920s to 1930s. Walter Laqueur discussed it in the book *Black Hundred: The Rise of the Extreme Right in Russia* (Laqueur, 1994).

The nationalist, anti-Semitic, neofascist, and skinhead groups are active and meet no resistance. Why? There are several subjective causes. Fascism, Nazism, and xenophobia fulfill the following functions for the contemporary Russian regime:

- Fascists and Nazi are good "monsters" or "bugaboo" for the Russian people. The contemporary Russian regime can say before future elections, "Either it will be *we* or will be *fascists*."
- "Strangers" and "foreigners" are scapegoats for people, who are very poor, lacking normal habitation, food, and perspectives. The income of more than 30% of the Russian people is lower than the official living wage; and more than 50% of the people are "excluded." Power structures are inaccessible for the excluded masses. They feel "humiliated and insulted" (F. Dostojevsky), and they find strangers or foreigners guilty of causing these problems.
- It is possible that Nazis and skinheads are the "reserve" of the regime against the so-called "orange revolution" (as in Ukraine).

Moreover, nationalistic opinion is widespread in the population, especially among police and other "power structures." According to a poll, 60–65% of the Russian population countenance the slogan "Russia for Russian!" It is a pity, but there are objective and subjective causes for hate crime in Russia. Consequently, hate crimes will continue to spread.

Terrorism

Terrorism is a great threat to human security in the contemporary world. There are three main signs of terrorism: the use of violence; with a political (religious, ethnic, and ideological) object; against noncombatants or civilians (for details, see Ganor, 2002). Terrorism is a very complicated phenomenon. It is the old question, "Is it terrorism or revolutionary violence? Is he a criminal or a fighter for independence?"

There is a difference between terror and terrorism. *Terror* is the violence of the power against the poor, dependents, and the "humiliated and insulted" (F. Dostojevsky). *Terrorism* is a reaction of the poor and dependents on the terror of power. Terrorism is a crime, but an unconventional crime. Terrorists are sure that they are fighting for freedom and independence. Therefore terrorism is, first of all, a political problem, not only an issue for the judicial system and police. This is very important to understand. For instance, the policy of France in Algeria is the "right decision" for the problem, while the actions of the United States in Iraq or those of Russia in Chechen is erroneous policy. The Russian population is a hostage of their own power, but not only of Chechen terrorists now. It is our tragedy with an infinite number of victims (remember the "North-East," Beslan, etc.).

"Defense" of the Russian People

Russian law enforcement is very corrupted and cruel. People fear policemen more than criminals. The results of our interviews provide evidence of that. Moreover, "the same number of people are afraid of attacks by terrorists and the tyranny of policemen" (Auzan, 2006, p. 12). Russian judges are very corrupted and dependent on the power of the regime. Russian people are absolutely defenseless. Private security defends only private firms and very rich men, not townspeople. Moreover, there is "war" sometimes between different private security services.

Conclusion

There are too many criminal risks for Russian people, in both the urban and rural populations. There are not enough means of providing personal security.

References

Abramkin, V. (1998). *In Search of a Solution: Crime, Criminal Policy and Prison Facilities in the Former Soviet Union* (2nd ed.). Moscow: The Moscow Center for Prison Reform.

Auzan, A. (2006). Agreement—2008: Agenda. *New Newspaper*, January, 25–28 (Russian).

Babichenko, K. (2005). *Discrimination and Hate Crimes: Qualification and Prevention.* PhD Thesis. St. Petersburg (Russian).

Barclay, G., & Tavares, C. (2003). International comparisons of criminal justice statistics 2001 // *Home Office Statistical Bulletin*, Issue 12/03.

Borodkin, F. (2000). Social exclusion. *Sociological Journal*, 3/4, 5–17 (Russian).

Christie, N. (2000). *Crime Control as Industry: Towards GULAG's Western Style?* (3rd ed.). New York: Routledge, Taylor & Francis Group.

Christie, N. (2004). *A Suitable Amount of Crime.* New York: Routledge, Taylor & Francis Group.

Corruption and Combat Corruption. (2000). Moscow: Russian Criminological Association (Russian).

Crime and Delinquency: Statistical Review (Annual) (1990–2008). Moscow (Russian).

Erokhina, L., & Buryak, M. (2003). The Problem of trafficking in persons according to Russian experts' estimates (sociological approach). *Organized Crime, Terrorism and Corruption. Studies, Surveys, Law Making, Statistics, Information. Criminology Almanac*, 3, 36–42 (Russian).

Finer, C., & Nellis, M. (Eds.) (1998). *Crime and Social Exclusion.* Blackwell Publishers Ltd.

Ganor, B. (2002). Defining terrorism: Is one man's terrorist another man's freedom fighter? *Police Practice and Research. An International Journal*, 3(4), 287–304.

Gilinskiy, Y. (1998). The penal system and other forms of social control in Russia: Problems and perspectives. In K. Aromaa (Ed.), *The Baltic Region Insights in Crime and Crime Control* (pp. 197–204). Oslo: Pax Forlag A/S.

Gilinskiy, Y. (2000). *Criminology.* St. Petersburg: Piter (Russian).

Gilinskiy, Y. (2005). Police and the community in Russia. *Police Practice and Research*, 6(4), 331–346.

Gilinskiy, Y. (2006). Crime in contemporary Russia. *European Journal of Criminology*, 3(2), 259–292.

Glonti, G. (2004). Human trafficking: Concept, classification, and questions of legislative regulation. In: S. Nevala & K. Aromaa (Eds), *Organised Crime, Trafficking, Drugs: Selected papers presented at the Annual Conference of the European Society of Criminology* (pp. 70–80). Helsinki: HEUNI.

Gurvich, I., Rusakova, M., Pyshkina, T., & Yakovleva, A. (2002). *The Commercial Sexual Exploitation of Children in St. Petersburg and Northwest Russia.* Stockholm: Save the Children Sweden.

Hall, N. (2005). *Hate Crime.* Cullompton, Devon, UK; Portland, Oregon, USA: Willan Publishing.

Index on Censorship. (1999). 7–8. St. Petersburg (Russian).

Jacobs, J., & Potter, K. (1998). *Hate Crimes: Criminal Law and Identity Politics.* New York: Oxford University Press.

Kanfler, J. (1965). *L'exclusion sociale: Etude de la marginalite dans les societes occidentales.* Paris: Bureau de Recherches sociales.

Kangaspunta, K. (2003). Mapping the inhuman trade: Preliminary findings of the database on trafficking in human beings. *Forum on Crime and Society*, 3(1,2), 81–103.

Laqueur, W. (1994). *Black Hundred. The Rise of the Extreme Right in Russia.* Washington, DC.

Ledeneva, A. (1998). *Russia Economy of Favours: Blat, Networking and Informal Exchange*. Cambridge: Cambridge University Press.

Lenoir, R. (1974). *Les exclus, un français sur dix*. Paris: Seuil.

Luneev, V. (1997). *Crime in the XXth Century: Global, Regional and Russian Trends*. Moscow: Norma (Russian).

Paugam, S. (Ed.) (1996). *L'exclusion, l'etat des savoirs*. Paris: La Decouverte.

Questions of Statistic. (2004). N 2 (Russia).

Repetskaya, A. (2003). Criminal exploitation of human beings in Eastern Siberia. *Organized Crime, Terrorism and Corruption. Studies, Surveys, Lawmaking, Statistics, Information. Criminology Almanac, 3*, 29–35 (Russian).

Satarov, G. (2002). *Diagnosis of Russian Corruption: Sociological Analysis*. Moscow: INDEM (Russian).

Stoecker, S. (2000). The rise in human trafficking and the role of organized crime. *Organized Crime and Corruption. Studies, Surveys, Information. Social and Legal Almanac, 1*, 57–66 (Russian).

Sungurov, A. (Ed.) (2000). *Civil Initiatives and Corruption Prevention*. St. Petersburg: Norma (Russian).

Tambovtsev, V. (Ed.) (2006). *Personal Safety as an Economic Good: Institutional Analysis and Institutional Design*. Moscow: IIF "Spros" KonfOP (Russian).

Vishnevski, A. (Ed.) (2006). *Russian Population, 2003–2004*. Moscow: Nauka (Russia).

Walmsley, R. (1996). *Prisons Systems in Central and Eastern Europe: Progress, problems and the international standards*. Helsinki: HEUNI.

Walmsley, R. (2003). *Further Developments in the Prison Systems of Central and Eastern Europe*. Helsinki: HEUNI.

Wewer, G. (1994). Politische Korruption. In H. E. Holtmann, H. U. Brinkmann, & H. Pehle (Eds), *Politic-Lexicon*. München, Wein: Oldenbourg Verlag.

World Development Report 2005: A Better Investment Climate for Everyone. (2005). New York, NY: Oxford University Press.

World Health Statistics (Annual) (1996). Geneva: World Health Organization.

Young, J. (1999). *The Exclusive Society: Social Exclusion, Crime and Difference in Late Modernity*. Los Angeles, London, New Delhi, Singapore: SAGE Publications.

Spatial Determinants of Crime in Poland

6

EMIL W. PŁYWACZEWSKI and
WIESŁAW PŁYWACZEWSKI

Contents

Sustained development of civilization, spontaneous urbanization processes, and constant increase in population of cities contribute substantially to crime and to decline in residents' feelings of safety. Current strategies and principles of designing a safe environment base on the following elements:

- *Natural surveillance*—the placement of physical features and the appropriate organization of the lighting system maximizes visibility and therefore enhances the possibility that an intruder can be noticed.
- *Natural access control*—the placement of entrances, exits, fences, landscaping, and other elements of physical environment in order to deter unauthorized access to the site and to increase the feeling of safety of the authorized persons. The possibility to enter and exit the site is limited through appropriate arrangement of parking spots and physical features as well as through the proper placement of a building and channeling pedestrian and motor traffic. Such an approach to environmental design creates opportunities for natural surveillance and as a result reduces crime risk.
- *Territorial reinforcement*—the use of physical attributes such as fencing, pavement treatments, signage, street benches, particular paint color, and landscaping. These elements not only allow to express ownership but also make it easier to distinguish the four types of space, that is, public, semipublic, semiprivate, and private. Clear

boundaries reinforce the perception of ownership and people tend to respect precisely defined property boundaries.

- *Maintenance*—poor condition of a property or its insufficient maintenance suggests lack of care and creates opportunities for illegal acts. The necessity to maintain the property should be taken into consideration in the designing process, for example, plants should be selected considering their maximum height, which may reduce the need to trim them too often. Using good-quality and damage-resistant materials (a lot of materials are given a special "vandal proof" label) also helps to lower maintenance efforts.

Worth noticing is that there is not a single homogeneous concept of how to prevent crime by designing the space. Since 1920, there have been as many as seven such concepts (van Soomeren, 1987). Each of them has already been criticized, and some, although successful in some countries, proved totally ineffective when transferred to other countries.*

Urbanization and Crime in Poland

The problem of designing safe, resident-friendly spaces as a research target is not a new issue in Poland. The results of a very interesting research project conducted in a few Polish towns[†] supported the theory stating that ill-considered urbanization leads to various negative consequences such as lack or inefficiency of public facilities and destructive influence on the community (Holyst, 2004).

A good illustration of that view is Mydlice Estate (Dąbrowa Górnicza—the area: 55 ha, population: 20,000, population density: 364 p/ha), which—according to Marek Stanisław Szczepański (1991a)—is a typical multistory block of flats district. Ten- and twelve-story buildings are placed very close to each other in such a small area that the residents are able to watch each other's lives through the windows. The "estate"[‡] is ugly, gloomy, and dirty. All buildings are grey, overwhelming; they lack style and look alike. There are not enough garages so the estate roads are crowded with parked cars. The

---

* This is the so-called *School of Chicago*. Research launched in Europe did not confirm the positive influence of the American model, which was elaborated on different causes of danger than the European ones.
† Among others, Tychy, Dąbrowa Górnicza, Siemianowice, and Ruda Śląska. The research was conducted in 1987–1989 by a team supervised by Professor Kazimiera Wódz (1991a).
‡ Szczepański uses the word "estate" in quotation marks to distinguish it from the original, positive connotation of the notion of a "social estate;" the term "estate" refers rather to urbanistic forms and has nothing in common or might be even in contradiction with the notion of the term "social estate."

pavements are very narrow and badly planned so it is very difficult to move along them. The "estate" lacks playgrounds, parks, and green spaces. According to sociologists, the community of Mydlice is disintegrated and anonymous. "After work people just sit at home and watch TV." "They feel lonely, lost, and helpless."

The Mydlice "estate," according to the police, is one of the most pathological districts of Dabrowa Górnicza. It is extremely difficult to control due to its character and disintegrated community. The original residents were young people from almost all parts of Poland. There are cases of extreme callousness and indifference to human suffering. Residents shout at each other, unattended children play in basements or around the blocks. A list of phrases that could be used to describe the "estate" would definitely include tall, dense, and overwhelming buildings; concrete desert; district of a neglected social infrastructure; callousness and anonymity; social disintegration; crowded shops, health centers and schools; incoming community; community susceptible to pathologies; high illness incidence rates; insufficient care given to the children and youth by their parents; and huge dormitory suburb.

Antisocial character of the matter constituting the environment for the residents of structurally disabled estates reinforces further social degeneration. Such estates are typical examples of so-called *empty areas* (Szczepański, 1991a) that can be characterized as a district of residents of no individual or collective identification with the shapeless area of an enormous estate followed by exaggerated orientation toward personal flat space. Such a phenomenon is described as shutting oneself away in one's own flat.* Paradoxically, the problem is getting more serious due to the current trend of protecting property with the use of technical means. Although physical barriers decrease crime risk, they may reinforce the problem of isolation and indifference to other residents.

Another phenomenon related to that problem is creating fortress-like estates—surrounded by fences, monitored by special systems, and security guards, areas that are meant to become an oasis of safety in surroundings overcome by crime.† The fenced and monitored estates are usually inhabited by well-off residents representing similar professions and often working in the same companies. Szczepański perceives such situations as "favorable conditions for the community to disintegrate." According to him, "such environment enhances the risk of creating a pathological social structure, resembling 'profession' ghettos. Residents are subjected to constant surveillance by their neighbours—coworkers, which generates gossip waves and results in carrying over professional attitudes into private relationships."

---

* See also Barkan (2001).
† Szczepański (1991a), p. 61. Isolation of groups of residents may enhance the emergence of "an empty area."

The problem of limiting everyday life space to someone's own home, work, and means of transport is a destructive influence on the feeling of safety and order in public places. There seems to be a strong link between those issues and the concept of "broken windows,"* which says that "when there are no people, the social supervision mechanism deteriorates, which also results in the "atomization" of society. Finally, the district of no city life or normal social relationships becomes an area in which crime develops (Kelling & Coles, 2000, p. 33).

Examples of antisocial character of the matter and of its criminogenic potential can be found in many Polish cities and towns, and it must be realized that many city districts resemble huge slums at the end of the twentieth century. One such district is "Za Żelazną Bramą" ("Behind the Iron Gate") in Warsaw, an estate attractively located in the center of the city. A lot of flats are rented by immigrants, and although the owners would like to sell them, it is very difficult because of the bad reputation of the area and poor condition of the buildings. In Wrzeciono, another district in the suburbs of Warsaw situated near Huta Warszawa, the residents contributed to the complete devastation of the site. Light switches torn out of walls, smoke-stained ceilings, and unmentionable graffiti are the dominant characteristics of the buildings. The estate was built in the 1960s and its original residents were people displaced from real slums in the suburbs of Annopol.

In other districts of Warsaw, such as Bemowo, Chomiczówka, or Gocław, there are drug dealer gangs that occupy the streets and come to schools. The police are helpless as the residents seem to be passive and to resign themselves to their fate while groups of juveniles armed with baseball bats terrorize their district. It is said that block housing estates "make" young people who live without an aim, just here and now. The "Report on the state of the city" prepared in Wrocław in 1994 says "a phalanx of youth is growing up. There is a justified fear that such districts as Nowy Dwór or Popowice will be turning to slums. Young people have a sad attitude to life, a kind of life pessimism which makes them willing to spend their lives in the blocks."

Sociological research conducted in Poland revealed that residents of big cities suffer from anonymity. "Neighborhood relationships are usually developed with one or a few families while contacts with other neighbors are very rare. Their closest, informal social contacts disappear. The 'Bs,' a sample family (45-year-olds, son—23) sold their flat in Bemowo, a Warsaw district,

---

* The broken windows theory first came to prominence in 1982, when criminologists George L. Kelling, and James Q. Wilson published an article on the subject in *The Atlantic Monthly*. The theory, as they explained it, holds that people are more likely to commit crimes in neighborhoods that appear unwatched and uncared for by residents and local authorities. Criminals are "emboldened by the lack of social control." See Kelling and Coles (2000).

and built a house in the country, near Kampinos Forest. They had previously waited a long time to move into the flat, and when in 1988 they received the keys they were very happy. Soon, they realized that the 'block life' was not for them. The building was gradually devastated, people threw their litter through the windows and cars were stolen even from manned car parks. Finally, several drug dealer gangs operating in the area and being a threat to the children were the last reason the Bs and five other families felt relieved to move out from their former 'dream flats'" (Pytlakowski, Socha, Urbanek, & Winnicka, 1999).

Urban Design

A concept contradictory to that of an antisocial "estate" seems to be a "communal estate." Marek Stanisław Szczepański, for the purpose of research, accepted the following model of the latter: (1) population of 5,000–6,000; (2) an area of 65 ha (25 families p/ha); (3) buildings not higher than 5 stories; (4) buildings of not more than 3 staircases;* (5) primary school serving a function of center of integration; (6) 10% of the area arranged as recreation areas and green spots; (7) necessary number of service points, such as shops, health centers or culture centers; (8) internal estate roads do not let extraneous through traffic; (9) public transport stop nearby; (10) relatively restricted character of the area; (11) prevalence of not very high buildings; (12) and importance of the estate's neighborhood.[†]

It is worth mentioning that the above model coincides with modern norms worked out through experiments and adopted within the Dutch program "Police Label for Safe Housing."[‡] According to the program, the estate that is able to enhance social control and resident engagement should have the following features:[§]

1. Blocks of flats not higher than 5 stories; higher tower-blocks acceptable only as elements meant to add variety to the urbanistic design.
2. One entrance to a building leads to not more than 10 flats.

---

* It can be assumed that the author meant to point out the limitations as to the number of residents rather than the number of staircases in a block.
† Szczepański (1991a), p. 55. His classification of research areas includes the division of communal estates in Poland into (a) communal estates from the socialism period and (b) communal estates from the 1970s and 1980s.
‡ Policyjny Znak Jakości Bezpieczne Mieszkanie.
§ The characteristics consider only those conditions that were mentioned by Szczepański. See also, Policyjny Znak Jakości Bezpieczne Mieszkanie [Police Label for Safe Housing], dz. cit., charter 2.2 Podstawowe wymogi urbanistyczne [Basic Urbanistic Requirements].

3. There is a multifunctional recreation area in the estate or on its outskirts, where children can play and various cultural events can be organized; smaller green spaces and playgrounds are distributed around the area of the estate (this requirement must be met if the population of the estate exceeds 500).
4. There is a shopping and service center in the center of the housing estate.*
5. Estate roads do not let extraneous through traffic and there is a limited number of them.†
6. Public transport shelters are well lit and made of transparent materials, so the waiting passengers are visible from nearby homes and streets.
7. Public places and buildings serving residents of other areas should be located on the outskirts of the estate so that they cause minimal disturbance to the residents.

An example of a Polish housing estate is the Estate of General Zawadzki‡ follows. The estate was built in the 1960s as an example of "architecture socialist in its content and national form." To realize that idea, designers and architects implemented ideal typological descriptions and parameters of a social housing estate. The empirical research revealed the following picture of the estate: built in the 1960s and developed in the next years; situated in a bigger district—Michałkowice; predominant buildings are 4–5 story blocks and standard design solutions. The whole housing estate, which was built mainly from traditional materials and partly from "modern" ones, looks clear and organized and the impression is reinforced by clear marking of streets, buildings, and staircases. The planning and spatial design of the estate are lucid, with shops and service centers in the middle and blocks of flats around, on the outskirts of the area.

One of the respondents wrote "the residents do their best to make their housing estate nice and well-kept." In the summer, balconies are decorated with flowers, squares are kept clean and tidy; a lot of work is done by residents themselves, though they often complain that their efforts are ruined (they planted a line of trees, which were later destroyed by employees of a sewage company). In the opinion of the estate residents, the area is safe and quiet, "not frequented by the dregs of society," and gives the feeling of being at home. Its infrastructure (shops, services, and medical facilities) seems to

---

* The mixture of functions: flats, shops, restaurants, libraries, post offices, health centers, banks, and so on guarantee the existence of social control at all times. The center can serve as a meeting place as well.
† A housing estate up to 500 flats has one or two main roads for motor vehicles. An area of more than 500 flats has 2–4 roads.
‡ Siemianowice, north of Poland, 18.4 ha; population of 5000; and density: 272 p/ha.

be good, although residents have to wait for nearly a month for those services that are in short supply (Szczepański, 1991a, p. 58).

In the years 2000 and 2001, following the Dutch example, a new housing estate was built in two stages in Pucka and Wejherowska streets in Szczecin—city in north-western Poland. Thirteen two-story blocks of flats form an enclosed area of the housing estate with only one road leading to it. The other two access roads have been closed with concrete flower beds, which enable natural surveillance of people entering the area as well as control of access to the premises. The district is designed for 900 inhabitants, and consists of 292 flats and 187 parking places. In the middle of the estate, there is a playground. However, the visibility is obstructed by overgrown vegetation. Staircases are equipped with house entry systems and lead to the maximum of 10 flats, which is expected to result in a decrease in anonymity and getting to know one's neighbors.

The estate is very well organized. Access to the estate, parking spaces, roads, pavements, and entrances to the stairwells are all very important markers of territoriality. Pavements, differing in color and texture, clearly indicate whether a given area is a private, semiprivate, semipublic, or public property. Balconies, with balustrades not obstructing the view, encourage inhabitants to spend their free time there, which obviously facilitates the surveillance of the area. The blocks have little gardens around them that can be accessed directly from the balconies of ground-floor flats, which is another factor that improves the surveillance. The gardens also make it impossible to approach the buildings from their direction, which results in giving a piece of public ground to a group of residents and their taking responsibility for the so-called "nobody's land." In this way, a large part of public space has been changed into semiprivate property, which is very beneficial from the point of view of safety and order in the area of the estate.

Although the designers of the estate followed a very successful model developed by the Dutch police, the Polish estate has not witnessed a similar decrease in crime. The local community police officer described problems faced by the residents as similar to those encountered in other areas of the beat. On the contrary, some of the threats are more acute, including those involving the youth. It seems possible that the reason for this is the fact that the estate is owned by the Board of Construction Association "Prawobrzeżne." As with other estates of this type, its residents can only rent their flats, and can never become their owners. Thus, it is possible that the residents do not take enough care of what is not their property. Another reason might be the fact that it costs quite a lot to rent such a flat, so the majority of residents go out to work. Their children spend a lot of time unsupervised, which might result in problems with the youth.

Since 2001, the influence of urban architecture on safety has been studied by researchers of the Prevention Institute of the Higher Police School in

Szczytno.* In 2003, they restored the local park in cooperation with the District Police Headquarters in Szczytno. In consequence, the threat of alcohol and petty crime stopped to appear there. It happened because after the trees and bushes had been trimmed, the park no longer offered secluded spots which, invisible to passers-by, used to be favored by those who would gather there to drink alcohol, or by the youth who wanted to escape the eyes of parents. In spots where the police or town wardens hardly ever appeared, anonymous young people had no moral restraints, which sometimes had led to their aggressive noisy behavior. All this had contributed to the sense of threat of crime among inhabitants who visited the places.

Urban Space

When discussing the problems of safety and public order, a few words should be said about other important issues that were considered in the research. The one that is of particular importance concerns is *the perception and valorization of elements constituting social order at the estate.* One of the features that influence the form and sustainability of the order is the sense of safety threat resulting from the spatial position. It appears that there is little sense of safety among residents of large urban complexes—complexes of blocks of flats and old downtown quarters. Only one out of every four residents considered the places safe or very safe, whereas every second resident of estates consisting of detached houses assessed their situation as positive (Szczepański, 1991b).

One of the weak points of modern urban space is its linear arrangement. In this architectural solution, buildings and parking spaces are arranged in lines, which contribute to the increase in anonymity and the lack of sense of ownership. The linear arrangement does not create public recreation spaces which make residents leave their homes and stay outdoors, thus ensuring the increase in the sense of safety. Parking spaces that are between buildings, or out of sight of residents doing their routine jobs, are considered unsafe. However, placing parking spaces in front of the houses or in busy streets makes them safer. Circumstances conducive to crime can be removed or reduced, among others by designing a space that improves relations between residents and helps notice illegal acts. Designing an estate that consists of small groups of buildings makes it possible. This way of designing and building estates develops the sense of territoriality, decreases anonymity, and strengthens the sense of ownership. The central positioning of public recreating spaces enables surveillance of the estate.

---

* Among others, see papers prepared by Krzysztof Łojek, published in journals of the Higher Police School in Szczytno: "Przegląd Policyjny" [*The Police Review*] 2004, Nr. 1, 2, and 3, and "Policja" [*Police*] 2006, Nr. 4.

The experience of countries such as Great Britain, Holland, Germany, Australia, Canada, and the USA as well as numerous analysis and research results shows that "safety-oriented" spatial design plays an important part in reducing the risk of crime and may considerably enhance the feeling of safety. As a result, a significant improvement in quality of residents' life can be achieved. The possibility of committing a crime can be eliminated or reduced if the physical environment is designed and organized in such a way as to create favorable conditions for strengthening friendly relations among citizens and therefore increases the possibility that a crime (or a potential offender) will be notified to the police. Of course, it is connected with many questions and a lot unsolved problems. Many of them were discussed during the third International Meeting of the UN Commission of Crime Prevention and Criminal Justice held in Vienna on November 28, 2006. The Commission prepared a brief paper outlining points for discussion titled "Crime prevention and criminal justice responses to urban crime, including gang-related activities, and effective crime prevention and criminal justice responses to combat sexual exploitation of children."*

References

Barkan, S. E. (2001). *Criminology. A Sociological Understanding* (2nd ed.) (pp. 40–41). Upper Sadle River, NJ: Prentice-Hall.

Holyst, B. (2004). *Kryminologia* [Criminology]. Warszawa, s. 1161.

Kelling, G. L., & Catherine, M. C. (2000). *Wybite szyby. Jak zwalczyć przestępczość i przywrócić ład w najbliższym otoczeniu* [Broken Windows: How to reduce crime and restore order in our communities]. Poznań.

Pytlakowski, P., Ryszard, S., Marian, U., & Winnicka, E. (1999). Blok polski [Polish Block]. *Polityka*, issue 24.

Szczepański, M. S. (1991a). *Procesy planowe i życiowe w czterech miastach Górnośląskiego Okręgu Przemysłowego—charakterystyka obszarów badawczych* [Planned and vital proccesses in four cities of Górnośląski Okręg Przemysłowy—description of the research areas]. In K. Wódz (Ed.), *Przestrzeń wielkiego miasta w perspektywie badań nad planowaniem i żywiołowością* [Big city space in the perspective of research on planning and spontaneity]. Warszawa.

Szczepański, M. S. (1991b). *Ecological values of space and place. The result of research.* In K. Wódz (Ed.), *Przestrzeń wielkiego miasta w perspektywie badań nad planowaniem i żywiołowością* [Big city space in the perspective of research on planning and spontaneity]. Warszawa.

van Soomeren, P. (1987). The Physical Urban Environment and Reduction of Urban Insecurity: A General Introduction. Conference on the Reduction of Urban Insecurity. Barcelona.

* E/CN.15/2007/CRP.3.

Wódz, K. (1991a). Prace Naukowe Uniwersytetu Śląskiego w Katowicach'. *Katowice,* issue 1205.

Wódz, K. (Ed.). (1991b). *Przestrzeń wielkiego miasta w perspektywie badań nad planowaniem i żywiołowością* [Big city space in the perspective of research on planning and spontaneity]. Warszawa.

Drug Problems in Peshawar, Pakistan

7

FASIHUDDIN

Contents

The drug problem has existed for centuries, but has never been so serious, so complex, so widespread, and so transactional in nature as we have it today. It has a linear dimension and a horizontal proliferation. It has its roots and branches. It is a local police issue and a matter of international concern. It starts from cultivation and laboratory processing and ends up in money laundering and hospital admissions, with a dozen criminal activities between the two ends (Figure 7.1). It is a crime, an associated crime, and also a source of a number of other crimes, though the relation cannot be so easily established on sound empirical basis.

The drug problem is one of the serious crimes and all serious crimes need a response, based on team concept and a multidimensional approach. Our response should be like a positive and progressive concerted effort, directed toward the multifaceted aspects of the drug problem.

We believe that serious crime investigation requires the collaborating of highly able personnel from a range of investigative backgrounds, who are both police and non-police specialists. We also believe that the scientific paradigm, developed by a number of key individuals in the last ten years, incorporating principles and methodologies derived from a number of different disciplines, including decision-making, leadership and management studies, forensic

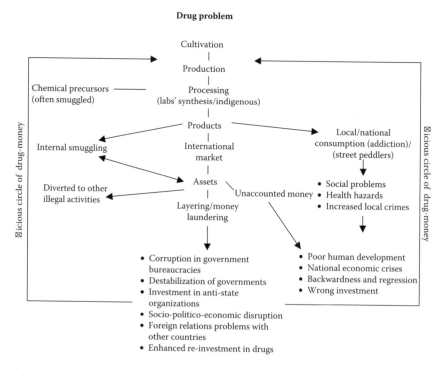

Figure 7.1 Linear and horizontal proliferation of drug problem.

psychiatry, forensic psychology and environmental psychology, has a pivotal role in this combined investigative endeavour (West & Alison, 2006).

To arrive at a more clear conceptual discourse of broader academic and international interest, I visited the offices of our local drug law-enforcement agencies and discussed with their investigators the various constraints (legal, financial, departmental, procedural, administrative, etc.) they face during investigation of drug issues. As Pakistan is an underdeveloped and transitional society, most of our investigation problems may not be similar to those being faced by the investigators of the developed countries. However, a list of common investigation problems will be of some help to make sense of the failure of our efforts in dealing with the drug problem.

Primary or Partial Responsibility of Drug Law-Enforcement Agencies

The "division of labor" or "span of responsibility" for drug offenses almost everywhere is indicative of "multidisciplinary" and "multijurisdictional" approach. The example of the United States could be more relevant. The U.S. Drug Enforcement Administration (DEA) has been working at the federal level since 1973 as a primary investigative unit, with the FBI having concurrent jurisdiction over drug offenses under the Controlled Substances Act, 1970. Domestically, the DEA works with other federal agencies, such as Customs, Border Patrol, Treasury, the Internal Revenue Service and the military, and with the state and local agencies to enforce the laws that cover controlled substances. Part of the DEA's mission is to work with foreign governments to detect and eradicate the cultivation of crops, processing labs, and shipping systems. There are currently over 4,000 investigators employed by the DEA. However, at the state and local levels, narcotics enforcement is a primary responsibility mostly of state, city, and county police departments and sheriff's offices. In addition, many district attorney or prosecutor's offices will have specialized narcotic units. The vast majority of these law-enforcement agencies participate in multijurisdictional task forces that foster cooperation and coordination across jurisdictional boundaries and governmental levels (Sonne, 2006).

Conversely, despite a similar vast majority of forces in Pakistan, the team spirit for a joint mission against drug is still an embryonic thought. Instead of sharing their knowledge and skills in drug law enforcement, these forces and departments rarely consult one another on the various dimensions of either "demand reduction" or "supply reduction" objectives. I could hardly see any formal or informal interagency cooperation in my country despite the fact that they work in an interconnected networking of administration (Figure 7.2).

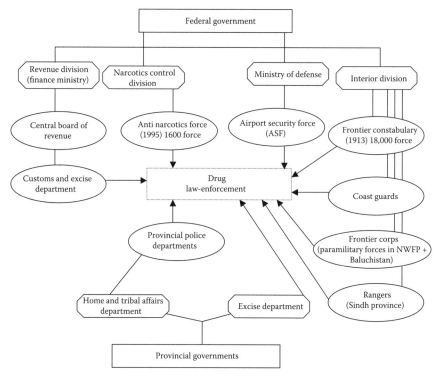

Figure 7.2 Various government departments having primary or partial responsibility for drugs-law enforcement in Pakistan.

This lack of interagency coordination is not limited to our country. The strain is present among law-enforcement organizations everywhere.

> By way of illustration, Levi and Osofsky (1995), speaking of the British police, say that their relationships with HM Customs are far from smooth for, among other things, they have different priorities. Customs are concerned with seizures, the police with developing informants. Herein lies the seat of the difficulty for, if co-operation cannot easily take place within national borders, it is even less likely to take place across national borders (Quoted in Bean, 2004).

Prevention versus Investigation

The Police Act 1861 and the Police Rules 1934 describe three basic police functions: prevention of crimes, investigation of crimes, and prosecution of the criminals. It is an old saying that prevention is better than a cure but in criminological studies it is very difficult, rather next to impossible, to determine whether crime is controlled/reduced through preventive strategies or through successful investigative processes. As modern crimes have become complex and difficult to detect, so some academics advise greater involvement in preventive measures whereas other may disagree with the costlier investment in preventive strategies. Sometimes, it seems to me "an egg and hen problem." Should we pursue extensive prevention policies or should we restrict ourselves to the criminals (the target of our investigation)? Interestingly, "crime prevention" itself is not easy to define. It is often used interchangeably with crime reduction, which means "any activity that seeks to lower the numerically measured instances of actions legally proscribed as criminal." Given that crimes are events proscribed only by legal statute, it is not surprising that there is a greater plethora of activities and initiatives associated with the term "crime prevention" (Hughes, 2006). At times, the term "crime prevention" is so widely and pervasively used by the academics that it even encompasses the whole of criminology and the complete criminal justice system including investigation, which by no means is an easy task to be achieved and accomplished without a compromise on "definitions." Ekblom (2005) observes,

> Prevention–intervening in the courses of crime and disorder events to reduce the risk of their occurrence and the potential seriousness of their consequences. Prevention (or reduction) can be done in two broad contexts. *Enforcement/ judicial prevention* acts, as implied, through police detection and investigation and the criminal justice and penal systems ... *Civil Prevention acts* through changes in everyday life. Enforcement/judicial prevention focuses on individual and occasionally corporate offenders; civil prevention covers both offender-oriented and situational interventions, acting at a range of ecological levels from individual victim, offender or place to family peer groups, institutions and communities.

If we look into the ingredients of prevention and investigation, we would rather tilt in favor of effective investigation which is more selective, targeted, and limited than prevention strategies that are mostly widespread, expensive, and, at times, counterproductive with a greater possibility of generating "fear of crime" and even "displacement of crime." Criminalistics may be costly but investment in situational crime prevention strategies at a large scale may be even costlier than scientific laboratory techniques. Investigation can be a failure but to identify and remove the causes of crime is more difficult to think about. However, this depends on the situation and the structure of the society and the delivery system of the criminal justice system, which will tell us what measures could be more effective in any given circumstances.

This "input–output system" seems to me an intellectual grafting or imitation of the "demands and supply" paradigm of economics. My aim in creating the ideal Crime System Model (Figure 7.3) is to look for the best available

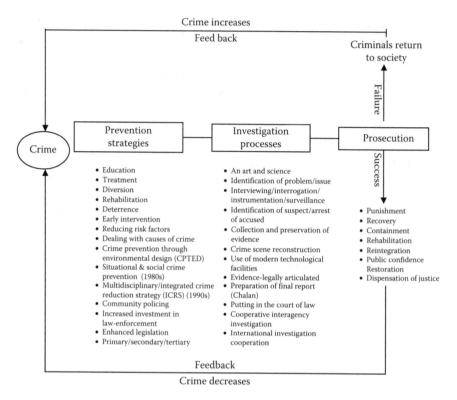

Figure 7.3 Crime system model.

strategy in dealing with the crime problem.* A system needs stability and equilibrium, which is necessary for its smooth functioning and for continuity of its desired production. Crime dealing, to my mind, is like a pendulum, which oscillates between the two peaks of prevention and prosecution with a middle equalizing force of investigation (Figure 7.4). If we intend to keep the pendulum away from disproportionate jerks or undesirable altitudes at both

---

*   "Any collection of elements that interact in some way with one another can be considered system. A system perspective or framework has several key characteristics, e.g; elements, parts or components, which are identifiable and having certain boundaries, and which interact with one another regularly and effectively in discernable ways. A system is a perspective on reality that is abstracted from that reality for purposes of analysis. A system is a framework with which an observer or analyst approaches, or a lens or perspective through which an observer or analyst chooses to view, some reality as politics" (Dahl & Stinebrickner, 2003).

I am confident that my Crime System Model beautifully fits into the system analysis theory, provided our criminologists give enough consideration to look for a new approach to crime management which is based on system analysis and with the purpose of finding the best available alternatives to address the issue in question.

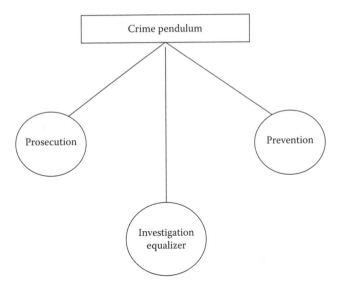

Figure 7.4 The crime pendulum.

ends, our endeavors will certainly be focused on the accelerating or retarding push at the middle. The stabilizing force of investigation will automatically keep the system intact and protected from dysfunctional jolts.*

Drug Production and Transit

Pakistan (total population 160 million and total area 796,095 km²) shares around 1,500 miles of its western border with Afghanistan—the largest

---

* For an academic interest, I reproduce the basic idea of stability factor in this systems theory, which may be given a fresh thought by the criminologists of our time. "In later work, Parsons provided a general theory of social systems as problem-solving entities, which sought to integrate sociological theory with developments in geology, psychology, economics and political theory. Every social system has four sub-systems corresponding to four functional imperatives, namely adaptation (A), goal attainment (G), integration (I) and pattern-maintenance or latency (L). These four sub-systems can be conceptualized at various levels so that, for example, the basic AGIL pattern also corresponds to the economy, polity, societal community and institutions of socialization. In adapting to their internal and external environments, social systems have to solve these four problems in order to continue in existence, and they evolve by greater differentiation of their structures and by achieving higher levels of integration of their parts. Parsons attempted to show the validity of the systems approach through a diversity of studies—of the university, politics, religion and profession. Although widely influential in the study of political processes, industrialization, development, religion, modernization, complex organizations, international system, and sociological theory, the theory has been extensively criticized ... After the death of Parsons in 1979, there was revival of interest in Parsonian sociology, especially in Germany. In turn, this development produced a re-evaluation of systems theory in the work of Niklas Luhamnn (1927–98)" (Abercrombie, Hill, & Turner, 2000).

producer of opiates in the world. In 2003, Afghanistan produced about 77% of the world's total opium but due to good weather conditions, the production from 32 kg/ha in 2004 increased to 39 kg/ha in 2005, thus Afghanistan accounted for 87% of the global opium production in 2005. The major portion of this production and the subsequent drug products are routed through Pakistan, Iran, and other Central Asian countries to Europe and America. The United Nations Office on Drugs and Crime (UNODC) has provided statistics for regional seizures of these opiates, generated from Afghanistan whereby the largest seizures are made by Iran (40%) followed by Pakistan (29%) (Table 7.1). An interesting remark by Macdonald (2007), author of the book *Drugs in Afghanistan*, is relevant while studying these figures:

> Seizure figures of opium and heroin from Afghanistan and neighbouring countries such as Iran, Pakistan and Tajikistan are less than reliable and may reflect the activities and methods of law enforcement officials or hidden political agendas more than any real increase in the amount of drugs being trafficked or a true reflection of trafficking routes. But such figures can still provide some evidence of broad trends in trafficking and cross-border smuggling.

This lack of reliable data has undoubtedly acted as a barrier to a comprehensive understanding and analysis of many pressing issues, as well as the development of realistic and culturally appropriate policies desperately needed to tackle the complex problems of countries like Pakistan and Afghanistan. At times, there are conflicting and confusing reports of cultivation and

Table 7.1 Regional Seizures of Opiates during 2005 (in kg)

Country	Opium Equivalent to Opiates	Morphine	Heroin	Total	Percentage of Total	Hashish
Iran	22,509.50	6,973.00	5,553.00	35,035.50	40.35	67,277.00
Pakistan	643.75	22,196.80	2,144.38	24,984.93	28.77	93,539.07
Afghanistan	8,659.20	201.00	7,771.00	16,631.20	19.15	67,277.00
Turkey	9.00	410.00	5,588.00	6,007.00	6.92	7,953.00
Tajikistan	110.44	0.00	2,344.60	2,455.04	2.83	1,164.40
Kazakhstan	66.89	0.00	625.70	692.59	0.80	284.10
Uzbekistan	10.77	0.00	466.80	477.57	0.55	454.70
Turkmenistan	74.86	0.00	180.80	255.66	0.29	154.00
Kyrgyzstan	11.65	0.00	202.60	214.25	0.24	2,114.80
Russian Federation	10.30	0.00	73.00	83.30	0.10	652.00
Total	32,106.36	29,780.80	24,949.88	86,837.04	100	2,40,870.00

Source: UNODC, Vienna, Austria. Estimates pertaining to Turkey and the Russian Federation are provisional + Anti-Narcotics Force (ANF).

eradication with contradictory claims by various stakeholders, nations, and organizations. This scribe has noticed that the same figure for poppy cultivation is sometimes expressed in metric tons and at other times simply in tons, even in the UNODC Reports.

As evidenced by the UNODC Report entitled *Afghanistan: Opium Survey 2006*, the area under illicit opium poppy cultivation reached a record level in 2006, with potential opium production estimated at about 6,100 tons, an increase of nearly 50% over the figures for 2005. The alarming scale of that illicit activity, in which 2.9 million persons (12.6% of the population) are engaged, constitutes a major obstacle to achieving peace, security, and development in Afghanistan and poses a continuous threat to countries in the neighboring area and beyond [International Narcotics Control Board (INCB) Report 2006]. The INCB Report 2006 further identifies a wide range of problems for these countries related to large-scale drug trafficking, such as organized crime, corruption, and relatively high demand for illicit opiates. For example, the Islamic Republic of Iran has the highest rate of opiate abuse in the world (2.8%) (INCB Report 2006). According to a UNODC and World Bank Report, Afghanistan's annual narcotics trade has risen to US$3 billion, accounting for one-third of total economic activity (UNODC Annual Report 2007, p. 36).

Pakistan's total production also saw an upsurge during 2002–2003 to 2004–2005 due to a number of reasons, including the unrest in tribal, semi-tribal, and border areas of Pakistan and due to the over occupation of law-enforcement agencies in antiterrorist operations. Some observers may not agree with this statement and may object to the professional commitment of the law-enforcement agencies. However, it is pertinent to compare the poppy production of Afghanistan and Pakistan since 1990, which provides a panoramic view of the problem on both sides of the Durand Line between Afghanistan and Pakistan (Table 7.2).

Actions against Drugs at National Level

Not mentioning the national and international efforts for poppy destruction, we restrict ourselves to the results of actions of various law-enforcement agencies against such a large production in or transit through Pakistan. According to Macdonald (2007), "It should not be the role of law enforcement to focus on eradication of poppy fields. Rather, its main role should be to focus on trafficking and drug processing and the successful arrest, prosecution and punishment of those engaged in such activities, no matter their official rank or social status."

The statistics provided to us by the Anti-Narcotics Force (ANF) show that the number of seizures made in Pakistan dropped from 49,279 in 2004 to 42,025 in 2005, indicating a decline of 15%. Likewise, the number of persons

Table 7.2 Global Illicit Cultivation and Production of Opium (1990–2007)

	1990	1991	1992	1993	1994	1995	1996	1997	1998	1999	2000	2001	2002	2003	2004	2005	2006	2007
Cultivation[a] in Hectares																		
Southwest Asia																		
Afghanistan	41,300	50,800	49,300	58,300	71,470	53,759	56,824	58,416	63,674	90,583	82,171	7,606	74,100	80,000	131,000	104,000	165,000	193,000
Pakistan	7,488	7,962	9,493	7,329	5,759	5,091	873	874	950	284	260	213	622	2,500	1,500	2,438	1,545	1,701
Subtotal	48,788	58,762	58,793	65,629	77,229	58,850	57,697	59,290	64,624	90,867	82,431	7,819	74,722	82,500	132,500	106,438	166,545	194,701
Potential Opium Production[b] in Metric Tons																		
Southwest Asia																		
Afghanistan	1,570	1,980	1,970	2,330	3,416	2,335	2,248	2,804	2,693	4,565	3,276	185	3,400	3,600	4,200	4,100	6,100	8,200
Pakistan	150	160	181	161	128	112	24	24	26	9	8	5	5	52	40	36	39	43
Subtotal	1,720	2,140	2,151	2,491	3,544	2,447	2,272	2,828	2,719	4,574	3,284	190	3,405	3,652	4,240	4,136	6,139	8,243

Source: UNODC World Drug Report (2008). From www.UNODC.org
[a] Opium poppy harvestable after eradication.
[b] All figures refer to dry opium.

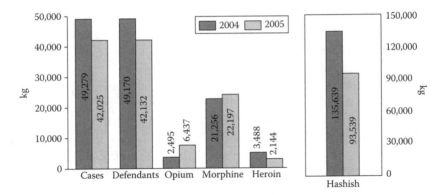

Figure 7.5 Seizures of drugs by all law-enforcement agencies. [Adapted from Anti-Narcotic Force. (2006). *Yearly Digest 2005–2006*. Rawalpindi, Pakistan: Directorate General of Anti-Narcotics Force (e-mail: anf@anf.gov.pk, Web site: http//www. anf.gov.pk).]

arrested has also fallen from 49,170 in 2004 to 42,132 in 2005, indicating a decline of 14%. Looking at the smuggling/trafficking trends, the seizures of opium and morphine base have increased by 158% and 4%, respectively in 2005 as against levels reported in 2004, whereas those of heroin and hashish have decreased by 39% and 31%, respectively in 2005. The overall results of all law-enforcement agencies in the country are shown in Figure 7.5.

Performance of Various Agencies at Provincial Levels

If we have to believe the findings, statistics, the yearly reports, and publications of the ANF, which is the only specialized agency for the purpose of controlling drugs production and smuggling and has greater powers, jurisdiction and resources than any other agencies, then we are compelled to appreciate the role and services of other law-enforcement agencies in this respect, who have meager resources but larger responsibilities and wider professional duties of some other kind. Police and Customs are the two other major agencies, which, besides their routine tasks, have rendered valuable services in taking meaningful actions against illicit drugs.

Pakistan has four provinces [Punjab, Balochistan, Sindh, and North-West Frontier Province (NWFP)]. If we omit the relatively small number of cases in the northern areas and in the capital city of Islamabad, we observe that police have a greater share of seizures in all the provinces except the province of Balochistan where the police jurisdiction is very limited due to larger tribal areas. It shows that police have greater success in seizures of opium or hashish as compared to heroin or other sophisticated products, which are generally costlier, and their interdiction requires greater information/intelligence, for which the police have no special budget. I would like to reproduce the statistics given by the ANF for all the law-enforcement agencies in all four provinces of the country (Tables 7.3 through 7.6). These statistics for the year 2005 provide us an opportunity to compare and contrast the performance of various agencies within the same province or with other provinces. Some patterns and trends can be deducted from such comparison.

We are compelled to admit that certain law-enforcement agencies like the Frontier Constabulary and the Frontier Corps, which are traditionally posted in the semitribal areas or deployed at international/tribal borders, are generally underutilized for this purpose. In the good old days, these forces used to carry out very effective operations against such antisocial elements involved in drugs activities. Today they have very little contribution in this respect.

A special feature of all these efforts is that almost all law-enforcement agencies achieved significant triumphs over foreigners involved in narcotics trafficking from Pakistan during 2005. A total number of 225 foreigners from 31 different countries were arrested at various locations, carrying drugs in various covers. They were carrying a total of 288 kg of heroin, 249 kg of hashish, and 12 kg of opium. Crystal heroin happens to be their drug of choice for trafficking. Nigerians were the most conspicuous on the list of heroin traffickers. As many as 114 Nigerians (51% of the total foreigners) were arrested with 141 kg of heroin and 10 kg of hashish. Nigerians were followed by South African (total arrests, 19), Ghanians (15), Tanzanians (12), and Afghans (11). An important and new trend is the smuggling of heroin from Pakistan into China, both by air and by land. There is information, according to INCB, indicating that, in addition to being used for the increasing domestic market, heroin entering China is smuggled further to markets in Europe through the Hong Kong SAR of China. In 2005, 23 seizures were made from departing passengers at international airports in Pakistan, compared with only three seizures in 2004. The traffickers were bound for several different airports in China (INCB Report 2006). Interestingly, over 37% of the total heroin seizure by the ANF was made at the various airports in Pakistan (ANF, 2006).

As far as the foreigners-cum-drug smugglers are concerned, Pakistan has signed 26 MOUs (Memorandum of Understanding) and 28 Extradition Treaties with foreign countries. Pakistan is trying to fulfill her obligations and commitment honestly as a signatory to the "UN Single Convention on Narcotic Drugs and its 1972 Protocol," the "UN Convention on Psychotropic Substances 1971," and the "UN Convention against Illicit Traffic in Narcotic and Psychotropic Substances 1988."

Five Years Performance of Police, Customs, and ANF in the City of Peshawar (NWFP)

The NWFP (total population 14 million and total area 74,521 km²) is surrounded by the eight Federally Administered Tribal Areas (FATA), almost

Table 7.3 Actions against Drugs in NWFP

			Opium		Heroin		Hashish	
Agency	Cases	Defendants	Quantity Seized (kg)	% Achieved	Quantity Seized (kg)	% Achieved	Quantity Seized (kg)	% Achieved
ANF	89	138	120.6	18.0	115.4	50.9	4,653.6	20.8
Airports Security Force	2	2	0.0	0.0	2.6	1.2	0.0	0.0
Customs	5	4	0.0	0.0	31.4	13.9	623.3	2.8
Frontier Constabulary	1	1	0.0	0.0	0.0	0.0	0.1	0.0
Frontier Corps NWFP	16	16	5.3	0.8	0.0	0.0	1,599.0	7.1
NWFP Police	22,065	22,005	544.4	81.2	77.1	34.0	15,519.8	69.3
Total	22,178	22,166	670.3	100	226.5	100	22,395.8	100

Source: Anti-Narcotic Force. (2006). *Yearly Digest 2005–2006.* Rawalpindi, Pakistan: Directorate General of Anti-Narcotics Force (e-mail: anf@anf.gov.pk; Web site: http//www. anf.gov.pk).

Table 7.4 Actions against Drugs in Punjab

			Opium		Heroin		Hashish	
Agency	Cases	Defendants	Quantity Seized (kg)	% Achieved	Quantity Seized (kg)	% Achieved	Quantity Seized (kg)	% Achieved
ANF	215	373	251.3	29.4	211.2	41.1	7,932.1	30.0
Airports Security Force	6	6	0.0	0.0	8.3	1.6	0.0	0.0
Customs	42	26	1.3	0.2	33.6	6.5	5,775.7	21.8
Excise	657	621	198.8	23.3	63.4	12.3	2,649.1	10.0
Punjab Police	17,085	17,165	403.5	47.2	197.5	38.4	10,112.3	38.2
Total	18,005	18,191	854.8	100	513.9	100	26,469.2	100

Source: Anti-Narcotic Force. (2006). *Yearly Digest 2005–2006.* Rawalpindi, Pakistan: Directorate General of Anti-Narcotics Force (e-mail: anf@anf.gov.pk; Web site: http//www. anf.gov.pk).

Table 7.5 Actions against Drugs in Balochistan

Agency	Cases	Defendants	Opium			Heroin			Hashish		
			Quantity Seized (kg)	% Achieved		Quantity Seized (kg)	% Achieved		Quantity Seized (kg)	% Achieved	
ANF	62	36	3,261.3	68.2		343.9	36.6		6,748.4	27.6	
Frontier Corps Balochistan	88	34	1,200.6	25.9		510.5	54.3		6,002.4	24.6	
Coast Guards	37	41	75.1	1.6		5.0	0.5		7,324.0	30.0	
Customs	8	8	5.0	0.1		2.9	0.3		2,904.0	11.9	
Excise	55	55	0.0	0.0		0.4	0.4		58.8	0.2	
Baloch Police	165	164	245.0	5.1		70.5	8.3		1,381.3	5.6	
Total	415	338	4,787.0	100		933.2	100		24,418.74	100	

Source: Anti-Narcotic Force. (2006). *Yearly Digest 2005–2006.* Rawalpindi, Pakistan: Directorate General of Anti-Narcotics Force (e-mail: anf@anf.gov.pk, Web site: http//www. anf.gov.pk).

Table 7.6 Actions against Drugs in Sindh

Agency	Cases	Defendants	Opium			Heroin			Hashish		
			Quantity Seized (kg)	% Achieved		Quantity Seized (kg)	% Achieved		Quantity Seized (kg)	% Achieved	
ANF	136	141	20.9	22.1		222.3	49.0		7,850.6	39.8	
Customs	134	75	14.0	14.8		161.0	35.4		6,066.0	30.8	
Excise	148	175	26.2	27.7		48.6	10.7		5,562.1	28.2	
Sindh Police	782	850	31.4	33.2		19.2	4.2		116.7	0.6	
Sindh Rangers	19	33	1.5	1.6		2.0	0.4		21.6	0.1	
Railway Police	25	25	0.5	0.5		0.7	0.2		103.1	0.5	
Total	1,244	1,299	94.6	100		453.9	100		19,720.1	100	

Source: Anti-Narcotic Force. (2006). *Yearly Digest 2005–2006.* Rawalpindi, Pakistan: Directorate General of Anti-Narcotics Force (e-mail: anf@anf.gov.pk, Web site: http//www. anf.gov.pk).

Table 7.7 Total Strength of Force (All Ranks) in Peshawar District

Year	Police	Customs and Excise	ANF
2001	4,727	137	48
2002	4,727	125	52
2003	4,732	110	55
2004	4,815	80	59
2005	4,905	80	63

Source: Local Offices of Law-Enforcement Agencies.

all of which are near Afghanistan and known for major production of opiates in Pakistan. Peshawar is the capital city of NWFP, with a total population of 2 million and a total area of 1257 km^2. I have personally visited the offices of the three major law-enforcement agencies in the city of Peshawar and the Central Jail of Peshawar for looking into their working, targets, achievements, and the difficulties they face in their normal activities or during their actions against drug criminals.

If we look at the total strength of these agencies, very little re-enforcement has taken place in these forces for the last five years (Table 7.7). They only fill the vacancies every year due to retirement, dismissal, death or promotion, and so on. Surprisingly, in the Customs and Excise Department in the District of Peshawar, no new recruitment/enrollment has taken place since 1994, and now the average age group of their lower ranks/foot constable is 45, which is relatively an advanced age to fight the armed drug smugglers in a real encounter or ambush. The number of police has also not been increased considerably. However, the performance of the police vis-à-vis registration of cases or arrest and recovery is really encouraging despite the fact that police are overburdened with other serious crimes in the city, such as robbery, theft, murder, and now bomb blasts, target killings, suicide attacks, explosions, and terrorism. A comparative statement of relative performance of these agencies can be seen in Tables 7.8 through 7.11.

Table 7.8 Recoveries of Narcotics in the Jurisdiction of Peshawar District

Year	Opium (kg)			Heroin (kg)			Hashish (kg)		
	Police	Custom	ANF	Police	Custom	ANF	Police	Custom	ANF
2001	517	62	110	154	27	181	7,013	744	6,778
2002	340	189	234	152	10	65	12,908	4,540	3,428
2003	514	69	128	77	52	73	10,798	1,161	8,276
2004	798	40	57	118	77	68	16,492	8,131	14,858
2005	557	—	120	66	31	115	16,366	1,943	4,653
Total	2,726	360	649	567	197	502	63,577	16,519	37,993

Table 7.9   Total Cases Registered against Drug Offenders

Year	Agency			
	Police	Customs and Excise	ANF	Total
2001	4,703	17	146	4,866
2002	5,967	19	80	6,066
2003	5,060	14	64	5,138
2004	5,758	19	66	5,843
2005	4,704	21	88	4,813
Total	26,192	90	444	26,726

Table 7.10   Total Arrests of Drug Offenders

Year	Agency						
	Pakistanis			Foreigners			
	Police	Customs	ANF	Police	Customs	ANF	Total
2001	4,713	27	115	20	01	69	4,945
2002	5,974	31	106	08	—	10	6,129
2003	7,075	20	83	04	—	08	7,190
2004	5,735	18	97	02	—	03	5,855
2005	4,703	10	121	16	02	19	4,871
Total	28,200	106	522	50	03	109	28,990

Some agencies, especially the ANF, concentrate more on the refined form of drugs like heroin, which makes greater sensation and coverage in the media whereas the police feel happier in the recovery of hashish and alcohol (the latter not included in this present comparison). The ANF also generates greater ripples in the media by their actions against foreigner-pushers at airports or in discovering some strange way of trafficking like parcels, letters, or swallowed pills, filled with narco substances. Some private TV channels telecast special antismuggling programs related to the performance of the ANF. Impartial observers may regard it a "media campaign" for "improving ones' image." However, its educative role demands our appreciation. Customs and Excise are generally more concerned with the non-customs paid (NCP) vehicles, smuggled from other countries via Afghanistan, contraband items, smuggled goods, and of course, narcotics. The police generally disperse large crowds of drugs addicts, mostly hashish and heroin addicts, who are known homeless, unemployed, socially marginalized but sit together at some relatively invisible places like under city bridge/over flying, around a tunnel, along a railway track, or in the corners of a general bus stand.

Table 7.11 Punishments Claimed by Various Agencies

Year	Imprisonment			Fine (Rupees in Million/Billion)			Forfeiture of Assets (Rupees in Million/Billion)		
	Police	Customs	ANF	Police	Customs	ANF	Police	Customs	ANF
2001	75[a]	18	130	3.5 m	1.20 m	8 m	—	—	11 m
	3,906[b]								
2002	91	25	88	7.1 m	5.11 m	2 b	—	—	4 m
	5,221								
2003	80	22	50	6.0 m	4.30 m	1 b	5 m	—	9 m
	4,429								
2004	65	10	55	3.2 m	0.30 m	5 m	—	—	17 m
	4,767								
2005	88	20	77	4.0 m	1.50 m	7 m	12 m	—	180 m
	3,495								
Total	399	95	400	23.8 m	12.41 m	3.020 b	17 m	—	221 m
	21,818								

Source: Central Jail Peshawar, NWFP. (2007). Crime statistics for five years. Peshawar, Pakistan: NWFP.

[a] Persons imprisoned in Central Jail at the moment.
[b] Total Number of imprisoned/punished culprits claimed by local police but now released from custody/jail.

However, as far as the performance of the Police, Customs, and ANF in the city of Peshawar is concerned, we observe that police have a greater role and achievements in terms of recovery of opium and hashish and the ANF has greater delivery in terms of heroin. The arrest and registration of criminal cases is also more by the police. However, it is pertinent to note that the prosecution and forfeiture of assets as required under the law is higher for ANF and Customs (Table 7.11). The reason for this successful conviction rate in cases registered by Customs and ANF is the availability of greater national and international financial resources to these agencies for proper prosecution and investigation. Police is rather overwhelmed with other security duties, and after the separation of prosecution, investigation, and preventive branches in the new Police Order 2002, the police feel relaxed or rather unable to achieve the desired results in terms of conviction. It may be due to shifting responsibilities, lack of coordination among its various branches, or lack of specialized units. The police need extra financial support and professional/technological assistance for prompt investigation and prosecution.

The most important thing is that despite the highest number of arrests and registration of cases by the police, the actual conviction in terms of protracted imprisonment is extremely low. The reasons for this sharp contrast are to be looked into, including faulty investigation, poor prosecution, and other influencing factors. Moreover, civil witnesses never come against drugs pushers/users to the court of law due to fear and wastage of time. Many are given bail during trial/custody. Another strange phenomenon is the nature of imprisonment and fine. For the last five years (2001–2005), the police claim that 21,818 people were convicted and imprisoned for drugs-related offenses in the city of Peshawar but we find only 399 people convicted and imprisoned in the Central Jail of Peshawar (Table 7.11). Actually, the police rarely arrest big drug pushers/smugglers and normally the police clearance rate/arrest is for the small street users/addicts. The recovery is in minor quantities and, therefore, the accused are awarded a few days or a month or so imprisonment with or without a negligible fine. This practice adds to the police conviction rate but the crime itself is not addressed positively. These and other problems are discussed in detail in the section on challenges and constraints of investigation.

The cases registered by the police are sent to the courts of District and Session Judge of the concerned district/area; those registered by the Customs are sent to the court of a Special Judge Customs (equivalent to Session Judge), and those by the ANF are heard and decided by their own Special Judge ANF (again equivalent to Session Judge). All have the High Court of the province as their appellate court. This multiplicity is fraught with risks of uneven punishments for a similar nature of offenses and therefore needs revision and replacement by a uniform legal process.

As we all know that we do not have readily available data or interagencies exchange of information, so I had to use my personal contacts for getting the requisite information and statistics from the local offices of law-enforcement organizations. I was told by an officer of the Customs department that, "due to public resentment against excessive checking on main roads at the customs checkpoints and by mobile squads, the provincial and local governments have ordered to avoid unnecessary stoppage to the public, hence very little checking by our agency in 2006." There is no doubt about it that checking at so many places and simultaneously by so many agencies on one main Grand Trunk (GT) road caused unbearable inconvenience to the general public. But this is also not appealing that only this one instruction or ban by the government on this excessive checking/patrolling could be a plausible reason for the poor performance of the law-enforcement agencies in 2006 and 2007, especially, in terms of their actions against illicit drugs and narcotic substances (Table 7.12). The police, as usual, claim greater arrest and greater conviction with successfully completing the final report (what we call Chalan) against the accused. The conviction rate is also very high for the arrests made by the police; however, we should not ignore the fact that the accused in the police cases are generally small street peddlers, drugs users, and "unaware drug pushers," who do not know in reality what

Table 7.12 Drugs Offenses in the City of Peshawar, 2006–2007 (Comparative Statement under CNSA + 3/4 PO, etc.)

Name of Agency	Total Cases Registered		Total Accused/ Criminals/Abusers Arrested		Investigation Completed/Final Report (Chalan) Submitted		Under Investigation/ Final Report (Chalan) Not Submitted		Pending Trial (Put-in-Court)		Conviction (If Any)	
	2006	2007	2006	2007	2006	2007	2006	2007	2006	2007	2006	2007
ANF	91	82	140	102	89	82	2	—	75	82	14	—
Customs	2	15	3	15	2	3	—	6	1	3	1	—
Police	4,867	6,139	4,795	6,188	4,775	6,135	92	4	1,473	605	3,302	5,530
Total	4,960	6,236	4,938	6,305	4,866	6,220	94	10	1,549	690	3,317	5,530

items they are carrying from one place to another. Due to many legal lacunae and investigative problems as explained later, these initially punished/convicted people are either released at the appeal stage or their sentence is reduced by the appellate courts. Examples in this respect are numerous and appear in the newspapers every day.

Some Intrinsic Problems of Law-Enforcement Agencies

In addition to many intrinsic difficulties, being faced by all the departments, many complain of discriminatory treatment by the foreign/donor agencies in terms of resource allocation or specialized/technical assistance. For example, police, despite their valuable services against drugs menace, as we observed in the preceding tables, have never been regarded as a focus of attention or an agency for better utilization against drugs problem. An official of the Customs department told me that "the Narcotics Affair Section (NAS) of the U.S. Embassy has provided us only two vehicles for anti-smuggling activities in the last ten years whereas the ANF has been given fifteen vehicles only last year." He further complained that "the secret service fund for informers is about three lac rupees (US$5,000) for the entire province whereas an average informer for heroin seizure is never satisfied with less than one lakh rupees (US$1,666) for a single interception/identification." Such disparities in resource allocation for the major organizations are expected to reflect in their desired efficiency and performance.

Another problem is the absence of clear-cut role descriptions for these agencies. The police are drawing their legal powers from the Control of Narcotics Substance Act (CNSA) of 1997 and the Prohibition (Enforcement of Hadd) Order of 1979. The Customs department depends on the Customs and Excise Act, 1969 whereas the ANF works under the ANF Act 1997. Though all of them derive most of their antidrugs authority from the CNSA, 1997, yet the overlapping of powers and intermingling roles result in many fault lines in their usual working. For example, some cases are referred to the ANF by Customs, provided they feel that intervention of another agency is necessary, which may also result in some legal lacunae. For a brief introduction, I have made a comparison of these laws and their various provisions, which shows the overlapping and multiplicity phenomenon (Table 7.13).

Identification of responsibilities is another big issue at certain places. At international airports, passengers are checked both by the ANF and Customs which not only result in inconvenience for the passengers but also invoke a rebuke for the staff of one agency if some drug smuggler is caught by another subsequent sister agency. A need for positive collaboration and joint effort is suggested in this respect.

Table 7.13 Some Basic Anti-Narcotic Laws in Pakistan

S. No	Law	Crime (Kinds)	Penalty (Various)	Agency
1	Prohibition (Enforcement of Hadd) Order, 1979 (P.O. of 4, 1979)	• Manufacture of intoxicants • Import/export of intoxicants • Possession of intoxicants • Drinking	• Imprisonment up to five years/life imprisonment • Up to 30 stripes (whipping) • Fine	• Police • Customs
2	CNSA 1997 (XXV of 1997)	• Prohibition of cultivation of narcotic plants (Section 4) • Prohibition of possession of narcotic drugs, etc. (Section 6) • Prohibition of import/export of narcotic drugs, etc. (Section 7) • Prohibition on trafficking or financing the trafficking of narcotic drugs (Section 8) • Prohibition on owning, operating premises or machinery for manufacture of narcotic drugs, etc. (Section 10) • Prohibition of acquisition and possession of assets derived from narcotic offenses (Section 11) • Prohibition on aiding, abetment or association in narcotic offenses (Section 14)	• Upto seven years imprisonment + fine or both • From two to seven years to life imprisonment depending on quantity of drugs • Death sentence • Upto 25 years imprisonment + fine not less than Rs 1 million for Section 10 violation • Imprisonment upto 14 years + fine equivalent to the value of assets + forfeiture of those assets	• Police • Customs • ANF
3	ANF Act, 1997 (Act No. III of 1997)	All crimes given in CNSA, 1997 + Prohibition Order 1979 + Special Powers for the Director General of the ANF	All penalties given in CNSA 1997 + Prohibition Order 1979 + Freezing the Assets gained from narco-business after enquiry/investigation/tracing	• ANF
4	Customs Act, 1969 (Act IV of 1969)	Prohibition and restriction of importation/exportation of certain goods, smuggled goods, narcotic/psychotropic/controlled substances (Section 2, 15, 16, etc.)	Detention + seizure + confiscation + imprisonment upto 25 years + life imprisonment + death sentence + fine not exceeding two times the value of the goods (Section 156 8(i) (ii) and Section 9(i) (ii) (iii) (v) (vi)	• Customs

Constraints in Investigation of Drug Offenses

Criminal investigation is generally defined as, "the collection of information and evidence for identifying, apprehending, and convicting suspected offenders." Professor Ralph Turner of Michigan State University prefers: "A criminal investigation is the reconstruction of a past event." Either definition may be classified further by examining the specific responsibilities of the investigator (Osterburg & Ward, 2004). Pakistan Penal Code, 1860 in its section 4 (l), defines investigation as, "all the proceedings under this Code for the collection of evidence conducted by a police-officer or by any person (other than a Magistrate) who is authorised by a Magistrate in this behalf."

Some serious crimes may require a different approach and a different set of investigation processes. For example, Sonne (2006) while lamenting "the dim prospects for a total victory in the war on drugs" and while admitting the fact that "the investigation of this crime requires different tools and methods at various stages and geographical location" enumerates that, "investigations (of drugs offenses) can be initiated through intelligence, complaints from concerned citizens, surveillance, use of informants, infiltration, buy operation (undercover), and wiretaps or even by a routine traffic stop that results in the seizure of drugs or currency." All these can be summarized into five specific areas, namely traditional investigation, surveillance, undercover and informant operations, cooperative interagency investigations, and international investigations involving two or more countries—all have their own merits and difficulties. The investigative techniques, tools, and laws have also evolved over time and now include the conversion of illegally gained currency or other assets, commonly known as "assets forfeiture." The tracking of ill-gotten money is a challenging aspect in such investigative activity as most transactions occur in cash and the "laundering" techniques are extremely complicated. From our local perspective, we observe the following problems/challenges to our investigation processes.

Difficulty in Registration of Criminal Cases against Poppy Growers

The first and foremost difficulty in registering a criminal case against the growers of illicit narco plants is that most of the growers belong to the tribal or *de facto* tribal areas where a different set of administration exists and where most of the lands are illegally occupied. If the cases are registered in the settled/urban police stations, then it becomes very difficult to establish the ownership for these growers in the court of law. The revenue record does not show them as owners. Moreover, the authority of the local police administration is always challenged and not established in these *de facto* tribal areas of the districts of Peshawar, Charsadda, Haripur, and so on. After the "war on terror" in 2001 against Al-Qaeda in Afghanistan and the military operations against religious militants in the tribal agencies/areas by the Pakistan Army, it has become almost impossible for the administration of tribal areas to engage in punitive action against illegal growers. There seems an anarchical situation in our tribal territories. The local tribal population has cleverly exploited this situation and thus has increased poppy growing.

Multiplicity of Laws

A lot of confusion exists among the law-enforcement agencies due to three major separate laws, which are simultaneously applicable. These laws are the CNSA, 1997, the Prohibition (Enforcement of Hadd) Order, 1979, and the Customs Act, 1969, as shown earlier in Table 7.13. The law-enforcement people may, at times, apply less severe sections of law or play a "legal mastermind" in order to evade, compound, or misrepresent a case. These laws need a thorough study, and a single comprehensive drug law is recommended.

Capacity Difficulties/Malpractices by Law-Enforcement Agencies

There are some anomalies in the existing multiple laws. For example, officers below the rank of Subinspector have no jurisdiction/authority to search and detain under the CNSA, 1979. If the recoveries are made by another officer during random checking or on some information where the competent officer could not possibly be available at the time of operation, then most of the cases registered by the police end up in failure under the CNSA, 1979 due to the seize and search made by police officers below the rank of Subinspector. The local police may "play with the law" on this pretext due to certain reasons (e.g., corruption or pressure from higher offices or political elites or threats from drugs barons, etc.).

As a police practitioner, I can say without hesitation that such malpractices are not unexpected in our police system. Recoveries are not properly made as per law and rules. The recovery memo should be made on the spot and signed by the witnesses thereof. In practice, the recovery memos are generally prepared in the police stations/offices. During court proceedings, the civil/police witnesses give contradictory statements about the recovery memos, leading to the failure of the cases. Civil witnesses do not come forward to witness the recoveries or recant their statements or deny their signatures during examination in the court. People are afraid of wasting their time and money in litigation, which takes a lengthy period in the courts. Resultantly, the police have to depend solely on their police witnesses whereas the courts insist that the recoveries should be made in the presence of respectable witnesses from the public. Due to haste at the scenes of crime or illiteracy in the lower ranks, the recovery memos are sometimes not signed by the witnesses or concerned officers, leading to another difficulty during trial in the court. Such anomalies or malpractices done advertently or inadvertently provide a leverage to the accused for "benefit of doubt" and thus acquittal by the courts.

Problems in Laboratory Testing

As said, the recoveries, most often, are not made according to the laid down procedures, but more importantly the sample for the laboratory testing is not separated in time and with proper legal documentation. The law-enforcement agency, due to one or the other reason, may send it to the Forensic Sciences Laboratory (FSL) at the provincial headquarters after a lapse of sufficient time. This "delaying tactic" or "ignorance of law" creates doubt in the mind of the judicial officers. Sometimes, the corrupt officials in the law-enforcement agencies play a "foul game" by sending a low-quality narcotic substance or some other apparently similar substance or an adulterated/mixed substance (e.g., powder mixed with heroin or low-quality heroin or cannabis, all available in the drug-markets). If a seizure consists of 30 boxes of similar substances, sample from each box is required legally, but police think that a single sample is sufficient, which creates problem later on during trial proceedings.

The laboratory officials may also not be trusted completely in this context. Sometimes, their biased opinion is of tremendous help to the accused. The minimum punishment for tampering the "case property" or making changes in "case registration record" is dismissal from the service, as given in the Police Rules, 1934, but I have seen only one case of such dismissal in my 11 years of service where the heroin (case property) was replaced by "flour" by a lower police official and he got dismissed after departmental enquiry. Even the recoveries and their samples are neither preserved, properly sealed, properly weighed, and counted, nor properly made parcels with unbreakable packing. The law-enforcement agencies, to be fair enough, do not have the facilities and resources for this technical preparation at the scene of crime. The basic idea is that the amount or quantity recovered is directly proportional to the prescribed punishment. A little quantity will ultimately mitigate the severity and gravity of the offense.

The financial, technological, and administrative constraints of the provincial FSL are another story of its kind. Obviously, the functions of FSL are affected. The FSL in this province was established in 1976 and the total sanctioned strength for the FSL, including the fingerprint bureau, was 78 officials in 1978 which has not been increased by a single new vacancy or post since then. I had an interview with the Director of FSL Nafeesul Islam, who is also a senior police officer. According to him, "the FSL examined a total of 2,500 cases in 1978 with the available/sanctioned strength whereas the same number of examiners analysed 54,700 cases only in 2006; this means that 701 cases are being examined by each examiner in 2006." The total cases include all kinds of offenses like narcotics, arms, explosives, rape specimen, vehicle tampering, and so on. The total budget for chemicals was increased from Rs 300,000 (US$5,000) to Rs 500,000 (US$8,333.33) in 2006. This is an extremely meager amount for the purchase of costly chemicals, the prices of which are always on the increase. It shows that the FSL was given an allocation of Rs 9.140 (US$0.152) for every single examination in 2006. This can be unbelievably surprising to the people in the west.

Problem of Witnesses

The general public is not bothered to engage in the activities of law-enforcement personnel. They are neither properly dealt and educated by the concerned agency on the points of legal importance nor apprised of their legal duties in a court of law. It is the prosecutor's duty to refresh his/her memory of being a witness at the time of seizure or during investigation, but this duty is rarely fulfilled. After a certain period of time, the prosecution witness may not be in a position to recall all minute details of the case. Here comes a "role failure" on part of the prosecution. Very often the witnesses do not bother to attend the court despite the repeated summons and warrants being issued by the courts and, due to this unwarranted nonappearance of the witnesses, the courts acquit the accused under section 265 (K) Criminal Procedure Code (CrPC) 1898.

This power has been exercised by Trial Courts as frequently as possible in order to avoid undue delay in disposal of cases and hardship to parties. In all drugs offenses, the aggrieved party is the state as it is not a crime against person or property. So the police feel relaxed after handing over the case to the prosecution whereas the police/civil witnesses are left at the mercy of the defense counsel, as the prosecution has been recently separated from the police and is still in its developmental stages with a low level of accountability. Prosecution is not a "disciplined" or "uniform" force and is vulnerable to all kinds of influences or vices prevalent in any underdeveloped society. In case of petty recovery of narcotics, the accused when bailed out does not take it serious to attend the court and the police think his production a mere "botheration." The police in such cases often inform the court that the accused is "not available" or of some "unknown whereabouts." The court in such cases returns the case file and stops the courts' proceedings under section 249 CrPC.

This practice adds up to the stockpiles of pending cases and no one is moved to take serious interest once the court bails out the accused.

Malpractices in Seized Narcotic Substances

The law-enforcement agencies, most often, have to depend on proper intelligence for interdiction or busting a gang of drugs pushers/smugglers. It is very rare to have successful seizure without a "valid informer." But it is also rarer to find one without an offer of handsome money or reward to such informer. The law-enforcement agencies, as far as I know, do not have enough allocation for that. What happens is that, at times, the law-enforcement people promise a reasonable share of narcotic substances to the informer. This "scratching back policy" works well as it gives a "performance show" to the law-enforcement agency and a "lion share" to the informer. The law-enforcement people have a bad record for keeping the "case properties" in proper shape and kind. This is entirely in the hands of the law-enforcement people to "deflate or inflate" the quantity of the seized items. If not at the initial stages, they may do whatever they like to do after exhibiting the case property in the court of law and after sending the same to the official storehouse (malkhana). During informal discussions, the law-implementing officials may tell you that the actual amount or quantity of seized items should never be destroyed by fire under section 516 (A)* CrPC.

It is in connivance with the prosecution department that a little quantity may be destroyed in presence of the general public, media reporters, and even foreign dignitaries, for showing "efforts" in the "war against drugs." This "over display" often accelerates the drug problem at the backdoor. However, no empirical research could be found in this regard.

Inadequate Investigative Facilities

The "drug-mafia" is extremely shrewd, well connected and invisibly operating in our day-to-day life with rapidly changing patterns, techniques, and with not so easily suspected ways of drugs trafficking. A few examples will show the concealment methods of drugs pushers:

  i. 2.5 kg of heroin were concealed in hard cardboard sheets, generally placed in readymade shirts. Small packets of the drug were sandwiched

---

* 516-A. *Order for custody and disposal and property pending trial in certain cases*: When any property regarding which any offense appears to have been committed or which appears to have been used for the commission of any offense is produced before any Criminal Court during any inquiry or trial, the Court may make such order as it thinks fit or the proper custody of such property pending the conclusion of the inquiry or trial, and if the property is subject to speedy or natural decay, may after recording such evidence as it thinks necessary, order it to be sold or otherwise disposed of: (Provided that, if the property consists of explosive substances, the Court shall not order it to be sold or handed over to any person other than a Government Department or office dealing with, or to an authorized dealer in, such substances) (CrPC, 1898).

between the two layers of cardboard glued together. (Recovery from a Ghanian lady named Briddet Sedofia, at Quetta International Airport on October 11, 2005. The larger number of shirts created suspicion of drug concealment.)

ii. 232 kg of cannabis recovered from the hidden cavities of a motor-cycle at Peshawar on February 21, 2005. Culprit Syed Haider Shah (motorcyclist) arrested on spot.

iii. 12 kg of heroin and 1,210 g of chemical precursors recovered were tactfully concealed in the wooden rods of a bed in Kohat on September 11, 2005.

iv. 5 kg of heroin were concealed in hairclips in the luggage of a foreign lady on September 8, 2005 at Peshawar International Airport.

v. 11 kg of heroin were recovered from a Ghanian national on September 29, 2005 at Peshawar International Airport. The heroin was skillfully concealed in a dry oven (sterilizer).

vi. Two ladies from Azerbaijan, destined for New Delhi, India were searched at Lahore International Airport in February 2005 and 1.2 kg of heroin were recovered from ladies' earrings, necklaces, and other jewelry.

vii. A leather jacket is often used as a method of safe concealment.

viii. Courier parcels carrying ladies' shoes were dissected and found heroin packs in cavities made in the soles of these shoes.

ix. On April 4, 2005, a Nigerian lady's private parts were examined by a lady constable and found an extraordinary huge capsule from her vagina, carrying 0.29 kg of heroin.

x. Trafficking in auto parts, wooden shields, swollen capsules, large baggage, fastening belts, shirts, buttons, hidden surfaces of suit-cases and briefcases, foot mats, stationery items, electric appliances, shampoo bottles, glue sticks, medicines, ornamental souvenirs, shoes, powder cartons, cosmetics, and many other innovative methods are generally seen in transnational trafficking. Within the country, the hidden parts of vehicles are used as the safest concealment areas. Sometimes, these vehicles bear fake official registration numbers with their drivers in official dress with fake identity. By this, they expect an easy escape or overlook at the check posts of law-enforcement agencies.

Owing to the above trends and techniques of national and international drug smugglers, drug law enforcement has become a challenge for all the con-cerned agencies. None of them can claim to have the skills, techniques, knowl-edge, or equipment for identification of these "ever-changing deceptive" and "smart" *modus operandi* of drugs traffickers. The law-enforcement agencies have no facilities of telephone call analysis, audio–visual accessories, scanners or x-ray machines for suspected items or people and the technical and professional know-how of DNA testing, finger prints, or footprint collection. Basically, all these facilities and provisions are to be made and supplied to every law-enforcement agency at some strategic station or at least at their most sensitive areas of operation or at their headquarters. Even our laboratories are not fully equipped with these modern facilities.

Difficulties in Investigating Drug Assets

The money gained and assets made as a result of drug production, possession, or trafficking are enormous, and the bigger these assets are, the more difficult is their identification and confiscation. The police have never done an investigation in this regard. Dealing with "money laundering" is extremely difficult for untrained, understaffed, and nominally educated police forces in Pakistan. The police are not fully competent to deal with ordinary drugs offenses, much less the highly sophisticated investigative process of money laundering. Police have never been trained for this either. Same is the case with customs. However, the ANF has made some achievements in chasing the assets of some people who could not give a proper legal account for such a large amount of money. Depriving criminals of their ill-gotten assets through forfeiture or freezing has a long-lasting effect on narcotic control efforts, as accumulation of wealth and maximization of assets are the ultimate goals of nearly all drug barons. The ANF has worked out a total of 179 cases so far, which has led to an asset forfeiture of Rs 472 million (US$7.8 million) and an asset freezing of Rs 4,258 million (US$71 million). The scenario at this front would have been more promising, had the police and customs been fully authorized and trained in investigating the assets of unknown sources.

A person's assets can be doubted/presumed as drugs assets if he is convicted for three years imprisonment on drugs offenses, but no tracing is seen in this respect by any of the agencies, despite the legal provision for doing so. Also, a separate application for freezing of assets of a person can be moved by the law-enforcement people, if the accused is convicted for a rigorous imprisonment of 5–14 years. Lack of professionalism in full utilization of these legal provisions is surprisingly evident.

Doubted/Fake Recoveries

Law-enforcement agencies sometimes recover very huge quantities of narcotic substances from disbanded houses, far-flung huts, and mountainous caves, with no arrest or nomination of a suspected drug pusher. A queer situation is recoveries from big cartons of narcotic substances, placed on a "donkey" or a "bicycle" where the owner of the donkey or bicycle makes his escape good. Most of the huge recoveries made by the police belong to this category. Even the ANF recovers huge quantities from such unclaimed places or deserts or forests. For example:

i. 1,001 kg of morphine and 64 kg of hashish were recovered by the ANF in Dalbandin, Baluchistan on February 1, 2005, which were "dumped in an unnoticed area." No arrest was made in this case.

ii. 1,024 kg of opium were dumped in a "mountainous area" near Bostan, Pishin (Baluchistan). The ANF recovered the same on February 11, 2005 with no arrest.

iii. 1,110 kg of opium were recovered from a "deserted hut" in Kharotabad, Quetta (Baluchistan) by the ANF on August 21, 2005. No arrest could be made for such a large recovery.

These recoveries often create doubts in the minds of free analysts and impartial observers. Public and media people generally cast aspersions on the "authenticity" of the information for such a big quantity of narcotics, left unattended in an open mountainous area. As these recoveries are mostly without any arrest, so the investigations of all these cases are usually "untraced." A senior officer who once served in the ANF for three long years narrated to me some "amazing stories" about such "unclaimed recoveries." Only fiction stories can be put as rivals to the stories of these "recoveries." All recoveries, whether fake or genuine carry a good cash reward also. Anyhow, the recoveries are spectacular, if the investigation is a failure.

No Special Investigative Units

Rarely do we notice a special investigative unit or cell for drug offenses in the law-enforcement agencies. The Frontier Constabulary (a force of 18,000 personnel) and the Frontier Corps (a big paramilitary force) have no such units or skills for dealing with drug offenses. The ANF has its own cell but even Customs has no separate unit of specialized officials for the purpose of such investigation. Actually, most of the law-enforcement agencies tend to concentrate more on "preventive actions," "commando actions," and "raids and ambush" for recoveries and arrest than on utilization of their investigative faculties on the whole criminal process or conviction of the accused. This "ad hoc" approach toward drug offenses leaves us with ever-exacerbating drug problems. It is also true that these other agencies have no legal authority for registering and investigating a criminal case against the drug pushers, except their "preventive actions" and handing over the accused and case properties to the concerned investigative agency.

Inadequate Funds and Staff for Investigation

The cost of investigation has never been an issue with our police before the newly enacted police law, the Police Order 2002. It is only after the police reforms that the prevention and investigation branches are being separated. The investigative branch is gradually evolving into an established wing of the police force. We have an extreme shortage of resources for all this new development and establishment. As a result, the cost of investigation is now included in our daily policing. The total registered crimes in the city of Peshawar were 17,840 in 2006 and the total budget for the cost of investigation was Rs 32,90,000 (US$54,833). So, the cost of any crime investigation, including drug offenses, was Rs 184.41 (US$3.07). The total drug offenses occurring in the city of Peshawar in 2006 were 4,867, and the total investigative staff is 306, so we have 58 cases (including 16 drugs cases) for each police investigator.

Local Consumption of Drugs

On the streets, parks and other public places of Peshawar, the dusty capital of NWFP in Pakistan situated about 50 km from the Afghan border, it is quite common to walk over the comatose bodies of drug users, both Pakistanis and Afghans. There is no way of calculating how many of these men have died over the years. There are no records kept, no official morbidity or mortality rates. It is estimated that over 65 percent are homeless, often without family contact, and that many are buried or disposed off after they die with few records kept of their passing (Macdonald, 2007).

The data on drug offenders appearing before the courts in the United Kingdom are described by John Corkery (1999) from the Home Office as "very complicated, old fashioned and time consuming." Clearly, the situation is worrying. How can it be that the data are so poor, and why has so little attention been given to them? (Bean, 2004). The writers in the developed world may be looking for the causes into their particular problems, but the situation in Pakistan is the same, maybe with similar causes and problems. Unfortunately, we also do not have a verified and authentic study for drug offenders/addicts in the streets, villages, and cities of our country. The Drug Assessment Surveys of 1980, 1993, and 2000 are also not comprehensive, rather based on small-scale samples and generally portray a trend or pattern and a sort of rough estimation. The global figures for drug consumption are also not comprehensive and even the statistics shown by international bodies are generally derived from respective countries.

Ignoring these difficulties, we observe that the total official estimated number of addicts in Pakistan is reported to be 4 million, out of the world's total estimated 200 million addicts (ANF, 2006). We have the world's highest rate of drug addiction, and most of the country's 500,000 heroin addicts are aged between 25 and 35 years with 60,000 among them using injectable heroin. (Human Rights Commission of Pakistan, 2006). Pakistan could face an AIDS epidemic as many of the heroin addicts are injecting the drug. (The total reported adult HIV positive cases in Pakistan, according to WHO/ UNAIDS estimates are 24,000–140,000.) For instance, according to one surveillance report of the National AIDS Control Program, in the total reported cases of 2741 HIV positive cases in a selected area (third quarter of 2005) there were 596 injectable drug users (IDUs). Drug abusers in Pakistan are 99% male (ANF, 2006). The AIDS–drugs nexus is more of a serious concern in the cities than in the rural areas. Similarly, heroin addiction is also regarded as an "urban phenomenon." According to a survey conducted by the Federal Ministry of Health in 2005, nearly 60% of Pakistan's urban population is "nervously afraid" of having public contact with a person who is HIV positive (ANF, 2006).

I would like to reproduce some facts from this survey, which is often quoted by the ANF, and which clearly depicts how rampant and prevalent is the menace of drug abuse at the national level, besides the production and transit of narco substances. Many NGOs and media essays also frequently quote these facts and figures. This is generally known as National Drug Abuse Assessment Study 2000:

i. Cannabis, in one form or the other (marijuana, hashish, etc.), is the most commonly used drug in Pakistan in terms of lifetime use and prevalence, followed by heroin, alcohol, and psychotropic substances.

ii. Eighty-one percent (81%) of respondents (283 key informants in total) reported that heroin caused "major problems" in their locale. In Punjab province, 88% of respondents reported "major problems" in their communities resulting from heroin abuse.

iii. Contrary to the findings of a 1993 survey which suggested that heroin was the most commonly used drug, the present survey (2000) reveals that cannabis-type drugs are reported to be commonly used in the locales (i.e., in 36 sampling sites).

iv. Among males in the age bracket of 15–45 years, there are 500,000 regular heroin drug users. Forty percent of the heroin abusers fall in the age bracket of 25–35 years.

v. Hashish (charas) is equally popular in urban and rural areas. Heroin abuse, however, is conspicuous as more of an "urban drug."

vi. On average, respondents had been using heroin for nearly five years before entering treatment. (Sample of survey in four major cities, that is, Karachi, Lahore, Quetta, and Peshawar was 1,049, only 12 among them were female.)

vii. The average age for first heroin use was 22. This figure was found lower for hashish/charas (18) and alcohol (19).

viii. Heroin abusers, on the average, have six years of education.

ix. Of the total number of heroin users, 43% are unemployed and 26% are engaged in full-time employment.

x. The frequency of drug abuse is highest among skilled and unskilled labor categories (47%), followed by business persons (16%), agricultural workers (5%), and students (3%).

xi. Insofar as women are concerned, psychotropic substances are the most common drugs of abuse. It has also been found that women comprise only 3% of the total number of patients being reported, making it an important area for intensive research.

xii. Among heroin users, 77% are reported to be using the drug on a daily basis, as for hashish, 41% use it on a daily basis and 34% occasionally. Alcohol consumption remains more varied. However, most of the respondents (76%) are reported to be consuming alcohol twice or thrice a week or less, with only 10% consuming five or more days a week.

xiii. Other significant drugs include opium and tranquilizers, which are currently being used by a quarter of all respondents. A majority of the hardcore drug abusers consume multiple drugs.

xiv. As many as 73% of the total heroin users either smoke the drug or inhale its fumes while 11% sniff it and 15% inject it. Cannabis is mostly used in smoking (96%). Injecting drug use is accompanied by high incidence of practices associated with the spread of bloodborne infections.

xv. Over half (66%) of subjects reported that at some time they had not been able to have access to treatment when they had needed help.

xvi. As far as treatment and rehabilitation is concerned, 64% of the respondents report difficulties in getting treatment. For an overwhelming majority (80%), treatment is unaffordable. Lack of in-patient facilities in government hospitals is cited as the major deterrent for treatment by 23% of the respondents; 44% have received treatment for a drug problem at some stage in their life. Most of the addicts have never received intensive or sustained therapy. Those who received treatment included vast majority (96%) for heroin treatment with far lower numbers reporting treatment for the abuse of opium (7%) and hashish (5%).

xvii. Thirty-five percent (35%) of the respondents are reported to have spent some time in prison for their alleged involvement in drug-related offenses.

We are told about a rough estimate of 3–5 million addicts in the country but, to be fair enough, the exact distribution and identification is still a task ahead. However, it is beyond doubt that the greater prevalence is seen in the mega/urban cities of Karachi, Lahore, and Peshawar. According to an estimate of an NGO, Drug-Free Society, there are more than 100,000 drug addicts in the city of Peshawar. Some may find it difficult to agree with the estimate of 100,000 as it is hard to locate such a large number of addicts either in the streets or being registered with the few rehabilitation centers in the city. The NGO found that in many cases, the addicts have shown an internal social mobility trend, and due to easy and cheap availability/supply of narco substances in the city of Peshawar, these addicts keep coming from other provinces and cities. They are then lost in these existing crowds and no one knows where they are destined to and how they earn their livelihood except menial jobs, begging, theft, and other crimes.

Another important issue is the "authenticity" and "validity" of this National Drug Abuse Assessment Survey. According to an official of the ANF, "this study was carried out as a Rapid Assessment Survey, but later on after compilation, it was presented and published as a 'National Survey/ Assessment,' which seems inappropriate on part of the authorities who, wittingly or unwittingly, had overstretched a 'selective study' to a broader national spectrum." No doubt, it gives a wrong impression and creates a sort of intellectual misrepresentation. The study admits that it cannot report comprehensively on the abuse of drugs by women in Pakistan (p. x). It also admits that the prevalence of cannabis abuse in Pakistan has not been a primary focus of the study, and though the prevalence of cannabis abuse is considerably greater, yet it is not possible to give a credible estimate of the magnitude of the abuse at this time (p. xiii). The study does present "collecting data on drug abuse" as "an end in itself," rather it emphasizes the fact that "the information is required for informing the debate on how best to develop target interventions designed to reduce drug abuse problems" (p. 2).

The difference between words and action is very evident from the fact that the Federal Government of Pakistan has not issued its much awaited Master Plan till September 2008, and even the only major responsible agency, the ANF has failed to publish its annual report for the year 2007–2008, whereas the UNODC Report 2007 says that "the UNODC assisted Pakistan in the preparation of its Second National Drug Control Master Plan for 2007–2011." No doubt this plan was submitted to the Federal Cabinet in early 2007 but till late 2008, the nation has yet to depend on the existing system for drugs control which has never been a promising one.

It is obligatory under the CNSA 1997 that the provincial governments shall register all drug addicts and establish as many treatment centers as necessary for detoxification, deaddiction, and rehabilitation of such addicts but no concrete efforts have been made so far in light of the following provisions:

> *Section 52: Registration of addicts*—(1) Each Provincial Government shall register all addicts within their respective jurisdiction for the purpose of treatment and rehabilitation of addicts. (2) The Federal Government shall bear all expenses for first time compulsory detoxification or deaddiction of an addict. (3) The addict shall carry a registration card in such a form as may be prescribed and produce it to any public authority on demand.
>
> *Section 53: Powers of the Government to establish centres for treatment of addicts*—The Provincial Government shall establish as many centres as may be deemed necessary for detoxification, deaddiction, education, aftercare, rehabilitation, social integration of addicts, and supply of such medicines are considered necessary for the detoxification of the addicts.

The country has a total of 76 Treatment and Rehabilitation Centres of which 21 are government-run, 42 are NGO-run, and 12 are owned by private persons, all having a total of bed capacity of 1806. A few NGOs/Rehabilitation Centres in the city of Peshawar have lofty claims and publish their colorful reports more than their actual services. Some critics observe that the NGOs normally concentrate on "attractive presentations" for "donors' interest" and inflate their figures of registered patients, obviously for gaining a good place in the record of funding agencies. However, it will be a little unfair to the efforts of community people in a society where the governments have failed to fulfill their duties that are legally binding on them vis-à-vis the registration and rehabilitation of drug addicts.

Recommendations

My recommendations are very simple, and I have already hinted most of them in my account in the whole chapter. Briefly, I would like to recommend:

 i. A general mass awareness campaign about the "demand reduction" and "supply reduction" policies, through all possible ways and means of communications.
 ii. A uniform drug law, which should be simple, single, and in accordance with international treaties and conventions.
 iii. All law-enforcement agencies should be given equal role and proper allocation of resources from the national and international funds for "war on drugs."

iv. A joint forum of all law-enforcement agencies where they should share information, the outcome of their efforts, and their constraints in dealing with drug offenses.

v. Specialized units in all departments of law enforcement for proper investigation, collection of evidence, and compilation of accurate data.

vi. Registration of identified addicts and efforts for their early treatment and rehabilitation.

Conclusion

The drug problem is neither a local issue nor can it be easily addressed by a single agency. It is a transnational problem with greater implications and challenges for national security and international peace and cooperation. Law-enforcement agencies in Pakistan have done much for the eradication, control, and interdiction of narcotics, despite their meager resources and routine overwork. Pakistan is intending to revise its Master Plan of 1998–2003 for Drug Abuse Control, and is committed to the international treaties and bilateral agreements. The society as a whole is expected to work for "freedom from narcotics," which not only enslave bodies but also souls. The support of the international community and established organizations is also expected to be meaningful and productive. Drugs and associated crimes should not be overlooked by all the law-enforcement agencies on the pretext of work burden, resource constraints, or role imperfection. We all stand committed.

References

Abercrombie, N., Hill, S., & Turner, S. (2000). *Dictionary of Sociology* (4th ed.). UK: Penguin Books.

Anti-Narcotic Force. (2006). *Yearly Digest 2005–2006.* Rawalpindi, Pakistan: Directorate General of Anti-Narcotics Force (e-mail: anf@anf.gov.pk, Web site: http//www.anf.gov.pk).

Bean, P. (2004). *Drugs and Crimes* (2nd ed.). UK: Willan Publishing.

Central Jail Peshawar, NWFP. (2007). Crime statistics for five years. Peshawar, Pakistan: NWFP.

Choudry, T. N., & Ghaffar, M. A. (2007). *The Major Acts with Short Latest Comments.* Lahore, Pakistan: Irfan Law Book House.

Crimes Branch, NWFP. (2007). Crime statistics for five years. Peshawar, Pakistan: Police Department, NWFP.

Dahl, R. A., & Stinebrickner, B. (2003). *Modern Political Analysis* (6th ed.). India: Pearson Education.

Ekblom, P. (2005). Designing products against crime. In N. Tilley (Ed.), *Handbook of Crime Prevention and Community Safety* (Chapter 8). UK: Willan Publishing.

Hughes, G. (2006). Crime reduction. In E. Mclaughlin & J. Muncie (Eds), *The Sage Dictionary of Criminology.* UK: Sage Publication.

Human Rights Commission of Pakistan. (2006). *State of Human Rights in 2006.* Lahore, Pakistan (e-mail: hrcp@hrcp-web.org, Web site: www.hrcp-web.org).

International Narcotics Control Board (INCB). (2007). Report, 2006. United Nations, New York. (e-mail: secretariat@incb.org, Web site: www.incb.org).

Macdonald, D. (2007). *Drugs in Afghanistan.* London: Pluto Press.

Osterburg, J. W., & Ward, R. H. (2004). *Criminal Investigation* (4th ed.). Cincinnati, USA: Anderson Publishing.

Sonne, W. J. (2006). *Criminal Investigation for the Professional Investigator.* UK: Taylor and Francis.

UNODC Annual Report for 2007 and 2008. From www.UNODC.org.

West, A., & Alison, L. (2006). Conclusions: personal reflections on the last decade. In L. Alison (Ed.), *The Forensic Psychologist's Casebook: Psychological profiling and criminal investigation* (Chapter 16). UK: Willan Publishing.

Organized Crime in South Africa

8

C. J. ROELOFSE

Contents

The introduction of democracy in South Africa had a definite influence on policing. The transition from the previous regime to the current democratic dispensation had strategic priorities that left organized crime (OC) virtually unattended as more pressing issues were pursued. This created ample opportunities for syndicates to establish their operations in South Africa. The preoccupation of the state with structural changes such as the creation of nine Provincial Governments, dismantling the Transkei, Bophuthaswana, Venda, and Ciskei (TBVC) state apparatus as well as those of the self-governing territories and the new local government initiatives allowed crime syndicates to go almost unchecked in the initial years of democracy. Reorganization included the amalgamation of 11 Police Forces and several Defense Forces and former liberation movements into the new South African Police Service and South African National Defense Force.

The aim of this chapter is to give an overview of the South African Police Services handling of OC. Almost 13 years into the new dispensation it is necessary to scientifically assess the policing of OC in the light of international conventions and treaties and to determine to what extent South Africa is complying with these conventions and treaties. It is also essential to study the police transformation since 1994 and how these changes affect the policing of OC.

Organized Crime

The term "organized crime" refers to crime that involves the cooperation of several different persons or groups for its successful execution.

> Organized crime is usually professional crime ... In a broad sense, the entire underworld may be said to be organized. It is set apart from the rest of society. It has its own standards, attitudes, and public opinion, and an informal, though effective, means of communication known as the 'grapevine' ... Organized crime as it now exists in the United States requires the active and conscious co-operation of a number of elements of respectable society. It requires the passive co-operation of many other elements (Lindesmith, 1941, p. 119).

OC constitutes any enterprise, or group of persons, engaged in continuing illegal activities which has as its primary purpose the generation of profits, irrespective of national boundaries (Huber, 2001, p. 216).

The author defines OC as a business with all the inherent practices of planning, hierarchy of authority, division of labor, intelligence, market research, organizational culture, discipline, and contracting, driven for profit and power but without legal and moral constraints. In this chapter, OC and transnational organized crime (TOC) have been used interchangeably but reference to OC always means TOC.

OC in South Africa

The first indications of TOC in South Africa can probably be attributed to Chinese Triad societies. The Chinese criminal elements that caught the attention of police during the 1970s were mainly those involved in the shark fin trade, smuggling of products from endangered species such as rhino horn, and illegal gambling operations. By 1990, police were convinced that OC groups were making a considerable contribution to the escalating crime problem in South Africa. One of the strategies devised at a police conference was to establish a national Organized Crime Intelligence Unit (Gastrow, 2001, p. 1).

Around the middle of the previous century, the government in South Africa faced an armed insurgency from various groups of whom the most prominent were the armed wings of the ANC (MK—Umkhonto we Sizwe) and the PAC (APLA—Azanian Peoples' Liberation Army). This led to: (1) the establishment of infiltration routes and courier networks through which arms were smuggled; (2) training in the east and connections with Russian, Chinese, and Korean as well as African revolutionaries; and (3) apartheid government counter strategies that also involved criminal activities. The result is that connections have been established with former Komitet Gosudarstvennoy Bezopasnosti (KGB) and Triad operatives that have been perpetuated into OC operations. Anecdotal evidence exists that former liberation fighters from Southern Africa are involved in cash heists, gun running, hijacking, and robbery.

Secondly, the transitional phase of the political dispensation in South Africa created for a number of years a policing vacuum. The metamorphosis from a politically motivated police force to a Civilian Police (CIVPOL) approach as well as the belated recognition of the OC problem created fertile soil for syndicates to establish themselves in South Africa. Comparative evidence suggests that OC grows most rapidly in periods of political transition and violence, when state resources are concentrated in certain areas only and gaps emerge in which organized criminal groups may operate. The most notable example is the former Soviet Union: The collapse of communist rule allowed the emergence of literally thousands of criminal organizations involving current and former members of the establishment (Sherr, in Shaw, 1998, p. 2).

In South Africa, these and other forces have been at play. Before the collapse of apartheid, South Africa was not considered to have had an OC problem. This was only partly true: In the Western Cape, increasingly organized gangs had forged links with foreign criminal organizations in East Asia in order to obtain narcotics, particularly qualoids or (in South African terminology) mandrax. Local gangs were often used to target antiapartheid activists in exchange for police turning a blind eye to their activities.

The advent of democracy in the country heralded an increase in organized criminal activity. Senior South African Police Service (SAPS) officers point out that, when apartheid ended, border controls were weakened, thus creating new potential areas of operation for OC. This also occurred at a time when transnational criminal operations were expanding; just like "legitimate" multinational businesses, East Asian, Nigerian, and East European groups bought into local South African criminal operations and expanded them, or contracted subsidiary organizations to conduct their work for them (Shaw, 1998, p. 2).

Minnaar (1999, p. 2) mentions a number of factors that contribute to the growth of OC in South Africa:

- Renewed investor interest.
- South Africa's favorable geographical location on the major trafficking routes between the Far and Middle East, the Americas, and Europe.
- South Africa's accessibility via land, sea, and air routes. To this can be added that a number of unmonitored air strips exist close to our Northern borders which makes illegal and unnoticed border crossings very easy (this has been exploited for instance to take abalone out of South Africa to neighboring states).
- A criminogenic market structure. Unsaturated demand for and readily available illicit commodities such as drugs, arms, vehicles, endangered species products, and body parts exist.
- The large-scale presence of illegal aliens/undocumented migrants notably from Southern African Development Community (SADC) countries, China, Taiwan, and Nigeria that are involved in OC adds fuel to the fire.

Syndicates Operating in Republic of South Africa

The increase in OC activities in South Africa is no more evident than reflected in comparative statistics. By the time the transitional government took charge, there were about 200 identified groups in South Africa. In his report to the 11th United Nations Congress on Crime Prevention and Criminal Justice in April 2005, the Minister of Justice indicated that the number of identified and infiltrated groups amounted to 341.

Chinese Triad Groups

In 2000, the legal Chinese population of South Africa was estimated at 100,000, and police estimated that the country was home to another 100,000–200,000 illegal Chinese. The Triad groups in Republic of South Africa are mainly Cantonese- and Mandarin-speaking groups of which the most notable are Wo Shing Wo, San Yee On, 14K-Hau, and 14K-Ngai groups (Gastrow, 2001, p. 3). Although Triad activities in South Africa probably surfaced as a result of shark fin trade, authorities were not concerned as it was believed that the sharks were caught outside of South Africa's territorial waters. However, some individuals were involved in the smuggling of rhino horn and also with illegal gambling. By 2001, however, authorities recognized that groups in the Western Cape also were trafficking in narcotics, laundering money, and dealing in prostitution but the main attraction for Triads was the marine delicacy, abalone.

Abalone is endemic to South African waters, but one species only, *Haliotis midae*, is of any commercial value. Known in South Africa as *perlemoen* (from the Dutch *Paarlemoer*, meaning mother-of-pearl), it was endemic to several hundred kilometers of South African coastline stretching from Table Bay to the Eastern Cape before overexploitation threatened it with extinction (Tarr in Steinberg, 2005, p. 1). Part of the problem is that communities are participating in the demise of the perlemoen. They include divers, transporters, and dealers. Many believe that under the freedom of the new government they have unrestricted access to marine resources. These community members directly feed the illegal Triad operations. There is however much more involved than harvesting this marine delicacy that calls for anywhere from $65 to $100 in the East. Triads are now involved in bartering operations trading abalone for drugs especially methaqualone and then selling it on the streets of South Africa and particularly in the Western Cape. This means that there is an explosion in their profits as they make astronomical profits on the difference of the buying price of abalone in South Africa and the price they fetch in the East. The drugs are then again sold at enormous profits in South Africa and elsewhere.

As indicated above, there are a number of unmonitored air strips in the North of South Africa. Information suggests strongly that the bulk of South African abalone is not smuggled through sea ports but across uncontrolled and commercial land borders and on illegal and unrecorded air flights. A number of hauls have been intercepted by the police as far North as Pietersburg (1,600 km from the Cape coast).

> There are no specific figures to verify this account, but there is a great deal of anecdotal evidence and some strong quantitative evidence. In a recently published paper, the organization TRAFFIC cites records of the Census and Statistic Department of Hong Kong which show that 200,000 kg of frozen, shucked *perlemoen* and over 100,000 kg of dried *perlemoen* were imported from Mozambique, Namibia, Tanzania, Swaziland, and Zimbabwe to Hong Kong between the beginning of January 2002 and the end of June 2003. As the authors of the TRAFFIC paper point out, *perlemoen* is endemic to none of these countries with the exception of Namibia. It is almost certain ... that all this *perlemoen* was illegally harvested in South Africa, smuggled into the other African countries, and then re-exported to Hong Kong (Willock, in Steinberg, 2005).

Nigerian Groups

According to Irish and Qhobosheane (2003, p. 9), there are between 40,000 and 100,000 illegal Nigerian aliens residing in South Africa. The main operations of Nigerian syndicates involve drug trafficking, prostitution networks, Advanced Fee Fraud (AFF), kidnappings, money laundering, and check and credit card fraud. According to a Telkom technician interviewed by the author, highly technically skilled Nigerians operate sophisticated computer networks from underground cable ducts, connecting their computers and phones to the network and accruing massive bills for unsuspecting legitimate users. Nigerian syndicates are also increasingly becoming involved in the trafficking of cocaine from South America. From West Africa, cocaine is then smuggled to South Africa and Europe.

Russian Groups

When the South African Minister for Safety and Security visited Moscow in November 1998, he told a media briefing that Russian criminals in South Africa were involved in arms smuggling, fraud, car theft, and drug trafficking. He provided the Russian authorities with a list of 23 names of persons, some of them known internationally, who were under suspicion for involvement in criminal activities in South Africa. He informed the media briefing, held in Moscow on November 24, 1998, that the South African police feared that Russian criminals could also be dealing in uranium (World Justice Information Network, 1998).

International Cooperation

On December 15, 2000, 124 of the 189 Member States of the United Nations signed the treaty "The United Nations Convention on Transnational Organized Crime" with close to 80 of them also signing the treaty's two accompanying protocols—one to prevent, suppress, and punish trafficking in persons, especially women and children, and the other against the smuggling of migrants by land, sea, and air (UN Press Release L/T/4359, December 2000). South Africa is one of the signatories to the treaty and has through legislation, policy, and actions given effect to a number of important international treaties. Some of the measures were already in place by the time of signing the above-mentioned treaty.

African Union

Africa has been ravaged by numerous conflicts in which corruption and crime flourished. The illicit diamond trade for instance has not only financed armed struggles but has been the source of many conflicts in itself. The African Union (AU) has adopted several resolutions and conventions to fight crime on the continent but the implementation has been sadly lacking due to a lack of resources. The New Partnership for African Development (NEPAD) that aims to economically develop Africa and the SADC are all contributing to regional initiatives in fighting corruption, conflict, crime, and poverty. The most significant declarations, protocols, and conventions adopted by the AU and SADC are listed below:

- 1996 Political Declaration and Drug Control Action Plan on the Control of Drug Abuse and Illicit Drug Trafficking in Africa, which was reviewed in 2002 at the 38th Ordinary Session of the Oraganization for African Unity (OAU, now the African Union), at which a revised action plan for 2002–2006 was adopted.
- The Declaration on the Prevention and Control of Organized Transnational Crime and Corruption, adopted on July 21, 1997 in Dakar, Senegal.
- The OAU's 2000 Bamako Declaration on the Common African Position on the Illicit Proliferation, Circulation, and Trafficking of Small Arms and Light Weapons.
- The Economic Community of West African States (ECOWAS) Political Declaration against Trafficking in Human Beings, and Sub-Regional Plan of Action, Regional Level, adopted on December 20–21, 2001, at the 25th Summit held in Dakar, Senegal.
- The ECOWAS Declaration on the fight against the Illegal Traffic in Persons and Action Plan for 2002/03.
- The East Africa and the Great Lakes Regions Declaration on the Proliferation of Illicit Small Arms and Light Weapons, signed in Nairobi, Kenya, on April 20 and 21, 2004.
- The 1996 SADC Regional Protocol on Illicit Drug Trafficking.
- The 2000 SADC Protocol on Corruption; 2002 SADC Protocol on Extradition; and 2002 SADC Protocol on Mutual Legal Assistance in Criminal Matters.
- The 1999 OAU Convention on the Prevention and Combatting of Terrorism (also known as the Algiers Convention).
- The 2003 AU Convention on Preventing and Combatting Corruption (Mashaba, 2005, p. 1).

Southern African Development Community

South Africa has been readmitted to the international community following the 1994 elections although it had been accepted as a member of Interpol in the preceding year. A Sub-Saharan Interpol office has been established in Harare, Zimbabwe and a very significant development has taken place subsequently with the formation of the Southern African Regional Police Chiefs Coordinating Organization (SARPCCO). The organization is comprised of the chiefs of policing agencies in the following countries: South Africa, Angola, Botswana, Lesotho, Malawi, Mauritius, Mozambique, Namibia, Swaziland, Tanzania, Zambia, and Zimbabwe. The secretariat for the organization is provided by Interpol.

> SARPCCO plays a particularly important function at the level of exchange of information, joint management of criminal records, and in providing support for joint operations. The body consists of a Council of Police Chiefs (the main decision-making structure) and a Permanent Coordinating Committee which comprises the Heads of the Criminal Investigation Services and handles all policing/investigation functions. The Legal Subcommittee attends to harmonizing of legislation and the promotion of mutual assistance on criminal investigations. The Training Subcommittee formulates systematic regional police training policies and strategies (Van der Spuy, 1999, p. 2).

South African Regimes in Combatting OC

South Africa complies with the United Nations Convention against TOC as far as the legislative requirements for criminalization of offenses contained therein are concerned, namely crime in respect of participation in organized criminal groups, money laundering, corruption, and obstruction of justice. South African parliament has enacted several pieces of legislation that are vital for the combatting of OC, while others are already prepared and being discussed (see *Country Report to the 11th United Nations Congress on Crime Prevention and Criminal Justice*, 2005, pp. 13–17).

> *Prevention of Organized Crime Act, 1998 (Act No. 121 of 1998)*: The Act took effect in January 1999 and introduced a number of measures to combat OC, money laundering, and criminal gang activities. The Act provides for the confiscation of criminal assets and also for the civil forfeiture of certain assets. It further provides for a Criminal Assets Recovery Account and a Criminal Assets Recovery Committee. One of the objects of the Committee is to advise Cabinet on issues around the rendering of financial assistance to law-enforcement agencies in order to combat OC, money laundering, criminal gang activities, and crime in general.
>
> *The Financial Intelligence Centre Act, 2001 (Act No. 38 of 2001)*: This Act provides for the establishment of the Financial Intelligence Centre (FIC) and is aimed at combatting money laundering, in particular, through the reporting of suspicious transactions to the FIC. The FIC is operational since February 2003. It serves as a coordinating body for the collection and distribution of information to law-enforcement

agencies in the country and notably to SARPCCO and Interpol as well as cooperating agencies in other countries. The Act makes it incumbent on certain individuals to report suspicious financial transactions to the FIC.

The Regulation of Interception of Communications and Provision of Communication-related Information Act, 2002 (Act No. 70 of 2002): This Act regulates the interception of certain communications, the monitoring of certain signals and radio frequency spectra, and the provision of certain communication-related information. The Act also regulates the applications for, and the issuing of directions for authorizing the interception of communications.

Firearms Control Act, 2000 (Act No. 60 of 2000) and the National Conventional Arms Control Act, 2002 (Act No. 41 of 2002): These two Acts deal with the licensing of fire arms, their possession, competencies, and also regulating the armaments industry in South Africa.

The Protocol to Prevent Trafficking in Persons: At present, South Africa has no legislation specifically criminalizing trafficking in persons. However, the Law Reform Commission has drafted a Bill and released it for comments during May 2006. There exists a plethora of laws and sections of laws dealing with trafficking, child prostitution, and addressing the wider issue of sexual offenses, rape, and the protection of vulnerable women and children. The Criminal Law (sexual offenses) Bill, 2003, also touches on child prostitution and includes male rape in its definitions. Sections 10 and 11 specifically criminalize the promotion of sexual offense with children and child prostitution.

The Protocol against the Smuggling of Migrants: At its meeting on November 5, 2004, The Portfolio Committee on Justice and Constitutional Development, having considered the request for approval by Parliament of the *Protocol against the Smuggling of Migrants by Land, Sea, and Air, Supplementing the United Nations Convention against TOC*, noted that "at present there is no current legislation to deal with the criminalization of the smuggling of migrants in terms of article 6 of the said Protocol." The Committee recommended that such legislation be adopted.

Law Enforcement in the New South Africa

Law enforcement in the New South Africa has been pivoted around the National Crime Prevention Strategy (NCPS) and the White Paper on Safety and Security.

National Crime Prevention Strategy

The NCPS had been adopted by Cabinet in May 1996. Obviously, after the democratic elections a different approach in dealing with crime was necessary. The approach was to shift from a "secureaucratic" society to one where there was emphasis on the social phenomena of crime and crime prevention. The NCPS argued that dealing with crime required a dualistic approach of development on the one hand and crime prevention measures on the other hand.

The NCPS was in favor of a synergistic approach to problem solving, involving role players from broader society where government, NGOs, and the public can work together to solve the crime problem. The NCPS was therefore aiming at providing the means through which SAPS and Municipal Police, other government departments, the private sector, and civil society could develop a progressive partnership in the fight against crime.

The NCPS evolves around four critical strategies:

- Changing the criminal justice system: The criminal justice system had to be made more efficient to cater for a system that is legitimate, has a culture of human rights, and can effectively deal with crime.
- Reducing crime through environmental design: Aimed at primary crime prevention by eliminating precipitating circumstances; situational crime opportunities had to be minimized.
- Community values and education: Aimed at optimizing community participation and involvement in crime prevention.
- TOC: Aimed at curbing the growing number of crime syndicates that flooded the country since the early 1990s.

The NCPS had set specific priorities to be pursued of which only those relevant to this study will be mentioned: Crimes involving firearms; OC; white-collar crime; vehicle theft and hijacking; and corruption in the criminal justice system (Pelser & Rauch, 2001, pp. 1–5). In order to pursue the NCPS objectives, there was a need to form a coordinating body and in 1997 this has been entrusted to the National Secretariat for Safety and Security (NSSS). In turn, the NSSS established a number of structures to further the objectives of the NCPS; these included a Ministers' and Directors' General Forum in order to provide high-level decision making concerning priority areas for action and a Departmental Coordinating Mechanism that enables such priorities to be integrated and implemented at the program and project levels.

Forthcoming from the NCPS and NSSS are a number of projects and programs pertaining to crime but also to OC, such as the Integrated Justice System (IJS) Program aiming particularly to ensure proper information management and coordination, and the Witness Protection Program. Following the restructuring of the Department of Safety and Security shortly after the appointment of the new Minister for Safety and Security and National Commissioner in 1999, the NCPS coordination functions have been transferred to the Central Coordinating Office that existed in the Secretariat for Safety and Security. The NCPS provided impetus for further developments. The most prominent outcome is the drafting of the White Paper on Safety and Security.

White Paper on Safety and Security

In 1998, Cabinet approved the White Paper entitled "In Service of Safety" with the intention to provide a policy framework for the provision of Safety and Security. The White Paper concentrates on three vital areas to meet the set objectives: law enforcement, crime prevention, and institutional reform.

Law enforcement. The focus areas identified in the White Paper to ensure effective law enforcement and service-orientated policing are intended to improve the investigative capacity of the SAPS; implement visible policing; and meet the needs of victims.

Crime prevention. As far as crime prevention is concerned, the White Paper advocates ambitious strategies involving multiparty/agency participation focusing on offenders and victims in an ecological setting that involves their environment and the root causes of particular crimes.

Institutional reform. Forthcoming from the international treaties and conventions as well as regional dynamics in Southern Africa and moderated by the NCPS and White Paper certain agencies and systems have been put in place. (Note: The following sections are virtually verbatim from Country Report to the 11th United Nations Congress on Crime Prevention and Criminal Justice.)

National Prosecuting Authority

The National Prosecuting Authority was established in terms of section 179 of the Constitution of the Republic of South Africa (Act No. 108 of 1996), and the National Prosecuting Authority Act (Act No. 32 of 1998). A National Director of Public Prosecutions heads the National Prosecuting Authority (NPA). It consists of a number of Business Units, some of which are discussed below: National Prosecution Service; Directorate of Special Operations (Scorpions); Asset Forfeiture Unit; Sexual Offenses and Community Affairs Unit; Specialized Commercial Crimes Unit; Witness Protection Unit; Priority Crimes Litigation; Integrity Management; and Corporate Services.

The National Prosecution Service. The National Prosecution Service is responsible for the management and performance of all the mainstream prosecutions in the courts in South Africa. A Deputy National Director of Public Prosecutions is in charge of the National Prosecution Service. Historically, all the Offices of the Directors of Public Prosecutions (formerly known as Attorneys-General) were independent and responsible for prosecutorial functions in their area of jurisdiction. The creation of a single National Prosecuting Authority brought these uncoordinated prosecutors under the control of the National Director.

Directorate of Special Operations. The Directorate of Special Operations, also referred to as the "Scorpions," had been established to effectively deal with all national priority crimes, including corruption. The Directorate intervenes in crime markets that have the greatest economic, social, or security impact on the citizens of the country. It will also, where appropriate, institute criminal proceedings in respect of offenses or any criminal or unlawful activities committed in an organized fashion or, such other offenses or categories of offenses as determined by the President by proclamation in a Government Gazette.

The Directorate's multidisciplinary methodology is underscored by the so-called "troika-principle," which amounts to the combining of prosecution, information gathering, and investigation. The Unit is structurally designed to give effect to this principle and therefore consists of prosecutors, special investigators, crime analysts, crime information gathering specialists, and forensic accountants. The Directorate achieved the following during 2004: (1) 234 investigations with a conviction rate of 90%; (2) 223.2 million rand (approximately US$38.4 million) worth of assets have been placed under restraint; (3) drugs with a street value of 4.4 billion rand (approximately US$758.6 million) were seized; and (4) 22 ongoing racketeering investigations were conducted with five convictions.

Asset Forfeiture Unit. The Asset Forfeiture Unit was established in May 1999 in the Office of the National Director of Public Prosecutions to focus on OC and the fight against money laundering. The Asset Forfeiture Unit provides support to the cases investigated by the South African Police Service and the Directorate of Special Operations in respect of the criminal or civil forfeiture of assets. A Deputy National Director of Public Prosecutions heads the Asset Forfeiture Unit and is assisted by a Special Director of Public Prosecutions, special financial investigators, and Deputy Directors of Public Prosecutions.

During the 2003–2004 financial year, the Asset Forfeiture Unit won 19 of 23 cases, a success rate of 83%. The Asset Forfeiture Unit has achieved exceptional growth as the number of new cases has grown at a rate of 65% per annum over the last four years, and the value of the cases increased by 25%

per annum. The Asset Forfeiture Unit has also increased the number of completed cases from 73 to 116, while the amount involved increased from 15 million rand (approximately US$2.5 million) to 48 million rand (approximately US$8.2 million).

Regional, Continental, and International Collaboration

The Southern African Regional Police Chiefs Cooperation Organization is used to address OC and other safety and policing-related issues within the SADC Region. The 9th SARPCCO Annual General Meeting took place in August 2004 and the meeting adopted resolutions relating to the conducting of coordinated cross-border operations, targeting the proliferation of small arms and OC groups in the Southern African region. The operations that have been conducted thus far have led to a number of successes, including the seizure of stolen vehicles, illegal firearms, and drugs and the arrest of persons involved in these crimes.

It has become evident that successes related to these operations increase as cooperation among countries improves and that these operations severely disrupt OC networks. In addition to cooperation within the SARPCCO structure, bilateral contact between policing agencies on the African continent takes place. Bilateral agreements have been concluded with Nigeria, Rwanda, and Egypt in addition to the multilateral agreement that forms the foundation of the SARPCCO. These cooperative initiatives will have a positive impact on the prevention, detection, and investigation of TOC in the SADC region and the African continent as a whole, specifically in respect of those crime phenomena where trafficking is a key element of the crime.

Multilateral Police Cooperation

The following police cooperation agreements were also concluded in the interests of preventing and combatting TOC:

- Police cooperation agreements relating to the combatting of drugs and drug trafficking between South Africa, Brazil, Argentina, and Chile.
- A memorandum of understanding in respect of the combatting of drugs and drug trafficking concluded with the Islamic Republic of Iran.
- General police cooperation agreements with the Russian Federation, France, Hungary, the People's Republic of China, Austria, Portugal, Turkey, and Bulgaria.
- South Africa is also an active member of Interpol and participates in all related Interpol activities. The National Commissioner of the South African Police Service was also elected as President of Interpol

in 2004, reinforcing South Africa's involvement in Interpol activities. (Country Report to the 11th United Nations Congress on Crime Prevention and Criminal Justice.)

Key Strategic Focus Areas

A National Security Policy was developed in order for the SAPS to fulfill its mandate as described above. The Policy is aimed at integrating crime prevention and crime combatting activities with the improvement of socioeconomic conditions. To implement this Policy, three phases were identified: A short-term stabilization phase (2000–2003), a medium-term normalization phase (2000–2005), and a long-term socioeconomic development phase (2000–2020). The first two phases are the primary responsibility of the SAPS in cooperation with other role players, but in the socioeconomic development phase the SAPS plays only a supporting and advisory role to departments in the Social Cluster.

The National Security Policy is being coordinated by the Justice, Crime, Prevention, and Security (JCPS) Cluster. The main objective of the JCPS is to focus their endeavors and resources jointly in addressing the incidence of crime, public disorder, inefficiency in the justice system, and all aspects of society that impact negatively on development. In order to realize this, the JCPS Cluster has identified several strategic interventions that are categorized under two themes: the transformation of the criminal justice system; and a joint crime prevention and crime combatting strategy (Strategic Plan 2002/2005|Strategic Direction of The SAPS).

Reorganization in SAPS

In January 2001, the SAPS announced that the specialized units as they existed at the time would be dissolved. The units would be reorganized into Organized Crime and Serious Violent Crime Units. This was done in accordance with "government's strategy to have an integrated approach to fighting crime." In addition, the National Commissioner of the SAPS was reported as saying that the police's "capacity to deal with OC syndicates should be coordinated in an integrated manner." Furthermore, there was a feeling that "local police stations should be empowered to effect expert policing. This would ensure that serious and violent crime was adequately addressed by those with the necessary expertise" (Mistry & Redpath, 2001, p. 2).*

---

* Quoting National Commissioner J Selebi quoted in an article entitled Revamp for Gauteng police units, written by Ernest Mabuza for Business Day, January 16, 2001.

To understand the rationale behind the decision to reorganize the police, it is incumbent that the status quo be reviewed as it was before the reorganization. Investigations were handled mainly by specialized units such as South African Narcotics Bureau, commonly known as the Drug Squad, which investigated drug-related offenses; Vehicle Theft Units; Murder and Robbery Units; Live Stock Theft Units; Gold and Diamond Units; Anti-Corruption Unit, and so on.

In OC, there is often more than one crime being committed in a particular operation. There may be narcotics, murder, stolen vehicles, and armed robbery involved in the same operation. This in essence is the crux of the problem. Which unit should coordinate the investigation and which unit should be first in handling the information available? A lot of information was not shared among units due to professional jealousy and sometimes just lack of insight. The scope of the proliferation of the semiautonomous specialized units becomes evident when the fact that over 500 such units existed countrywide is assessed.

In January 2001, SAPS announced that specialized units would be closed down and that investigations will be handled by two units, that is, Organized Crime and Serious Violent Crime Units. Detectives from the specialized units would be moved back to police stations. The closure of the specialized units meant that some 7,000 detectives had to be redeployed. This was done in three phases.

Phase one. This involved the identification of the units to be closed down and the establishment of the two main investigation units. Initially, just over 200 units were closed and 233 OC units were established around the country. The aspect of CIVPOL played an important role in the decision. The transfer of detectives to local police stations increases civil oversight through Community Police Forums. This was one aspect where the specialized units failed dismally.

The coordination needed to combat OC can be seen in Figure 8.1. This reflects international and regional cooperation as well as the role of intelligence and community participation. Connections to Interpol and SARPCCO are very important aspects of the SAPS's strategy to combat TOC.

Intelligence exchange among agencies and states is an absolute essential in combatting TOC. It is obvious that there exists a global exchange on information among responsible states. In the South African context, Interpol and SARPCCO play major roles in facilitating the flow of information. However, at an operational level there are severe problems in intelligence gathering. A country's Intelligence Service will obviously play a role when OC threatens the state. Intelligence gathering through informers and plants becomes very difficult when ethnic and language barriers exist such as with Triads and

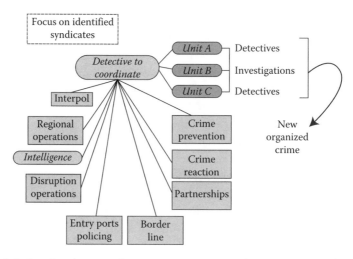

Figure 8.1 South African police service crime combatting concept for selected organized crimes. (Adapted from South African Police Services. (2002a). Strategic Plan 2002–2005. Pretoria: SAPS.)

virtually every other international syndicate. Language, ethnic affiliation, and rituals are protective barriers against plants and infiltration. Recruitment of existing members under lure of reward has been used successfully by all police agencies but brutal action against informers whose covers are blown are risks that limit the success when it comes to Triads in particular. A very serious complication with plants is that they may have to commit crime or at least be an accomplice in order to protect their cover. This is an issue for in-depth discussion and decision.

> *Phase two.* This simply entails a consolidation phase following phase one to evaluate the effects of the units that have been closed and to assess the performance of the enhanced OC units and the serious violent crime units.
>
> *Phase three.* This phase is still continuing and encompasses the further closure of specialized units.

Oversight

Democratic control over the police is regulated by Section 208 of the Constitution that calls for a civilian secretariat. Despite the reorganization and the high demand to cope with serious and TOC, the inherent desire and commitment to be accountable to the public is also strongly pursued. Constitutional oversight is ensured within the framework of the Bill of Rights and structures such as The Public Protector, Human Rights Commission, National and Provincial Safety and Security Secretariats, and Community Police Forums.

A further enhancement of accountability has been ensured by the creation of an Independent Complaints Directorate (ICD). The ICD is a government department that has been established in April 1997 to investigate complaints of brutality, criminality, and misconduct against members of the SAPS and Municipal Police Service (MPS). It has a national office as well as offices in the nine provinces. The ICD has a total of 51 staff members at its head office and 102 in its provincial offices. The ICD investigates the following:

- Deaths of persons in police custody or as a result of police action (such as shooting, assault).
- The involvement of SAPS members in criminal activities such as assault, theft, corruption, robbery, rape, and any other criminal offenses.
- Police conduct or behavior which is prohibited in terms of the SAPS Standing Orders or Police Regulations, such as neglect of duties or failure to comply with the Police Code of Conduct.
- Dissatisfaction/complaints about poor service given by the police, for example, failure to assist or protect victims of domestic violence as required by the Domestic Violence Act (DVA).
- Misconduct or offenses committed by members of the MPS (ICD brochure, 2006, p. 1).

Constitutionally, legally, and structurally there exists a pretty robust system to tackle OC. Unfortunately, as in all countries, corruption is a major problem. In addition, in a joint workshop between the ICD and the Center for the Study of Violence and Reconciliation, it was revealed that in the 30-month period from April 1997 to the end of January 2000 there have been 2,071 deaths in police custody or due to police action. In effect, on average every month in South Africa during this period there have been 60 of these deaths (approximately 20 in police custody and 40 police action deaths). (ICD/CSVR, http://www.icd.gov.za/documents/workshopcsvr.htm.)

Corruption

In South Africa, TOC has received great assistance from corrupt officials in Home Affairs. The acquisition of fraudulently issued identification documents, passports, work permits, duplicate birth certificates, and so on, has been a nightmare for the administration. Corrupt officials at entry points into the country were targeted by syndicates to allow gray goods, cigarettes, drugs, and so on into the country. Minnaar (1999, p. 5) states that corrupt policemen supply drug lords with police radios and keep them informed of police investigations so that they may evade arrest, elude the capture of evidence against them, or even "buy" or pay for dockets against them to be lost.

A former Commissioner of SAPS, George Fivaz, gave an instruction in September 1995 that a study be conducted on the feasibility of establishing anticorruption units at national and provincial levels. Judge Heath ran a special investigations unit with great effect but this unit was closed down. The anti-corruption unit (ACU) was established and at its full strength comprised a total of 240 staff members, made up of 201 police members and 39 civilian personnel.

As can be seen from Figure 8.2, as the profile of the unit increased, so did the number of allegations of police corruption that were reported to it. Between its establishment in 1996 and the end of 2001, the ACU had received a total of 20,779 allegations of police corruption, 3,045 police members were arrested, and 576 were convicted (Newham & Gomomo, 2003, pp. 2–3). With the reorganization of SAPS, the ACU is becoming part of the OC component. This is a highly contestable decision as the OC units are prime targets for corruption and bribery by crime syndicates.

The closure of the ACU means that the measure of autonomy enjoined by the unit as a separate investigation team has now been negated. In Figure 8.2, it can be clearly seen that the number of cases received, investigated, and the number of convictions dropped after the first units were closed down in 2000. Linked to this controversy was a debate that raged for some time until the Khampepe Commission came up with a compromise. The National Commissioner wanted the Special Investigation Unit (Scorpions) to be transferred to SAPS. The Khampepe Commission eventually recommended a dualistic responsibility, that the political accountability over the Scorpions

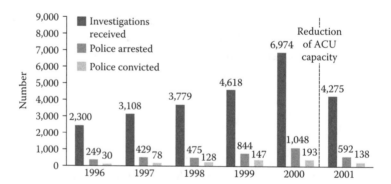

Figure 8.2 Investigations, arrests, and convictions undertaken by SAPS anti-corruption unit, 1996–2001. (Adapted from South African Police Services. (2002b). Annual Report of the National Commissioner of the South African Police Services 2001–2002. Pretoria: SAPS.)

will be split. The investigating arm now falls under the Minister of Safety and Security, while the prosecuting arm remains under the Minister of Justice. The ICD now really remains the only institution to deal with corruption in the police. With a total staff of compliment of 153, it is impossible to cope with the influx of complaints.

An additional concern is that the kinds of interventions currently entertained around the world to deal with OC can easily deteriorate into draconian laws and become a generator of state income. This applies especially to asset forfeiture before a court conviction has been achieved. The nonconviction or *in rem* forfeiture can occur without a conviction. Redpath (2001, p. 2) says in this regard, "Criticisms of this kind of law include that it is a punishment and punishments should not be meted out without a criminal conviction...."

Recommendations

South Africa is a fledgling democracy. It is playing a vital role in peacemaking and peacekeeping operations in Africa but the democratic changes also led to a relaxation of controls at our borders, an opportunity seized by syndicates. We need to

- Consolidate efforts to strengthen the criminal justice cluster
- Improve controls at our borders and at our harbors and airports
- Strengthen our crime intelligence gathering capacity
- Speed up training for investigators
- Do away with affirmative action in critical areas to enhance investigative and prosecuting capacity
- Strengthen our police/community partnerships
- Clamp down on corruption in government departments
- Make more money available for research on OC and criminal justice
- Jealously guard our civil liberties

Conclusion

The new dispensation in South Africa has also brought new opportunities for criminals. The country has experienced a tremendous influx of foreign nationals linked to OC syndicates. The study clearly indicates that South Africa complies to a very large extent with the UN conventions and treaties to fight OC. The AU and SADC and South Africa's participation in these organizations clearly indicate that international cooperation to fight OC is a priority for South Africa. Cooperation with Interpol and SARPCCO, as well as agreements with many countries, point toward a progressive approach in the SAPS to deal with OC.

As far as organizational changes in the SAPS are concerned, it should be noted that the closing of specialized units and the creation of the OC Units and the Serious Violent Crime Units, while closing down the Anti-Corruption Unit, cannot be defended within the context of general corruption within the country and the police.

References

Country Report to the 11th United Nations Congress on Crime Prevention & Criminal Justice. (2005) Viewed at saps.gov.za/docs_publs/legislation/country_reprt_ three.pdf

Federal Bureau of Investigation. Undated. Organized Crime. Viewed at http://www. fbi.gov/hq/cid/orgcrime/glossary.htm

Gastrow, P. (2001). *Triad Societies and Chinese Organised Crime in South Africa.* Pretoria: ISS.

Huber, B. (2001). England. In W. Gropp & B. Huber (Eds), *Rechtliche Initiativen gegen organisierte Kriminalität.* Freiburg, Germany: edition iuscrim. Viewed at http:// www.organized-crime.de/OCDEF1.htm#index#index

Irish, J., & Qhobosheane, K. (2003). *Penetrating State and Business. Organised Crime in South Africa* (Vol. 2). Pretoria: ISS.

Lindesmith, A. R. (1941). *Organized Crime, The Annals of The American Academy of Political and Social Science* (Vol. 217), September 1941. Viewed at http://www. organized-crime.de/OCDEF1.htm#index#index

Minnaar, A. (1999). A Symbiotic relationship? Organised Crime and Corruption in South Africa. Presentation to workshop, 9th International Anti-Corruption conference. Durban, October 10–15.

Mashaba, M. (2005). Organised crime and corruption. Fighting the problem within a Nepad framework. *African Security Review, 14*(4). Pretoria: ISS.

Mistry, D., & Redpath, J. (2001). The impact of the dissolution of specialized units on the investigation of crime in South Africa. 2nd World Conference. Durban, December 3–7.

Newham, G., & Gomomo, L. (2003). Bad cops get a break: The closure of SAPS Anti-Corruption Unit. *SA Crime Quarterly,* 4(June).

Portfolio Committee on Justice and Constitutional Development. (2005). Committee meeting resolution. November 5, 2004. Cape Town: Parliament.

Redpath, J. (2001). Papering over the Cracks: The Law and Organised crime, 2nd World Conference. Durban, December 3–7.

South African Police Services. (2002a). Strategic Plan 2002–2005. Pretoria: SAPS.

South African Police Services. (2002b). Annual Report of the National Commissioner of the South African Police Services 2001–2002. Pretoria: SAPS.

Shaw, M. (1998). *Organised Crime in Post-Apartheid South Africa.* Pretoria: ISS.

Steinberg, J. (2005). *The Illicit Abalone Trade in South Africa*. Pretoria: ISS.

United Nations. (2000). UN Press Release.

Van der Spuy, E. (1999). International and Regional Co-operation in Crime prevention. Centre for the Study of Violence and Reconciliation. Johannesburg.

World Justice Information Network (WJIN) News. (1998). Russia linked to arms and drugs in South Africa, November 25 and December 2. Viewed at www.wjin.net

Organized Crime and Safety in Azerbaijan

9

FAZIL GULIYEV and ORKHAN DADASHOV

Contents

Azerbaijan is one of the newly independent countries that emerged in the post-Soviet space. Azerbaijan, the heir of the Azerbaijan Democratic Republic of 1918–1920, gained its independence back in 1991 after 70 years under Soviet regime and started reforms in 1993 under the leadership of national leader Heydar Aliyev.

In 1988, during the Soviet times, Armenia SSR claimed a stake against the territorial integrity of Azerbaijan SSR in the Nagorny Karabakh autonomous region. Pursuing an ethnic cleansing policy, Armenia deported 200,000 Azerbaijanis living in Armenia. It proceeded to occupy 20% of Azerbaijan's territory including Nagorny Karabakh, the people of which were forced to flee to other regions as internally displaced people. On February 26, 1992, genocide targeted at Azerbaijanis in one of the small towns in Karabakh—Khojali—caused the brutal death of 613 people (including 63 children, 106 women, and 70 old men) simply because of their ethnic and religious belonging. Resolutions of UN Security Council on liberation of Azerbaijan's occupied territories 822, 853, 874, and 884 have not been executed. Resolution of the Council of Europe 1416 adopted in 2004 requires immediate withdrawal of Armenian troops from occupied Azerbaijani territories.

Although the ceasefire agreement reached in 1994 led to suspension of military operations, the conflict has not been fully resolved. Still, the achievement of ceasefire triggered political, economic, and legal reforms in our country and fueled huge oil projects. During these years, our country set the goal to run balanced policy of cooperation, integration to the world community, and secure national interests.

A strong state building process is underway in Azerbaijan on legal and secular, economic, and military aspects aimed at strengthening of democratic principles and state independence. Large-scale social economic and legal reforms and improvement of legislation and regulations have been progressing successfully.

During recent years, the capital and other cities experienced fast socioeconomic development, expansion caused by internal and external migration, and population increase. New institutions and production facilities are being established, renovations and construction of dwelling houses have been taking place, thousands of new job opportunities have been opened, and the employment rate is growing. Well-thought policy to speed up the socioeconomic development set by the country leadership preconditions the speedy development of the economy. Dynamic development of the Azerbaijan economy in 2006 placed it in a leading position in the world according to gross domestic product (GDP) growth.

Although GDP growth rate was 26.4% in 2005, results for 2006 showed growth to 35% and industrial production was about 37%. Currency reserves of the country reached 4 billion USD. Budget expenses were increased on average by 80% in comparison with 2005. Generally, as a result of economic reforms conducted during the last three years, the state budget increased for more than four times and it expected that it will reach 6.5 billion in 2007. Today international organizations as well approve that Azerbaijan is a leading country in the world in terms of pace of economic growth.

Apart from that, the volume of investments was on average 7 billion USD in 2006, including 3.1 billion USD for the nonoil sector. For the last 10 years more than 25 billion USD was invested in Azerbaijan's economy. A strong push for reduction of unemployment led to 173,000 new jobs in 2006, and in general for the last three years 520,000 jobs were created. Speedy growth of the economy of our country, including international projects on establishment of an East–West energy corridor, makes Azerbaijan a leading power of the region, provider of energy security in the Euro-Atlantic family, and lays ground for ongoing achievements.

Public Order and Public Safety

Expansion of cities under the above-mentioned circumstances raises the issues of public order and public safety. The increased number of criminal elements, juveniles, and youngsters belonging to risk groups in society requires a new, revised approach of prevention. In order to reduce the growing younger generation's contacts with criminal environment, it is necessary to provide a favorable environment for leisure time. Dynamic urbanization and demographic growth affect the operational environment in big cities and preconditions the police officers to fulfill their duties and functions put forth by legislation with high professionalism and in compliance with require-ments of modern times.

Legal reforms covered inclusion of more humanist elements in criminal legislation and measures to ensure that the rule of law and protection of human rights and freedoms are underway. According to the Constitution, protection of human rights and freedoms are stated as common state objec-tives and law-enforcement bodies follow these values as a guide.

The Ministry of Internal Affairs carries out well-defined and systematic measures to bring the law-enforcement system efficiently up to international standards and accommodate more advanced working methods. During recent years several positive changes were achieved in combatting crime, ensuring public order and safety. The positive position in providing political public stability is being developed and strengthened. Ensuring public order and public safety has become a goal in recent years.

Intensive works are carried out for prevention of potential internal factors, which may affect stability. Necessary organizational and practical measures were conducted for strengthening cooperation among state bodies dealing with public safety in the fight against crime. All efforts are directed to prevention and disclosure of especially violent crimes, search of persons committing them, protection of all kinds of properties from ille-gal actions and organization of efficient international cooperation in this direction.

During recent years, continuous improvement in the struggle against criminality has been observed. The number of crimes per 100,000 of popula-tion on average was 203 for the last five years. According to results of ensuring public order and fight against crime Azerbaijan continuously reshapes the image of a country with best figures in the Commonwealth of Independent States (CIS) and Eastern Europe. Within this period, 1,471 persons were held and extradited for committing different crimes.

Solely in 2002–2006 and the last year, 1,027 persons were rendered harm-less who committed murder, burglary, plunder, robbery, and kidnapping. Generally for that period, 62,534 persons for different crimes, including 1,080 for murder, 761 for burglary, 155 for plunder, and 856 for robbery were held criminally liable. For the period of more than 10 years, more than 34,000 illegally kept automatic weapons were collected and the number of crimes committed by weapons decreased by more than 10 times.

As a result of measures taken in 2006, decrease in the number of crimes committed in the capital and other nine cities of the country were observed including deliberate murder (−5.4%), attempt to murder (−13.8%), rape

(−13.3%), burglary (−14.4%), and crime by minors (−42.4%), in public places (−1.5%) including square and streets (−3.5%). Last year, the number of crimes committed by weapon in cities was decreased by 10% (40 to 36).

In 2006, 1,893 cases were disclosed in the fight against illegal circulation of narcotics, which is 8.4% or 147 more in comparison with the year 2005 and more than 146 kg narcotics were taken from illegal circulation.

Along with this in comparison with 2005, the relative number of crimes for 100,000 of urban population was increased from 296 to 317 (7.2% increase) including 7% increase in severe and especially severe crimes. One out of three serious crimes in Azerbaijan were committed in cities. There is special working group within the Ministry of Internal Affairs for eliminating such cases, which constantly follows the operational environment, studies negative factors affecting the criminal situation, conducts necessary analyses, and determines adequate measures.

Terrorism

It goes without saying that unexpected and severe results of terror attacks necessitate being alert to new threats and menaces. From this perspective Azerbaijan Republic takes an active part in the antiterror coalition by joining international conventions and protocols on fighting terrorism. Appropriate organizational practical measures were taken for prevention of terror acts according to provisions of UN Security Council Resolutions and Council of Europe's documents in this area.

The principal position of Azerbaijan is that terror organizations, as they threaten the coexistence, stability, and development of nations, shall always be appropriately punished without regard to the locations of terrorists' bases and pretexts they are covered under.

Today, in the period where new threats of terrorism exist, no one has insured against the attacks of terrorists, and all necessary measures must be taken for an effective struggle with it. In 2001, the Republic of Azerbaijan ratified the UN Convention "on combatting financing terrorism" of 1999 and consequently related to that in 2002 by making changes to criminal legislation hardening the responsibility for terrorism and added a new article on financing terrorism into the Criminal Code.

In order to strengthen the activities in this area in 1999, a law of the Republic of Azerbaijan "on financing terrorism" was adopted. The law determines legal and organizational basis of conducted measures, rules of coordination of activities of relevant state bodies, and also rights and duties of country's citizens and related state bodies. By that law, terrorism is defined as disturbing the public order, raising fears among the population, assassination, bodily harm causing considerable property damages and explosion, fire, or commitment of other acts which may result in occurrence of other public threats, including threatening to commit such acts.

It should be noted that lots of works are carried out in our country for an establishment of legal and functional mechanism for prevention of terrorism within UN and other international and regional organizations framework. But time demonstrates that all these measures are not enough for responding adequately to terror threats. The question of what should be done for improvement of activities in combatting terrorism and preparation of efficient proposals in this area also worries us.

To our mind, for an effective struggle against terrorism, at first the problem of its definition should be resolved. The lack of appropriate definition always appears as an obstacle impeding the uniting of efforts of the international community and makes it necessary to use one common definition of terrorism that can be used by all states. The harmonization of national legislations of separate countries can lead to increase of the level of mutual legal assistance in fight against international terrorism. This will enable the activities of law-enforcement bodies related to prevention of international terror acts to achieve more efficient results.

The comprehensive measures also are carried out to identify persons inclined to extremist appearances in Azerbaijan. Related to that, control over the work of issuing identification documents was intensified. The Ministries of Internal Affairs, Justice, National Security, General Prosecutor's Office, State Border Service, and other related bodies carry out their activities in close cooperation related to extradition of persons having direct relationships to terror organizations. Granting a shelter in our country or provision of any type of supplies by state bodies to such persons is illegal. Also, decisive measures are taken for seizure of financial means or other economic income sources of persons or organizations involved in terrorism.

During the last five years, 30 persons were caught by law-enforcement bodies, more than 20 participants of illegal armed groups were involved into court responsibility having connections with terrorist organizations such as "Al Cihad" and "Caucasus Islam Army." Fourteen members of the terrorists groups of the radical vahhabi movement in North Caucasus, who tried to hide in the territory of Azerbaijan after committing terror acts in different cities of Russian Federation which resulted in explosion of residential buildings and hundreds of death cases, were caught and sent back to that country. Another organized criminal group was caught on June 21, 2005 as a result of operational measures conducted by internal affairs bodies in Baku city, which was considered suspicious on engagement to terror activities.

Along with this, prevention of using the territory of Azerbaijan for committing terror acts in other countries is under the control of law-enforcement and special service bodies. As a result of well-thought out measures during last years, the Baku branches of six humanitarian organizations that were considered suspicious for passing financial means to terrorists were disclosed, their activities were ceased, and 43 related persons were deported.

It also should be noted that the Azerbaijan Republic became the target for numerous terror acts by Armenian special service bodies and Nagorny Karabakh separatists. It was proved based on procedural rules that 32 terror acts, which took place 100 km from the frontline, were committed by special service bodies of Armenia.

It goes without saying that, one of the important issues for our country, which has huge energy potential, is protection of energy resources, oil and gas industry objects, and transport lines from terror acts. Setting this purpose as a goal, necessary preventive–prophylactic works are carried out in our country and special antiterror measures are taken. These include measures to harden the protection of transport and communication systems, review the postpatrol service, strengthen the operational provision on those areas, ensure that international goods and passenger transport foreign transport means use the routes determined by the Republic, and increase passport and visa controls at border pass points, train stations, ports, hotels, and hostels.

In order to define mutual cooperation mechanisms, collect operational information and conduct information struggle, Ministries of Internal Affairs, National Security, Emergency Situations, Defense, State Border, and Special State Protection Services of the Republic of Azerbaijan carry out different measures. In order to disclose and prevent possible attempts of hijacking of air transport in the capital city and other cities, strengthen physical and operational protection in important state and industrial facilities, transport means, communication systems, cross-border facilities, and public places, trainings and trials are held by applying artificial explosive substances, and readiness and mobility of the staff is increased by activating regular alarms and protection of entities of special interest.

Practice proves that common efforts lead to big successes. That is why exchange of operational information, its exact analysis and purposeful usage, conduct of agreed events, special operations, efficiently responding to queries, application of advanced experience, and strengthening of cooperation in the form of implementation of existing technical, financial, and normative legal programs are considered basic conditions.

Generally, along with international terrorism, armed separatism, extremism, and entirely transnational organized crime create new threats to all world countries. It is obvious that response to such dangerous threats can be possible just by uniting common efforts and strengthening international cooperation. Azerbaijan Republic takes part in this work both in multilateral and in regional levels including bilateral levels. The constant exchange of information including operational character information is carried out with competent bodies of other states for prevention of terror acts.

One of the important issues to be noted is that in the modern world the problems of fighting crime put very serious challenges before humanity. Threats arising from organized crime, especially from its transnational types, does not just create obstacles to development of individual countries but generally to world union.

Organized Crime

Organized crime shatters the basis of the state, hypernegatively affects the economic, social, moral–psychological, cultural, and other processes in society. It appears in more dangerous and complicated form as a quality change of different crimes. Features such as adapting to national policy, justice system, and defense mechanisms of separate states are peculiar to organized crime. Organized crime, which involves different layers of society in most cases, possesses strong financial and economic opportunities, which cannot easily be controlled by state and society.

Organized crime, which appears in the form of close relations among criminal groups, is not only one of the potential factors disturbing internal stability but at the same time is an important issue that disturbs the international community. That is why the struggle against transnational organized crime and its separate organizations has become one of the important goals of international cooperation in the modern world.

Special provisions related to organized crime were added into criminal legislation of the Republic of Azerbaijan. Definitions of organized groups and criminal unions (criminal organization) are given in article 34 of the Criminal Code of the Republic of Azerbaijan. According to that article, an organized group is a steady group consisting of two or more persons, united for commitment of one or several crimes; the criminal union (criminal organization) is the creation of a steady organized criminal group with the purpose of committing minor, serious or serious crimes, or steady association of two or more organized criminal groups created for the same purposes.

The basis for a successful struggle against crime, including its organized types, was laid down in 1994 by decree of the President of the Republic of Azerbaijan dated August 9, 1994, on "strengthening the fight against criminality and measures on strengthening of the rule of law." The main duties of the Ministry of Internal Affairs and other state bodies were specified related to execution of operational service activities and prevention of crimes committed by organized groups, illegal armed unions, bribery, and corruption cases. According to decree, within the Ministry of Internal Affairs a Department on Combatting Organized Crime was established and the fight against the most dangerous form of crime was strengthened by a new organizational basis.

One of the forms of transnational organized crimes is illegal circulation of narcotics. This issue, including timely disclosing the smuggling channels of narcotics and its prevention, is always at the center of attention. In our country, in the area of combatting illegal circulation of narcotics, a set of measures reflecting activation of international cooperation and organization of the work of law enforcement in modern level were taken and that work is currently underway.

Azerbaijan Republic has signed the UN Conventions on "narcotic drugs" of 1961, "psychotropic substances" of 1971, "illicit traffic in narcotic drugs and psychotropic substances" of 1988, and in 2001 signed the "Paris agreement on use of narcotics and struggle against their illegal circulation" and it cooperates with international organizations. By respective decree of the President of the Republic of Azerbaijan in 1996, a State Commission on Narcotics and Struggle against their illegal circulation was established. Taking into account UN recommendations, a "national program on combatting spread of narcotism, narcotic drugs, psychotropic substances, and illegal circulation of precursors" was adopted and is currently underway. Along with this, new laws were adopted in 2001 on "narcological service and control" and in 2005 on "circulation of narcotics drugs, psychotropic substances, and their precursors."

For a successful solution of objectives faced in the struggle with illegal circulation of drugs, the Ministry of Internal Affairs takes organizational and practical measures in a planned way. A national information database on narco-traffic is available within the ministry. The information received from Ministries of Justice, National Security, Health, State Customs Committee, and others is placed there. This information database enables us to evaluate the narco-situation in the country in real and operative form and lets us determine main directions in the area of struggle against the illegal circulation of drugs.

In order to increase the efficiency of prevention of entrance of narcotics into the country in huge amounts and its delivery to other countries, in 1998–2001 regional departments on combatting narcotics of the Ministry of Internal Affairs were established in northern and southern regions of the Republic. For the last five years (2002–2006) 10,621 criminal cases related to narcotics including 3,496 related to their sale were disclosed by internal affairs bodies and about 966 kg of different types of narcotic drugs were taken out from illegal circulation (613.9 kg marijuana, 176.3 kg opium, 74.1 kg heroin, 70.8 kg hashish, and other different type of narcotics). Two tons of plants containing narcotics were destroyed in green mass.

Unfortunately, due to high latent character of this kind of crime, in the best case it becomes possible to confiscate up to 10% of narcotic drugs from illegal circulation—the rest is realized in "black markets." One of the important issues in the struggle against narcotics from the geopolitical perspective of our country is to prevent the using of our territory as a transit corridor for delivering narcotics to the west. Experience shows that transnational organized groups put much effort into using these routes, which looks extremely attractive.

Serious thoughts mainly can be said in regard to three routes:

1. Afghanistan → Turkmenistan → via Caspian sea to Azerbaijan → Georgia → Turkey → Europe.
2. Afghanistan → Iran → occupied territories of Azerbaijan → Nagorny Karabakh, Armenia → Georgia → Europe.
3. Afghanistan → Iran → Azerbaijan → Georgia → Turkey → Europe.

We try to prevent such attempts. Apart from this, continuous measures are taken toward destruction of narcotic character plants, arable lands, rehabilitation of drug addicts, legal enlightenment among the population, and public awareness. But, due to its occupied territory of 20% by Armenia, Azerbaijan is unable to maintain control over 132 km of its border adjacent to Iran, which favors planting of narcotics character plants and production of narcotics in those regions, including smuggling them into the region and creating favorable conditions for delivering them to other countries.

Other types of organized crime such as illegal migration and human trafficking are also in great concern of international community. Our country, as all other countries, carries out very serious measures in the area of struggle against such crimes, which has transnational character. Illegal migration and human trafficking have close ties to, and at the same time create favorable conditions for, narco-traffic, illegal circulation of weapons, smuggling, and other crimes, and are accompanied by rough violation of human and citizen rights.

Immigration

The fight against illegal migration is considered as one the important conditions for prevention of terrorism and other transnational crimes. Taking into account the fast development of our country and lack of local work force related to that, it is expected that new workers will come to Azerbaijan and this tendency is already observed. For regulating these processes and for controlling migration, relevant orders were given to state bodies and numerous important duties were set before the Ministry of Internal Affairs for regulating these issues. For complete execution of duties related to regulation of migration issues and for efficient provision of state interests in this area, by decree of the President of the Republic of Azerbaijan dated June 29, 2005, a Migration Service was established within the Ministry of Internal Affairs.

This service carries out prophylaxis of illegal migration, controls functions in the area of migration, reviews petitions in the area of migration and takes relevant decisions, issues relevant documents confirming the status of immigrants, controls the movement of migrants within the country, and carries out other authorities defined by the legislation of the country. The Migration Service also takes measures in regard to foreigners violating defined rules and take measures toward persons without citizenship according to legislation, conducts operational search activities in their surroundings, processes applications of foreigners and citizens without citizenship on their immigration to Azerbaijan, proceeds on issues related to Azerbaijan citizenship, prepares measures, and ensures their implementation for prevention of negative effects of uncontrolled migration processes. As a result of such work, 110 foreigners without legal permission (visa) or registration were deported from the country and 97 persons were fined in 2006.

Starting in 1997, within the framework of cooperation with the International Organization for Migration, a special program on Establishment of Migration Management potentials in the Azerbaijan Republic was implemented. Along with this, certain positive results were achieved in formulation of state migration policy, improvement of national legislation in the area of migration and its development, simplification of passing process in border pass points, and registration of migrants.

"State Migration Program of the Republic of Azerbaijan" covering the years 2006–2008 was approved by decree of the President of the Republic of Azerbaijan dated July 25, 2006. This program envisages the implementation of state policy in the area of migration, improvement of legislation according to international norms and requirements of modern times, development of a migration management system and improvement of its efficiency, more efficient protection of rights and freedoms of migrants and their family members, expansion of related social measures, prevention of illegal migration, strengthening of coordination among state bodies, and establishment of a single migration information bank and modern technical control systems on modern migration processes.

Human Trafficking

Prevention of human trafficking is another priority area in the struggle against transnational organized crime. These types of crimes are unlawful acts that violate the rights of citizens and humans in serious form and create threats to their security.

From this perspective, "National Action Plan on struggle against human trafficking" was adopted by decree of the President of the Republic of Azerbaijan dated May 6, 2004. According to the plan, a working group comprising of the members of numerous ministries of the Republic was established, at the same time, rules handing over cases of human trafficking without any impediment to special police units were developed. Several tasks were assigned to the Ministry of Internal Affairs in the National Action Plan and based on execution of the measures envisaged in the plan, a Department on Combatting Human Trafficking was established within the structure of the Ministry in 2004.

In order to regulate the issues of prophylaxis of human trafficking, legal and organizational basis of human trafficking, also protection of victims of human trafficking and rendering assistance to them, the law on "combatting human trafficking" was adopted in June 28, 2005. Human trafficking was defined in article one of the law as—involving, obtaining, storage, concealment, transportation, delivering, or accepting of people (involving, obtaining, storage, concealment, transportation, delivering, or accepting children for exploitation purposes shall be considered as human trafficking even if the means stipulated in this chapter were not used) for exploitation purposes by using force or under the threat of force, by threat or other methods of compulsion, by means of theft, fraud, deception, abuse of possibility to influence or victim's weakness, or by providing or obtaining material and other boons, privileges, or concession in order to get the consent of the person controlling another person. In order to strengthen the struggle against human trafficking and to improve the normative legal base in this area, changes were made to the Criminal Code on September 30, 2005 which included new articles that criminalized human trafficking, forced labor, and dispersing information on victims of human trafficking.

As a result of conducted organizational-practical and operational-search measures in the fight against human trafficking, 211 relevant criminal acts were disclosed, 192 criminal cases were investigated, and 207 were involved into responsibility for committing these crimes. Also, 77 victims of human trafficking were identified. As a result of conducted operational measures, four organized groups and 23 criminal groups were rendered harmless who deceived young women and girls via different means on the pretexts of travel, marriage, high living standards, and so on with the aim of sexual exploitation.

Corruption

One of the concerns of the world community is the state of struggle against corruption offenses. The fact that such criminal attempts and their different types are becoming complicated and dangerous, while at the same time becoming more transnational in nature, puts forth the necessity to carry out a purposeful and decisive fight toward such crimes.

The strategic basis of the fight against corruption in our country is determined by decree of the President of the Republic of Azerbaijan on "strengthening the fight against corruption" dated June 8, 2000. Azerbaijan Republic ratified the Council of Europe's "Criminal Law Convention on Corruption" and "Civil Law Convention on Corruption" on December 30, 2003. With the purpose of fulfilling the liabilities arising from these conventions on January 13, 2004 "law on combatting corruption" of the Republic of Azerbaijan was adopted. On September 3, 2004 "State Program on Combatting Corruption (2004–2006)" was adopted. Also Azerbaijan Republic joined to UN "Convention against Corruption" on September 30, 2005.

By the law of the Republic of Azerbaijan dated May 13, 2006, several changes and amendments were made to the Criminal Code and the name of Chapter 33 was renamed—Corruption Crimes and State Power, Civil Service Interests, Crimes Against Duties in Local Governments, and Commercial and Non-Commercial Organizations. Article 312-1 (trade in influence, illegally affecting the decision of public official) was added, also the content and the title of Article 311 (bribe taking—passive bribery) and Article 312 (bribe giving—active bribery) were changed.

Along with this, by decree of the President of the Republic of Azerbaijan dated March 3, 2004, on application of the law "On Combatting Corruption," the Department on Combatting Corruption within the General Prosecutor was established and by another decree dated October 28, 2004 the statute of that department was approved. The department deals with investigation of corruption cases as defined by legislation. An Operational Search Unit for Corruption Crimes was established within the Head Department on Combatting Organized Crime of the Ministry of Internal Affairs, the Government body for operational search on March 7, 2005 to ensure professional arrangements for combatting corruption. For the sake of information it should be noted that, 232 criminal cases were registered during the year of 2006 confirmed by investigations.

Money Laundering

One of the important means of prevention of organized crime is struggle against legalization of proceeds obtained through criminal ways. Our country has productive cooperation with the international community in this area. Azerbaijan Republic signed the UN Convention "on transnational organized crime" in 2000 and in November 2001 signed European Conventions "on laundering, search, seizure, and confiscation of the proceeds from crime." An example of conducted measures in this direction in our republic was taking a decision on a state level on closing illegally acting casinos, night bars, and other business objects favorable for money laundering.

According to the law of the Azerbaijan Republic dated May 13, 2006, on "changes and amendments to some legislative acts of the Republic of Azerbaijan in connection with combatting corruption," the new article 193-1 on "legalization of money proceeds and other property obtained through criminal acts" was added into the Criminal Code. An expert group on "measures against money laundering and financing terrorism" acting within the Cabinet of Ministers prepared a draft law on "the prevention of the legalization of illegally obtained funds or other property and financing of terrorism," taking into account international experience. Also the establishment of a Financial Intelligence Unit in our country is envisaged.

Transport Safety and Security

Security of public transport in the Azerbaijan Republic is perceived as protection of people, society, utmost interests of the state, and in general transport facilities and infrastructure from internal and external threats. There is common policy conducted by our state directed to prevention and disclosing of crimes in transport sector including terrorism, prevention of natural or technological accidents, decreasing to minimum the amount of damage caused as a result of criminal and emergency cases, sustaining ecological state of transport system, and increasing the ecological security of deliveries.

Transport security conception of our country comprises of defining national interests in this area, disclosing the factors threatening those interests, establishment of common struggle system toward them, and bringing the transport security system of Azerbaijan Republic into conformity with world standards and measures directed to improvement of its quality. The establishment of an effective security system in transport is possible only through uniting the efforts of numerous countries in this area, studying and applying international experience on combatting terrorism in transport.

Terror acts taken place in Baku metro in 1994 confirm transport as one of the main objects subject to terror acts. Apart from this, the events of 11th September of 2001 and numerous terror acts conducted by using automobiles equipped with explosives prove that terrorists already involve transport as a means. Taking this into account, the special operational measures plan is approved for prevention of occupation and hijacking of air, water transport means, and railway trains. By Presidential decree a "headquarters for management of antiterror acts" was established to provide direct and single management for operation against terror acts in the transport sector.

It should be taken into account that fighting terrorism in the transport sector is one part of the problem of ensuring transport safety of the country.

The other threats in this area are illegal interventions (putting things on rails, dismantling of railway equipments, illegal isolation of airports and other transport highways, etc.) impeding normal functioning of transport, criminal acts toward passengers and cargo, and emergency cases (events) related to violation of ecological safety rules, including transportation maintenance, also accidents taken place as a result of natural factors and resulting in material damage and human loss.

Along with protection of public order in fighting criminality, the Ministry of Internal Affairs of the Republic of Azerbaijan also conducts necessary organizational practical measures for ensuring traffic safety, which is one of the main directions of the activity of ministry. Statutes are prepared and put into implementation along with international contracts to which our country is party, including UN Convention "On Road Traffic." At the same time, respective rules, standards, and technical norms are prepared by Commissions established at the government level.

Structural improvements were conducted in traffic police service according to international experience, and purposeful measures were taken to increase the responsibility of employees for assigned areas. Generally, much attention is paid to ensuring control over traffic safety, administrative proceedings on relevant offenses and events, organization of reproof measures, conduct of state technical control and registration of automobiles and trailers, issuing state number signs, conduct of exams on traffic rules and driving habits, and organization and development of issuing of driving licenses according to modern requirements. The improvement of professional training of staff and duties in the area of human rights and freedoms is always given special attention.

As a comparison, 1992 saw 1,265 deaths, 3,432 injuries out of 3,045 traffic accidents; in 2002, all three figures (deaths, injuries, accidents) increased. During that period the death rate per each 100,000 decreased 2.3 times. But since 2002 it has been observed that the number of dead and wounded persons in road traffic accidents is increasing. In comparison with the year 2001, the number of registered road traffic accidents in 2005 increased 60%, two times the number of persons died as a result, and injured persons increased 65%. During the last five years one out of four registered accidents resulted in death, and the death rate per 100,000 increased from 7 to 12. Vehicle-pedestrian accident cases account for half of the accidents.

As a result of preventive measures carried out in 2006, almost 2 million road traffic violations were detected, including 50,000 speeding violations and 6,384 drunk drivers. The growth of road traffic accidents was 0.6% in comparison with the year 2005, the number of deaths as a result of accidents was increased 3.6%, and the number of injured was decreased 1.7%.

Analysis proves that the main reasons for the growth in the number of road traffic accidents and problems in regulation of transport flow are (1) speeding violations, (2) driving the opposite way, (3) drunk driving, and (4) increase in the number of automobiles in the country. At the same time, according to "Action Plan on improvement of transports system in Baku city for the period of 2006–2007" prepared by the government for prevention of traffic jams, important measures are carried out. Currently, pedestrian subways and different level road guides are constructed in main transport hubs, new streets are built, roads are expanded, special places for parking were determined, and multistoried garage and stopping places are constructed.

During recent years, necessary measures are taken in capital for provision of road safety according to world standards. Automatic management systems covering crossroads are applied, cameras for centralized control over violation of road traffic rules and mobile radar equipment with photo description of relevant offenders are installed, and towing is used for increasing the efficiency of struggle against drivers violating the parking rules.

Conclusion

In conclusion, provision of political–public stability, fast socioeconomic growth, and political, economic, and legal reforms have strengthened our state independence and ensured independent policy in the region. Respecting territorial integrity and independence of all other countries, the Azerbaijan Republic, defining human rights as its main values, is always loyal to its peaceful policy and successfully continues democratic reforms. Our country is ready for close cooperation with all other countries, currently fulfills and decisively commits to fulfill all international obligations in the future as well.

Traffic Administration in Hyderabad, India

10

ADKI SURENDER

Contents

India is one of the ancient civilizations of the world and has witnessed urbanization as far back as 2500 BC. Accounts of urban life, including the administration of security in urban areas, can be found in Kautilya's "Arthashastra" of fourth century BC.

Although modern India is a country with a predominantly rural population, there has been a progressive increase in urbanization. Independent India has brought about remarkable changes in urbanization. The capital cities of provinces in federal India have registered a dramatic growth in urban character. The reorganization of states in 1956 later brought about yet another wave of change in urban development. Urbanization has registered a rapid growth since 1961. The dawn of globalization in the 1990s triggered even speedier development of urban areas.

Urban areas in India can be divided into three categories: towns, cities, and metropolises. About 30% of India's population is urban. In 2001, more than half the urban dwellers lived in 393 urban agglomerates or cities consisting of more than 100,000 people. By 1991 India had 24 cities with populations of at least 1 million.* By that year, Bombay (or Mumbai), in Maharashtra State, was ranked seventh in the world at 12.6 million people, and Calcutta (or Kolkatta), in West Bengal State, was ranked eighth at almost 11 million. According to the census reports of 2001, there were 35 metropolises in India whose minimum population was 1 million or more. Among the Indian metropolises, Mumbai, Kolkatta, Delhi, Chennai, Bangalore, and Hyderabad are considered the most populous.

India is a populous country and occupies the second position in the world, with a 1.27 billion population. Table 10.1 shows the total population growth and urban population growth since 1951.

Among the notable factors responsible for increased urbanization are industrialization, rise in employment, growth of trade and commerce, failure of an agrarian economy to support a rural workforce leading to migration, and migration of students and their families to avail of urban educational facilities. The growth of six metropolises is more rapid than the other centers of urban India. Over 50% of the population of the 35 metropolises in 2001 lived in the five giant cities of Mumbai (16.3 million), Calcutta (13.2 million), Delhi (12.8 million), Chennai (6.5 million), Bangalore (5.7 million), and Hyderabad (5.6 million).

Table 10.1 Growth of Urban Population in India

Year	Total Population (M)	Urban Population (M)	% Urban	Number of Metropolitan Cities
1951	350	62	17.62	5
1961	425	78	18.26	7
1971	529	107	20.22	9
1981	685	159	23.73	12
1991	846	218	25.7	23
2001	1,027	285	27.8	35
2006	—	—	30.0[a]	50[a]

Source: Census Reports of India 2001 and India Development Report 1999–2000.
[a] Estimated.

---

* Criminal Procedure Code 1973, Section 8, defines any city whose population exceeds 1 million as a metropolitan area.

Traffic Growth

The urban transportation in India is dominated by motor vehicles, with an increasing use of two and three wheelers, minibuses, buses, and trucks. Large cities have major urban bus systems and metro rail systems. Bullocks, camels, elephants, horses, and other beasts of burden are also seen throughout India. Combined with a wide mix of high- and low-speed vehicles, increased road usage is posing problems to urban traffic management.

Contemporary urban life in India is throwing up challenges to its public administration, policymaking, and law enforcement. These have become formidable concerns of modern public administration in India. One such concern, posing a threat to the security of urban life, is the remarkable increase in vehicular population in urban areas. Table 10.2 gives details of vehicular population growth in India.

It can be seen that the growth of vehicular population was slow in the initial decades, rising in the 1980s and acquiring phenomenal growth in the last 6–7 years. The impact of economic and social liberalization in the wake of globalization since the 1990s significantly added to this growth. Further, the study noticed that the percentage of mass transportation was negligible. The rapid growth in motor vehicles has also led to the rise in road accidents.

Road Accidents in India

An estimated 1.17 million deaths occur each year worldwide due to road accidents. The majority of these deaths, about 70%, occur in developing countries. Sixty-five percent of deaths involve pedestrians and 35% of pedestrian

Table 10.2   Total Number of Registered Vehicles in India 1951–2001 (in Thousands)

Year as on 31 March	Total Vehicles	% Growth
1951	306	—
1961	665	217.3
1971	1,865	180.4
1981	5,291	183.7
1991	21,374	304.0
2001	54,991	157.3
2006	70,000[a]	27.3

Source: Reports of Ministry of Road Transport and Highways, Government of India.

[a] Estimated figures.

Table 10.3   Road Accidents in India

Year	Number of Road Accidents	Number of Persons Killed
1970	114.100	14,800
1980	153.200	24,000
1990	282.600	54,100
2000	351.999	70,781
2003	406.726	85,998

deaths involve children. Over 10 million people are crippled or injured each year.* The majority of road crash victims (injuries and fatalities) in developing countries are not motor vehicle occupants, but pedestrians, motorcyclists, bicyclists and non-motor vehicle (NMV) occupants. India is no exception. Table 10.3 shows the rate of road accidents in India.

Approximately 85,000 people are killed in road accidents and 1.2 million meet with serious injuries every year in India, causing an annual social economic loss of Rs 55,000 crore ($550 billion).† Further, the study analyzes that during 2003 one accident took place for every 165 vehicles and one person was killed for every 779 vehicles. Every hour almost 10 persons are killed on Indian roads.

Focus and Scope of the Study

An attempt is made in this chapter to focus on the various steps taken by the government and administrative agencies to counter the threats posed by growing vehicular traffic to public security and peaceful living. One of the objectives of the chapter is to comprehend and evaluate the level of adequacy of the steps taken by the government in harmonizing safety, security, and sustainability in relation to urban transport, with a special focus on the metropolitan city of Hyderabad.

The scope is limited to highlighting major issue areas, related problems, and a review of reformative measures. The literature on urban administration reveals that the area of traffic administration has not received adequate attention. Therefore, this is an exploratory study to bring out the salient features of prominent traffic-related issues. The study is based on both primary and secondary data. The data available in various public and private publications have been used to understand the existing state of affairs. A few discussions have been held to gain insights into the problems at the operational level.

* http://www.worldbank.org/fpd/transport/roads/safety.htm
† Reports 2005, Ministry of Surface Road Transport, Government of India.

The administration includes all those organizations that are actively involved in securing public safety and security in administrating vehicular traffic movement in the city. It may be stated that the police force is one of the major agencies entrusted with the task of meeting challenges to public safety and security on the roads, and takes the measures necessary to discipline traffic movement.

Part I: Traffic Law and Structure of Administration

The Motor Vehicle Act of India 1914 as amended in 1939 and 1988 is the principal legal instrument of the country through which road transport is regulated. The Motor Vehicle Act of 1988 represents an integrated approach toward traffic administration throughout the country. The Act provides for steps like pollution control, fitness of vehicles, prevention of misuse of vehicles, provision for insurance cover for accidents, system of issuing driving licenses, and so on.* No state government has ever attempted to bring out an enactment to suit its own specific requirements. Thus the legislative measures introduced by a single Act continue to serve the complex needs of the growing metropolises.

Under this Act a Road Transport Authority (RTA) has been constituted by the Andhra Pradesh State Government as an implementing agency. A senior officer belonging to the All India Services is designated as Road Transport Commissioner. This authority is assisted by a number of senior officers at the headquarters level and motor vehicle Inspectors at the field level. Each Inspector has a fixed jurisdiction area, which coincides with that of the Revenue Division of a district. At the middle management level there are officers at the regional and district level to exercise supervision and control over the field-level officers. The minister for road transport administers the RTA. The minister is assisted at the secretariat level by a senior IAS officer who is designated as secretary in policymaking and coordination.

Technically speaking, the RTA has exclusive jurisdiction over traffic management. However, the State Police Department is empowered by a system of convention and usages to exercise control over traffic. An officer of the rank of Police Inspector, under the Motor Vehicle Act of 1988, is empowered to check driving licenses but is not empowered with prosecution powers. Under the Indian Police Act of 1861, police officials exercise wide-ranging powers, including imposition of fines and collection of penalties. In other words, exercising control over traffic regulations and enforcement to facilitate

---

* The Central Motor Vehicle Rules 1989, Government of India, Section 139, Chapter VI, Deepak Publications 1993, p. 94.

the orderly movement of traffic and action to prevent and investigate road accidents is a police responsibility.*

It can be seen that police officials derive much of their traffic powers from legislation concerning the police and not from laws related to road transport. Under police legislation, traffic enforcement is an integral part of the Law and Order enforcement functions. All the metropolitan cities fall under the same system of administration as outlined.

The city administration related to police matters at the metropolitan level is handled by a senior-level officer of Indian Police Services cadre, which is drawn from All India Services. The Police Commissioner of the city is responsible for Law and Order enforcement for the metropolis. In relation to traffic matters, a specialized unit at the headquarters level assists him. This unit is manned by a senior officer of the rank of Inspector General of Police who holds a status more or less equivalent to that of Police Commissioner.

Traffic enforcement units of the police at the field level are called Traffic Police Stations. An officer of the cadre of Inspector is responsible for Traffic Law enforcement. The Inspector is assisted by junior officials of the rank of Sub-Inspectors and Assistant Sub-Inspectors. The subordinate staff known as Constables are posted at field level to exercise vigilance and make reports to the police stations. Head Constables exercise control over the Constabulary.

General Characteristics of Indian Traffic

After discussing the administrative arrangements, it may be necessary to throw light on the characteristics of Indian traffic. Firstly, Indian roads are characterized by limited width and length. The Indian Road Congress has recommended that 20% of the land available in any metropolis be allocated for the laying of roads. The minimum width of roads is put at 100 ft. In most of the metropolises, the road length and width do not conform to these specifications. On an average percentage, the land allocated to road purposes stands between 5% and 15% with the average width at 30–40 ft, which is 60% less than the recommended norm.

Secondly, vehicular traffic is heterogeneous in nature. There are no less than 25 types of vehicles moving on the roads. The physical dimensions of these vehicles vary drastically. Some vehicles like trucks and buses occupy almost 50% of the width and thus become a cause of concern for both road users and law enforcement.

Thirdly, the potential speed of these vehicles also varies. A number of vehicles are slow moving, such as man-driven carts, animal-driven carts,

---

* Indian Police Act 1861, Section 31—stipulated that "it is the duty of the police to keep order on public roads, streets, thoroughfares, ghats, landing places, and all other places of public resorts and to regulate assemblies and procession."

bicycles, and so on, and these vehicles share the road with fast-moving modern vehicles. There is no bifurcation of space on the road for fast-moving and slow-moving types.

Lastly, large numbers of vehicle drivers have only an average education because the minimum qualification prescribed for driving license holders is the ability to read and write at least one Indian language out of those specified in the VII schedule of the Indian Constitution and English.* This limited knowledge of English does not enable drivers to understand the complexities involved in traffic rules and regulations. In other words, lack of awareness of rules is a major attribute of Indian traffic, which is overcome only through trial and error.

Part II: Metropolis of Hyderabad

The 400-year-old historical city of Hyderabad is the sixth largest city in India and the 45th largest in the world. It was founded on the bank of Musi River, a tributary of the Krishna River in south India. Many contemporary writers on that period have pointed out that Quli Qutub Shah, the fifth ruler of Qutub Shahi's dynasty, saw that the city of Hyderabad was built in 1591 AD in order to reduce the congestion in the fortress town of Golconda, which was too small to accommodate the growing population of those times.

Hyderabad, also called the twin cities of Hyderabad and Secunderabad, was a planned city. Nizam rulers (1724–1948) engaged the services of English technical experts for the purpose of city planning and development. Most of the landmarks of today were laid down by Osman Ali Pasha, the last Nizam. These include Patherghatti, M.J. Market, Abids, Tankbund Road, Bombay Highway, Madras connectivity road, Bangalore connectivity road, and Nagpur connectivity road. Most of the bridges across the Musi River and a number of culverts across the drain line of famous lakes were constructed by the Asaf Jahi (Nizam) rulers.

Politically, Hyderabad enjoyed relative autonomy before 1948. British administration in India under various treaties and agreements had supported this autonomous nature. This factor paved the way for the fast growth of Hyderabad city both geographically and demographically.

Today's government of Andhra Pradesh has plans to declare Hyderabad as "greater Hyderabad." According to the proposed plan of action, the city may grow almost threefold to 630 km^2, covering the total area of agglomeration of Hyderabad, including the area of Municipal Corporation of Hyderabad (MCH), cantonment, and 10 surrounding municipalities. The area covered by the city at present is 217 km^2, which includes MCH and the cantonment area.

---

* The Central Motor Vehicle Rules 1989, section 8-9/1, Chapter II, Deepak Publications, New Delhi, 1993, p. 3.

Population Growth

From the beginning, the Hyderabad city population has been cosmopolitan in nature, and plural and multicultural in composition. Although the administration represented a theological state with Islam as the official religion until 1948, the people did not experience any noticeable discomfort in its growing styles and patterns. In other words, secular values were nourished even during monarchic rule. After independence, various factors turned Hyderabad into a point of attraction for people from various walks of life. These include political activity, industrialization, trade and commerce, religious festivities, cultural growth, the spread of higher education, and growth of media and entertainment.

As a consequence of all these developments, the city of Hyderabad registered a very substantial growth in its population, more than tripling from 1951 to 2001 (Table 10.4). Growth was fairly continuous, with the fastest increases from 1961 to 1991.

Figure 10.1 shows that there was an extraordinary increase in the density of population, as indicated by the increase in density from around 6,000 residents per km^2 in 1961 to 21,000 in 2001. This increase in density also contributed to the rise in concentration of vehicles and increasing traffic strength over time. As the infrastructure, such as roads and communication systems, could not keep pace with the population rise and density, a recurring problem of traffic congestion resulted.

There are a number of factors that are responsible for the growth of Hyderabad city. An important factor seems to be affluent families from various parts of the state and country shifting to the city as the central place of their activities. Other reasons for the growth of population are the following:

- The reorganization of states in 1956 had an impact on the population size of Hyderabad after 1961.

Table 10.4   Population Growth of the Core City since 1951–2001 (in Thousands)

Year	Population	Difference	% Increase	Density per km^2
1951	1,083.624	—	—	5,429
1961	1,191.687	108.063	10.0	5,970
1971	1,682.537	491.850	41.3	9,748
1981	2,251.089	567.472	33.8	13,042
1991	2,945.939	694.930	40.0	17,068
2001	3,632.586	686.647	23.3	21,046

Source: Census Reports 2001.

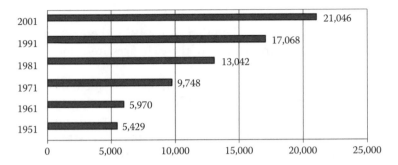

Figure 10.1 Density of population growth, 1951–2001 (per km²).

- Hyderabad became the capital city of the new State of Andhra Pradesh, bringing in its wake an increase of employees, officials, students, entertainment workers, and so on, in the city.
- The rapid growth of economic activities was one of the factors for growth of the population.
- Further, population growth could be attributed to the problem of migration of people from other parts of the state. It is interesting to note that the average migration per annum was estimated at 112,000. It is noticed that around 307 new persons are migrating to the city every day.*

It may be necessary at this point to mention the literacy level of the population concerned. Although Hyderabad is ranked as the third most important urban agglomeration, its level of education has not been significant. The majority of migrants to the city are not literate, and even among literates many were not provided with English education. As a result, people here have a traditional orientation in their thinking and are conservative in their actions. These city residents are also characterized by economic underdevelopment.

Vehicular Growth

Hyderabad and its twin city of Secunderabad have witnessed rapid growth in all respects. This growth is quite alarming to say the least, as the transport system is not able to keep pace with the growth of the city. Prior to 1956, the transport system was a mix of rudimentary and modern patterns. In other

* Hyderabad 2020 (2003), Draft Master Plan for Hyderabad Metropolitan Area, HUDA, Hyderabad.

words, there existed *tongas, rickshaws,* and bicycles on the one hand, and trains and motor vehicles on the other. After 1956, there was a change in the mode of transportation. Features of these changes are as follows:

1. The animal transport system (mostly carts), which was popular during the period of the eighteenth and nineteenth centuries, has largely disappeared. *Jatkas, buggies,* and *tongas,* mostly *horse driven,* also came to be replaced by a mechanical transport system.
2. Rickshaws and bicycles, which replaced *tongas* and *jatkas,* reduced as faster modes took over.
3. Two-, three-, and four-wheeler motor vehicles registered increasing growth from the 1960s and 1970s.
4. The public mass transportation system (buses) has given way to private, personalized transport.

Today, Hyderabad city roads and bylanes are littered with as many as 24 types of vehicles; many are fast moving and several are slow moving. The common sight today is that as one type of vehicle tries to overtake the other types, traffic flow turns particularly chaotic. At the time of the formation of the State of Andhra Pradesh in 1956, vehicle strength was only 7,133 in the city. However, by 2006 vehicle strength had increased to nearly 2 million. Table 10.5 shows that since the formation of the state, the growth of traffic has been more than 100% in each decade. The most dramatic increase came in 1981–1991, when the number of vehicles increased by more than fourfold. The average increase from 1991 to 2001 was 80,000 vehicles per annum.

Table 10.6 shows that the number of vehicles has continued showing a rapid increase since 2001. But, road length growth has remained static.

Table 10.5 Decadal Growth of Vehicles since 1956 (in Thousands)

Year	Total Vehicles	Growth	% Growth
1951	5.224	—	—
1961	15.000	7.867	110.3
1971	38.000	23.000	153.3
1981	88.270	50.270	132.3
1991	518.258	429.988	487.1
2001	1,327.287	809.029	156.1
2006	1,997.000	669.713	50.4

Source: Municipal Corporation and Road Transport Authority of Hyderabad.

Table 10.6   Vehicle Growth, 2002–2006 (in Thousands)

Year	Road Length	Total Vehicles	Growth of Vehicles	% Growth	Vehicles Per km
2002	235	1,313.408			5.589
2003	235	1,492.327	178.919	23.5	6.350
2004	235	1,595.889	103.562	57.9	6.791
2005	235	1,823.308	227.419	14.2	7.759
2006	235	1,997.000	173.692	9.5	8.497

Source: Road Transport Authority Department, Hyderabad.

At the end of 2006, the total number of motor vehicles registered stood at 1,997,000 as against 518,258 in 1991. The growth rate of 1991–2006 is more than 385%, with a yearly average vehicle increase of almost 100,000, which means that every day about 270 new vehicles are registered in the city.

Every third person in Hyderabad city area is the owner of a vehicle and the density of vehicles per km reached 8,497.8 during the year 2006. The high and steady growth in vehicles in conjunction with increases in population and mobility has resulted in high traffic volume on all types of roads. Table 10.7 explains details of the different categories of vehicles in the city during the year 2006.

The table shows that there are about 442,000 cars and more than 69,000 autorickshaws that are being operated in the city and a phenomenal 1.42+ million two wheelers. Almost 96% of these vehicles are privately owned and operated. The mass public bus transport system has not developed

Table 10.7   Share of Vehicles (in Thousands)

Vehicle Category	Number of Vehicles	Percentage
Two wheelers	1,420.820	71.1
Cars	442.150	22.1
Autorickshaws	69.080	3.4
Goods	48.020	2.4
Private buses	6.480	0.3
Seven-seater autos	3.768	0.2
Public buses	2.675	0.1
School buses	2.356	0.1
Maxicabs	1.985	0.1

Source: City Traffic Branch, Hyderabad, Andhra Pradesh.

much. Hyderabad city* has the highest share of two wheelers among major metropolitan cities of India. In the absence of public transport growth, the demand for autorickshaws is on the increase. This mode of transport carries a million commuters a day. This means a very high utilization of autos in the absence of satisfactory means of public transport.

Further, it may be observed from the above analysis that one person out of every 12 persons in Hyderabad city is the owner of a car. At least 225 new cars enter the city roads daily, indicating increases in the affordability of more and more city dwellers. It should be noted that cars occupy more space on the road than a two or three wheeler. Such an increase in cars could only add severe congestion on the roads of Hyderabad.

Further, the data reveal that every fourth Hyderabadi has a two-wheeler vehicle, and daily more than 400 new two-wheeler vehicles are added to the city. This phenomenal increase is one of the reasons for the frequent road transport problems and spurt in traffic congestion and also for the number of accidents in the city.

A good network of roads and an efficient mass urban transport system make significant contributions to improving the working efficiency of a city and its environs. A poor urban transport system not only constrains urban economic growth but also degrades quality of life through congestion, pollution, accidents, and so on.

Heavy Traffic Volume Locations in the City

In order to reduce traffic congestion, it is necessary to identify pockets where there is more congestion. Such an effort requires a scientific approach. The researcher of this study has undertaken a ride, to identify such areas where there is a heavy concentration of traffic volume. This was designed to make a field study so as to make use of participatory observation. During five consecutive working days in the first week of July 2006, the researcher visited the following important junctions: Green Lands, M.J. Market, Afzalgunj, Chaderghat, Khairatabad, Patny Center, Lakdikapool, Ameerpet, and RTC X Road. Using the stop clock method of F. W. Taylor (1911), a count of vehicles was conducted. The findings of the study are as follows.

Table 10.8 indicates that the Green Lands intersection is the place where the largest number of vehicles pass per hour, followed by M.J. Market, Afzalgunj, Chaderghat, and Khairatabad crossroads. All the other areas also contained certain pockets where there was heavy traffic volume.

---

* Hyderabad 2020 (2003), "A plan for sustainable development," Draft Master Plan, HUDA, Hyderabad, p. 36.

Table 10.8   Locations with a Heavy Volume of Vehicles (per Hour)

Sl. No.	Intersection	Vehicle Volume per Hour
1	Green Lands	31,142
2	M.J. Market	30,122
3	Afzalgunj	29,332
4	Chaderghat	29,231
5	Khairatabad	28,732
6	Patny Center	28,267
7	Lakdikapool	27,362
8	Ameerpet	23,345
9	RTC X Road	22,363

Method Adopted to Reduce Traffic Volume

Several methods have been adopted to reduce traffic volume. These methods include the prevention of four wheelers from entering the Central Business District (CBD), banning three wheelers in the city center areas, construction of flyovers, and collecting entry fees and parking fees. A discussion with officials of the traffic and transportation section of MCH reveals that Hyderabad city administration has adopted some of these methods in a phased manner. Flyovers, for instance, are being constructed in areas where more than 10,000 traffic volumes are present. However, at present there are no flyovers in areas of heaviest traffic volume.

Further, it may be noted that the increase in the car population has caused a number of problems. First, the space occupied by cars is disproportionately higher than that occupied by other vehicles. This has caused traffic congestion and frequent traffic holdups. It is general public knowledge that roads get congested during peak hours (8:00–11:00 a.m., 4:00–7:00 p.m.). Traffic management personnel find it extremely difficult to clear traffic jams during these periods. Also

- The government is required to deploy more and more human resources to regulate traffic flow. It is difficult to meet this requirement because of the lack of funds.
- The government is required to set up more and more Traffic Police Stations to monitor observation of traffic rules. This is also not easily accomplished due to financial constraints.
- There is an increase in air pollution.
- There is a need for new roads, bridges, subways, and flyovers. Needless to say, the creation of such structures requires heavy financial outlays.

Road Accidents in the City

Accidents in Hyderabad city were recorded by the traffic police up to the year 1981. Subsequently the law and order department took over the responsibility of accident recording. The road accident trend for the last five years is shown in Table 10.9. The number of accidents has increased each year, except for 2005, and the number of injuries has increased each year.

Currently, on average, each one person is killed in a road accident every day in Hyderabad and 10 people are injured. Out of every 10 persons killed in road mishaps in the state, one is from the city. The number of accidents in the city is on the rise, with vehicular traffic growing abnormally. Hyderabad city has registered the highest number of accident cases as compared to other metropolises.

Traffic reports show that 78% of accidents in the city are due to the negligence of drivers, followed by bad roads (15%) and vehicle conditions (7%). It appears that the lack of education and proper training to drivers are the causes for such traffic accidents. The present study conducted fieldwork to elicit the opinion of road users through the questionnaire method. It was found that out of 500 respondents, 342 (68%) were license holders without any prior driving test being conducted. This means that lack of proper traffic awareness among road users is on the increase.

Traffic Police in Hyderabad Metropolis

Law and order and traffic are two inseparable functions. In fact, the Police Act does not make any distinction between traffic-related offenses and other criminal acts. However, the traffic function is organized into a separate branch, which functions in close association with the law and order branch. The traffic branch has a very chequered history of more than 65 years.

Prior to the formation of Andhra Pradesh State in 1956, the Government of Hyderabad State established, for the first time, a separate official traffic cell in 1952, under the charge and supervision of a Deputy Commissioner of

Table 10.9   Road Accidents, 2002–2006

Year	Road Accidents	Deaths	Injuries
2002	3,039	411	3115
2003	3,427	451	3373
2004	3,525	419	3643
2005	3,088	344	3741
2006	3,477	426	3874

Source: Traffic Cell, Hyderabad.

Police. With the formation of Andhra Pradesh State, the city traffic police was reorganized and strengthened from time to time.

Before venturing into a discussion on the present administrative arrangements of the city traffic branch, it may be necessary to have a look at the objectives of the traffic police of Hyderabad city. At present, the traffic police of Hyderabad city has the following objectives:

- To prevent violations of traffic laws.
- To achieve safe and efficient movement of traffic and prevent accidents.
- To take persuasive action to prevent road users from violating traffic laws.
- To punish those who violate traffic laws.

It may be stated that whatever applies to law enforcement is equally applicable to enforcement of traffic law. In Hyderabad city, the traffic wing looks after only regulatory work, and does not investigate traffic offenses like fatal road accidents (304-A IPC cases). The One Man Police Commission of Andhra Pradesh State (1984) has recommended that the traffic wing should be entrusted with investigation of all traffic offenses.* The same opinion has also been expressed by the traffic personnel. But, action has not been taken by the government to provide powers of investigation of accident cases to the traffic police.

Traffic police enforcement has several characteristics, of which the following few are some of the most important:

1. Traffic enforcement aims at the administration of traffic in pursuit of the goals as set by the competent authority.
2. It is a collective human action involving various groups, including the police, politicians, bureaucrats, road users, and members of the public.
3. Cooperation forms the essential base of traffic enforcement.
4. Deliberate coordination becomes the livewire of traffic enforcement.
5. Information and communication technology as a facilitating factor is a very essential element of traffic enforcement.

The goals of traffic administration are set up by higher officials of the traffic police who conduct that activity within the broad guidelines provided by the public policy. With the active interaction and participation of politicians, bureaucrats, and technicians, these goals are revised from time

---

* Report 1984, "The One Man Police Commission of AP," Chairman, Sri. K. Ramachandra Reddy, Government of AP. Recommendation 15.48, p. 181.

to time. The police organization undertakes the administrative functions in pursuit of these goals. However, much depends on the way it secures cooperation from various constituents of society in general and persons concerned with traffic administration in particular. Coordination takes care of the problems flowing from overlapping and duplication of administrative action. Finally, the communication network, supported by information and communication technology, provides much needed support to decision making, supervision, and control.

Functions of Traffic Police

Although traffic enforcement constitutes an independent element of traffic control (others being traffic education and traffic engineering), it cannot be treated in isolation. It is a well-known fact that the efficiency of traffic enforcement is conditioned by traffic engineering and traffic education as well. Therefore, enforcement may be treated as an integrated element with traffic engineering and traffic education as components.

The police force, it has been observed, is the most visible arm of the government as it deals with such vital social issues as protection of life and property and administration of justice. Within the various police functions, control of automobiles is one of the most visible police functions. Traffic control overshadows, in magnitude, every other police regulatory task in metropolitan cities, and Hyderabad too is part of this.

In regulating urban social life in Hyderabad city, city traffic police play an important role. Their concern can be seen during the morning and evening (peak) hours, especially in the context of the rush of both the school-children and office goers. On an average, the operative employee of traffic police is too busy to talk to others during morning hours. During peak hours, the police constable cannot afford to move away from his place of work. On festive occasions the role of traffic police becomes very crucial. Observation of the Ganesha festivities and Moharram processions of the last five years indicated that a few human errors on the part of traffic police resulted in a major law and order problem.

The work done by traffic police in Hyderabad is found to be an important factor in facilitating the movement of state machinery. It may be interesting to note that failure on the part of the police to prevent traffic congestion was viewed by the highest functionary of judiciary as a serious offense, and judicial proceedings were initiated against erring officials of the traffic police.

The administration of traffic enforcement is a complex phenomenon. It has been found that the traffic administrator uses the following tools and techniques: personal observation; deliberate direction (signaling); road

Table 10.10   Number of Cases Booked and Compounding Amounts Collected under the Motor Vehicle Act and C.P. Act during 2002–2006

Year	Motor Vehicle Act Cases		C.P. Act Cases	
	Cases Booked	Fine Amount	Cases Booked	Fine Amount
2002	904,447	80,622,070	16,657	1,649,150
2003	963,947	71,507,800	14,638	1,629,350
2004	845,961	67,922,600	17,873	1,783,750
2005	1,175,422	106,190,700	23,120	1,850,800
2006	2,214,145	156,703,200	10,074	1,382,600

Source: Records of City Traffic Police Branch, Hyderabad.

engineering; random checking; education and counseling; regulating facilities; insisting on safety devices; and controlling drivers' behavior. The traffic police of Hyderabad city, while employing these techniques, have been imposing penalties and collected sizable amounts as compounding fees under the Motor Vehicle Act and City Police (C.P.) Act, details of which are given below.

Table 10.10 shows that traffic cases have been on the increase, except for a slight dip in 2004. In 2005 violations were substantially increased and then during the year 2006 violations under the Motor Vehicle Act increased enormously (100%) when new safety devices like helmets and seat belts were made compulsory. During 2006, 411,502 cases were booked under helmet violations and 120,817 cases under seat belt violations.

To sum up, the traffic police constitute an important wing to reckon with in the context of both sociopolitical activity and administrative work. The omissions and commissions on the part of the traffic police can prove to be fatal to the working of the administrative machinery. The role, therefore, of traffic police is not a static one. It keeps changing and several factors induce such changing roles in varied situations.

Organization

The traffic branch of the city is under the control of the Additional Commissioner of Police (Traffic) who is of the rank of Inspector General of Police. The City Traffic Branch is divided into two wings: the Operational Wing or Enforcement Wing, and the Administrative Wing. The Operational Wing is divided into two districts: North and South. These district areas are further divided into five enforcement zones, which are coterminus with law and order zones. These are (1) North zone, (2) West zone, (3) Central zone, (4) South zone, and (5) East zone. These zones are presently administered by six

Table 10.11   Sanctioned Strength of Traffic Police in 2006

Sl. No.	Category of Posts	Strength
1	Additional Commissioner of Police	1
2	Deputy Commissioner of Police	2
3	Additional Deputy Commissioner of Police	2
4	Assistant Commissioner of Police	7
5	Inspectors of Police	20
6	Reserve Inspectors	3
7	Sub-Inspectors of Police	121
8	Reserve Sub-Inspectors	21
9	Head Constables	206
10	Police Constables	791
Total		1,174

Divisional Offices. An officer of the rank of Assistant Commissioner of Police heads each zone (Division). Two Deputy Commissioners of Police with the rank of Superintendent of Police have supervision over the Zonal Divisional Officers. These DCPs are assisted by two Additional Deputy Commissioners of Police who are of the rank of Additional SPs. Each Traffic Division is again divided into 2–4 Traffic Police Stations. At present, there are 18 Traffic Police Stations in the City of Hyderabad. An officer of the rank of Inspector of Police heads each Traffic Police Station; he is assisted by Sub-Inspector of Police and Head Constables and Traffic Constabulary. Particulars of the existing strength of traffic police are given in Table 10.11.

Besides the above sanctioned strength, there are a number of home guards, who are casual employees. Their number varies from time to time as they are employed on a need-based consideration. The present strength of home guards is 871.

Disproportionate Increase

Table 10.12 compares data regarding the increase in traffic police and the increase in vehicular traffic. The table shows that vehicular strength was

Table 10.12   Growth in Police and Vehicle Strength

Year	Police Strength	Police Growth	Vehicles	Vehicle Growth	Police Vehicle Ratio	Ratio Growth
1995	846	—	553,000	—	1:654	—
2006	1,174	328 (39%)	1,997,000	1,444 (261%)	1:1,701	1,047 (160%)

553,000 in 1995 and rose to 1,997,000 in 2006. This is an increase of more than 261%. However, the strength of police has increased by only 39% during the same period. The ratio of police and vehicles was 1:654 during 1995 and it became 1:1,701 in 2006. This means that the work pressure and burden on the police has increased enormously.

Survey on Job Satisfaction: Police Perception

On the basis of primary data, it may be stated that most people working in the traffic branch at different levels are not willing to remain in the traffic branch. In this connection, the researcher has interviewed 86 traffic police personnel of subordinate services who were actually involved in traffic regulation activities: 17 Sub-Inspectors, 17 Head Constables, and 52 Traffic Constables covering 17 Traffic Police Stations of four traffic zones.

More than 83% (72 out of 86) of police personnel expressed their unwillingness to continue in the traffic branch. During interaction with the personnel, the researcher found various reasons for such an attitude.

- Firstly, there is a serious health problem faced by the police on account of the high levels of noise pollution. Traffic personnel standing at traffic junctions have reported a serious impact on hearing abilities. According to Apollo Hospital doctors, 76% of city traffic personnel of the operational wing suffer from "noise-induced hearing loss," which is a permanent disability.* Further, it was found that traffic personnel who have put in more than six years of service were the worst affected.
- They have to spend more time on the roads and there are no fixed working hours.
- There is a lack of investigation activities.
- There is a lack of promotional benefits in the organization.
- Finally, they are not permanent base staff of the branch; therefore, they are not serious about their duties.

When requested to identify solutions to these problems, traffic police responded as follows: providing proper facilities like medical aid, seasonal allowances, extra-duty allowances; providing uniforms on a regular basis; proper transportation facilities; restroom facilities, recreation facilities, and

---

* Apollo Hospital Jubilee Hills Hyderabad has conducted a hearing assessment test for odd traffic cops in the city since 2002–2005, under the supervision of Dr. E. C. Vinay Kumar, Head ENT Department. (*Deccan Chronicle*, English Daily, Hyderabad, dated 11-6-2005, *Hyderabad Chronicle*, p. 25.)

so on; promotional benefits; and creating a separate cadre of traffic police. Suitable changes may also be made in the composition of recruitment agency, methods of examination, and conducting of interview. It is necessary to place more emphasis on preference for relevance insofar as knowledge of traffic rules is concerned.

Governmental Response

Government from time to time has responded to this problem in various ways. New administrative units were added to the existing structure of administration. A number of autonomous and semiautonomous bodies such as Hyderabad Urban Development Authority, Quli Qutub Shah Urban Development Authority, Airport Development Authority, Cyberabad Urban Development Authority, Municipal Corporation of Hyderabad, Housing Board, Hyderabad Metro Water Works and Sewerage Board, Hyderabad Regional Road Transportation Corporation, Multi Model Transit System (MMTS), and so on have come onto the scene. The government has enacted a number of laws such as the City Police Act Fasli 1348, the Municipal Corporation Act of 1955, the Urban Development Act of 1975, and so on. The government has formulated a number of policies such as Master Plan for 2020 and Pedestrian Development Plan 2004, and has implemented numerous programs that include the construction of inner and outer ring roads, urban community development, road widening, gardenization, improved water supply, modernization of drainage facilities, and street lighting development of suburban areas to counter immigration rural areas.

All these developments have given varying levels of results. Although improvements have been noticed in some specific areas (e.g., construction of flyovers and fly walkers, modernization and synchronization of the signaling system, computerization of RTA and its licensing system, introduction of one-way traffic, and diversion of traffic during peak hours), the problems in core areas still remain threaten public safety and security. Traffic congestion and the marked increase in the rate of road accidents have not been addressed with the seriousness that they deserve.

Public Perception (Road Users)

The author carried out a survey of selected road users to elicit their perception of the role and performance of traffic police. Five hundred road users were picked up at random and divided into groups of 125 each from four traffic zones of the city. Only 23% reported that they were satisfied with traffic management in the city, with some variation between zones (Table 10.13).

Dissatisfaction with traffic control by the traffic police was by and large uniform across all the traffic zones (Table 10.14). It was found that road users

Table 10.13   Public Satisfaction with Traffic Management

Zone	Yes (%)	No (%)	Total
South zone	17.6	82.4	125
West zone	27.2	72.8	125
East zone	20.8	79.2	125
North zone	24.8	75.2	125
Total	22.6	77.4	500

Table 10.14   Satisfaction over Traffic Control by Traffic Police

Zone	Yes (%)	No (%)	Total
South zone	22.4	77.6	125
East zone	24.8	74.2	125
North zone	31.2	68.8	125
West zone	28.8	71.2	125
Total	26.8	73.2	500

blame traffic police for disorder and mismanagement, although they are not the only agency responsible for such a state of affairs. This could be because the traffic policeman is the only agent physically visible on the road and hence road users consider him/her responsible.

Quite a number of road users feel that the traffic police try to execute wrong priorities, such as collecting penalties for not possessing papers or for wrong driving, instead of ensuring smooth traffic movement by bringing about order into an otherwise disorderly, congested, on clogged situation of vehicular movement/nonmovement. It would be instructive to carry out a survey of road users' perception of their own allegiance to rules and norms that ensure smooth traffic without the police having to enforce the same.

Part III: Findings

Police personnel on their part suffer from various limitations. In police organizations, there is no noticeable stress on dichotomy between traffic law enforcement and common law enforcement. The top brass of police hierarchy overemphasizes common law enforcement to the neglect of traffic law enforcement. Consequently, personnel concerned with traffic law enforcement are given lesser importance. One adverse consequence of this dichotomy has been damage to the morale, moral fiber, and motivation of the average traffic policeman. In a number of interviews with police personnel, it was found that they do not feel comfortable for various reasons. They are found to be more interested in quickly shifting to nontraffic areas of police administration. It may be stated that such a dichotomy is irrational because enforcement of traffic law is equally important. In fact, in some cases it is more important than the implementation of common law, considering that criminals and militant organizations use vehicles to carry out attacks and escape apprehension. It would be correct to look at traffic law enforcement more seriously and invite a more interventionist role for traffic police.

An important finding of this study is that in India the physical enforcement of traffic law by the police is of paramount importance. For instance, it was found that in all metropolises signals are manned by police personnel notwithstanding the level of sophistication of the signaling apparatus.

"Heterogeneity" (Riggs, 1964) is a prominent feature of road users of Hyderabad city. The vehicular population ranges from bullock carts to sophisticated high-speed automobiles. This heterogeneity has contributed to some problem areas like traffic congestion, rash driving, accidents, air and noise pollution, and violation of law for petty reasons.

There are also pressure group tactics adopted by a set of road users, which adds to the traffic problems. (1) In Hyderabad city, the owners and drivers of three wheelers have very strong unions; often they bring pressure on the government in order to gain advantage of one type or another, more often than not targeting the "behavior" of traffic police personnel. (2) Secondly, the power elite through their own brand of pressure tactics compel traffic personnel to take a softer view of their own traffic violations.

The administrative system associated with traffic administration reflects the features of the SALA model (Riggs, 1962). There are too many organizations to look after roads, road users, and law relating to movement of traffic on the roads. Consequently, a lack of coordination is casting its telling impact. Frequent digging on the roads, for instance by agencies such as Water Supply, Telephone Department, Electricity Department, and so on, have contributed to traffic jams and avoidable accidents.

Development of awareness among road users requires a massive drive. The government is not able to focus its attention here, as it is preoccupied with many pressing needs of political nature. Nongovernmental organizations (NGOs) and civil society organizations have not shown much interest in strengthening traffic education. As stated earlier, police suffer from the lack of funds and facilities to involve themselves in extension activities concerning traffic education. Thus traffic education has emerged as a deemphasized area.

With regard to jurisdiction of operation, it may be stated that there is lack of unity of command. Although there are several agencies to look after traffic problems, the major burden falls on the police. Besides, they have to prioritize many sundry duties like VIP *bandobust*, disciplining of processions, rallies, bundhs, mob actions, public meetings, and religious festivals, and so on.

As recruitment of new staff is becoming more and more difficult and road-related development activities are facing setbacks owing to the government showing more interest in populist programs, the element of traffic engineering is getting deemphasized stress. While technology seems to be the answer, the compliance factor is a hard nut to crack under Indian conditions.

The multiple laws that have an impact on traffic administration such as the C.P. Act of 1348 F., the Motor Vehicle Act 1988, the MCH Act 1955, and the Road Transport Corporation Act of 1959 have become dated as they were enacted long back. Besides, the laws and manuals do not provide sufficient authority and powers to suit the requirements of traffic police administration.

An important finding of the study is that traffic administration is not able to evolve career development plans for its officers and subordinate staff, as is evident from their large-scale discontent, frustration, and pessimism. Consequently, subordinate-level officials and staff are alienated from the goals and values of traffic administration. It is found that they discharge their duties in a ritualistic manner. This finding is duly substantiated by the perception held by road users too. Besides, Sub-Inspectors and the Constabulary are reported to have developed health-related problems on account of lack of occupational satisfaction.

Suggestions

The researcher suggests that the following measures may go a long way in strengthening traffic administration.

1. Setting up a coordination and policymaking body, which may be called "Traffic Planning and Development Council," with a broad-based membership is needed. It would be appropriate if the Council is chaired by the Minister of Municipal Administration and Urban Development. Members may include the Chief Executives of all organizations that have concern for the administration of Hyderabad city. The Council may be supported by the "Traffic Planning and Development Board" for effective implementation of policies of the Council.
2. A comprehensive legislation covering all aspects of traffic administration such as traffic enforcement, traffic engineering, and traffic education is needed. The traffic police may be given powers to implement the provisions of the proposed law and the Sub-Inspector of police may be allowed to function as investigation and prosecution officer.

3. Traffic police may be made responsible for registration and processing of road accident cases, in which traffic police presently have no say.
4. There is a need for modernization of Traffic Police Stations, strengthening them with infrastructure and improved technology. Areas like office management, records management, and communication management may be supported with electronic equipment and computers so that the station house officer is relieved from the burden of routine duties and can concentrate on traffic planning and control.
5. In view of the findings that traffic administration suffers from a financial crunch, 50% of proceedings related to fines and penalties imposed on road users may be assigned to the traffic police. Besides, project-specific special funds may be released to strengthen engineering and educational aspects.
6. There is a need to set up traffic engineering and management boards with the involvement of engineers, planners, and police to prepare traffic management schemes.
7. Road length and other infrastructural facilities on the road should be improved, and encroachments on the roads should be removed.
8. Finally, the participation of people is the most effective solution to ease the traffic problem in the city.

References

Riggs, F. W. (1962). *The Sala Model: An Ecological Approach to the Study of Comparative Administration*. Boston: Houghton Mifflin.
Riggs, F. W. (1964). *Administration in Developing Countries: The Theory of Prismatic Society*. Boston: Houghton Mifflin.
Taylor, F. W. (1911). *Shop Management*. New York, USA: Harper and Bros.

Urban Mass Evacuation in the United States

11

MICHAEL DOYLE

Contents

Recent events of both man-made and natural origins have resulted in nations and governments developing emergency response plans to protect their populations. In fact, most American cities have prepared for local and regional emergencies and have some sort of plans in place to respond to them. However, many emergency response plans are still being developed or are in the process of evolving to meet expected needs. The questions that remain are: Have American cities prepared in detail for serious or "doomsday" possibilities like hurricanes or extensive terrorist attacks that could require evacuating people from threatened areas? Are these plans capable of evacuating millions of people from danger areas at relatively short notice? What variables should be considered by regional planners when developing an evacuation plan as part of a comprehensive emergency plan?

The purpose of this chapter is to provide a look at some of the variables that affect urban evacuations and the plans for handling them. The chapter will also address the importance of planning, communication between all stakeholders, and regular examination and review in developing and maintaining emergency and evacuation plans.

Evacuation

The first thing we need to do is define an evacuation. Simply put, an *evacuation* is an organized movement of people from an area that is at risk to an area that is safe, when necessitated by emergency conditions. Evacuations can take two forms, *limited* and *large-scale*. Limited evacuations apply to a very specific geographic area, and are in response to areas threatened by a localized danger. Examples of localized dangers are fires, gas leaks, and local flash floods. Large-scale evacuations apply to large geographic areas, including cities or regions, threatened by wide-spread danger. Examples of these dangers include a major hazardous material spill, an event involving nuclear materials, a terrorist attack, extensive flooding, and extreme weather (such as a hurricane).

The next thing to consider in evacuation planning is defining what it is that people will be evacuating from. To be effective, evacuations and their plans must be *event driven*. Evacuation plans must be formulated to account for the effects of different emergencies, which would in turn require different evacuation strategies. For example, Los Angeles, California is located in an area that is at risk for tsunamis. It is also located on an earthquake fault line, and is in an area known for wildfires. Each of these dangers requires its own unique evacuation plan. Any evacuation plan for the Los Angeles area must also take into account the mountain ranges that lie to the east of the city, since these mountains will affect the speed at which people can move over them. This is especially true in the winter when mountain snowstorms can become an issue.

As another example, San Francisco, California has two bridges and a subway under the bay, which are major transportation routes into and out of the city. It is also a city located on an earthquake fault line. Philadelphia, Pennsylvania relies on a series of bridges and elevated highways as integral parts of its transportation infrastructure. The east coast and Gulf of Mexico states of the United States are in hurricane-risk areas and rely on the interstate highway system to move evacuees out of harm's way. As these different examples show, there is no "one-size-fits-all" evacuation plan that can deal with all threats and emergencies. Evacuation plans must be developed in anticipation of each anticipated threat, and the plans must account for the effect that the threat will have on the evacuation route's transportation infrastructure.

Evacuation Planning

When planning for emergencies and related evacuations, it is crucial that regional entities plan and work together as a team when formulating and carrying out these plans. All government and support services must be clear about the regional emergency and evacuation mission and their own specific roles in responding to the emergencies according to the plans. What one city does in response to an emergency can affect neighboring cities in their emergency responses, and vice versa. If all the entities plan together for emergencies, it is less likely that the evacuation actions of one city will interfere with the emergency activities of surrounding cities.

A major consideration in emergency evacuation planning is how to determine if evacuation is the best strategy for a particular situation. There are many times when the best way to keep people safe in an emergency is to have them stay put or *shelter in place* in response to that emergency. People can shelter in place inside their homes or in designated public or private buildings instead of evacuating an area. This strategy was a large part of American civil defense planning during the cold war years, with buildings designated as "fallout shelters" being equipped and able to shelter people from radioactivity in the event of a nuclear event. To the present day, many people, cities, and rural areas maintain shelters to protect people from severe weather or natural events such as tornadoes and hurricanes. The benefits of sheltering in place include keeping people in an area that they are familiar with and keeping them from being exposed on open roadways as the danger approaches. Furthermore, by keeping the roadways less congested, government agencies are better able to use the roadways to bring resources and support to the people who are sheltering in place.

Human Behavior

When preparing emergency and evacuation protocols, planners must consider the *human response to emergencies* when formulating them. People respond to emergencies with varying emotional responses, ranging from confusion all the way through to different levels of panic. People under emotional duress cannot be counted on to simply comply with all the official evacuation directives. For example, some people who are not in the primary danger area and should shelter in place will still choose to evacuate, even though evacuation is not necessary. Some people who are in the danger zone and who should evacuate either refuse to do so or resist complying with evacuation directives. Then there are also people who may want to comply with an evacuation order but who are unable to do so due to health concerns, including hospital or nursing home confinement, poverty (having no car or means to evacuate), or incarceration. In these cases governmental entities must plan to use other modes of available transportation to remove them from the threatened areas.

Understanding the levels of human evacuation behavior is crucial to emergency planners when designing emergency and evacuation protocols. This knowledge can help prevent *spontaneous evacuation*, an evacuation event that is a true goal of a terrorist attack. Spontaneous evacuation occurs when citizens in a threatened area choose to evacuate without official notification or direction. Their movement is unorganized and unsupervised, and they find themselves in the dangerous position of evacuating without a plan or final destination in mind. Spontaneous evacuation is dangerous in an emergency because it not only clogs roadways and escape arteries but also reveals chaos and a major disconnection between the public and government agencies (which are supposed to be protecting them). Instead of governmental direction and feedback to evacuate in this scenario, people end up being guided by rumors, observations, and perceptions when making their decisions. Fortunately, spontaneous evacuations have been rare occurrences so far. However, emergency planners should be aware of the fact that spontaneous evacuations can and will occur without careful planning and dissemination of plans.

Another evacuation phenomenon that has occurred in past emergencies is *shadow evacuation*. Shadow evacuation occurs when there is an evacuation directive for a specific danger zone, but people outside the danger zone evacuate when they do not have to. Shadow evacuation causes the roadways to become clogged with vehicles, which can block those trying to evacuate from a danger area and can prevent emergency vehicles from reaching the danger area. Shadow evacuation took place in Pennsylvania in 1979 when a partial meltdown of the nuclear reactor at the Three Mile Island power facility caused an evacuation to be ordered for a specific radius around the facility. Instead of the limited evacuation that officials had anticipated, the evacuation grew to mammoth proportions. Because the evacuation had to do with a nuclear event, people outside the evacuation area decided to evacuate as well out of fear. The resulting traffic jam made people who were supposed to evacuate turn around and return home.

Another example of shadow evacuation took place in Houston, Texas in 2005 when Hurricane Rita was approaching the American Gulf Coast. Again, officials who called for the limited evacuation of areas in danger of being flooded assumed that only residents of the danger area would flee. However, residents outside the danger area chose to evacuate as well, especially since images of the destruction of Hurricane Katrina three weeks before were fresh in everyone's mind. As a result of this shadow evacuation, the roadway infrastructure in and around Houston had more than twice the traffic that was anticipated.

Infrastructure

When formulating an evacuation protocol, planners must also consider the impact of evacuations on infrastructure and must remember that roadways were not designed to handle evacuation-level demand. Not only does evacuation overwhelm the roadways, it also takes a toll on a variety of en route services. For example, in the Hurricane Rita evacuation, people were stuck in traffic jams for up to 14 hours. Not only did they burn up their fuel, but they also needed food, water, medical care, toilets, and gas station services. All of these services were overwhelmed by the number of people needing them. Additionally, gas stations were unable to refuel vehicles because the stations ran out of fuel. In many cases, fuel trucks were unable to reach the gas stations to resupply them with fuel. In other cases, fuel station workers walked off the job as a result of *role conflict*. Role conflict is when a worker decides which role he/she will play in an emergency: either as a service worker or as a husband, wife, parent, son, daughter. It is a situation where a worker decides that his/her family duties take precedence over work duties. This conflict can also affect other public and private workers, further taxing en route service delivery. Finally, overwhelmed transportation infrastructures hinder the very reason why evacuations are ordered: to protect people. When people are stuck for hours in an evacuation traffic jam, they are also exposed and vulnerable to the very danger that they are supposed to be evacuating from.

These scenarios do not have to happen this way. With careful planning, design, and resource allocation, these kinds of effects can be minimal, and the mission of getting people to safety can be attained.

Communication and Preparation

The best emergency and evacuation plans in the world are of little value if they are formulated in a vacuum and not disseminated to the public they are designed to protect. Communication is key to the success of any emergency plan. When emergency and evacuation plans are regionally prepared and implemented, they must be shared with the public in an ongoing dialogue. Citizens must understand what is expected of them in an emergency. In addition to dialogue, government entities must conduct regular warning tests and emergency drills to familiarize the public with the process. When an actual emergency does occur, the government entity must take special care not to alert the public in a manner that will overly alarm them and add to the panic, which can lead to shadow or spontaneous evacuation. In the short term, the plan should focus on evacuating people safely from danger zones while planning on dealing with anticipated crowd behaviors such as shadow evacuation. The long-term goal is to have a public that is well informed and practiced in emergency and evacuation procedures. A population that is prepared to respond to a well-designed emergency plan will also be confident in its government's directions in times of emergency. This confidence will make implementation of emergency procedures, including sheltering in place and evacuations, more efficient.

In addition to planning, government entities should make related preparations in advance of emergencies to the extent possible. This is especially necessary when preparing the roadway infrastructure for emergency evacuations so that necessary evacuations will occur effectively. In addition to the benefit that these preparations will have during emergency evacuations, they will also benefit the cities and regions in dealing with other transportation challenges that they will face on a regular basis.

An example of infrastructure evacuation preparation has to do with the institution of a *contraflow* plan. A contraflow is a reversal of the inbound lanes of a limited-access divided highway (e.g., American interstate highways). Instituting a contraflow during an emergency allows for increased outbound traffic capacity away from the danger area. To make a contraflow effective, preparation must be in place to allow vehicles to enter the contraflow lanes at entry or "loading" points, which makes the transition to a contraflow smooth and synchronized with the traffic already traveling in the lanes. Otherwise, each loading point becomes a separate bottleneck that adds to the congestion on the evacuation route.

Houston experienced these kinds of bottlenecks during the Hurricane Rita evacuation. After the emergency was over, the Houston region examined their contraflow plan to find a better way of activating it in future emergencies. What the planners came up with were premade contraflow loading points that called for replacing selected portions of the cement median barrier with temporary median barriers that consisted of water-filled plastic barrels. When the next emergency contraflow becomes necessary, all the officials need to do to open the median to contraflow is to have the temporary barriers drained and removed. The result is that the contraflow route has evenly spaced loading points that are less likely to cause traffic bottlenecks. Additionally, the region around Houston also installed signage that directs motorists to the contraflow lanes when an emergency situation arises and a contraflow is ordered by the designated authority. These are examples of advance preparations that help people evacuate more effectively in the face of danger. By having the evacuation route prepared for contraflow, regional authorities will have helped the evacuees reach their safe destination rather than have them stuck and vulnerable on a roadway

Evaluation

Once emergency evacuation plans have been developed and implemented, the job is not over. Ongoing evaluation of the plan is a necessary component of public safety. A good rule of thumb is for an entity or region never to be satisfied with its emergency and evacuation plans. The plans and evacuation routes should be constantly examined, evaluated, and revised to reflect any physical or procedural changes that have taken place. Planners have the opportunity of building on the *lessons learned* from other regions and entities who have experienced emergencies and their effects on their emergency plans. Sharing of information between agencies and regions helps all parties in developing realistic and up-to-date emergency and evacuation plans.

In conclusion, it is wise to remember that no plan is perfect, no plan is all-encompassing, and absolutely no plan will stand up 100% to reality. The emergency situations that the plans will face will contain events that cannot be planned for. Emergency response agencies will have to optimize the plan in the best way they can and will have to adjust their activities as conditions change. However, the emergency plan will provide a strong framework for protecting citizens from the danger they will be facing. This framework will make emergency responses and evacuations possible, regardless of what surprises the emergency situation has in store for the region. Finally, the public should be kept informed on what their duties and expectations are in times of emergency. As they are an integral part of emergency and evacuation plans, they must be encouraged and assisted in taking an active role in planning for their own safety.

Police Responses

II

Reforming Policing in Victoria, Australia

12

CHRISTINE NIXON

Contents

I see my role as Chief Commissioner of Police primarily as a strategic leader, operating within the public sector, accountable to the government and the community, and with a duty to make the very best of the authority, money, resources, and above all, the people given to me to manage and lead. Victoria Police is a large public institution employing more than 13,600 people: 11,500 are sworn police, and the rest are public servants and protective security officers. We have an annual budget of 1.4 billion AUD (i.e., about 1.2 billion USD or 575 million GBP). We serve a population in excess of 5 million. Most of these people live in Melbourne, the second largest city in Australia, with a population of 3,300,000. The rest are scattered across a vast hinterland of towns and rural communities.

While the core roles of the public police may be unchanging, actually identifying what these are in concrete terms and in order of priority, within a complex and ever-changing environment, and then mobilizing organizational capacity to achieve these is a continuous intellectual and moral challenge. I want my police force to be the best it possibly can be in meeting the priorities and needs of all the people of Victoria in the most decent and fairest way. How to achieve that, or rather, moving toward that ideal, is what drives me forward.

I did not arrive as Victoria's Chief Commissioner of Police with a detailed blueprint for reform. Working on police reform in New South Wales in the aftermath of the Wood Royal Commission on police corruption, I left the one we developed there behind. But I brought with me to Victoria the principles and ideas about good policing, good strategic management, and good people management and leadership that I personally believed in and brought to the work of developing that plan.

My arrival as a complete newcomer and outsider enabled us all to start with a clean sheet, with no hostages to fortune, no history, no hidden agendas. Before my arrival the force had gone through a difficult time. Under the pressure of neoeconomic public management, the force, among other things, had to endure significant drops in police numbers to pay for technical advances. Morale was low, the attrition rate was at a historic high, and there were many officers trapped within the organization who would have left if they could. They were looking for leadership and direction.

A new government wanted its police to be seen as modern, progressive, effective and honest, and, most certainly, not to be a political liability when it came to the polls. The public wanted reassurance that all those dollars they paid for policing from out of their taxes were being spent wisely, to good effect. They wanted a police force they could be proud of.

So you can see that I had to work on three fronts. First, to have a conversation with the public including all those agencies and groups with a stake in policing; second, with the government I was accountable to; and third, with a large group of officers who wanted to be treated decently as skilled and committed professionals.

These conversations had to be genuine. This meant above all that I asked the right questions and then listened respectfully and carefully to the answers. It also meant that I had to be open and honest about where I was coming from, about what I believed in, what I thought about policing and its management. This approach requires strong self-belief but also strong belief in people. I go along with the idea that the overwhelming majority of people are decent and well meaning most of the time, and that they know when a person is genuine.

Operational Police

With my officers, the conversation took place early on, with me touring police stations and rooms right across the state, meeting on a face-to-face basis with officers, 8,000 of them in all. It meant standing there, looking them in the eye, white board marker in hand, and asking them what they thought were the important issues we should be addressing. This might seem commonsense— but believe me, in the context of Victoria Police in 2001 it was revolutionary. Throughout its long, varied (and occasionally scandalous) history, one major constant has been that the Chief Commissioner was a remote and aloof leader, insulated from operational police officers by layers and layers of hierarchical levels and a mountain of rules and regulations. For these frontline officers, this was the first time they had been empowered to express opinions and ask questions without threat by a chief commissioner who told them that we all had our different jobs to do, but forget about the mystique that surrounds rank and inhibits conversation. I told them that I was no better than anyone else, so let us talk.

And they did, and we did and we still do. I promised to listen, to record, and then to circulate to each and every one of them my account of what they had identified as the issues and problems they wanted addressing. I asked them to volunteer to sit on project groups to address these issues and to come up with solutions. They needed to know that I regarded them as responsible adults, knowledgeable practitioners, and imaginative innovators. They put their hands up in large numbers, project groups were formed and supported and asked to move quickly to come up with recommended solutions. These recommendations, for the most part, I acted quickly to implement.

That, of course, was just the start but it was a matter of us getting to know each other and building trust in each other. Only then would I be in a position fairly to challenge my officers to engage in a sustained and radical set of changes in the way we did business and how we measured our success.

The Public

The second conversation was with the people of the state of Victoria, which of course included all of my police colleagues who read newspapers, listen to the radio and watch television, and talk with neighbors and friends. So as I set out to meet and communicate with as many members of the public as I could, from meetings in small community halls, or at plush dinners with the movers and shakers at the top end of the town, and to be interviewed at length by all the various media, I knew that my new police colleagues would be very attentive.

Again, talking to the people through the media is a critical part of strategic leadership in an open society. In a culture in which deference is not the name of the game, public leaders engaging with the public media had better be prepared to be completely open and honest, about what they know, about what they do not know, about what they believe and do not believe, about what they stand for. People are smart. They know that even the experts do not know it all. They know life is complicated, messy, and uncertain and that we are all fallible. Therefore, in as positive, optimistic, and confident way as I could, I told the public what I represented, what were my hopes and aspirations for them and their police, and what sort of person I was.

People responded to that, and over that first year I could sense (and opinion polls confirmed) a huge surge of support and commitment from the public for their police, and this put me and Victoria Police in a very good position to draw upon strong support from our key stakeholders and partners and our government.

However, successful strategic leadership is not like winning a popularity contest. I learned that a leader cannot escape the responsibility of making some hard decisions that would have terrible consequences for some people. But again, we are there to make the right decisions. Being open, inclusive, supportive, nurturing, and collegiate does not mean being soft. I never flinch from making hard decisions.

Government and Police Leaders

Along with my initial conversation with operational police and with the larger public, I had to engage with two other hugely important groups—first, the government in the shape of the Police Minister, the Premier, and Cabinet (and not forgetting Treasury and Finance) and second, my operational managers and supporting staff.

Governments today have moved to a user-pays model and they want effectiveness and value for money from their public sector. But I have got to say, especially because of the way public debate about policing is mediated through the media, that governments' thinking about their police can be narrow, thin, cautious, and very short term. Contrary to that, I wanted my government to have a rich and ambitious set of expectations about what we could deliver, given its support in terms of finance, technology, legislation, and so on. A key point about conversation with government is to educate ministers and policy makers (and treasurers) about the capabilities and limits of what policing can deliver given the powers, resources, and legitimacy and the support it is given.

When I started, Victoria Police was regarded as a good but rather old-fashioned command and control, hierarchical and process-driven bureaucracy with a leadership style perhaps best described as management by exception, although that had begun to change in the mid- to late 1990s. Since comparative crime statistics became available, and for no self-evident reasons (but clearly connected to the history and culture of its people), the state of Victoria enjoyed significantly lower official rates of reported crime as measured against the Australian national average. Being a skeptical ex-New South Wales police officer, I was quick to get independent confirmation that the Victoria Police system for measuring these things had full integrity—and it did.

I wanted to promise the government results and outcomes that demonstrated they were getting value for their money and for the authority and powers they vested in their police. Such a system was lacking. When I arrived, Victoria Police's performance indicators, as described in its business plans, included goals such as promising to conduct so many hours of road patrol per year—all process, very little product.

Now I know that, for example, in the United Kingdom, many senior police have regarded their new public management-driven government's emphasis on police performance indicators as a bit over the top in terms of numbers, and of creating too much tension between the centre and local priorities and needs. Some have even warned of the danger of a comparative competitiveness being encouraged between forces that threatened things such as adhering to due process and not cutting corners for short-term gain. I note that the United Kingdom Home Office has recently signaled an appreciation of these concerns with, among other things, a promise to reduce the number of performance indicators it will use to hold its police to account.

But I have long believed that policing can and should make a difference to the communities it serves, and this difference can be measured, not completely, not perfectly, and not always directly, but that we should not be frightened by such a measurement of outcomes. I have never been a subscriber to the nothing works negative philosophy of policing. Such a philosophy is not just wrong. It is a recipe for going through the motion, of engaging in bad faith, and, most outrageous of all, it is an excuse for not thinking, not changing, not inventing and innovating, and not trying to be better.

I know that much of what we do as police has yet to be sufficiently evaluated and tested by robust research and experimentation. And that such research and experimentation itself can be contested and can never substitute for good political debate and values about what is important and what is not. I also appreciate that many, if not all, of the outcomes we strive for are caught up in forces, circumstances, and the actions of others over which we may have little control. But that our work is complex, intertwined, and embedded in the lives and actions of others only means that we have to put more thought and invention into what we do, not less.

Above all we have to challenge the assumptions upon which we act, and think through what we do. My experience has taught me that people can become locked into ways of thinking by their histories and the systems they operate within so that they come to firmly believe that this is the way the world is, that nothing much can be changed, and anyway, that significant change is unnecessary. So I was keen on getting my government to think about police success in terms of valuable social outcomes—measurable increases in community safety, for example, in terms of numbers of road deaths and serious trauma cases, reductions in residential burglaries, reductions in numbers of cars stolen, increases in people's perception of safety, and increases in people's trust and satisfaction with their police.

The government agreed to hold us to account for the differences we promised to make. However, when we developed a strategic plan built around measured outcomes and values, their official external expectations of us were quite modest, because, I suppose, anything more ambitious might appear too much a hostage to fortune. In our strategic plan of 2003–2008, for example, we were set a target of a 5% reduction of the overall crime rate and required merely to "reduce" the road toll and incidence of road trauma (Victoria

Police, 2002). Free to be much more ambitious internally, I was able to persuade my colleagues to aim much higher, to go for "stretch goals."

What we actually achieved greatly exceeded our official targets. For example, within five years the overall official crime rate fell by 21.5%. Robberies fell by 36.8%. Burglaries dropped by 39%. Theft of automobiles, which previously had a rate soaring upward, reaching a peak of 48,000 per annum, nearly 1,000 per week in 2001, fell to 21,000.

Of course, it was not always us police, by our solo efforts, who achieved these outcomes. Sometimes it was just a matter of bringing a new intensity of attention to them and, where we could, making sensible changes to our practices, for example, in relation to evidence-gathering for volume crime. But we could bring pressure to bear upon others to change their practices, for example, car manufacturers with regard to vehicle safety, and those organizations responsible for managing large public car parks. In this way, we caused the differences to come about through partnerships and "third party policing" strategies (Mazzerolle & Ransley, 2005).

Strategic Planning

Development of our strategic plan—The Way Ahead 2003–2008—took nearly the first two years of my commissionership. It took that time because its process exemplified the organizational transformation reform approach that I favored, one that was, I believed, necessary for the plan to succeed. In other words, I did not assign development of a plan to a small group of policy makers locked up in some room somewhere, and then noisily herald the arrival of the new plan to the world. The plan's development took the form of structured and focused conversations—with the public, our stakeholders, government, government and nongovernment agencies, and with all our officers. The process was inclusive, sustained, and conversational.

It started with us consulting with a number of eminent international police scholars on their thoughts, ideas, and theories about the future of policing—people like Clifford Shearing, David Bayley, Mark Moore, and John Braithwaite. Out of this consultation came a discussion paper on the possible future of policing, which was widely circulated. In this fashion, in as inclusive and as fair a way as possible, a very large number of people and organizations contributed toward our strategic direction, our blueprint for reform. I call this process "conversation." Some experts use grander concepts and refer to such things as "empowered participation" (Feng, 2004).

You can try to impose reform upon an organization by driving down through the organization, pulling your weight about and making lots of noise. But when the outcomes you want to achieve are only deliverable through the practices and behaviors of your people, and they do not get to own these changes, then invariably, reform attempts fail, or at any rate, only partially succeed. That is all too common in the history of reform in policing in my experience. It has simply not been understood sufficiently that people can not only help develop solutions, but are essential to their delivery.

I cannot but help noticing, in so much talk about police reform implementation, that perhaps there is too much emphasis placed on rigorous and intrusive supervision. For example, a major report by Her Majesty's Inspectorate of Constabulary was recently published—on citizen satisfaction with call room, incident management, and initial response—which lamented the poor quality of some patrol officer practices and saw the solution in top-down supervision (HMIC, 2007). I certainly want supervisors to supervise, to support, to mentor, to inform, and to provide feedback to their constables. But I also know that constables themselves want to feel valued and to acquire professional satisfaction from their work, to participate in change. How many of our police reforms do they contribute to?

All organizations, and especially old and large police ones, are built upon history and tradition, on the beliefs, achievements, and practices of earlier generations. There is no escaping from that. The past should be honored and respected. When I arrived in Victoria Police, I knew that constables and their managers had long learned about how they were expected to behave, how their success was to be measured, what values they needed to subscribe to. Through such learning they had made considerable investments in the status quo, and why would not they? Was this investment to be rendered instantly valueless by a leader who simply ordered that a different currency was to circulate? That, I knew, would be a recipe for disaster.

But it is just because people have commitments developed over time, and made investments in their careers to date, that there is no avoiding conversation. That conversation should be increasingly laced with reference to evidence, evidence of what current ways of thinking and doing were achieving and evidence of what different and perhaps better ways of thinking and doing were available.

My aim is to change the ways in which Victoria Police managers interface with each other and with their people. Foundationally, they need to treat all with respect and dignity. Walking the talk in terms of values and behavior has become a serious topic of the conversation in Victoria Police, and we have started to measure these things through surveys. I want us to move from being "deference-based" in the way we talked to each other to "evidence-based," within a strong normative framework about what good policing should strive to achieve and about how we should treat each other.

Our consultation-based strategic plan paid respect to the past and used this as the foundation for moving forward. It also drew support from the wider framework of government policy, especially Victoria government's policy on developing social cohesion and justice—"Growing Victoria Together." This came to shape our sense of what our mission was.

Our plan is based on four key value areas and for each of these we spelled out the kinds of changes we would need to embark on to achieve what we wanted. These were

- *Intelligent policing* aimed at developing an organizational culture and strategic capability to identify emerging issues and opportunities, and introducing integrated systems to acquire, store, use, and secure information.
- *Confident policing* that encourages innovation and creative problem solving. It is about a people-centered and enabling management style that aims to create police as community leaders who are capable, ethical, and high performing.
- *Community policing* focused on local level service needs and delivery to achieve maximum impact upon local priorities and safety outcomes.
- *Partnership policing* that collaborates and works with other agencies and groups in the pursuit of common community safety outcomes through developing and strengthening community partnerships across the State.

The plan is a license for making decisions, for everyone, and especially for our managers. But the four value areas could not be fully realized until we began changing our way of doing business, our support, and delivery systems. This meant that we had to *institutionalize* the conversations that I have talked about in this chapter, that is, make them part of the routine way we do business. This meant tackling a whole host of things, including the rank system and command and control.

Institutionalizing Change

I have to say that, of course, when leading an emergency operation, handling a disaster or a large-scale public order event, or responding to a terrorist act, the time and luxury for conversation will be usually absent. Every group of professional practitioners—the military, emergency services, and surgeons— knows that. What is to be hoped is that the systems you possess to deal with these events are well designed and can be effectively applied, generally through a system of command and control. Policing will never be able to abandon that. But a system of command and control is there to shape the way an operation is handled. It is *not* a general and appropriate way of managing the people who conduct and deliver such operations.

To succeed in delivering on our strategic plan I had to convince my colleagues to help transform the management systems through which they thought and within which they operated. We needed a new system of organizational governance. Developing this new system has taken time and is still evolving.

In terms of reporting and accountability it was agreed that I delegate my legislated authority for setting policy to a board, or a corporate committee, chaired by me, and consisting of all my most senior managers. All its members would have to learn to think corporately, to make decisions about strategy and policy for the good of the people of Victoria and Victoria Police, not their own departments. This decision making had to be informed by strong social and corporate values and by relevant and available evidence.

Setting performance standards for senior department heads and day-to-day executive decision making went to a smaller executive management group composed of myself and my most senior people. We broke decisively with direct face-to-face one-on-one reporting. The two deputy Chief Commissioners, for example, were taken out of the line of command and took on corporate-wide portfolios, mentoring, and public advocacy roles. All my senior managers took on the championing and sponsoring of corporate-wide issues and areas—prolific offenders, auto theft, assaults, violence against women, burglaries, and so on—another way of encouraging them to think organization-wide. One of our regions experimented with being run by a board of management with a rotating chair rather than an assistant commissioner of police. This piece of organizational learning has started to extend across the organization.

A powerful enabling tool for these kinds of reforms is a strong internal accounting mechanism; and, hats off to Bill Bratton, we found that in Compstat. Our version of Compstat, which is still developing in lots of very interesting ways (e.g., we are using them to look at emerging problems and themes across the organization—recent ones include looking at youth issues, human resource management, and most lately, what could be the beginning of an interesting but worrisome rise in assaults against women in public places), holds managers accountable not just for results, but for the human costs of how these are achieved. We are as much interested in work-based accidents as in traffic accidents. When unplanned leave rates go up, we want to know why. When public complaints spike in a division or area, we ask the relevant managers for explanations. When spectacular results are achieved we are very keen to know how these were achieved, not just to offer our congratulations but so that good practices can be shared across the organization.

As Compstat started to work a year or two ago, we became confident enough to begin another major phase of reform. As with other progressive modern police bureaucracies, Victoria Police had developed an approach to organizational reform that consisted of identifying a big ticket issue, for example, community policing, youth at risk, and intelligence-driven policing; then giving policy formation responsibility to a senior officer and a project team; waiting a year or so for them to report; and then, slowly but implacably, imposing a new way of doing things onto the organizational landscape; a corporate-wide model, a one-size-fits-all this-is-how-you-will-do-it approach.

I suppose some good has come from such an approach. But I believe it has serious deficiencies in these more dynamic and complicated times. First, the pace of change has quickened up. Now we need to do more of our routine business through a project team approach and to do this much more quickly, or invite the possibility of our reforms being overtaken by changing times. Second, in this approach, innovation and inventiveness and problem-solving gets to be the responsibility of an elite few rather than the activities of the many. The message is no need to think, just follow this new way of doing things.

Third, developing corporate-wide models, badging them (giving them brand names), and making them highly valorized and visible, we are likely to create sacred cows, develop strong factional interests, and end up with our proud reforms actually getting in the way of further change. For example, in Victoria Police, earlier, we invented a local police service delivery model that had to be the same everywhere, although our neighborhoods and communities are highly diverse, with different priorities and different needs. Another example: we developed a school-based youth program that ended up with us giving expensive, special, and privileged service to a small minority of the state's low-risk children while largely ignoring the kids not at school and at most risk. When we set out to change it, we had to overcome entrenched vested interests to obtain a better, fairer, and more effective approach to the problem in place.

So, when it came to reviewing our way of delivering police services to local communities, we needed an approach that overcame these deficiencies, one that delivered on a number of fronts:

- Devolving decision making to the lowest possible level so that local knowledge informed it.
- Engaging our neighborhoods and communities so that their priorities and needs surfaced, their voices were heard, and their rights were respected.
- Empowering constables to be leaders and problem solvers for their local client groups.
- Avoiding a decentralized anarchy by ensuring that everyone knows the limits within which decision making and innovation had to take place by providing support, capacity, and accountability from the centre.

We knew that these ideas were being explored and applied elsewhere. For example, we had kept a careful eye on the Chicago Alternative Policing System (CAPS), a devolved system involving empowered participation and local democracy in the delivery of policing services (Skogan, 2006). But we did not want a badged model, we did not want another flavor of the month, fad or fashion, or another sacred cow. I notice that the latest Chicago Police Department website does not refer to CAPS. It is no longer an alternative way of policing. It is how they do all their business.

So we asked our project team to come up with not a model with a fancy name and a marketing logo, but are with a set of principles that ought to underpin any good, fair, responsive, innovative local delivery of police services (the bread and butter stuff that constitutes about 70% of what we do, day in, day out, and throughout the year on a 24/7 basis).

The project team ended up with a 70-page report and hundreds of pages of appendices (Victoria Police, 2006). But within that, along with a few structural change recommendations, they came up with no more than a page or two containing just four service delivery principles. These we are currently communicating and explaining to our 56 police service area managers and their teams (the precincts, districts, beats, and police stations). They now know that they need to base the way they shape, manage, and deliver services to their local communities upon these four principles and that they will be held accountable for their gradual and supported compliance with them.

We require from them

- delivery of local services that is equitable, responsive, and client focused.

We promise them that

- all decisions made by them that are lawful, ethical, and reasonable will receive corporate support.

We expect from them that

- their local policing priorities will be determined and communities strengthened through high-quality, effective internal and external collaboration and networks.

We want them to manage and lead their teams in ways that encourage the emergence of

- a professional work environment that supports our people to use their capabilities and resources efficiently, effectively, and fairly.

The realization of these principles as operational realities will take time, and no doubt will be uneven in their development across the organization.

The process will require careful monitoring and support from the center. But I am confident that these principles will create the space within which all the people can realize their full potential as professional practitioners.

I have not neglected some other big corporate-wide issues and problems—they have not let me. Within months of my arrival, the Drug Squad imploded with dramatic evidence of serious corruption, with high-profile much-admired role-model detectives revealed to be trading in large quantities of illegal drugs. Soon after this, and really making my first year or two in the job very interesting indeed, an organized crime gang war erupted in Melbourne that saw the rapid accumulation of 30 plus gangland killings.

Now an old friend and colleague of mine, Professor Mark Moore of the Kennedy School of Management, apart from explaining very clearly why the strategic management leadership approach I try to apply can work (Moore & Stephens, 1991), has often remarked that sometimes the only way to get public reform really moving is through the occurrence of the equivalent of corporate bankruptcy—then everyone can see that change is required. But, having gone through the trauma of the New South Wales Wood Royal Commission, and having seen the pain and paralysis stemming from such happenings as the Mollen inquiry, the Los Angeles Ramparts scandal, and the Rodney King beating (Skolnick & Fyfe, 1993), I know that there have got to be better ways of police reform than the seemingly endless cycle of corruption, scandal, and rule-tightening reform (Neyroud & Beckley, 2001). Of course, we should tackle these issues in open and transparent ways, but also in ways that allow us to own the solutions to them, while operating within a wider context of effective external oversight so that our political masters and the community are reassured.

Mark Moore has also suggested that sometimes, perhaps, a series of smaller scandals and misfortunes can provide the reforming leader with the urgency and opportunity to move forward. This has happened in Victoria. We do not have any comfort zones. But we have been able to keep delivering to high standards and thereby retain the support of our citizens.

We applied our conversational model to the organized crime problem. Within a few months, we had harnessed a team of experienced practitioners and international experts and realized that our organized crime strategy was based on an out-of-date and now false set of assumptions about how organized crime actually works. We changed accordingly, and did so in ways that brought what Mark Moore (1995) calls our "authorizing political authority" (the people without whose support we would not have the legitimacy to pursue our social mission) into the very process of reform. With a new draft Organized Crime Strategy we brought our stakeholders and politicians, our judges, our media, our senior managers, and our international experts together for a two-day closed conference and sought and got their endorsement of the plan.

We then proceeded to bring the same approach to bear upon the Crime Department as a whole. We have very good detectives but they had been operating within a system of management that exposed them to moral danger and which did not encourage them to innovate, self-critique, and which did not hold them to robust and transparent account.

And so it goes. There are other important elements I have had to neglect in this account, for example, the role that partnerships with university research groups is playing in our program of evidence-informed continual improvement and reform. My approach is represented in Mark Moore's (1995) strategic triangle: my duty is to use the resources entrusted to me to add to public value. The vision for this is our social mission: creating a more just society (which is a broad government policy) by enhancing social cohesion, safety, and the rights of citizens in our community and improving citizen satisfaction with police service. This is achievable only if I can draw upon the support and resources of my authorizing community, the people of Victoria, my government, my key stakeholders, the courts, interested groups, and the media. And it will only be effective, can only possibly succeed, if I can build an organizational capacity to deliver what I have promised. This capacity resides in the hearts and minds and hands of my police colleague members—the men and women, sworn and nonsworn, of Victoria Police.

References

Feng, A. (2004). *Empowered Participation: Reinventing Urban Democracy*. Princeton, NJ: Princeton University Press.

HMIC (Her Majesty's Inspectorate of Constabulary). (2007). *Beyond the Call: A Thematic Inspection of Police Contact Centres' Contribution to Incident Management*. London: Home Office.

Mazzerolle, L., & Ransley, J. (2005). *Third Party Policing*. Cambridge, UK: Cambridge University Press.

Moore, M. (1995). *Creating Public Value: Strategic Management in Government*. Harvard University Press.

Moore, M., & Stephens, D. (1991). *Beyond Command and Control: The Strategic Management of Police Departments*. Washington, DC: Police Executive Research Forum.

Neyroud, P., & Beckley, A. (2001). *Police, Ethics, and Human Rights*. Cullumpton, Devon, UK: Willan Publishing.

Skogan, W. (2006). *Police and Community in Chicago: A Tale of Three Cities*. New York: Oxford University Press.

Skolnick, J., & Fyfe, J. (1993). *Above The Law*. 1st edn. New York: The Free Press.

Victoria Police. (2002). *The Way Ahead*.

Victoria Police. (2006). Fit For Purpose: Principle-Based Police Service Policing.

Urbanization and Community Policing in Nigeria

13

AMOS OYESOJI AREMU

Contents

The Nigeria Police is one of the legacies associated with British colonial rule in Nigeria. The Nigerian nation became an independent country on October 1, 1960. Prior to this period, the first ever presence of the then British empire was the annexation of Lagos in 1849 through the Chartered Royal Niger Company. And by 1900, the British government revoked the charter granted to the Royal Niger Company and took over the direct administration of its Lagos colony.

Then, there were other protectorates in Nigeria (e.g., Northern, Southern, and the Niger Coast). These were all united in 1914 and became known as Nigeria during the administration of Lord Lugard. Throughout this period the two protectorates (Northern and Southern) and the Lagos colony were without security measures provided for formally by the Nigeria Police. However, what is now known as the Nigeria Police came into existence in 1914, following the unification of the North and South. There was the presence of police forces prior to this period.

The first ever police force and administration in Nigeria started with a 30-man consular guard in Lagos in 1861. Similarly, the armed paramilitary Hausa constabulary was formed in 1879. In 1888 and 1894, similar forces were established in Lokoja and the Niger Coast protectorate. Fundamentally, what is now known as the Nigeria Police Force came into existence in 1930, when the Northern and Southern forces were merged and came under a single administration in Lagos, the then federal capital city.

Ever since, the Nigerian nation, which now has 36 states with the seat of government in Abuja, has developed, with many urbanized cities (e.g., Lagos, Abuja, Ibadan, Kaduna, Port Harcourt, Kano, Benin, Onitsha, and Ogbomoso) and its attendant consequential effects (e.g., armed robbery, assassination, violence of all forms—religious, political, ethnic, and social). These have not only stretched the police, but their effects on the psychological well-being of citizens and noncitizens have made sociopolitical commentators and analysts begin to question the efficiency of the Nigeria Police in curtailing the rising tide of urbanized violence.

Urbanization and Community Policing

Urbanization

Urbanization is a complex process in which a country's organized communities become larger, more specialized and more independent. More elaborately, it is the result of many variables—economic, technology, demographic, environmental, and so on—and it is inevitably accompanied by other changes in society. More succinctly, urbanization can be viewed as the process in which the number of people living in cities rises rapidly compared with those living in rural areas. Operationally, therefore, a country is considered urbanized when over 10% of its population live in urban cities.

For a better understanding of the concept of urbanization, highlighting the modalities of evolution of cities in human history is germane. The first city in human history is believed to have emerged around 3200 BC in Sumer, Mesopotamia, between the Tigris and Euphrates rivers, as a consequence of the Neolithic Revolution, which saw a shift in food production from hunting and gathering to agriculture, based on domesticated plants and animals (Childe, 1950).

Bairoch (1988) then reaffirmed that the emergence of cities in Sumer marked the beginning of an "urban revolution" that came rather slowly. Another scholar, Wrigley (1987), contended that the emergence of cities and, by extension, urbanization is not peculiar to Mesopotamia. He reasoned that cities also emerged independently in at least two other places—China and the New World (i.e., places where major domestication of plants and animals arose independently). Archeological evidence also shows that there may have been as many as 15 city-states by 3000 BC, and a typical city-state may have a population of 25,000 with a rural population of about 50,000 (Hammad, 1992).

Here, it should be noted that in the context of earlier definitions given on urbanization, early cities do not fit into the modern context of urbanization. However, with further evolution of cities from the period of the Roman world through the era of the Middle Ages (between 100 BC and 1500 BC) to the rise of Western Europe, and then the modern period, cities began to attract global attention for pertinent reasons (Bairoch, 1988; Brewer, 1998; Vries, 1984). Indeed, governments became concentrated in cities given that the efficiency of military and government operations required the collection of enormous information (Brewer, 1998).

Modern urbanization in most African countries is dominated by the growth of a single primary city, the political and commercial center of the nation, and its emergence was, more often than not, linked to the shaping of the country during the colonial era. Unlike most other nations, however, Nigeria had not just one or two but several cities of major size and importance, a number of which are larger than most other national capitals in other African countries.

From the foregoing, it is apparent that cities would require a greater presence of police than rural areas. The reason is that in urban areas with its increasing trend for population growth, social vices will predominate due ostensibly to the convergence of people with shady characters. Thus community policing would become necessary for people's safety.

Community Policing

Wilson and Kelling (1982) posited that community policing operates (from a theoretical perspective) on the assumption that increased police and community cooperation and partnership aimed at improving the quality of life at the neighborhood level will reduce the fear of crime. The inherent reduction in the fear of crime occasioned by community policing has been established in previous studies (Cordner, 1997; Dietz, 1997). Zhao, Scheider, and Thurman (2002) reported that police presence had an impact on fear reduction with respect to fear regardless of the modalities of its implementation.

Arguably, police presence when complemented with community policing strategies tends to yield a greater reduction in crime. Trojanowicz and Buqueroux (1990) defined community policing as a new philosophy of policing, which emphasizes a working partnership between police officers and citizens in creative ways in order to solve community crime and neighborhood disorders. Bennet (1994) defined it as a belief or intention held by the police that they should consult with and take account of the wishes of the public in determining and evaluating operational policing and that they should collaborate with the public in identifying and solving local problems.

Benefits of Community Policing

A 1993 survey of over 2,000 U.S. law-enforcement agencies, police chiefs, and sheriffs believed that community policing would result in

- Reduction of problems on issues of concern to citizens.
- Improved physical environment in neighborhoods.
- Better public attitudes toward law-enforcement agencies.
- Decreased potential for conflict between citizens and police.
- Increased officer/deputy satisfaction.
- Reduction of crime rates (National Institute of Justice, 1995, p. 1).

From the foregoing, the belief is that when community policing is adopted in urbanized cities, the crime level often associated with urbanization will be reduced. This implies that community policing is an idea whose time has come, and which is seen as a "revolution" and/or "paradigm" in effectively policing urban areas that are no longer safe for law-abiding citizens (Oliver & Bartzis, 1998). Although in Nigeria community policing has not been fully integrated into Nigeria Police practice, the philosophy has been accepted and is being experimented with in three (Enugu, Ogun, and Plateau) out of 36 states. Community policing as a philosophy has also been stressed by the current police leadership in Nigeria through its slogan "to protect and serve with integrity." Apparently, community policing is an idea in the right direction in the Nigeria Police.

Since it is an evolutionary concept in the Nigeria Police, police scholars and commentators are yet to subject it to empirical investigations. This notwithstanding, Aremu and Emehinola (2006) reported that the import of community policing is seen as a paradigm shift, needed by the Nigeria Police to situate it in the contemporary policing approach and move away from the traditional policing method, that has always brought it into collision with the public. Adebayo (2005) referred to it as prosocial policing.

Police scholars (e.g., Adebayo, 2005; Cordner, 1997; Thurman & McGarrell, 1997) have agreed that community policing represents a substantial paradigm shift in policing rather than a mere passing fad. In the light of this, phrases such as "organizational change," "paradigm shift," "new paradigm of policing," "organizational commitment," "institutionalizing change," "prosocial policing," and "policing cynicism" appear to be on the increase in police literature (Aremu & Jones, 2007; Cordner, 1997; Weisel & Eck, 1994; Zhao & Thurman, 1997; Zhao et al., 2002).

The real police paradigm shift requires the police to purposefully combat crime professionally. This requires what Zhao et al. (1999) referred to as change at all three levels of police organization—what individuals do, how groups interact, and organizationally (i.e., what the agency redefines as its primary mission). Thus, Turner and Wiatrowski (1995) remarked that community policing is in fact the paradigm within which the public now put its understanding of policing. This underscores the notion that community policing accords the police positive perception.

In line with this viewpoint, Bayley and Shearing (1996) advocated that community policing must become the organizing paradigm of public policing. In essence, public policing requires the absence of crime, and given the inevitability of crime, its reduction must be apparent and appreciable. If implemented appropriately, the community policing philosophy designed to place the police in good stead in the public consciousness, improve the public–police partnership, and thus reduce crime.

As good as this seems, the desired results (reduction in crime and police–public cooperation) are still far from being achieved. This still leaves a gap in the modalities needed to achieve the desired paradigm shift in the police, most especially in Nigeria where policing is still being traditionally practiced. Moving the police forward would therefore require "emotional intelligence."

Emotional Intelligence as a Catalyst for Paradigm Shift

Oliver and Bartzis (1998) observed that the concept of community policing is itself a paradigm, not in the one large-scale theory sense, but rather as an evolving mix of theories that describe enhanced methods for delivering police services. Thinking within the context of Oliver and Bartzis (1998), Kelling and Moore (1998), in their "Broken Windows," theory noted that neighborhood disorder is a source of public fear and "Unrepaired Windows" invites social disorder and criminal activity into a neighborhood. Moreover, if the police are to reduce crime and social disorder in neighborhoods, they must bring the community together: restore civility, drive down the high rates of crime, ensure stability in the polity, and reduce fear. These are central to emotional intelligence in the police.

Emotional intelligence as defined by Goleman (1998) is a learned capability based on the manipulation of feeling and emotions that result in outstanding performance at work. In another work, Goleman (1995) referred to it as the ability to sense, understand, value, and effectively apply the power and acumen of emotions as a source of human energy, information, trust, creativity, and influence. Salovey and Mayer (1990), who were reputed to have coined the term "emotional intelligence" in 1990, described it as a form of social intelligence that involves the ability to monitor one's own and others' feelings and emotions, to discriminate among them, and to use this information to guide one's thinking and action.

In the contemporary psychological literature, emotional intelligence is one of the concepts that has gained prominent mention among psychologists who are keen to keep abreast of evolution and development of knowledge in their field. As a matter of fact, emotional intelligence is a new paradigm of the competencies of being SMART. These involve Self-awareness, Mastering negative emotions, Attitude of optimism, Reading the emotions of others, and Training to maximize results. Salovey and Mayer (1990) offered the following in their emotional intelligence framework: self-awareness, self-regulation, motivation, empathy, and social skills (or handling relationships).

Self-awareness: This, according to Goleman (1995), means recognizing a feeling as it happens. That is, the ability of an individual to monitor feelings from moment to moment. This further underscores the importance of insight and self-understanding on the part of the individual.

In the context of this chapter, a police officer is required to be self-aware and manage his/her emotion when on duty. The police organization in Nigeria as a paradigm shift would rely on people (i.e., community policing) more than before to combat urbanization crime. The police therefore must be ready to lead a system-wide organizational change by encouraging its officers and the rank and file to individually have self-awareness.

Self-regulation: Emotional intelligence enables people to lead with courage and demonstrate passion. Police, more often than not, encounter difficulties and also work with difficult members of the public. These situations (most especially when fighting crime) can generate frustration, anxiety, and could even lead to "accidental discharge." Through self-regulation, however, members of the police organization would be able to manage their thoughts, actions, and reactions when on duty.

Motivation: This is the ability to use emotions to take positive action and to continue to persistently pursue goals even in the face of significant adversity or difficulty. In Nigeria, to say that the police work in an unfriendly environment is to say the least. Aremu and Jones (2007) have reported that police in Nigeria lack organizational commitment. Thus, emotional self-motivation would be required in order to be positive, confident, and persistent when on duty.

Empathy: Using empathy would enable the police to effectively communicate with the public and understand the public viewpoint. This would also generate trust from the two parties. Empathy would enable the police to be more insightful and to solve problems. Goleman (1995) was of the opinion that people who have empathy are more attuned to the subtle social signals that indicate what others need or want. Empathy is also known to contribute to occupational success (Pilling & Eroglu, 1994; Rosenthal, 1977).

Social skills: This involves developing and nurturing relationships. It is also the ability to demonstrate sincere care for others, and setting a positive tone of cooperation with others. Goleman (1995) was of the opinion that people who excel in these skills do well at anything they attempt. Aremu (2006) did report that police who are exposed to social skills training did better than those not exposed. This underscores the importance of social skills in policing.

Emotional Intelligence: Why It Matters in the Nigeria Police

With increasing challenges facing the Nigeria Police, police effectiveness and its acceptance have come under serious public debate in recent times. As observed earlier, one of the cardinal principles of the Nigeria Police under its present leadership is to "serve and protect with integrity." This slogan has further challenged the policing integrity of the Nigeria Police.

Jackson and Wade (2005) have noted that the impetus to examine alternative variables for understanding proactive police behavior is once again becoming a major thrust in policing literature. Emotional intelligence is therefore one of the catalysts needed to reposition the police in the twenty-first century. Policing should not be practiced again as it is in the contemporary time. The world and the people inhabiting it are changing. For the police to cope with these challenges, they must be amenable to education that emotional intelligence provides.

Recently, police researchers (although very few) have taken the challenge by empirically and conceptually investigating the influence of emotional intelligence on police behaviors. The works of Aremu (2005), Aremu and Lawal (2006), Aremu and Tejumola (2007), Bellamy and Bellamy (2003), and Donna (2003) are a pointer in this direction. For example, Aremu and Tejumola submitted that emotional intelligence in the Nigeria Police leaves much to be desired. They then concluded that Nigeria Police personnel do not have sufficient emotional intelligence to make them undertake the policing job as is expected of them.

Earlier, Aremu (2005) reported the positive influence of emotional intelligence on the career commitment of young police officers in Nigeria. Similarly, Bellamy and Bellamy (2003) noted that emotional intelligence has an influence on police leadership in the American police. More recently, Aremu and Lawal (2007) reported the influence of the hypothesized model investigated (gender, self-efficiency, emotional intelligence, mentoring, and emotional labor) on the career aspirations of Nigeria police trainees; emotional intelligence as a variable also impacted and contributed significantly to the career aspirations of police trainees.

In summary, the main aim of this chapter is to theoretically advance the submission that urban crime can be reduced by the Nigeria Police if they adopted community policing and, more importantly, if they are emotionally intelligent. Although this submission is not in itself an absolute policing method that could help reduce urbanized crime, nevertheless the influence of emotional intelligence combined with the community policing approach could help the police address the urban crime reduction problem. The point here is that the expected paradigm shift that is being canvassed for by the public, and which the Nigeria Police is also aware of, will enable the latter to gain the confidence of the public and to be more alert to its primary responsibility, that is, protection of life and properties.

The police must embrace emotional intelligence and practice community policing in order to maintain public order (absence of crime). In line with this submission, Walker (1998) suggested that police, who constantly confront communities demonstrating high levels of social disorganization, high crime, and low levels of social capital, begin to recognize their inability to control the area. Crank (1998) frankly pointed out that police inability to control an area is a negative mark against them. This is what emotional intelligence should overcome in the police. And all the more reason why it matters in policing.

Conclusion

One of the challenges this chapter has provoked is how, where, and when would police embrace emotional intelligence. What matters most is starting, that is, implementation. Therefore, it could start in the training of police cadets and recruits. It could also be through in-service training, seminars, workshops, and organized lectures. The main theme of this chapter is that combatting urbanized crime by the police can be made less stressful if community policing is adopted and if police personnel are emotionally intelligent. This is because a growing body of research, as enunciated in this chapter, has empirically shown that police job success can be influenced by their ability to adopt self-regulation, perceive their job positively, and identify and manage emotions of the public when combatting crimes.

References

Adebayo, D. O. (2005). Ethical attitudes and pro social behavior in the Nigeria police: Moderator effects of perceived organizational support and public recognition. *Policing: An International Journal of Police Strategies & Management, 28*(4), 684–705.

Aremu, A. O. (2005). A confluence of credentialing, career experience, self-efficiency, emotional intelligence, and motivation on the career commitment of young police in Ibadan, Nigeria. *Policing: An International Journal of Police Strategies & Management, 28*(4), 609–618.

Aremu, A. O. (2006). The effect of two Psychological Intervention Programmes on the improvement of Interpersonal Relationships of Police Officers in Osogbo, Nigeria. *Criminal Justice Studies, 19*(2), 139–152.

Aremu, A. O., & Emehinola, S. A. (2006). Correlates of psycho-social variables on community policing of the Nigeria Police. Unpublished M.Ed. thesis, University of Ibadan, Nigeria.

Aremu, A. O., & Lawal, G. A. (2006). A path model investigating the influence of some personal-psychological factors on career aspiration of police trainees in Oyo State, Nigeria. Unpublished manuscript, Department of Guidance & Counseling, University of Ibadan, Nigeria.

Aremu, A. O., & Jones, A. A. (2007). Predicators of organizational commitment of Nigerian police in Lagos: Some counseling Implications. Unpublished manuscript, Department of Guidance & Counseling, University of Ibadan, Nigeria.

Aremu, A. O., & Tejumola, T. O. (2008). Assessment of emotional intelligence among Nigerian police. *Journal of Social Science. 16*(3), 221–226.

Bairoch, P. (1988). *Cities and Economic Development.* Chicago: Chicago University Press.

Bayley, D. H., & Shearing, C. D. (1996). The future of policing. *Law and Society Review, 30,* 588–607.

Bellamy, A. R., & Bellamy, A. R. (2003). Emotional intelligence and transformational leadership: Recursive leadership processes within the context of employee work attitude. *Midwest Academy of Management, 23*(3), 19–31.

Bennet, T. (1994). Community policing on the ground: Developments in Britain. In D. P. Rosenbaum (Ed.), *The Challenge of Community Policing: Testing the Promises* (pp. 224–248). Thousand Oaks, CA: Sage.

Brewer, J. (1998). *The Sinews of Power: War, Money and the English State, 1688–1783.* Cambridge, MA: Harvard University Press.

Childe, V. G. (1950). The Urban Revolution. *Town Planning Review, 21*(1), 3–17.

Cordner, G. W. (1997). Community policing: Elements and effects. In G. P. Alpert & A. Piquero (Eds), *Community Policing: Contemporary Readings* (pp. 435–465). Prospect Heights, IL: Waveland Press.

Crank, J. P. (1998). Civilianization in small and medium police departments in Illinois, 1973–1986. *Journal of Criminal Justice, 28*(1), 85–100.

Dietz, A. S. (1997). Evaluating community poling, quality police service and fear of crime. *Policing: An International Journal of Police Strategy & Management, 20*(1), 83–100.

Donna, R. (2003). Emotional intelligence, negative mood regulation expectancies professional burnout among police officers. Unpublished Ph.D. Thesis, Rutgers University, New Jersey.

Goleman, D. (1998). What makes a leader? *Harvard Business Review,* November–December, pp. 93–102.

Goleman, D. (1995). *Emotional Intelligence: Why It Can Matter More Than IQ.* New York: Bantam Books.

Hammad, M. (1992). *The City in the Ancient World.* Cambridge, MA: Harvard University Press.

Jackson, A. R., & Wade, J. E. (2005). Police perceptions of social capital and sense of responsibility: An explanation of proactive policing. *Policing: An International Journal of Police Strategies & Management, 28*(1), 49–68.

Kelling, G. L., & Moore, M. H. (1998). From political reform to community: The evolving strategy of police. In J. R. Greene & S. D. Mastrofski (Eds), *Community Policing: Rhetoric or Reality.* New York: Praeger.

National Institute of Justice. (1995). Community policing strategies. *National Institute of Justice—Research Review*, November, Washington, DC: U.S. Government Printing Office.

Oliver, W. M., & Bartzis, E. (1998). Community policing: A conceptual framework. *Policing: An International Journal of Police Strategies & Management, 21*(3), 490–509.

Pilling, B. K., & Eroglu, S. (1994). An empirical examination of the impact of salesperson empathy and professionalism and merchandise salability on retail buyers' evaluation. *Journal of Personal Selling and Sales Management, 14*(1), 55–58.

Rosenthal, R. (1977). The PONS Test: Measuring sensitivity to nonverbal cues. In P. McReynolds (Ed.), *Advances in Psychological Assessment*. San Francisco, CA: Jossey-Bass.

Salovey, P., & Mayer, J. D. (1990). Emotional intelligence. *Imagination, Cognition, and Personality, 9*, 185–211.

Thurman, Q. C., & McGarrell, E. F. (1997). *Community Policing in a Rural Setting*. Cincinnati, OH: Anderson Publishing.

Trojanowicz, R., & Buqueroux, B. (1990). *Community Policing: A Contemporary Perspective*. Cincinnati, OH: Anderson Publishing.

Turner, R., & Wiatrowski, M. D. (1995). Community policing and innovation: The "new institutionalism" in American Government. In P. C. Kratcoski & D. Dukes (Eds), *Issues in Community Policing*. Cincinnati, OH: Anderson publishing.

Vries, J. (1984). *European Urbanization 1500-1800*. Cambridge, MA: Harvard University Press.

Walker, S. (1998). *A Critical History of Police Reform*. Lexington, MA: D.C. Heath.

Weisel, D., & Eck, J. (1994). Toward a practical approach to organizational change: Community policing initiatives in six cities. In D. Rosenbaum (Ed.), *The Challenge of Community Policing: Testing the Promises* (pp. 53–72). Thousand Oaks, CA: Sage.

Wilson, J., & Kelling, G. (1982). The police and neighborhood safety: Broken windows. *Atlantic Monthly, 249*, 29–38.

Wrigley, N. (1987). The concentration of capital in UK grocery retailing. *Environment & Planning, 19*, 1283–1288.

Zhao, J., Lovich, N.P., & Thurman, Q. (1999). The status of community policing in American cities. *Policing: An International Journal of Police Strategies and Management, 22*, 74–92.

Zhao, J., Scheider, M., & Thurman, Q. (2002). Funding community policing to reduce crime: Have COPS grants made a difference? *Criminology and Public Policy, 2*(1), 301–322.

Zhao, J., & Thurman, N. P. (1997). Determinants of minority employment in American municipal police agencies: The representation of African officers. *Journal of Criminal Justice, 26*, 267–277.

Policing Multiethnic Societies

14

BRANISLAV SIMONOVIC and
UROS PENA

Contents

Policing in multiethnic and multidiverse societies all over the world has had a long history of problems, nonacceptance, violation, disrespect of human rights, and other difficulties. Today, a great deal of policing research is being conducted and published in western literature on diverse societies (multirace, multiethnic, etc.). The results show that tensions between minority communities and the police are a widespread problem in many states (Brunson & Miller, 2006).

For example, many research studies show that drivers from minority communities are stopped and searched at proportionally higher rates than they are represented in the community (Withrow, 2004). Home Office figures from 1998 for the United Kingdom suggest that blacks are five times as likely to be stopped by the police as whites (Body-Gendort, 2004, p. 137). A degree of disproportionality of police use of stop powers based on ethnicity is a real fact in many countries (Wild, Hallsworth, Higwan, & McGuire, 2006). Many critics of policing consider this prima facie evidence of institutional racism.

The problem in relationships between police and race (ethnic) minorities is complicated with respect to security questions. The war on drugs, gangs, and terror has often been connected with minority societies, which complicates the police job and intercitizen relationships. Tanovich (2006, p. 474), who deals with these issues, concludes that "It is reasonable to assume that they (the police reports) influence who is most likely to attract police attention ... In essence, the war on drugs is a war on blacks. The war on gangs is a war on Asians and Aboriginals, and the war on terrorism is a war on Arabs." On the one hand, the problem is how to preserve police efficiency in fighting against criminality, especially drugs and terrorism, and on the other hand, the problem is how to enable the police to render police services justifiably and at the same time respect human rights and generally adopted democratic society's principles relating to equality of citizens, and correct and fair treatment.

There is no doubt that some facts are indisputable and that they have a large influence over police activities in multinational, that is, diverse, communities:

1. There is a mutual lack of confidence in multinational communities and a misunderstanding between the police and minority groups arising out of numerous historical strains and prejudice. Nevertheless, in American society (and all over the world) prejudice and discrimination still exist and have an impact on minority police officers (Sullivan, 1989). Too often, a dichotomy of "Us and Them" articulates police and minority relations in their respective cultures within a context of unequal power relations (Body-Gendort, 2004).

2. Minorities (ethnic, racial, and others), in principle, have fewer opportunities for advancement, success, and equal competition in comparison with the majority population. Unemployment, of young people particularly, and bad housing and living conditions, in most diverse communities, are crime factors. "People of colour living in disadvantaged urban communities have been shown to be the disproportionate recipients of both proactive policing strategies and various forms of police misconduct" (Brunson & Miller, 2006, p. 613).

3. It is minority communities, especially neglected and poor ones, that show a rise in criminal offenses committed primarily by young members of the community (drug trafficking, violence, and, lately, terrorism), which represents a huge security problem and challenge for police all over the world and calls for implementation of proactive strategies. For example, some research in the United States found a correlation between race affiliation of stopped drivers (African Americans and Hispanic Americans) and illegal transportation of particular types of drugs. The finding lent some support to the notion that race may be correlated with the type and amount of drug discovered during motor vehicle stop-and-search operations (Lichtenberg, 2006). Now the question is, how can the police respect

human rights of minority members and simultaneously react to obvious crime problems arising in these communities, particularly taking into account threats of terrorism and organized crime? The police force faces a dilemma on whether to emphasize fairness or efficiency.

The findings suggest that the relationship between race and suspect demeanor is very much complicated by the way the police interact with members of poor minority communities (disproportionate experiences with surveillance and stops; disrespectful treatment and verbal abuse; the use of force, including excessive and deadly force; police deviance). When they compared the rates of disrespects for minorities and whites, they found that minorities were twice as likely to receive disrespect from the police. In fact, scholars have argued that one of the most harmful elements of aggressive policing strategies is their disproportionate targeting of both minority citizens and poor minority communities (Brunson & Miller, 2006, pp. 613–616).

The definition of institutional racism used in the Macpherson Report (after the Lawrence case in England) perceived public institutions to be collectively failing minority ethnic individuals by not providing "an appropriate and professional service ... Because of their colour, culture, or ethnic origin. Institutional racism could be seen in processes, attitudes, and behavior which amount to discrimination through unwitting prejudice, ignorance, thoughtlessness and racist stereotyping" (Phillips, 2005, p. 358).

Unlike the West, exact research relating to specific police activities in multiethnic and minority communities has not been done in the Balkan countries. For decades, it has been a taboo subject so that there have not been many writings focused on the topic nor practical research. The civil war that was fought in the last decade of the twentieth century in countries of the former Yugoslavia caused terrible suffering to a large number of members of minority communities. In many cases, police actions were not impartial and professional. All the warring sides perpetrated crimes and brought anguish to minority groups. Very often, the police did not prevent crimes but closed their eyes to them, encouraged them, and even committed them. Only in a few cases have legal actions been taken in The Hague or in the home courts. The Balkan states have been trying lately to improve relations between the police and minorities and to introduce new standards of police activities.

Traditional Concept of Policing and Multiethnic Diversity

A long time ago, it was noticed that the traditional concept of policing and police organization—which is basically bureaucratized in a rigid hierarchical system—is not suitable to specific circumstances that are very obvious and easily noticeable in some local communities. Centralized management of the police has not produced good results in multinational and multiconfessional communities as it is neither suitable nor ready to adapt itself to diversities (Simonovic, 2006). The traditional concept of policing produces a system of police culture that leads to isolation and inability to conform to the circumstances of a particular community. "And the phenomenon involves an institution, the police that is a closed culture, almost monastic" (Bender, 1991, pp. 56–57). Chan (1996) reviews prevailing approaches to police culture, such as those outlined by Skolnick and Reiner, and suggests that they tend to regard it as monolithic, unchanging, and universal (Rowe & Garland, 2003). Many authors write about cynicism and a sense of isolation in police departments all over the world. Police officers in many departments band together for support and understanding. One result of this group identity is the police "code of silence" (Bender, 1991).

Police officers often confront people who are not only of a different race, but of a different ethnic and economic background. These social factors, combined with the nature of police work, often foster feelings of racial prejudice and cultural misunderstanding. It is not surprising that the vast majority of police brutality cases are committed by white police officers against nonwhite victims (Bender, 1991, p. 13). In the mid-1960s in America, there were a series of very violent urban ghetto riots that resulted in numerous deaths, thousands of injuries, and millions of dollars in damage. Most of these riots were triggered by incidents in which white officers were policing in black ghetto areas (Sullivan, 1989).

The traditional style of police work does not pay enough attention to establishing new, friendly relations with the community and to problem solving of these communities. It results in special problems in nationally and racially diversified social environments. In these social strata, police forces are often perceived as "occupying forces, racists or even fascists whose presence and practice threaten citizens in the community and increase further ethnic polarization" (Hüttermann, 2003, p. 388).

The few studies to examine these issues among adolescents suggest that juveniles have even fewer favorable attitudes toward the police than adults. Minority youths consistently express more negative views of the police than whites, and race/ethnicity was the strongest predictor of perception of fairness and police discriminations. The authors report that individuals who believe they were victims of racial profiling have more negative attitudes toward the police (Brunson & Miller, 2006). "Even good kids now see police as the enemy. They shun cops" (Bender, 1991, p. 65).

After it was realized that the classic policing style might be troublemaking and unacceptable in minority groups, "the western world" commenced to develop programs that improved relations between the police and those strata. A large number of the programs had no effect (many of them were very naive) as they did not speak of the problems that the minority groups were facing. Some pointed out the need for the police to be more sensitive to minorities. Various ways that would promote greater cooperation between the police and the community were sought (Goldstein, 1990). Police units concerned with public relations and civic representative bodies tried to reduce minorities' widespread dissatisfaction with the police (Eck & Spelman, 2000). Unfortunately, this problem has not yet been resolved.

Is Racial/Ethnic Discrimination System-Conditioned or an Individual Excess?

There is a dilemma as to whether racial/ethnic profiling is institutional or not. Most politicians, a large number of police leaders, and only a few scientists all over the world have denied racial/ethnic profiling in police work. For decades, in America, racist violence perpetrated by law-enforcement personnel has been covered up, or explained by job-related stress (which causes police brutality). Excessive police force against blacks has always been tolerated and is a regular method in the paramilitary style of fighting crime (Bender, 1991).

In France, race relations, ethnic discrimination, and racism have been neglected by most social scientists until recently. A culture of denial indeed characterizes French administration, including police (Body-Gendort, 2004). The French system is so immersed in an equalitarian and universalist ideology that it cannot perceive the problem of discrimination. Political parties, trends, movements, and people are blamed, but no one admits that the way in which French institutions function produces discrimination.

Some English politicians refused to accept scientists' critique that police conduct and racism against colored persons was *institutionally established* (institutional racism), arguing that racial prejudice was evident occasionally in the behavior of a few officers on the streets but that it was not the outcome of practices, culture, or more institutional phenomena. Screening out racist recruits and better training for new officers was recommended (Body-Gendort, 2004). The Stephen Lawrence murder (committed by hooligans) followed by inefficient, uninterested, and ineffective police performance demonstrated "a form of institutional racism" defined as "the collective failure of an organization to provide an appropriate and professional service to people because of their color, culture or ethnic origin" (MacPherson, 1999). The commissioner of the Metropolitan Police at the hearings acknowledged that "individual officers can be, and are overly racists," but he failed to accept that "institutional racism was a concept of direct relevance to his organization" (Body-Gendort, 2004, p. 137).

The former Yugoslavia (and other states in the Balkan region) always denied any discrimination that could be seen in the police treatment of national minorities and ethnic groups. If excessive police force was used in some incidents, it was justified by other reasons. These cases were covered up or were given a different political background that diminished the responsibility of official institutions, and subsequently police responsibility. There was neither scientific research nor official statistics. After the war operations—in the course of which there were extreme and various violations of minority human rights by the police forces, especially in the war zones—some attitudes and practices were changed. It should be pointed out that all sides in all states and regions that took part in the war operations have still not admitted that their police forces violated human rights institutionally during the war and police operations. At the same time, each involved side shifted the blame of institutional and police violation of human rights to the other side. Even if some cases of human rights violations have been admitted, or if some law suits against perpetrators have been brought (in cases of multiple murders of prisoners of war, children, and women), they are treated as single incidents.

One thing is certain. Any cover-up of single cases of minority rights violation, and any denial of institutional framework supporting racism and ethnic discrimination in a community, neither leads to progress nor gives the police an opportunity to become aware of their mistakes and to correct them. Denying the institutional framework of discrimination in a society neither leads up to a critical rethinking nor contributes to more egalitarian society building. On the other hand, it is obvious that paramilitary, central, and traditional concepts of the police open the door to police abuse of minority (race/ethnic) groups.

Basic Causes of Minority Group Discrimination

A society wishing to institute unbiased police work (based on respect of proclaimed human rights) and efficient police actions in multiracial/multinational communities is not limited only by a traditional concept of police organization. The fundamental determinant is the basic position of minorities within the majority community. Democratic (western) countries adopted international (commonly accepted) norms that protect minority human rights—but actually, as is often pointed out, it is everyday discrimination that is a real fact. Economic welfare of minority groups, their political power, and their influence over society are considerably weaker than those of members of the majority community. Economic, political, and social deprivation of minority groups (unemployment, bad urban conditions, economic endangered conditions, cultural differences, and prejudice) determine their marginal place in the community and lead them to poverty, isolation, segregation, and frustration. Such a position intensifies minority group revolt, extremism, terrorism, and criminal conduct, especially of young people.

All these events result in prejudice against minorities, lack of tolerance, reduced direct communication between majority and minority citizens, mutual lack of understanding, discriminatory conduct of the majority community, and the request that those who do not respect the values of a "democratic society" should be treated harshly. This "vicious circle" finally causes intensified police repression. Thus, the intensified police repression of the traditionally organized and militarized police arises as a consequence of the objectively neglected and stigmatized minorities and racial diversities in a society. When an excess occurs, it is very easy to blame "a frustrated individual from the police" for brutality, but rarely does one blame the police organization or the actual causes that lie in the society as a whole.

Waters (1990) stresses that despite the progress of the past three decades, racism is still endemic in the United States. Yet for many white Americans, for whom race plays little or no role in their everyday lives, race has little meaning. This social reality creates a huge barrier for teaching about racism (Husiman, Martinez, & Wilson, 2005). David Bender (1991, p. 65) noticed that "the bulk of police forces are white males of the middle class. Yet we send them into large urban centres that are black and Hispanic and poor, with no understanding of the cultural differences, to enforce white, middle-class moral laws. Doesn't that create a clash?" Arun Kundnai has written in a similar way about the United Kingdom (Amin, 2002, pp. 4–5):

> The fires that burned across Lancashire and Yorkshire through the summer of 2001 signaled the rage of young Pakistanis and Bangladeshis of the second and third generations, deprived of futures, hemmed in all sides by racism, failed by their own leaders and representatives and unwilling to stand by us, first fascists, and then police officers, invaded their streets ... It was the violence of communities fragmented by colour lines, class lines, and police lines. It was the violence of hopelessness. It was the violence of the violated ... The trigger was the sheer accumulated anger and frustration of pockets of Pakistani and Bangladeshi young men with their life circumstances and their marginalization, the paternalism of their so-called community elders, vilification in the media, heavy-handed or intensive policing, and the incursion of "outsider" claimants.

According to a piece of research conducted in England after racial riots in Brixton, there were several characteristics common to areas where riots occurred: racial disadvantage and discrimination; unemployment—especially among young blacks; urban deprivation; political exclusion; decline of civil consent; and hostility toward the police (Body-Gendort, 2004). The creation of negative relations between police and ethnic minorities in Brixton came from police stereotypes of blacks as criminals or drug offenders and from fundamental ideas in the culture of policing about the absolute control of a geographical territory. The report recommended that the police should tackle racial prejudice and harassment, improve their methods of policing inner-city multiracial areas, and develop new methods of managing urban disorder.

Research conducted in Australia shows a typical stereotyping of minorities as either high-achieving, law-abiding "model minorities" or threatening, alien criminals. The intersection of youth and membership in a minority ethnic or racial group problematizes the relationship between police and young people of Indo-Chinese background (Dixon & Maher, 2002). The popular media have constructed an image of a group that is alien, threatening, dismissive of "Australian values," and linked to organized crime. It suggests that Vietnamese communities in particular differ from "normal Australian" communities in attitudes toward violence, the value of human life, police, and the law.

Similar or almost identical problems arise in other countries constituting western democratic societies such as France, Canada, Germany, and so on when the question concerning police work in minority and racial/ethnic communities is raised (Tanovich, 2006). Police work in a diverse society is limited by global economic, social, political, religious, and cultural characteristics that exist in a society. It is necessary to have an influence on basic factors of discrimination that exist in a society (economic, political, social, cultural, and legal), although this is a very slow, long-lasting process and hard work. It is essential to be realistic and admit that there are participants belonging to all sides who are not honest and who have different, very often incompatible, opposite, and extreme goals.

If a society really wants to enhance police work in multinational communities in the shortest possible period, in spite of all the diversities and difficulties in the given society, it is necessary to emphasize the following strategies: (1) To operate on the general basic conditions that make a social framework of racism and discrimination in a society. Reforming of the police can only be successful when the focus is not only on police culture, but also on the external milieu of the police, which inevitably forms the functional conditions of day-to-day policing (Hüttermann, 2003). (2) To introduce antidiscriminatory regulations. (3) To make organizational changes in the police that will be adjusted to the work in a multinational community. (4) To study foreign practice, and to adopt and adapt foreign solutions that have proved to be efficient in other communities.

Community Policing as a Chance of Improving Policing in a Diverse Society

"Can police change?" Monique Marks (2003, p. 236) puts forward this question. It requires a move away from a partisan and repressive police force to a police agency that provides impartial service and has a firm adherence to human rights principles. Such a shift demands change at three levels—structure, behavior, and attitude.

Today, the only promising alternative is the concept of community policing. Only community policing gives a chance to change the role of police from "police force" to "police service." Unlike the classic concept, in which the police keep their distance from a community and in which they are alienated from minority communities and opposed to them, in the concept of community policing they aim at the *improvement of positive relations with a community and at constituting an effective partnership*, which is a completely different notion of the approach to police activities.

The notion that there is a connection between public perception of the police and their ability to achieve goals and objectives is reflected in the British ideal of "policing by consent." Simply stated, this notion holds that the police can only achieve their goals and objectives when they have public support and cooperation (Schafer, Huebner, & Bynum, 2003). Police often rely on the citizenry in the performance of their duties, and community residents are more likely to cooperate when they view the police positively and with legitimacy. Negative citizen perceptions may threaten the efficacy of community policing efforts. Consequently, if organizations are going to enact community policing, they must be aware that negative contacts with the public may hamper the level of success they achieve. The police need to maximize positive voluntary contacts with the public and minimize negative interactions.

Community policing implements *problem-oriented work* in neighborhoods and society. It establishes an approach that involves all residents of a community. It neither isolates nor discriminates individuals or even whole entities as conflict-oriented policing does. Community policing introduces a team approach. This is an approach in which the community and its police work together to carefully analyze problems, in order to develop and implement solutions tailored to those problems. This approach brings police officers closer to the community (Bender, 1991). Community policing includes many activities such as problem-oriented work, meetings with citizens, discussing problems, improving communications, and using police foot patrols that can decrease police brutality. Community policing is also a deterrent to the improper use of force.

A huge security problem in minority communities is the high rate of criminal activities of its individual members. Facing a life of economic deprivation and belonging to a different pattern of cultural values, some members of minority communities, mainly youth, adopt criminal behavior as a model and a solution to their problems. An often repeated justification for the harsh performance of police in multinational communities is the war on drugs and the war on terrorism. An unselected use of force and repression that does not make any difference between a criminal individual person or an individual person from the community but involves all the members of the community and equates them with potential or actual criminals is counterproductive because it makes a united front of one against the other. On the one hand, the police, majority public, and the media see the minority population as potential drug dealers and terrorists; on the other hand, all members of a minority group feel stigmatized, suspected, and endangered, which inevitably leads to ethnic (racial) polarization. Taking into account that the classic concept of police work is fundamentally reactive, that it is not problem oriented, not individualized in accord with the problems, and that it does not tend to establish partnerships with the community in order to notice and solve problems before they escalate, it can be concluded that the accomplishments of this concept are very limited. Basically, it is "conflict-oriented policing."

Murray (2006) cautions that after September 11, the so-called "war on terror" had the potential to distance police from the rest of the community and undervalue the principles of community policing and its emphasis on prevention. Some governments have put pressure on police commissioners to adopt (or revert to) the more traditional model in the context of the so-called "war on terror." Traditional policing is authoritative and has the tendency to distance police from the rest of the community. National security, of course, is important but police commissioners should be alert to the inappropriateness of moving back to traditional policing, for to do so would be counterproductive. Such a move would tend to reduce the high standing in society policing has enjoyed under a community policing philosophy (Murray, 2006).

By establishing tight connections with minority communities, a partnership approach, and problem-oriented work, community policing is better able to separate perpetrators of potential crimes from citizens who have a clear criminal record. Apparent goodwill and readiness of the police to help members of a minority community and their families, and not only to arrest or apply nonselective force, should attract lawful members of society and encourage them to cooperate. In this way, police work strives to achieve legitimacy in minority communities.

Martin Innes notes that neighborhood-policing processes can be used for detecting subtle indicators of suspicion that people may develop about activities connected to terrorism in their communities. Better relationships with members of the minority community also provide a communication channel into these communities to counteract rumors. The number of contacts that the police maintain needs to be increased in an effort to monitor the activities of people who might be a risk or at risk. Thus, building a network of community intelligence contacts provides a more effective way of maintaining surveillance over groups and communities that are especially hard for the police to penetrate either overtly or covertly (Innes, 2006).

Establishing International Standards of Policing in Multiethnic Societies

Europe has made efforts to create international standards based on positive practices in police work in multiethnic communities. The standards are founded on the bases of international conventions regulating human rights. Since this problem is very complex and specific, some international documents and recommendations dealing exclusively with the introduction of standards for police work in multiethnic communities are being adopted. We believe that *the Rotterdam Charter*, one of the first documents, and *Recommendations on Policing in Multi-Ethnic Societies*, one of the latest, deserve our special attention.

The Rotterdam Charter document was designed at an international conference on "Policing for a multi-ethnic society" held in Rotterdam (May–June 1996). The main objective of this Charter is to enhance organizational commitment to the issue of policing a multiethnic society. The first requirement is a clear mission statement for the organization specifying its commitment to equal treatment and to combatting racist and xenophobic violence. The Rotterdam Charter emphasizes the need for partnership among the police, nongovernmental organizations (NGOs), and local authorities, but most importantly it assists police organizations throughout Europe to respond to ethnic diversity in a positive and proactive manner. The Charter sets out the principles on which this response should be based, together with the main actions that are required to turn these principles into a reality. The Rotterdam Charter covers five different topics: (1) recruitment and retention, (2) training, (3) implementation of antidiscrimination laws, (4) building bridges between ethnic minorities and the police, and (5) avoiding criminalizing migrants.

A very important international legal act has been passed recently. This is *Recommendations on Policing in Multi-Ethnic Societies* (2006) designed in February 2006 by the Office of the High Commissioner on National Minorities (HCNM). The position of HCNM has been established by the Organization for Security and Cooperation in Europe (OSCE) in its Helsinki Decisions of July 1992. This mandate was created largely in reaction to the situation in former Yugoslavia, which some feared would be repeated elsewhere in Europe, especially among countries in transition to democracy.

The recommendations aim to provide states with some practical guidance in developing policies and law in accordance with international norms and standards, and based on international experience and best practice that can balance and meet the needs and interests of all sectors of the population, including those of persons belonging to national minorities. The recommendations are divided into six subheadings, which group the 23 individual recommendations: (1) general principles, (2) recruitment and representation,

(3) training and professional support, (4) engaging with ethnic communities, (5) operational practices, and (6) prevention and management of conflict.

In addition to the above-mentioned documents, it is necessary to mention the *Action Plan on Improving the Situation of Roma and Sinti within OSCE Area*, designed by OSCE 2003 (Action Plan, 2003). This document suggests some strategic measures that are important for police work (developing antidiscrimination legislation as well as establishing antidiscrimination bodies, ombudsman offices, commissions for combatting discrimination, police disciplinary commissions, and other relevant bodies that can alleviate tensions between Roma and Sinti and non-Roma communities). A particular headline of the document is devoted to police management in protection/security, equal treatment of these categories of persons with regard to others, as well as overcoming the gap between international standards and existing police practices in some countries. It is also recommended that, besides the state, national, and local police, the media, representatives of Roma and Sinti, NGOs, and OSCE should also be involved in these activities.

OSCE activities related to the enhancement and standardization of police work all over the European area are very intensive and important. The document entitled *Guidebook on Democratic Policing* should also be mentioned because, among other things, it gives important guidelines on police work in multinational communities of European countries (*Guidebook on Democratic Policing*, 2006).

One of the latest and most promising practices is *the implementation of antidiscriminatory regulations* relating to all aspects of the minority position in a society, so that some members of minority communities are employed with the police. In this way, the minority position within the police organization will be improved (Body-Gendort, 2004). Another modern practice is the formation of *unique and standardized databases recording all incidents and criminal offenses based on a racial and ethnic basis* resulting from the practices of police actions and the penal policy of courts that have competence in such cases. A good practice, which should be taken as a role model, comprises drafting a *national plan for the enhancement of police work in multinational communities*. For example, the Home Secretary (United Kingdom) drew up a national plan for police race relations. It included a commitment and important strategic recommendations: race relations should be at the center of their work, changing the culture of the police as well as its practices. The police were required to regain minorities' trust and to tackle the problem of institutional racism (Body-Gendort, 2004). Home Secretary's Action Plan (1999) has its explicit targets and milestones established for improving the recruitment, retention, and progression of minority ethnic staff across criminal justice services (Phillips, 2005).

One example of good world practice is the formation of *different professional associations*. Some police officers from minority backgrounds may feel that there are benefits in coming together to form their own professional associations. Police authorities should, in principle, support such initiatives and be willing to facilitate their establishment. The formation of such associations is a human right and can provide mutual personal support for minority police, especially when they are small in number and geographically isolated. They can also provide a channel of communication between police authorities and police officers from minority backgrounds and be a source of valuable advice to the authorities on minority issues (*Recommendations on Policing in Multi-Ethnic Societies*, 2006).

Police *organization adjusting to* the needs of multinational, multireligious, and multicultural milieus is also an activity targeting problem reduction. Among other things, it implies that representatives of members of all minority groups, religious congregations, and NGOs dealing with human rights protection should be involved in community policing projects. It also entails support in employing members of minority groups with the police (Sanders, 2000). This thesis has been supported by good results and practices. Research has confirmed that the perception of police of the same minority affiliation differs, to a degree, from the perception of police belonging to the majority group (Brunson & Miller, 2006).

Special attention is being paid to *the communication advancement* of the police and citizens living in multinational, multireligious, and multicultural milieus. Projects on multiethnic (racial) tolerance confirm that numerous efforts have been made around the world aiming at the improvement of relations between the police and a minority community, and its inclusion in a majority society. Many projects have produced good results so that they should be taken into account as they comprise various forms of companionship, roundtable sessions, regular meetings of the neighboring police and citizens, youth sports clubs, entertainment centers, disco clubs, where they can communicate and exchange ideas, child-care facilities, youth projects, different scholarships, and so on. Suggested next measures include community forums, public meetings, community advisory boards, joint police–community workshops, community contact points at police stations, and dedicated patrol officers regularly visiting particular communities (*Recommendations on Policing in Multi-Ethnic Societies*, 2006).

The police in multinational communities are expected to learn various cultural and communicational patterns typical for these communities, which is the fundamental condition of successful police performance (Palmiotto, 2000). Here is an example of an experiment of the Holland police conducted in several cities. The experiment included the strategy of establishing positive relations and problem-oriented work with young Moroccans inclined to crime. The program consisted of many synchronized activities such as establishment of direct contacts and companionship, face-to-face talks relating to their problems, building a network of aid and surveillance on teenagers (in which the parents were included), schools, a center for social work, giving lectures on the cases when the police may arrest them, and police training concerning specific features of communication with such persons (Wouter, Stol, & Bervoetes, 2002).

Improving the system of police outer and inner control connected to issues of police minority relations is another method that should better the position of minority group members hired by the police. It is important that effective internal complaints mechanisms are in place, so that police officers who experience discrimination do not have to endure such behavior in silence. Managers need to encourage minorities to make complaints when they experience discrimination or other forms of ethnically motivated behavior, so that they are aware of such problems and can deal with them directly (*Recommendations on Policing in Multi-Ethnic Societies*, 2006). Heterogeneous commissions are being appointed to judge complaints related to race or ethnic discrimination within the police or between the police and a minority community, or changes to the police discipline code, so that racially prejudiced behavior was classified as a particular offense, which seeks organizational change via reconfiguring police culture (Rowe, 2003). For example, in the United Kingdom, the Race Relations (amendment) Act 2000 was passed. Initiatives included reviewing and assessing policies and practices to assess their impact on race equality, rigorous ethnic monitoring for particular service elements, and improving the recruitment, retention, and career progression of minority ethnic staff (Phillips, 2005, p. 368).

Special attention is being paid to education of *the police working in a multinational, multiconfessional, and multicultural environment.* Old programs are being critically reexamined, and a large number of improvements are being integrated in police education at all levels. Among other things, representatives of minority groups having (good or bad) experiences with the police and NGOs dealing with the improvement of minority status are being incorporated in the educational process and various workshops (Huisman, Martinez, & Wilson, 2005).

In order to define police professional standards, *codes of conduct* need to be drawn up, and competences that enable the professional to achieve those standards need to be identified. This principle should be applied in the context of police training, and in particular to police training for working in multiethnic environments (*Recommendations on Policing in Multi-Ethnic Societies*, 2006). It is particularly important that individual states draw up codes of conduct and specific practice with regard to policing in multiethnic environments due to the particular challenges such work may entail and its potentially controversial nature. Examples of potentially challenging and controversial policing tasks include managing overt ethnic conflict, deescalating ethnic tensions, conducting stop-and-search operations in ethnically sensitive areas, or conducting police operations generally in minority residential areas. Detailed codes of practice should provide specific guidance and support for police who undertake such tasks (*Recommendations on Policing in Multi-Ethnic Societies*, 2006).

Policing in Multiethnic Societies in Former Yugoslavia

Police work in multinational communities in former Yugoslavia passed through three phases. *The first phase* started in 1918 when the Kingdom of Yugoslavia was founded and when all the peoples who had taken part in its formation had been given constituent status and the same rights all over the newly formed state (Serbs, Croats, and Slovenians). During World War II, when the country was occupied by Germans, the country's territory was disintegrated so that some areas separated and became independent units, which simultaneously resulted in a multidimensional war: the civil war between, up to then, constituent people and national minorities, the struggle against German conquerors, and the Communist Party power struggle. After World War II, the whole territory of the (first) Yugoslavia was saved, but with new social and political system (the period of communist Yugoslavia). Besides Serbs, Croats, and Slovenians, some large national groups were promoted to the status of constituent peoples such as Muslims, Macedonians, and Montenegrins.

National equality of all peoples and national minorities were promoted strongly until 1989, when socialist Yugoslavia collapsed. Most national minorities were equally appointed and included into the central and local authorities; they could use their mother tongue on all levels. Minorities had the same opportunity and right of finding a job, and taking part in politics and self-governing bodies. Official ideology emphasized "unity and brotherhood of nations and national minorities" as one of the main political values. This was necessary due to the mixture of national groups within former Yugoslavia.

The basic function of the police (they were then called militia) in socialist Yugoslavia was to maintain the socialist political system, while the second function was to prevent crime. Basically, the police was party and ideologically oriented so that it greatly resembled militia forces of other states of Eastern Europe. The idea of a socialist society development was dominant and it united all political resources so that the national and religious diversity was subdued and kept in the background. The whole state, authorities, and police were brought together under the same banner of the Communist Party. In this way, ideas about socialism, unity, and brotherhood had control over separatist forces and ideas. The dissolution of the Yugoslav Communist League in the late 1980s opened the door to nationalism, religious bigotry, narrow-mindedness, intolerance, separatist ideas, state dismantling, and civil wars.

During the period of the former socialist Yugoslavia, police were decentralized and special attention was drawn to ethnic equality in the police. At that time, all nations and national minorities were equally represented in the police at all levels of police organization, from top to bottom. Then, local police practiced in their work many elements of the current concept of community policing (by employing representatives of minorities with the police, holding meetings with citizens, supporting contacts, improving their relations with members of all ethnic groups, and participating in sports and cultural events). Owing to the above-mentioned conduct and activities, the police enjoyed high reputation. They reacted strictly to nationalistic incidents. During the 46-year existence of socialist Yugoslavia, there were only serious clashes between the nations that were cleared up primarily by political means, very rarely by the use of a limited police force.

In the course of that period, only the status of Roma communities was completely neglected and marginalized. Roma did not have the status of a national minority but only the status of an ethnic group. Actually, they were excluded from social life, lived in very bad conditions in shanty towns, or had a nomadic way of life. Society showed strong prejudice against this category of citizens, but this attitude was considered to be normal. Roma had the same position in all countries all over Europe.

The second phase of police approach to minority issues took place in the last decade of the twentieth century, during the civil wars and when former Yugoslavia was falling apart. Some republics of former Yugoslavia had voted for secession and proclaimed their independence. Some people/nations homogenized on national or ethnic basis and some opposing trends emerged. One nation was supporting the separation and formation of a new national state, while the others were striving to maintain federal Yugoslavia and links with their mother countries. That is why the newly formed national minorities (up to then they had had the status of a nation) homogenized in the newly set-up states and were trying bitterly to join their parent country. Political and territorial enclaves were formed by Serbs in Croatia, Serbs in Bosnia and Herzegovina (B&H), and Croats in Bosnia and Herzegovina, while Kosovo Albanians attempted to separate and form their own independent state. Civil war broke out in Croatia, Bosnia and Herzegovina, and later in Kosovo and Metohia, which resulted in an enormous exodus of millions of refugees who started moving to their mother countries.

As former Yugoslavia was falling apart at the national seams, the police forces of the newly formed states were growing into nationally pure police. National communities formed their own national police on the territories on which they held political power. Thus the police of the Serbian people, the police of the Croatian people, and Muslim police were formed on the territory of Bosnia and Herzegovina. As one nation was at war with other nation(s), the police were used as part of military forces carrying out classic military tasks. Police maintained public order and kept peace in the territories under their control. After the national police had been incorporated into the national armed forces, the police were taken under strict central control and command, militarized, bureaucratized, and stripped of their peacetime activities.

The very essence of the tragedy of the people (and their police) of former Yugoslavia lay in the socialist-ideology phase characterized by a lack of strong democratic institutions and the domination of the Communist Party over the police. This phase was followed by state breakdown and a period of growing separatist and nationalistic ideology. The police of the newly formed states or enclaves were not ready to change quickly. Under dominant personnel and strategic influence imposed by nationalistic politics under the war conditions and in the war environment, the socialist police transformed from a servant of the Communist Party into the guard of national states and nationalistic ideologies.

All these elements have contributed to abuse by different police forces in the regions, polarization of the police force of all states, the increased rate of crimes committed by the police, unprofessional conduct of the police, inadequate training and selection of personnel, and expansion of organized crime in the Balkans. In the division of people, religions, and cultures, national minorities got the worst of it, especially in the regions of war operations, as they were the victims of numerous war crimes and other criminal offenses. War crimes committed by majority groups against minorities in some communities resulted in retaliation to other communities so that the spiral of violence was increasing in quantity and brutality.

Instead of preventing violence against minority groups, police of the newly established entities seldom took effective action. Media and politicians supported violence and intolerance, while the paramilitary and parapolice forces were perpetrating them. The regular police forces that did not take part in violence and numerous crimes did little or nothing to stop them.

A drastic example of bad criminal intelligence and police antiterrorist strategy in multinational communities is the example of the conduct of Serbian police in Kosovo during the period immediately preceding escalation of the crises. In the 1980s, before Milošević came to power, the Kosovo police were multiethnic. Serbs and Albanians participated at all levels of police. In mixed communities, the number of policemen of each nationality matched the national distribution of residents. Most Albanians employed with the police were loyal to the then Yugoslavia. Criminal intelligence operations successfully covered all sources of terrorist and separatist activities. When Milošević came to power in Serbia and when nationalism started growing, the majority of Albanian policemen left the police forces of Serbia and formed their own Albanian police. During the 1990s, Kosovo was supervised by two police forces—Serbian and ethnically pure Albanian police, which acted illegally. While Serbs were confident about their (official) police, Albanians experienced them as the Serbian occupation army, hated them, and organized terrorist attacks on them. Channels of communication, within the security system, between Serbs and Albanians were completely broken. In this way, security and antiterrorist control turned only into repression.

The third period of police work in multiethnic communities began after the wars had ended and when democratic changes emerged in the states formed on the ruins of the former socialist Yugoslavia. This movement continues; at present it is characterized by opposite processes, some of which slow down while others speed up police reform. The processes that slow down police reform in the states of former Yugoslavia are backward relics of the previous period surviving in the collective and individual life of these communities. They are numerous and limiting, and they comprise nationalism, traditionalism, narrow-mindedness, unwillingness to make some changes and resistance to some changes in politics, the society as a whole, and some changes in the police. Economic crisis, unemployment, poverty, and corruption induce negative personnel selection and harden police upgrading and prosperity of the society. They narrow an individual's views and spread the lack of hope and national threat. Many political, economic, and criminalized centers of power, even today, seize their chance in backwardness, isolation from the international community, and refusal to accept world standards in the society, economy, and police.

There are progressive forces in all newly established states at all levels and in all backgrounds. These forces seize their chance and future in cooperation with the world and Europe, fostering world standards being applied in most societies, economies, and the police. It is the international community that influences the adoption of international standards in police reform in the Balkan states. In Bosnia, the largest influence has been the European Police Mission, while in Serbia it is the influence of the OSCE. Their marked impact on the induction of new standards, and current changes, relating to police work in multinational communities is going to be dealt with in the following part of the chapter.

Policing in Multiethnic Society in Republika Srpska and Bosnia

After the Dayton Peace Accords had been signed, and especially after the international peacekeeping forces had come to Bosnia and Herzegovina, such as the International Police Task Force (IPTF) and the European Union Police Mission (EUPM), the reform processes in police organizations of Bosnia started. Recognizing the importance of establishing professional democratic police forces that respect international standards, human rights, and fundamental freedoms, UN Security Council Resolution 1035

(December 21, 1995) articulated the mandate for the IPTF, which developed a three-point plan concentrated on (1) restructuring a postwar and post-paramilitary police force, (2) reforming the police through training, selection, certification, and depoliticized procedures, and (3) democratizing the police forces by establishing a depoliticized, impartial, accountable, multi-ethnic police force that abides by the principles of community policing. Following deployment in late 1995 to early 1996, the IPTF's initial activities during the Implementation Force (IFOR) phase of the peacekeeping operation focused on monitoring local police authorities for compliance with internationally accepted standards in their daily operations and treatment of minorities (King, 2001, pp. 37–38).

At the end of 2004, the EUPM and Republika Srpska (RS) police started to implement the project entitled "Strengthening the local police capabilities with respect to the security of returnees." The project particularly encourages returnees of different ethnic and minority groups. The operational objectives of the project are not only to establish a standardized system of maintaining the data encompassing returnees and refugees, but also to increase trust in the police, select police officers who will work with the community, and develop public relations concerning returnee problems. In the course of project implementation, security information relating to returnees and refugees was gathered and special attention was paid to preventive actions by sending larger police forces to areas to which refugees of all nationalities were returning. In a relatively short period of time, great help was given to the prevention of victimization of minority groups and returnees.

Mission (IPTF) has launched important initiatives to accelerate changes in the ethnic composition of local police, improve interentity police cooperation, depoliticize local police administrations, and advance the establishment of court of police. Agreement on Police Restructuring and Democratization in RS (1998) limits the number of RS police to 8,500. Furthermore, the Agreement established an ethnic quota that requires, by December 2000, that 25% of all new RS police recruits should be minorities (21% Bosniak, 3% Croat) (King, 2001, pp. 41–42). The latest indices show that 6,766 police employees consisting of 512 Bosniaks (6.9%), 69 Croats (0.9%), and 40 members of minority ethnic groups (0.5%) were hired by the Ministry of Interior of RS in 2006. In total, the percentage of police officers who are not Serbs amounts to less than 8%.

Although considerable advancement has been made since the Dayton Peace Accords signing, it is not yet satisfactory owing to the general circumstances in RS and the whole of Bosnia and Herzegovina. Due to economic problems, members of the police forces in RS have considerably lower salaries than police members in the B&H federation and the District of Brčko, so that policemen of Bosniak and Croatian nationality are not interested in employment with the Ministry of Interior of RS. More and more frequently, members of non-Serbian nationality who graduated from the Police Academy, after a short-time work for the Ministry of Interior of RS leave it and join other police organizations of B&H such as State Border Service of B&H, State Agency for Investigation and Protection of B&H (SIPA), and other security agencies. Low salaries have caused a large loss of educated personnel, regardless of nationality.

The Bosniak federation has a quota to hire 20% of Serbs and 8% of other nationalities in its police force. But these quotas have not been fulfilled yet. For example, only 5% of the required number of Serbs was hired by October 1999 (King, 2001, pp. 41–42).

Police training in Bosnia and Herzegovina was carried out by a large number of police coming from different countries such as Germany, Austria, Sweden, and France. It is important to mention the International Criminal Investigative Training Assistance Program (ICITAP). This U.S. Justice Department program was largely responsible for drawing up and distributing guidelines and standards for "democratic policing," including orientation to democratic principles adherence to the code of conduct worthy of public trust; protection of life; public service; respect for human dignity; and nondiscrimination. IPTF organized completion of induction training involving an introduction to "international standards for policing, human rights" (King, 2001, p. 39).

In order to professionalize the police, the quality of training and professional advancement has been raised in the Ministry of Interior of RS. At the High School of Interior Affairs in Banja Luka, 819 students of the basic police training have acquired the first degree of the Police Academy since 1999. The majority of them, 548, are Bosniaks, others including 202 Serbs, 53 Croats, and 16 students of other nationalities. At the moment, the 11th class is being attended by 60 trainees, out of whom 37 are Bosniaks, 20 Serbs, and 1 Croat. In order to further professionalization, and especially to promote performance in multiethnic environments, a large number of seminars and courses have been organized for management personnel and police officers.

In spite of intensive activities in police training in RS and Bosnia on the whole, there are some objective obstacles.

Training post-conflict police forces is a difficult task, as the orientation of the police may not be different from the military. It is common phenomenon that during the course of conflict, police forces often assume military roles. With the cessation of conflicts, they are characteristically inept in professional and technical skills, and they may continue to carry out human rights abuses and have strong loyalties to political or ethnic affiliation. Professionalization processes for police seek to achieve: reorganization, training, internal oversight, external civilian oversight, higher standards, increased technical capabilities, implementing codes of conduct and international standards etc. It is not to say that police training is purely a technical task, as it may take a generation or more to change attitudes. The strategic documents say that "The police must realign their missions from the protection of the state to the protection of citizens' right" (King, 2001, p. 39).

Members of the Ministry of Interior of RS are devoted to the development of communication and cooperation with minority groups, trying to build mutual confidence and trust at the local level and at the entity level. There are many examples showing that good international relationships have been established in local communities of the RS area. Noticeable progress was made in the Prijedor municipality, during the implementation of the pilot project "Police work in a community and the community security," which was carried out from the second half of 2003 till December 2005. In Prijedor, members of the Unit for Police work in a community, together with sector leaders, other police officers, and management staff, have greatly improved common life in this heterogeneous national environment.

In comparison with the period before 2004, when several incidents on the grounds of nationality were recorded (attacks on religious facilities), such incidents have not been recorded for almost two years in the municipality of Prijedor. The security state has been improved in the municipalities of Kozarac and Ljubija, where the largest number of refugees has returned. Now, weekly football matches between the police and the residents as well as casual companionship in Ljubija are normal events.

The municipality of Brod recorded an important improvement, too. During 2001, there were many burglaries in the houses of Croat refugees who were rebuilding their houses at that time. Better police preventive performance and the residents themselves completely rooted out such incidents so that the local parish office sent an official acknowledgment to the Brod police and thanked them for their successful cooperation.

A major step toward the improvement of cooperation in multiethnic environments was made by a higher degree of transparency in police work. All citizens have at their disposal different mechanisms that help them in influencing and directing the work of police officers, asking for the help of competent bodies in cases of law breaking or discrimination, and reporting such incidents publicly or anonymously to the local police stations. At the same time, police patrols have been frequent in mixed communities. The patrolling teams are carefully selected so that they are ethnically mixed.

Up to now, 30 municipal security forums have been formed over the area of RS. The municipal security forums are made up of representatives of all ethnic and confessional communities and are organized on a multidisciplinary basis. Their goal is to discuss the items on the agenda in a problem-oriented way as well as to spread multiethnic tolerance and understanding. Citizens are encouraged to take part in the regular meetings of these operating groups so as to resolve numerous local security problems, and to report all criminal offenses, incidents, as well as any forms of harassment grounded on interethnic hatred, discrimination, and intolerance.

Members of the police of the Ministry of Interior of RS regularly attend all public meetings in their environments and take part in advisory associations, common workshops, roundtable conferences, and soapboxes, while in the offices for Police work in a community they come into direct contact with local residents. The implementation of the project "A school policeman" contributed to improvement of police activities in this area, owing to direct contact with pupils, their parents, and teachers. Cooperation with other social institutions, centers for social work, courts, and bodies of local administration and local self-government has also been improved, so that adequate police, legal, or humane help is available to victims of interethnic discrimination.

Police members, special police units particularly, are trained regularly to acquire the necessary theoretical and practical knowledge so as to be able to intervene properly, professionally, impartially, and using minimal force in case of conflict situations such as civilian clashes or potential interethnic incidents. The Information Bureau of the Ministry of Interior of RS takes many steps and actions to open the police toward the public, to obtain fuller cooperation with the media, and to persuade inhabitants of mixed ethnic communities to live together. It is worth mentioning that lately some mechanisms of constant surveillance and monitoring of police activities in the community and the performance of members of the Ministry of Interior of RS in nationally heterogeneous environments have been set up.

A step that had to have far-reaching effects was the formation of a working group to draw up "Strategies for police work in a community in B&H." The group was formed in May 2006, and comprised representatives of all security agencies in B&H. A final version of the draft has been made recently, and it should become a basis for the future work of the police in a community in B&H as well as in RS. This document incorporates four basic strategic goals:

- To improve police capabilities in order to prevent and reduce the crime rate, giving priority to problems that cause insecurity of citizens and the community.
- To upgrade the competence and skills of police management so that they can manage changes successfully.
- To enhance the cooperation with the community by promoting partnership between all subjects in the community and by rebuilding links between them.
- To build up mutual trust of the citizens and the police through cooperation and participation in activities of consulting, communication, and involvement of citizens.

Table 14.1 Police Discrimination

In the course of their activities …	Number of Those Polled	
	f	%
The police do not discriminate against anybody	229	38.68
The police discriminate on the grounds of national and religious affiliation	24	4.05
The police discriminate on the grounds of party loyalty	17	2.87
The police discriminate on the grounds of social status	121	20.44
The police discriminate on the grounds of sex and age	39	6.59
The police discriminate against everybody except against policemen	32	5.41
Other	41	6.93
I do not know/I have no attitude	71	11.99
Reserved comment on that	18	3.04
Total	592	100.00

In an attempt to obtain at least a partial insight into the effects of achieved changes, the High School of Internal Affairs in Banja Luka conducted an opinion poll in several towns in RS in 2006. The answers to many questions were obtained, but we present only two. One question was: "In the course of their activities, the police discriminate/do not discriminate against …?" (Table 14.1).

Out of 592 citizens who were polled, 39% said that the police do not discriminate against anybody. It can be concluded that most citizens believe that the police tend to indulge in various kinds of discrimination, among which discrimination on the grounds of social status is most prominent. Out of 592 polled citizens, only 24 of them (4%) are convinced that the police discriminate on the grounds of national and religious affiliation.

Another question was: "What are your experiences with the police?" The distribution of answers on the basis of nationality is given in Table 14.2.

The obtained answers assert that the experiences of members of various nationalities with the police of RS are positive in the largest percentage. There is no doubt that great advancement has been made, especially if the experiences from the last decade are taken as zero points from which the reform processes have started.

The report on the state of human rights in Bosnia and Herzegovina for 2005 refers to the police twice in a favorable context and their activities and actions with reference to resolving and preventing crime offenses containing elements of assaults on members of minority communities or their property. The report stated that the police managed to greatly facilitate the security of returnees. The only critical remark was that the projected quotas on

Table 14.2 Experiences with the Police

Nationality	Excellent	Relatively Good	Mainly Good, Though I Had Some Bad Ones	Mainly Bad	I Had Only Bad Experiences	Other	I Do Not Know/I Have No Attitude	Not Declared	Total
Serbian	50	206	158	37	6	8	15	4	484
Bosniak	11	27	27	4	3	1	0	0	73
Croatian	2	7	5	0	0	0	0	0	14
Others	3	8	5	0	1	0	0	0	17
Noncommittal	0	3	0	0	0	0	0	1	4
Total	66	251	195	41	10	9	15	5	592

2. Question: What are Your Experiences with the Police?

employment of members of minority nations with the police had not been ful-filled (*Report on the Status of Human Rights in Bosnia and Herzegovina*, 2005).

Aside from that, the state of human rights on the whole territory of Bosnia was estimated as very difficult and not satisfactory. It was stated that returnees and displaced persons were in a rather difficult position. There are no precise records about such persons. It is estimated that around 2.2 million persons changed their address of residence during the war in Bosnia. The return of refugees has been very slow, and in many cases the return is tempo-rary because they return in order to sell their property. Only the aged have been returning. There are no records of the volume of real estate exchanged or sold by returnees. It is even a greater problem for returnees to find a job. There are cases where local persons in power hamper refugees from return-ing to their homes, and in every way possible—trying to find some excuse for delay—make the life of returnees difficult by not supplying refugee settle-ments with water or electricity.

Only about 9,000 Serbs have returned home out of 39,000 Serbs who escaped from Herzegovina during the war. Today, about 10% of Bosniaks live in Bijeljina. Before the war they made up 36.7% of the inhabitants of this town. About 20,000 Bosniaks have returned to Prijedor, while there were around 50,000 Bosniaks in the town previously. During the war, 82,000 Serbs ran away from the Tuzla canton, and only about 8,000 of them returned.

A very difficult position of the Roma population in Bosnia is pointed out in the 2005 *Report on the Status of Human Rights in Bosnia and Herzegovina*. Only 1.5% of working-age Roma are employed in comparison with 50% employed before the war. Roma's living conditions do not even meet minimal standard. In most cases, they live in shacks, without sanitary facilities, running water, or electricity. Only 15% of Roma children complete compulsory ele-mentary education, and, as a rule, girls drop out of school in the 5th form of elementary education. The Roma illiteracy rate is very high. Most have neither health insurance nor any legal income.

In summary, it can be concluded that the process of police reforms relat-ing to minority issues in Bosnia and RS has made noticeable progress. However, regardless of new mechanisms of control, education, police train-ing, and employment of new methods of cooperation between the police and minorities, the situation is still very problematic. The results show that the process of improvement of police work in multiethnic communities is better in the police teams that gradually, but successfully, foster the community policing project, an example of which is the police in Prijedor. Good police activities can be a catalyst in reducing interethnic tensions and returnee problems, but only to a limited extent (*Report on the Status of Human Rights in Bosnia and Herzegovina*, 2005).

Economic difficulties, bitter memories of past events, deep-rooted preju-dice of one nation/minority against another, and political climate represent important and essential limiting factors of a national reconciliation. Everybody who knows the situation in Bosnia and Herzegovina can confirm the thesis that different peoples and members of different religions of Bosnia live one next to the other and not one with the other. They cooperate only when they have to and as much as they have to. When asked about mixed marriages in Bosnia, people reply: "Mixed marriages? There haven't been any. It's too early!"

References

Action Plan on Improving the Situation of Roma and Sinti within the OSCE Area. (2003). DECISION No. 566, Organization for Security and Co-operation in Europe. http://www.osce.org/documents/odihr/2003/11/1562_en.pdf.

Amin, A. (2002). *Ethnicity and the Multicultural City, Living with Diversity*, Report for the ERC CITIES Programme and the Department of Transport, Local Government and the Regions, January University of Durham.

Bender, D. (1991). *Police Brutality: Current Controversies.* San Diego: Greenhaven Press, Inc.

Body-Gendort, S. (2004). Police race relations in England and in France, policy and practices. In G. Mesko & M. Pagon (Eds), *Policing in Central and Eastern Europe: Dilemmas of Contemporary Criminal Justice* (pp. 134–145). Slovenia: Faculty of Criminal Justice, University of Maribor.

Brunson, R., & Miller, J. (2006). Young black men and urban policing in the United States. *The British Journal of Criminology, 4,* 613–638.

Chan, J. (1996). Changing police culture. *The British Journal of Criminology, 1,* 109–134.

Dixon, D., & Maher, L. (2002). Anh Hai: Policing, culture and social exclusion in a street heroin market. *Policing and Society, 12*(2), 93–110.

Eck, J., & Spelman, W. (2000). Problem-solving: Problem-oriented policing in Newport news. In Alpert-Piquero (Ed.), *Community Policing: Contemporary Readings.* Illinois: Waveland Press (ISBN 1-57766-155-9).

Goldstein, H. (1990). *Problem Oriented Policing.* New York: McGraw-Hill, Inc.

Guidebook on Democratic Policing. (2007). Secretary General, OSCE, Vienna. http://www.osce.org/publications/spmu/2007/01/23086_795_en.pdf

Home Secretary's Action Plan: Stephen Lawrence Inquiry. (1999). http://police.homeoffice.gov.uk/publications/equality-diversity/stephen-lawrence-inquiry/home-secretary-action-plan-1999?view=Binary

Huisman, K., Martinez, J., & Wilson, C. (2005). Training police officers on domestic violence and racism, challenges and strategies. *Violence against Women, 11*(6), 792–821 (DOI: 10.1177/1077801205276110).

Hüttermann, J. (2003). Policing an ethnically divided neighborhood in Germany: Day-to-day strategies and habits. *Policing and Society 1*(4), 381–397.

Innes, M. (2006). Policing uncertainty: Countering terror through community intelligence and democratic policing, *ANNALS, AAPSS, 222,* 605 (DOI: 10.1177/0002716206287118).

King, J. (2001). *Building Peace in Bosnia: Reintegration and Civilian Police Capacity—Building*. Department of Foreign Affairs and International Trade, International Security Research and Outreach Programme International Security Bureau.

Lichtenberg, I. (2006). Driving While Black (DWB): Examining race as a tool in the war on drugs. *Police Practice & Research: An International Journal, 7*(1), 49–60.

MacPherson Report. (1999). http://www.archive.officialdocuments.co.uk/document/cm42/4262/4262.htm

Marks, M. (2003). Shifting gears or slamming the brakes? A review of police behavioural change in a post-apartheid police unit. *Policing and Society, 13*(3), 235–258.

Murray, J. (2006). Criminal exploitation of women and children and the important role of community policing. *Police Practice & Research: An International Journal, 7*(2), 125–134.

Palmiotto, P. (2000). *Community Policing*. Maryland: Aspen Publishers, Inc.

Phillips, C. (2005). Facing inwards and outwards? Institutional racism, race equality and the role of Black and Asian professional associations. *Criminal Justice, 5*(4), 357–377.

Police Reform in Serbia. (2004). Law Department OSCE Mission to Serbia and Montenegro, January, pp. 22–15.

Police Reform in Serbia: Towards the Creation of a Modern and Accountable Police Service, Annex 1 of the Document. (2004). Law Enforcement Department OSCE Mission to Serbia and Montenegro, January, pp. 80–89.

Recommendations on Policing in Multi-Ethnic Societies. (2006). Office of the High Commissioner on National Minorities. http://www.osce.org/documents/hcnm/2006/02/17982_en.pdf.

Report on the Status of Human Rights in Bosnia and Herzegovina. (2005). Helsinki Committee for Human Rights in Bosnia and Herzegovina.

Rotterdam Charter. (1996). http://www.rotterdamcharter.nl/read/the_rotterdam_charter.

Rowe, M., & Garland, J. (2003). Have you been diversified yet? Developments in police community and race relations training in England and Wales. *Policing and Society, 13*(4), 399–411.

Sanders, J. (2000). Racial and ethnic minorities in San Diego, United States. *Policing and Society, 10*, 131–141.

Schafer, J., Huebner, B., & Bynum, T. (2003). Citizen perceptions of police services: Race, neighborhood context, and community policing. *Police Quarterly, 66*(4), 440–468.

Simonovic, B. (2006). *Rad policije u zajednici* [Community Policing]. Banja Luka: The High Police College.

Sullivan, P. (1989). Minority officers. In R. Dunham & G. Alpert (Eds), *Critical Issues in Policing: Contemporary Readings* (pp. 331–345). Illinois: Waveland Press, INC (ISBN 0-88133-390-5).

Tanovich, D. (2006). The colour of justice: Policing race in Canada, review: John Martin. *Police Practice & Research, An International Journal, 7*(5), 472–475.

The Ministry of Internal Affairs of Bosnia and Herzegovina: The State Border Service. (2005). Project No. 6.6.12. of 5.

The Role of Community Policing in Building Confidence in Minority Communities. (2002). Serbia, Report of the International Helsinki Federation for Human Rights (IHF) to the OSC Supplementary Human Dimension Meeting on the Role of Community Policing in Building Confidence in Minority Communities, Vienna, pp. 28–29.

The Vision Document. (2003). Belgrade: Ministry of Interior of the Republic of Serbia/ Danish Centre for Human Rights.

Waters, M. C. (1990). *Ethnic Options: Choosing Identities in America.* Berkeley, CA: University of California Press.

Wild, R., Hallsworth, S., Higwan, K., & McGuire, M. (2006). Police stop and search: Examining proportionality and disproportionality in relation to ethnicity. In G. Mesko & B. Dobovsek (Eds), *Policing in Central and Eastern Europe: Past, Present and Future* (pp. 153–154). Ljubljana, Slovenia: Faculty of Criminal Justice University of Maribor.

Withrow, B. (2004). Driving while different: A potential theoretical explanation for race-based policing. *Criminal Justice Policy Review, 15*(3), 344–364.

Wouter, W., Stol, Ph., & Bervoetes, E. J. A. (2002). Policing Dutch-Moroccan youth. *Policing and Society, 12*(3), 191–200.

Urbanization, Security, and Human Rights

15

CARMEN LEE SOLIS and
PATRICIA L. GATLING

Contents

Urbanization and security issues are inextricably intertwined with race, ethnicity, poverty, and economics in many countries, including the United States. A sizeable body of research suggests that minorities, the formally incarcerated, and those who live in poverty have less access to power and resources, including police protection in their communities (Walker, Spohn, & Delone, 2007; Zatz & Portillos, 2000), and in urban cities they experience higher rates of victimization, arrest, crime, and employment inequalities. This impacts security, because unemployment, crime, and poverty are significant factors in urban violence (Krivo & Peterson, 1996; Parker, 2004; Walker et al., 2007). Consequently, fear of violence, concern for personal safety, incarceration, unemployment, and the proliferation of urban crime create a sense of insecurity.

According to Brennan (1999) crime and violence in urban cities do not just happen; they are the result of inequality, class struggles, the economic situation, values, and poor communication, as well as a lack of cooperation and collaboration with government agencies like the police. Some studies have indicated that lack of communication with government institutions and poorly implemented policing strategies, even when well intended, can serve as forms of social–political control that ultimately may pose real threats to civil liberties and human rights for minorities and immigrants in the United States and throughout the world (Gonzalez & Portillos, 2007; Romero, 2006; Solis, Portillo, & Brunson, 2009). Critical Race Theory and its counterpart Latino Critical Race Theory (LatCrit) have allowed scholars to explore how connections between power, privilege, domination, racism, sexism, classism, and other forms of oppression influence the historical and daily experiences

257

of people of color living in the United States (Solis et al., 2009; Soloranzo & Delgado Bernal, 2001).

LatCrit theory in particular "has been used extensively to explore how the legal and criminal justice system create inequitable outcomes for Latinos/as, and more recently has revealed how disparate police practices shape police–community relations" (Solis et al., 2009). Romero (2006), in assessing immigration roundups in Chandler, Arizona with a LatCrit framework, maintains that policing is a key vehicle for controlling public spaces viewed as dangerous. Gonzalez and Portillos (2007) employ a LatCrit framework to describe how national and state education and criminal justice policies continue to oppress and criminalize Latinos based on views or preconceived notions that their communities are beset with crime. Such structural inequalities are discernible in everyday contacts and exchanges and can only be addressed via clear communication and collaboration (Solis et al., 2009). However, establishing communication and cooperation within urban communities, particularly in minority and poor communities, is a task that requires a great deal of sensitivity, creativity, and credibility. For law-enforcement organizations in particular, this can serve a number of important purposes. For example, information can be obtained regarding criminal actions, hazardous or suspicious conditions can be reported, and a sound sense of security can be developed.

Sound policing strategies have always required communication and collaboration. Yet the process of establishing these interpersonal dialogues in urban minority and immigrant communities may be difficult. First, there has always been stress and friction between police and minority communities (Goldstein, 1990). In New York City, for example, African-American and Latino communities have increasingly viewed the New York City Police Department (NYPD) and its strategies as "excessive policing-distant and brutal" (Silverman & Della-Guista, 2001). Secondly, many police departments in the United States continue to struggle with issues of race, ethnicity, cultural sensitivity, and equal access to effective services especially for communities of color. Thirdly, the United States has characterized poor and minority communities as criminal, making them suspicious, dangerous, and insecure. Such depictions endorse a more aggressive style of policing and encourage greater arrest and incarceration (Solis et al., 2009).

Minority communities, particularly African-American and Latino, continue to deal with issues of trust, bias, and abuse in police practice (Menjivar & Bejarano, 2004; Solis et al., 2009). This view of the police leads the community to consider most, if not all police actions as violations of their human dignity and/or rights. This perception is a major factor in creating an "us versus them" mentality, which is ultimately harmful to both sides. Ideally, attention to the concerns of others reflects an organization's recognition of their worth and a respect for their human dignity and rights. How the police interact with the public in daily situations will go a long way toward developing or harming the relationship between the two. Interaction without courtesy and respect sends a message to urban minority communities that law-enforcement organizations are not interested in working with them to solve problems that plague their neighborhoods or to secure their quality of life (Solis et al., 2009).

This chapter delineates a human rights model that can foster a sense of security in urban communities by opening up lines of communication, cooperation, and collaboration with law-enforcement organizations.

Violence, Fear, Trust, and the Police

In America and worldwide, scholars are reporting that violence and other types of crime are influenced by urbanization, politics, the economy, cultural conditions, the media, and inadequate security (Dammert & Malone, 2006; Vanderschuern, 1996). The rise of crimes such as theft, selling and carrying of illegal firearms, acts of terrorism, and drug and human trafficking affects individuals, families, and communities and increases fear of violence. According to Dammert and Malone (2006), academics suggest that fear of crime must be addressed by examining not only how crime occurs but also by assessing the effectiveness of the practice, methods, and strategies of law-enforcement agencies. These researchers posit that the occurrence of crime by itself is not the sole compelling force behind fear of crime. Other, equally important factors are the unsuccessful attempts of police to gain the public trust (p. 32). In other words, communities may experience greater fear of violence or crime if they do not trust those who are sworn to protect and serve them.

Silverman (1999) points out that some police departments, such as the NYPD recognize that crime reduction efforts are minimized if the community's trust in police is lost. Despite such a recognition and some well-intentioned strategies, most law-enforcement agencies fall short of their effort to build community trust (Brown, 1991; Solis, 2004). This is important because research asserts that trust is a significant factor in establishing community assistance. Devoid of community trust, the daily job of police officers is inherently difficult. However, if they treat people with dignity and respect their rights, they ultimately achieve community support. Thus, if police organizations actually incorporate respect for human dignity in their practice and treat even their own members with the dignity they deserve, they can connect more effectively to the community and improve overall police morale (Donato, 1999; Solis, 2004). Other studies on the issue of trust between the police and communities indicate that the public tends to view police "as part of a system that cannot be trusted" (Peak & Glensor, 1996, p. 211).

A train-the-trainer program in the Dominican Republic conducted using the Human Dignity/Rights Course developed in partnership between John Jay College, International Criminal Investigative Training Assistance Program (ICITAP), and the FBI in 1994 can serve as a good example of this. In this course, police and community members discussed issues of trust, corruption, abuse, and overall service. The community group members in the Dominican Republic initially perceived their police force as corrupt, with members who could not be trusted. In a similar vein, the police did not trust the community and was opposed to their involvement. It was only through the process of listening, communicating, and working collaboratively with each other that both groups gained an understanding of the other's perceptions and concerns. The focus on dignity in the collaborative participatory process enabled both the police and the community to respect each other, candidly talk about issues and, in the end, gain trust in each other. Once trust was established, the group was able to clearly identify problems and develop solutions (Solis, 2008).

Daily exchanges between police officers and the public can also influence trust in police. Consider a typical interaction between the NYPD and the community that occurs hundreds of times a day in New York City:

> The police get a call of a man with a gun standing in front of a particular address in a poor neighborhood in Brooklyn. The description is a dark-skinned male, in his 30's, approximately 6 feet tall, wearing a black t-shirt, blue jeans and white sneakers. As the police approach the location they see that the only guy standing there is a perfect match to the description they were given three minutes earlier. Obviously, to protect themselves—they are going to approach fast—securing the guy on the ground or on the wall immediately—and as the man is being searched—someone approaches you and says "What are you doing? He wasn't doing anything wrong."

A police officer who has no respect for the community might say: "Mind your own business and get out of here before I arrest you for obstruction of justice." A properly trained police officer who has respect for the community and values communication and a solid relationship might take a minute to explain that he/she got a report that a guy fitting this exact description, standing in this exact location had a gun. In order to protect ourselves, we put him on the ground to search him. If you want the matter to be investigated further you should feel free to call the Internal Affairs Bureau (an arm of the NYPD that investigates allegations of abuse or corruption involving police officers) or the Civilian Complaint Review Board (a city agency with a similar function). The person can walk away with the belief that the officer was doing the right thing and trying to protect the community by getting guns off the street.

Similarly, assuming that the individual does not possess a weapon (as is the case in the vast majority of these interactions), how the officer handles him is equally important. Although this is a potentially dangerous situation, the officer should attempt some courtesy at the outset. Speaking to the individual while the search is occurring, explaining why you are doing what you are doing, apologizing for the inconvenience and offering the numbers of the agencies or organizations that investigate police abuse will be extremely helpful in having that individual, even though he was accosted by the police, walk away feeling like the police were doing their job to protect him.

Initial data from the NYPD indicates that the department stopped and frisked over 500,000 individuals in 2006. These stops resulted in just over 50,000 arrests; this means that 90% of the time the police did not recover evidence to establish that the individual was involved in criminality. The same data reveal that out of the half million individuals who were stopped and frisked, over 85% were people of color [American Civil Liberties Union (ACLU) website].

According to a report conducted by the Office of the Attorney General (Spitzer, 1999) in precincts in which blacks and Hispanics each represent less than 10% of the total population, individuals identified as belonging to these racial groups nevertheless accounted for more than half of the total "stops" during the covered period. Blacks accounted for 30% of all persons "stopped" in these precincts; Hispanics accounted for 23% of all persons "stopped." Some researchers are indicating that in such stops, people of color were more likely to experience use of force (Walker et al., 2007). This raises questions of police misconduct and increases negative community perceptions of police.

In the above scenarios, open communication from the officer could result in either or both of the individuals involved in the scenario telling friends about their positive interaction with the police. Such a communication would lead to the officer receiving a reputation as a fair cop. This in turn will help community members feel comfortable in approaching the officer and providing information that can prevent or solve crime, making the area and everyone (including the officers) safer. Imagine similar relationships throughout your city and how much better life would be for everyone involved, and it all began with courtesy and respect for human dignity.

Current research continues to address issues of race, social capital, and trust in analyzing the relationship between the community and law-enforcement organizations. These studies indicate that police need to form collaborative relationships to help repair the damage created by lack of trust, anger, and "racially charged issues" experienced by urban communities of color (Solis, 2004). Macdonald and Stokes (2006) further maintain that measures to build community partnerships should involve objectives that facilitate better community connections, particularly in neighborhoods deprived "of strong social ties to local government entities [like the police]." Similar to Dammert and Malone (2006), these scholars submit that community partnerships should serve as links to developing trust. The premise is that as the level of trust increases in the neighborhood and in the police, the fear of crime decreases. Since the poor and minorities in urban cities are the primary victims of violence (Brennan, 1999) and victimization increases fear of crime, and those same neighborhoods have the least amount of constructive communication with the police department increasing their actual and perceived fear, it follows that appropriate policing strategies must include crime prevention, as well as community participation. This two-tiered approach will reduce actual fear and perceived fear and may aid in the ultimate goal of crime reduction.

Urban Security, Incarceration, and Recidivism

New York City and many other cities in the United States will be facing major security issues in the beginning of the twenty-first century. Crime is down throughout the country and one of the major reasons for that reduction is that the United States has spent the past two decades incarcerating offenders (Western, 2004). Since the vast majority of reported crimes occur in poor, minority, and immigrant neighborhoods, the majority of police officers are assigned to patrol these areas, resulting in the majority of those arrested being people of color. Travis (2005) posits that black and Latino communities have suffered greater levels of incarceration partly due to the rise in violence and drugs that grew out of the crack epidemic of the 1980s.

It is estimated that 30,000 individuals (mostly people of color) return to New York City after being released from prison each year (NYS Criminal Justice 2006 Crime Stat Report). When individuals have served their time and comes home from prison, they should have the opportunity to move ahead—to get a job and move on with their lives. While we need to address the policies of incarcerating our way out of social problems, we must also develop programs *in* prison to give inmates the education, skills, and support they need so they come out in a better position than they had when they went in. If we do not do that, it will be a short time before the same offender commits another crime. Travis (2005) points out that the "... recidivism rate of former prisoners has historically been high and many of them commit crimes that warrant a new prison term."

In 1972, 330,000 Americans were in jail or prison. In the 1990s, the average prison population had grown to 1.2 million. Today, over 2 million Americans are incarcerated, more than four times the number in 1972 (Western, 2004). The increase in our nation's prison population translates into an increase in these formerly incarcerated individuals returning to society with little education, few employable skills, old or new substance addictions, and/or the same undiagnosed and untreated mental illness that led them to prison in the first place. Now they have the added stigma of being ex-convicts. It is a huge problem. About 600,000 people are released from prison each year in the United States. That is over 1,600 a day (Travis, Solomon, & Waul, 2001).

The old adage, "out of sight, out of mind," seems to describe our country's prison policy. Lock offenders away and we will deal with them later. The fact is that we will have to deal with them later and, more likely than not, we will be dealing with the same offender after he or she commits another crime, enhancing the public's actual and perceived fear, further eroding a positive relationship between the community and the police. The majority of the people arrested in the United States have had prior contact with the criminal justice system and of those approximately 60% had been previously incarcerated. The message is clear: people who have served time are liable to commit crime again unless we do something to break the pattern of recidivism (Reaves, 2006).

This increase in incarceration is creating a situation where more generations within a family are going to prison. More than 1 million children are growing up with at least one parent in prison. These children are three times more likely to end up in prison than children whose parents were not incarcerated (Glaze & Maruschak, 2008).

Drugs, guns, and violence thrive in disadvantaged communities—communities with low median incomes, poor-performing schools, high dropout rates and truancy, few employment opportunities, and weak social and community support systems. The proliferation of drugs and drug-related crime in these neighborhoods has led to increased police presence. Critical Race Theory and LatCrit frameworks suggest that this leads to the use of more aggressive policing tactics, which only further marginalizes communities of color as unsafe and criminal (Solis et al., 2009). Higher levels of police activity result in higher numbers of arrests sending more people from these neighborhoods to prison and putting into play the cycle of the formerly incarcerated returning home.

Since most of the enforcement occurs in neighborhoods where people of color live, it also follows that people of color are incarcerated at a higher rate than other Americans. African Americans constitute 12.3% of the U.S. population, but represent 49% of prisoners nationally. In 1999, the Bureau of Justice Statistics estimated that in New York City, 58.3% of the prison population is African American (Bureau of Justice Statistics). Tragically, in recent years, more African American and Hispanic males in the United States have been incarcerated than have attended college (Walker et al., 2007).

Although less discussed, the number of Latinos in prison has more than quintupled since 1980. Latino Americans constitute 12.5% of the national population but account for 20.9% of the national prison population, and 30% of the New York City prison population, second only to African Americans (Walker et al., 2007). While the vast majority of prisoners are men, the number of women inmates has increased 600% since 1980—mostly as a result of mandated sentences for drug offenses. At this rate, by 2010 there will be more women in prison than inmates of both sexes in 1970 (Western, 2004).

The numbers do not lie. Prisoners are unprepared to navigate their return to society upon their release. They were not and are not being rehabilitated adequately. Most have not acquired any new insights, education, trades, or skills during their imprisonment that will expand their employment options or family stability.

One successful option to reducing this growing problem is an alternative to prison programs for nonviolent crimes. These programs identify the cause of the criminal behavior such as drug addiction and/or mental illness, treat the individual, and then require them to continue their education to develop employable skills. The relationship, however, does not end upon graduation from the basic 2-year program. Employment and other support services are provided for years to come with the ultimate goal of making the individual a productive member of society. This approach creates positive change instead of locking the individual away and continuing the pattern of recidivism (ComALERT: Kings County District Attorney's Office, 1999; Western, 2003).

The consequences of prison-life experience or a felony record can be disastrous for the returning inmate seeking to re-establish in the community. Researchers state that the unemployment rate is as high as 50% for people with criminal records, even when the unemployment rate nationwide is as low as 6%. For the few who are employed, their average annual wages are exceedingly low. Western (2002) has found that even when paroled inmates are able to find jobs, they earn only half as much as people of the same social and economic background who have not been incarcerated. He theorizes that economic inequality of the African-American community may be due, in part, to the rise in the number of incarcerated young African-American men. African-American men are seven times more likely to be incarcerated than their White counterparts.

More often than not, the largest obstacle formerly incarcerated individuals face in obtaining employment is the simple refusal of many employers to even consider hiring an "ex-con." Pager and Western (2005) conducted tests to determine the effect of a criminal record on employment opportunities. The conclusion of their study, both in Milwaukee and New York City, have broad implications for the fate of those 600,000 individuals returning home from prison yearly: "employers are extremely reluctant to hire a job applicant with a prison record no matter how qualified ... employers are only one-half to one-third as likely to consider applicants with felony convictions relative to equally qualified men with no prison record."

Pager and Western's (2005) research involved sending pairs of young men matched by age, race, appearance, and qualifications to apply for unskilled low-level entry positions throughout New York City. One tester presented himself as having been recently released from prison for a felony conviction. The other presented the same qualifications for the position, but no criminal record. Testers were African American, Latino, and Caucasian. She believed that employers used the preliminary pedigree information as a screening mechanism to weed out applicants at the onset of the hiring process. In most instances, the applicant with the criminal record was given no opportunity to explain the conviction or to demonstrate rehabilitation. Pager and Western summed up the results of their testers experience by saying, "as soon as an employer sees the box, 'Criminal history' checked 'yes', they're out." Their research highlights the difficulty formerly incarcerated individuals have in securing employment: They cannot get a foot in the door because they are boxed in by the word "yes" to criminal history. They conclude: "We know that finding quality, steady employment is one of the strongest predictors of desistance from crime, yet these men have very little opportunity to obtain legitimate work ... the inability to obtain employment may have been a condition that led to crime in the first place."

This study, which included 1,500 entry-level employers in New York City, revealed that a high school educated Caucasian male in his 20s, with a nonviolent felony conviction, had an equal chance of obtaining employment as a similarly situated African-American applicant without a conviction. The Caucasian applicant with a record was five times as likely to get an offer as the similarly situated African-American applicant. Anecdotal evidence indicated that African-American applicants were assumed to have a criminal record. Latinos in the study faired slightly better than the African Americans, but were still well behind the Caucasians (Pager & Western, 2005).

Even if a formerly incarcerated individual manages to meet with a potential employer, the experience of surviving prison may manifest itself during the course of a job interview. Western (2004) argues that the increasingly violent and overcrowded state of prisons and jails are likely to produce certain attitudes, mannerisms, and behavioral practices that "on the inside" function to enhance survival, but are not compatible with success in the conventional job market.

Akabas (2000, personal interview), in reviewing the importance of work in people's lives, states "employment is viewed as a right fundamental to Americans ... and ... unemployment is followed by socially bad outcomes." Furthermore, "having work contributes to well-being and being without work contributes to anti-social behavior and physical and mental decline," but first, "we need to be work-ready." While the problems facing a formerly incarcerated individual returning home are clear to understand and measure, the problems or damage to community residents in neighborhoods where large numbers of prisoners return are more difficult to assess. One approach to looking at community impact is to investigate the ties between individuals and their potential to help each other. For example, Putman (2000) discusses how Americans have generally become increasingly disconnected from family, friends, neighbors and our democratic structures. He stresses the importance of social networks or "social capital" for job placement and other economic needs. Your *human capital* may be what you know, but your *social capital* is *who* you know. And collectively, a community becomes stronger with these bonds among its members. Social capital can be found in neighborhood friendships, churches, schools, civic associations and even bars. Life is easier in a community that has a substantial stock of social capital. And social capital will fortify a community and encourage its economic development (Walker et al., 2007).

Our well-intentioned public policy of enhanced police enforcement in communities ravaged by street narcotics dealers has, as a consequence, destroyed social capital in those targeted communities. Now, high numbers of formerly incarcerated individuals will be returning to those neighborhoods and unless something is done, the pattern of recidivism will continue. According to Spence (1993), "an individual unfortunate enough to live in a neighborhood whose social capital has eroded is more likely than not to end up hooked, booked or dead."

In 1999, the Brooklyn District Attorney's Office began a new program, ComALERT—Community and Law Enforcement Resources Together—to support the re-entry of individuals leaving prison and returning back into their communities. The program increases an individual's social capital by providing a support network through community-based service organizations. Another aspect of the program targets members of street gangs or at-risk youth to substitute the negative social capital of gang membership with the positive social capital that will enable these young people to reach their potential and become productive members of society.

The network of referrals provided by ComALERT includes: job training, referral, and placement; education; substance abuse treatment; mental health treatment; and housing assistance. Social workers at the District Attorney's Office refer the program's participants to community-based organizations, some faith based, that identify and assist the formerly incarcerated with their particular needs, providing them with social capital to help break the pattern of recidivism. A large part of ComALERT is the collaborative relationship between the justice system (including police and corrections), political leadership, and community service organizations already in place. These organizations/resource partners have experience serving court-involved youth and the formerly incarcerated population (ComALERT: Kings County District Attorney's Office, 1999).

The program coordinates a growing network of community-based organizations, approximately 150 strong, available to provide services to targeted individuals. The organizations included: New York Theological Society (Youth Turn Project), the Doe Fund, CAMBA, Center for Employment Opportunity (CEO), Fortune Society, Osborne/South Forty Association, City

University of New York, Catch, the Rite Program, the Legal Action Center, Catholic Charities Diocese of Brooklyn and Queens, and CADC (Community Associates Development Corp.), to name a few. Most program participants have not completed high school or its equivalent and were not working full-time jobs when arrested. Most have substance abuse histories, either acquired while incarcerated or prior to and continuing through incarceration. Despite these obstacles, this program is working.

ComALERT serves 200 Brooklyn participants a year. All of them come out of prison looking for work: 60% are directed into "transitional employment" options because they are not "work ready." They do not have a high school diploma, General Education Diploma (GED), or a work history. They need to build a work routine and resume, and they need help doing it. The Doe Fund's "Ready, Willing, and Able" program is an outstanding example of a transitional placement. It offers paid work, a savings plan, housing, food, and substance abuse treatment. The other 40% are directed into a "permanent labor" track and referred to job developers in Brooklyn community organizations. ComALERT has reduced the recidivism of its Brooklyn clients by 60%. Their 1-year recidivism rate has dropped from 16% to 6.6%. Brooklyn's current 3-year recidivism rate is 41%; for ComALERT clients, that rate falls to less than 17%.

ComALERT reflects the belief that we can no longer "imprison our way out" of our nonviolent crime problem. It offers counseling, referral, and case management services to break the cycle of recidivism and serve the larger social goal of expanding economic opportunities through educational and employment programs. But with all that said, ComALERT is just one program. It is not right for everyone. We need to foster a range of programs to tackle such complex human and social problems.

Blumstein and Beck (1999) indicate that the number of prisoners in the United States is not necessarily reflective of the crime rate. In fact, the number of crimes committed is so far from those actually resulting in convictions and prison that we are left wondering if those numbers mean anything at all. In 1992, the Council on Crime in America found that of the 10 million violent crimes committed, only 4 million were reported to the police. And of those reported to the police only 641,000 led to arrests. That means only six in 100 even entered the system. Once in the system, only 165,000 led to convictions—only 165,000 convictions out of 10 million crimes (Council on Crime in America, 1996).

The same proportions are reflected in New York City. Zeisel's (1982) study from the 1970s still holds true. Of every 1,000 felonies committed, only 540 are reported to the police leading to 65 arrests. The 65 arrests result in 36 convictions. And of those 36 convictions, only three of those felons are sentenced to prison for one year or more. So if the number of prisoners does not reflect the crime rate, what does it reflect? Blumstein and Beck (1999) conclude that the number of prisoners is more reflective of how we as a society view these individuals and how the policy makers view the purpose and goals of incarceration.

We must begin to address the needs of the prison population and the formerly incarcerated more effectively. Failure to do so will continue to increase our prison population and its multibillion dollar price tag. But more importantly, failure to do so will have a detrimental effect on the public safety of our neighborhoods. Criminal justice policy must consider the loss of social capital experienced by our neighborhoods that have endured years of mass incarceration. If we fail as a civil society to assist the formerly incarcerated with their reintegration and stabilization, we will all suffer. If we are unable to assist in the economic development of these bankrupt communities, public safety and security remain vulnerable.

Human Dignity/Rights Model

A human rights model that supports security in urban areas needs to consider various perspectives. It must consider how to develop collaborative efforts, partnerships, support networks, and social capital in communities. There has to be honest and ongoing discussion on how to undertake human and social issues and develop more programs with missions similar to ComALERT and the Human Dignity Course. Such a model must incorporate intergroup dialogues and address issues that secure the enforcement of human rights and rule of law.

Intergroup dialogue is a method involving democratic approaches that assist people in working together to solve problems. The methods involve "face-to-face, focused, facilitated" discussions of issues that are problematic. The conversation requires honesty, and an obligation to listen to the concerns of everyone (Schoem, Hurtado, Sevig, Chesler, & Sumida, 2004). It is expected that in such dialogue sessions participants will have different opinions, political beliefs, values, race, ethnicity, and socioeconomic or class status. Such variations could assist in creating change for individual ideas, stereotypes, and perceptions about race, ethnicity, class, incarceration, and socioeconomic status. This kind of dialogue can open lines of communication, develop a respect for differences, human rights, dignity, issues affecting the formally incarcerated, and a breakthrough for real talk about problems that affect the entire community.

Similar to ComALERT and the Human Dignity Course, there are a myriad of training programs that have been developed by private, public, and governmental institutions that advocate peace, democratic principles, social justice, alternatives to incarceration, and human rights education (Scanlon, 2002; Solis, 2008). A good deal of this training makes use of pioneering approaches that focus on best practices and professional growth as a means of preventing violations of human rights, civil liberties, supporting peace efforts, and addressing criminal behavior. However, a few of these models bring members of the community into the development process so that they may become cofacilitators with professional law-enforcement personnel. Intergroup dialogues can assist in generating discussions infused with "human rights lessons" that create an understanding of human dignity as an innate quality that all people have (Curran & Rothlien, 1999; Das & Verma, 2002).

A human rights training model aimed at focusing on urban security issues must facilitate an assessment of human rights, morality, personal integrity, alternatives to incarceration, collaborative efforts with criminal justice agencies, and professional ethics. It should provide an opportunity to consider and carefully analyze our experiences and behavior in an effort to create positive institutional change by examining values, behavior, ethical decision making, and creative implementation strategies that focus on human dignity and the rule of law (Curran & Rothlein, 1999; Solis, 2008).

The model should incorporate methods developed to assist participants in evaluating institutionalized violations to their dignity as well as their community. The objectives should be for participants to develop self-awareness by recognizing how their own behavior and attitudes impact public and political perceptions of the criminal justice system and of specific neighborhoods. Participants should be able to share experiences and evaluate how negative behaviors and treatment could lead to human dignity violations that in turn result in social scars (Curran & Rothlien, 1999; Solis, 2008). The model should ultimately help participants develop a plan to implement strategies in their respective organizations and communities that demonstrate how respect for human dignity, human rights, and the rule of law would be strengthened and reinforced to promote improved methods of security in urban areas.

The aspects of collaboration and assessment that are key tools in the Human Dignity Course developed by John Jay College, ICITAP, and the FBI in combination with the ComALERT model developed by the Kings County District Attorney's Office can be utilized in this model. The major premise is to establish greater communication, collaboration, and cooperation within urban communities, especially communities of color and institutions of criminal justice including the police. The model provides an opportunity to reflect on our experiences and to assess behavior, conditions of urban neighborhoods, issues of social capital, and the need for partnerships between stakeholders. It will assist participants to look at what they do, why they do it and the role that values and professional ethics play in our lives and in our work (Curran & Rothlien, 1999). The dialogue that results from the model supports participants in examining the unique power police and other government institutions have to either protect or violate the dignity and rights of people and communities in urban areas.

In the first part of the model, law-enforcement personnel work together with community members in intergroup dialogues to create an understanding of human dignity by developing a group definition. Human rights are then examined based on the group's conception of human dignity (Curran & Rothlien, 1999). A brief historical review will assist in establishing that the pursuit of human dignity and human rights is not unique to any era or any part of the world. The focus of this initial effort is to have participants define human dignity and human rights with sufficient precision to move on to look at the concept in their work and in their lives.

The second part of the model has participants engaged in discussions on issues of privilege and power. Using the cited literature from Johnson (2006), facilitators lead the discussion into various occurrences: what people think about them, feel, and how they react. Participants discuss avoidance, exclusion, oppression, and blaming victims. The intent of exercises in this area is to profoundly and personally examine how such issues affect us all, create divisions in society and in the long run impact security. In discussing dignity violations, criminal justice professionals and community members learn to appreciate the importance of human dignity, the pain of its denial and the power and impact of authority figures. Curran and Rothlien (1999) posit that it helps participants "recognize that dignity violations can leave permanent scars and that those in authority can do a great deal of harm, as well as a great deal of good, in carrying out their responsibilities."

This section also serves to recognize the impact of vulnerability. Discussing the nature of vulnerability encourages empathy and understanding of how negative perceptions of certain groups, such as the formally incarcerated or African Americans and Latinos, can put them in jeopardy. Exercises in this section assist participants in discussing the ways in which law-enforcement agencies and the criminal justice system as a whole can better serve vulnerable populations. Participants can identify and discuss group or class discrimination and the negative impact this has on the effective delivery of services in the criminal justice system.

In confronting and examining a variety of issues related to personal integrity and professional ethics, law-enforcement officers and other professionals in the criminal justice system can get a sense of how their professional interactions in urban communities can affect security measures. This analysis will also allow participants to understand that while behavior is the product of multiple influences, ultimately actions result from personal decisions for which each individual is responsible. Ethical decisions, in addition, often involve issues related to the dignity, rights, and security of individuals, be they victims of crime, perpetrators, or fellow law-enforcement personnel. Thus, it is important in this model for participants to examine a variety of issues related to personal integrity and professional ethics.

In recognizing and respecting the human dignity and rights of all persons while carrying out the responsibilities of law-enforcement and criminal justice, this model reinforces, through practical application, the importance of security in urban neighborhoods (Curran & Rothlein, 1999). Throughout the different stages of the model, law-enforcement and criminal justice practitioners, in concert with community members, work on issues that assist them in assessing behavior and values that impact their day to day work. The final step is developing and later implementing a professional ethical code of conduct. The United Nations' Universal Declaration of Human Rights and Code of Conduct for Law Enforcement Officials are provided to participants as references in creating this task. The mission is to stimulate learning about how law-enforcement and other criminal justice practitioners should behave and practice in order to maintain safety and security in urban communities. The development of a work plan via a candid assessment of codes of conduct and professionalism will also assist these professionals in changing policies and practices within their agencies.

While this model is not a panacea for solving security issues in urban communities, it is a method that can bring criminal justice personnel and residents of urban communities together to collectively work on addressing the problems that affect their safety and security. The issue of protecting urban communities is becoming the focal point of security approaches. In some respects national and local security issues have been viewed from a strictly military standpoint (Ullman, 1983). Only recently have we begun to address the effectiveness of law-enforcement agencies and promote coalitions to establish greater security for residents in urban environments (Rojas Aravena, 2002).

The United Nations has spearheaded this effort by encouraging deference for international rule of law in communities and in prisons. The main objective for the United Nations is developing a peaceful, fear-free humanity. To do this effectively, countries, states, and cities have to cooperate, collaborate and communicate efficiently with each other. Rojas Aravena (2002) explains it in the following way:

> The basic concept that enables security to be understood in the post-Cold War period is the concept of cooperation. This concept emerges in all reports systematizing progress and interpreting the changes in the world. It also plays an important role in divergent views, both for preventing and for promoting peace and international security. New problems that must be incorporated into the concept go beyond military aspects; hence, elements of cooperation are essential. The development of human security concepts must be placed within this framework.

Thus, the security of communities, individual people, the formally incarcerated, the environment, economy, states or nations depends on enhanced collaborative and cooperative efforts. Without these efforts human security is threatened (Rojas Aravena, 2002). Cooperation and collaboration through focused facilitated dialogues is then the key to achieving solutions to the problems of security in urban cities.

References

American Civil Liberties Union (ACLU) Web site. (2007). Racial Justice, Racial Profiling: Flawed report glosses over racial disparities in NYPD's stop-and-frisk practices 11/20/07. On-line at www.aclu.org/racialjustice/racialprofiling/33245 prs20071120html.

Blumstein, A., & Beck, A. J. (1999). Population growth in prisons, 1980–1996. In M. Tonry & J. Petersilla (Eds.), *Prisons* (pp. 17–61). Chicago: University of Chicago Press.

Brennan, E. M. (1999). Population, urbanization, environment, and security: A summary of the issues. *Environmental Change & Security Project Report*, Issue 5.

Brown, L. (1991). *Policing in New York City in the 1990's*. New York: New York City Police Department.

ComALERT. (1999). Office of the Kings County District Attorney Charles J. Hines, Brooklyn, New York. Unpublished report.

Council on Crime in America. (1996). *The State of Violent Crime in America*. First Report, Part I. New York: Manhattan Institute.

Curran, J. T., & Rothlein, M. D. (1999). Course development and evaluation. In G. W. Lynch (Ed.), *Human Dignity and the Police: Ethics and Integrity in Police Work*. Springfield, IL: Charles C. Thomas.

Das, D. K., & Verma, A. (2002). Teaching police officers human rights. *International Journal of Human Rights*, 6(2), 35–48.

Dammert, L., & Malone, M. F. T. (2006). Does it take a village? Policing strategies and fear of crime in Latin America. *Latin American Society*, 48(4), 27–51.

Donato, R. (1999). Human dignity and the police: A practitioner's view. In G. W. Lynch (Ed.), *Human Dignity and the Police: Ethics and Integrity in Police Work*. Springfield, IL: Charles C. Thomas.

Glaze, L. E., & Maruschak, L. M. (2008). *Special Reports: Parents in Prison and their Minor Children*. Washington, DC: Bureau of Justice Statistics (NCJ 222984).

Goldstein, H. (1990). *Problem Oriented Policing*. New York: McGraw-Hill.

Gonzalez, J. C., & Portillos, E. L. (2007). The Undereducation and Overcriminalization of U.S. Latinoas/os: A Post-Los Angeles Riot LatCrit Analysis. *Educational Studies*, 42, 247–266.

Krivo, L., & Peterson, R. (1996). Extremely disadvantaged neighborhoods and urban crime. *Social Forces*, 75(2), 619–648.

Macdonald, J., & Stokes, R. J. (2006). Race, social capital and trust in police. *Urban Affairs Review*, 41, 358–375.

Menjivar, C., & Bejarano, C. (2004). Latino immigrants perceptions of crime and police authorities in the United States: A case study from the Phoenix Metropolitan area. *Ethnic and Racial Studies*, 27(1), 120–148.

Pager, D., & Western, B. (2005). Race at work: Race and a criminal record in the NYC job market. Princeton University (not published).

Parker, K. (2004). Industrial shift, polarized labor markets and urban violence: Modeling the dynamics between economic transformation and disaggregated homicide. *Criminology, 42*(3), 619–645.

Peak, K. J., & Glensor, R. W. (1996). *Community Policing & Problem Solving.* Upper Saddle River, NJ: Prentice Hall.

Putman, R. (2000). *Bowling Alone: The Collapse and Revival of American Community.* New York: Simon and Schuster Inc.

Reaves, B. A. (2006). *Special Report.* Washington, DC: Bureau of Justice Statistics (NCJ 205289).

Rojas Aravena, F. (2002). Human security: Emerging concept of security in the twenty-first century. In *Human Security in Latin America,* Vol. 2, pp. 5–14. Chile: Facultad Latino Americano de Ciencias Sociales (FLASCO).

Romero, M. (2006). Racial profiling and immigration law enforcement: Rounding up of usual suspects in the Latino community. *Critical Sociology, 32,* 2–3.

Schoem, D., Hurtado, S., Sevig, T., Chesler, M., & Sumida, S. H. (2004). *Intergroup Dialogue: Deliberate Democracy in School, College, Community and Workplace.* Ann Arbor, MI: University of Michigan Press.

Silverman, E. B. (1999). *NYPD Battles Crime: Innovative Strategies in Policing.* New York: Northeastern University Press.

Silverman, E. B., & Della-Guistina, J. A. (2001). Urban Policing and Fear of Crime. *Urban Studies, 38*(5), 941–957.

Solis, C. L. (2004). The Impact of Community Policing in New York City's Puerto Rican Communities. Dissertation, City University of New York, Graduate Center. ProQuest Company. UMI No. 311529.

Solis, C. L. (2008). Human dignity/human rights and the police: Training that manifests rule of law operations. In K. Aromaa & R. Slawonir (Eds), *For the Rule of Law: Criminal Justice Teaching and Training across the World.* European Institute for Crime Prevention and Control, affiliated with the United Nations (Helinski, Finland, and Seoul, Korea).

Solis, C. L., Portillos, E. L., & Brunson, R. K. (2009). Latino youths' experiences with and perceptions of involuntary police encounters. In L. J. Krivo and R. D. Peterson (Eds), *Race, Crime, and Justice: Contexts and Complexities. The Annals of the American Academy of Political and Social Science.* Vol. 263, pp. 39–51.

Solorzano, D. G., & Delgado Bernal, D. (2001). Examining transformational resistance through a critical race and LatCrit theory framework. *Urban Education, 3,* 308–342.

Spence, L. (1993). Rethinking the social role of public housing. *Housing Policy Debate, 4*(3), 355–368.

Spitzer, E. (1999). *The NYPD Approach to 'Stop and Frisk'.* Albany: Office of the Attorney General.

Travis, J. (2005). *But They All Come Back.* Washington, DC: Urban Institute Press.

Travis, J., Solomon, A., & Waul, M. (2001). *From Prison to Home.* Washington, DC: Urban Institute Press.

Ullman, R. H. (1983). Redefining security. *International Security, 8*(1), 129–153.

Vanderschuern, F. (1996). From violence to justice and security in cities. *Environment and Urbanization, 8*(1), 93–112.

Walker, S., Spohn, C., & DeLone, M. (2007). *The Color of Justice: Race, Ethnicity and Crime in America.* Belmont, CA: Wadsworth, Thompson Learning.

Western, B. (2002). The impact of incarceration on wage mobility and inequality. *American Sociological Review, 67*, 526–546.

Western, B. (2003). Lawful re-entry. *The American Prospect, 14*(11), 54–56.

Western, B. (2004). Mass imprisonment and the life course: Race and class inequality in U.S. incarceration. *American Sociological Review, 69*, 151–169.

Zatz, M. S., & Portillos, E. L. (2000). Voices from the Barrio: Chicano/a Gangs, families and communities. *Criminology, 38*(2), 369–401.

Policing Protests in New York City

16

ALEX S. VITALE

Contents

This chapter looks at the ways in which police discretion functions at political demonstrations by focusing on how the New York Police Department (NYPD) handled six demonstrations at the 2004 Republican National Convention (RNC). The analysis shows that to understand the police response during these demonstrations four factors need to be considered. These are (1) the posture that demonstrators took toward the police, (2) the overall styles of policing used by the NYPD, (3) the legal frame within which the police operate, and (4) the political environment in which the policing occurred. This four-part framework implies that responsibility for the decisions the police make at demonstrations lies not just with individual police officers or police commanders at the scene, but also with top police executives and political leaders, who set the parameters within which on-the-ground decisions are made.

In a democratic society, the police must balance the demands for insuring public safety and security with those of maintaining social legitimacy. One of the primary mechanisms for achieving this balance is to act within "the shadow of the law." This is a difficult task as the exact status of the law is often unclear to the police, who must make discretionary judgments as they encounter a wide variety of both routine and unexpected situations in a complex legal environment. In addition, the police, and especially police commanders, operate within a political context dictated by elected leaders, whose goals are subject to political as well as legal constraints.

Most research about police discretion has focused on the decisions made by patrol officers, whether engaged in random patrol or responding to citizen calls for service. This research has dealt with decisions about whether to make arrests (Davis, 1975; Skolnick, 1969), the use of force (Seron, Pereira, & Kovath, 2004; Skolnick & Fyfe, 1993), and traffic stops (Langan, Greenfield, Smith, Durose, & Levine, 2001; Schafer & Mastrofski, 2005). While some work has been done on the discretionary decisions of detectives in investigating crime (Corsianos, 2003), a few other aspects of policing have been analyzed.

One area where police discretion is of growing concern is the policing of demonstrations. The role of discretion in this context is especially important and complex: important, because demonstrations can be a charged environment in which the actions of the police can have a significant impact on the political process and complex, because top police commanders and political officials may become involved in the process of making decisions about how demonstrations should be policed. Since 1999 there has been a significant increase in large contentious demonstrations around such issues as global trade, military interventions, and climate change. Analyzing police reactions to these demonstrations has highlighted the differences in policing approaches in different local political contexts (della Porta & Reiter, 1998; della Porta & Peterson, 2005; della Porta, Peterson, & Reiter, 2006). A few of these studies, however, have looked closely at the role of discretion in this process.

Police Discretion

The police must balance the need to respect due process rights, while using coercion to gain compliance with legal requirements. In addition, they are often saddled with the task of maintaining order in ways that are either not covered by the law or at times are in conflict with the law. As Bittner (1970), Reiss (1971), Goldstein (1977), and other early policing scholars have pointed out, the police are expected to use force to maintain public order, but their legitimacy depends on their ability to do this within the bounds of the rule of law. Early police forces were a product of exactly this tension. The "Bobbies" of the London Metropolitan Police were created as an alternative to the use of soldiers or local militias, who operated completely outside of a legal framework (Skolnick & Fyfe, 1993). As such, the new police established the ideal of public legitimacy through legal accountability.

Early American police forces, however, were much more oriented toward order maintenance than due process protections or law enforcement (Skolnick & Fyfe, 1993). Brawls were broken up, public drunks sent home, and threats to suspicious characters made with limited regard to the contours of the law. By the 1960s, however, the police increasingly came to see themselves as the front door of the criminal justice system and were encouraged to do so as part of a broader trend toward professionalization (Walker, 1977). The Supreme Court decisions of the 1960s that expanded the right to counsel (*Miranda v. Arizona*) and strengthened the exclusionary rule (*Mapp v. Ohio*) further pushed the police into a legal framework.

Demonstrations present an especially challenging situation for the police since they often create a direct tension between the desire for order and the need to uphold constitutional standards. Many police view demonstrations as inherently disorderly and have tended to control rather than facilitate or protect them. Even though the last 30 years has seen a decline in violent suppression of demonstrations in the United States and Europe, more aggressive policing of demonstrations is on the rise in these areas and remains a constant in much of the developing world (Das & Jiao, 2004). As a result, further investigation is needed into the factors that influence police decisions about how to balance law and order during demonstrations.

Theoretical Models of Protest Policing

Police commanders, especially in large departments, have a wide variety of strategies and tactics available to them for policing demonstrations. Many cities have dedicated units with specific training and specialized tools such as riot shields and water cannons available. Even small departments, however, must make decisions about whether to handle demonstrations in an aggressive or accommodating manner. Research to explain the differences in how the police handle demonstrations can be placed in three main categories. The most common approach looks at the development of a particular style of protest policing used by specific police forces. These studies show how the police respond to a wide variety of protest events in a consistent fashion given a department's overall policing philosophy. McCarthy and McPhail (1998) and McPhail, Schweingruber, and McCarthy (1998) argue that there has been an important transition in the style of protest policing from the 1960s to the 1980s. In the 1960s and the early 1970s, the police operated under a philosophy of *escalated force* in which the militancy of protestors was met by increased militancy by the police. Any show of force or violence by the protestors was met with overwhelming force in return (McPhail et al., 1998). In response to the growing violence at demonstrations during this period, a new doctrine of *negotiated management* emerged based on greater cooperation between police and demonstrators and an effort to avoid violence. This approach called for the protection of free speech rights, toleration of community disruption, ongoing communication between police and demonstrators, avoidance of arrests, and limiting the use of force to situations where violence is occurring (Schweingruber, 2000). This new philosophy is now in place in much of the United States and Europe (della Porta & Reiter, 1998; McPhail et al., 1998; Waddington, 1994).

Winter (1998) also claims that police attitudes and tactics are organized around a coherent policing philosophy. In his review of West German protest policing tactics from 1960 to 1990, he identifies internal debates among police executives about the best way to orient their assessments of and responses to demonstrations. Overall, he notes a shift away from a more repressive form of policing characterized by a police philosophy that is tied to strongly supporting the stability of the state as an institution, which he calls *staatspolizei*, and toward a more tolerant form of protest policing, *burgerpolizei*, which is oriented toward protecting the stability of civil society. This overarching philosophy organizes the police assessments of the nature of the threat posed by any particular demonstration as well as the appropriate range of responses. During the *staatspolizei* period of the 1960s, the police were much more likely to view political demonstrations as a threat to the authority and legitimacy of the state and thus use more repressive measures. By the 1980s, many demonstrations were treated more leniently because they had come to be seen as a legitimate part of the democratic process now that the police viewed a healthy democracy as extending beyond formal governmental authority to civil society.

During the last 10 years, however, American protest policing has become at times more aggressive and repressive in response to the growth of more contentious protest activity (Boghosian, 2007; Vitale, 2007). Noakes and Gillham (2006) argue that a new style of protest policing has emerged, which is influenced by broader shifts in criminal justice philosophy. Building on the work of Garland (2001), they argue that there has been a transition from a welfare state-oriented *penal modernism*, which prioritizes reform of individual offenders to the neoliberal and neoconservative *new penology*, which is based on managing the risks of crime through the strategic control of suspect populations deemed to be a greater potential threat to social order. This new approach is characterized by a rejection of rehabilitation in favor of incapacitation and an intolerance of disorder. Unlike premodern criminal justice forms, it does not strictly focus on punitiveness because it lacks faith in deterrence. Instead, it utilizes information to assess which individuals and populations pose the greatest risk to society and uses mechanisms of control to isolate and discipline them in the Foucaultian sense of micromanaging their actions under constant surveillance.

In the policing of demonstrations, this has been translated into an intolerance of disruption in the form of the denial or restriction of the right to assemble, heavy reliance on surveillance, public vilification of protest groups, preventative and preemptive arrests and detentions, and extensive use of barricades and designated protest areas isolated from the targets of protests. In its most extreme forms, it calls for the use of mass arrests, extended detentions, and very high levels of force used against even nonviolent crowds as a way of restoring order rather than specifically enforcing the law or respecting political and human rights.

This approach, sometimes called the *Miami Model*, emerged nationally in response to the disruptive protests at the World Trade Organization meetings in Seattle in 1999 and is named for the Miami Police Department's handling of protests at the Free Trade Area of the Americas meetings in 2002 (Getzen, 2004; Scahill, 2004). This style is characterized by the creation of no protest zones, heavy use of less lethal weaponry, surveillance of protest organizations, negative advanced publicity by city officials of protest groups, preemptive arrests, preventative detentions, and extensive restrictions on protest timing and locations.

Sometimes the philosophies that underlie the policing of demonstrations are more directly tied to the strategic orientations guiding a broad range of local policing practices. In New York, the policing of demonstrations in the last 10 years has been organized around the principle of "zero tolerance" order maintenance stemming from their adherence to the "broken windows" theory (Wilson & Kelling, 1982). This has produced a *command and control* approach toward the policing of demonstrations that emphasizes the micro management of all aspects of demonstrations and the willingness to use force in response to even minor violations of the law (Vitale, 2005).

A second approach to understanding protest policing has been to look at the specific factors before and during a demonstration that give rise to a particular police response. These studies attempt to understand the interaction between the posture of the demonstrators and the posture of the police. Earl, Soule, and McCarthy (2003) reviewed press coverage of protests in New York State from 1968 to 1973 to evaluate the factors that were correlated with different levels of police aggressiveness. They found that as the size and militancy of demonstrations increased, they constituted a greater threat in the minds of the police and, as such, evoked more aggressive police responses. This approach suggests that the level of police aggressiveness occurs on a continuum in response to specific factors confronting them before and during the protest event.

della Porta (1998) takes this approach further by arguing that "police knowledge" is at the center of police responses to demonstrations. She argues that police decision making at demonstrations is not based on a straightforward assessment of threat and appropriate response, but is instead mediated by assumptions the police hold about the nature of political demonstrations and the institutional and political pressures at work. The police like any other social institution exist in both internal and external political contexts. Internally, the police have a *professional culture* that structures the way they respond to emergent events based on their preexisting attitudes toward demonstrators as well as their knowledge of available tactics and resources. In addition, they have an *environmental culture*, which encompasses the assumptions they hold about the political pressures they face in responding to contentious demonstrations. This is an effort to penetrate the "black box" of police decision making by understanding the way they classify both the level of threat a protest poses and the risk of political discord over how the event is handled.

The third approach argues that police discretion occurs within legal frames that structure how the police respond to each unique demonstration. Bjork (2005) compares police practices in Denmark and Sweden toward contentious antiglobalization demonstrations and argues that the differences in the legal statutes that govern police responses to disorder in those two countries played a central role in how demonstrations were policed. In the case of Denmark, the police are given a great deal of discretion under the law, allowing them to make on-the-spot decisions about whether or not to aggressively enforce the law in the face of illegal protest activity. In this case, the Danish police decided against a heavy-handed reaction. In Sweden, on the other hand, police statutory guidelines call for a stricter universal application of the law, and provide little guidance about the range of acceptable responses to disorderly demonstrations. This left the police without a clear legal shadow, which caused them to have uncertainty and fear. This, in turn, led to numerous bloody confrontations with demonstrators including the shooting of three participants.

Each of these approaches has strengths and weaknesses. The continuum approach's advantage is that it shows that not all demonstrations are handled in exactly the same fashion depending on the posture taken by protestors and external pressures. Even within a particular style of policing there is room for variation in the exact constellation of tactics used and their intensity. Most of these studies, however, fail to look at the ways in which police tactics are often grouped around a coherent approach. While police forces all have a variety of tactics available to them in any given situation—such as using metal barricades, ordering dispersals, or using less lethal weapons—in practice their response to demonstrations is patterned according to their strategic objectives and overall philosophy of policing. This is especially true in situations where command control of officers is maintained. Reiner (2000) has shown that individual officers have political beliefs that can affect their discretionary treatment of demonstrators, but only when they are able to act independently—as in a police riot as seen in New York on several occasions during the 1960s. The concept of police knowledge, however, begins the process of assessing the ways in which the different approaches used by the police are structured by coherent philosophies that exist in a political context.

The strength of the legal frames approach is that it takes into account the role of law in structuring the style of policing being utilized. The NYPD and other large departments have legal bureaus that advise commanders on the legality of different crowd control tactics and are involved in defending the police from civil actions by demonstrators who feel that their rights have been violated during protests. This in-house expertise creates a well-developed legal framework for commanders to operate within; and in fact at most large demonstrations in New York, including all six of the cases in this study, members of the NYPD Legal Bureau were either present or were consulted before or during the event.

The weakness of the legal frames approach is that the police do not always act within the confines of the law. In some cases, they develop interpretations of the law that are later found by the courts to be inaccurate. In other circumstances, they choose to act outside the law in the interests of larger political goals, such as preventing disruptions of politically sensitive events or what Waddington (1993) describes as "dying in a ditch." He points out that sometimes police choose to suffer "in the job" difficulties in order to avoid "on the job" problems. By this he means that sometimes the police are willing to violate their own procedures in order to avoid external censure from political leaders. He gives the example of police suppression of protests near royal events, despite the absence of a legal basis to do so (Waddington, 1994).

Each of these approaches provides an important part of the puzzle in trying to understand the nature of police practices toward demonstrations. I have distilled these insights into four primary factors that influence police discretion at demonstrations:

- *Demonstrator posture*: The ways in which the demonstrators prepare for and carry out the demonstration.
- *Style of policing*: The repertoire of tactics and strategies regularly used by the police.
- *Legal framework*: The legal context within which the police operate.
- *Political context*: The influence of elected officials in framing the police orientation toward the protestors.

These factors take into account microlevel interactional dynamics, internal institutional factors as well as macrolevel legal and political pressures.

In the rest of this chapter, I will review how each of these elements contributed to the nature of police actions directed toward demonstrations at the RNC in New York City in 2004. This exercise will show that traditional notions of police accountability through civilian complaint review boards and individual litigation are inadequate. Instead, a more comprehensive approach is required that takes into consideration the role of political pressure external to the police and the need for greater policy oversight of police departments.

The 2004 RNC

During the last week of August 2004, the Republican Party held its annual nominating convention in Madison Square Garden in midtown Manhattan. This gathering became a focus point for over a week of demonstrations of various sizes dealing with a variety of social issues including the war in Iraq, homelessness, and funding to fight AIDS. This represented a significant challenge for the NYPD as over 250,000 people were expected to participate in the largest of these demonstrations and several smaller events, some of which called for the use of civil disobedience and other tactics to attempt to disrupt the convention. Following on the heels of several years of large disruptive protests at trade summits and political conventions, the police had reason to be concerned about the potentially disruptive effects of these demonstrations. In the end, the NYPD deployed a variety of tactics to deal with these demonstrations from mass arrests and preventative detentions to facilitating unpermitted marches and closing off large sections of midtown for marches and rallies.

In order to review the factors affecting the policing of the demonstrations at the RNC, I directly observed a number of demonstrations as well as reviewed a variety of first-hand accounts, media coverage, and raw video footage. I used these observations and accounts to document the police tactics that were used at each demonstration as well as the tactics used by demonstrators. This is an inherently subjective process that relies on the expertise and experience of the observer. In this case, my own first-hand assessments are based on 20 years of close observation of political demonstrations. Unfortunately, I was unable to interview police officers or commanders directly. In part because of ongoing litigation, the NYPD has been unwilling to respond to academic inquiries about their methods and decision-making processes in dealing with demonstrations. Recent litigation, however, has generated some documentation about the police preparations for the RNC, especially the use of surveillance (Dwyer, 2007b).

While there were dozens of demonstrations of varying sizes, addressing numerous different issues, I decided to limit my investigation to the six largest demonstrations that took place at least in part near the convention center, since these events tended to most clearly require the use of specialized demonstration units and tactics. In contrast, some smaller demonstrations further from the RNC location were handled by neighborhood precinct details. One large march not included in the sample began in Brooklyn and ended in lower Manhattan two days before the convention began. The six events in the sample, in order of occurrence, were (1) the Critical Mass (CM) bicycle ride, (2) The United For Peace and Justice (UFPJ) march, (3) The Still We Rise (SWR) march, (4) The March for Our Lives (MFOL), (5) the A31 direct action, and (6) the Central Labor Council (CLC) rally. Each of these events had over 1,000 participants, was well advertised, and received extensive media coverage.

Demonstrator Posture

Earl, Soule, and McCarthy (2003) argue that the primary determinate of police practices at demonstrations is the nature of the demonstration the police are facing. They determined this by looking at the size, politics, and militancy of the group planning the event and correlating those factors with the aggressiveness of the police response. Their approach assumes that the police make judgments about the level of threat a demonstration poses to public order and public safety and respond in keeping with that assessment using a variety of tactics arranged along a continuum of forcefulness.

In order to test this approach at the RNC, I used eight factors to measure the posture of the demonstrations and seven factors to measure the posture of the police. The protestor factors are (1) the cooperativeness of negotiations prior to the event, (2) advanced public statements by demonstration organizers, (3) the openness of the organizing process to public scrutiny, (4) the level of logistical organization provided by demonstration planners, (5) the history of the relationship between the police and demonstration organizers, (6) the presence of demonstration permits, (7) the tactics and other actions taken by demonstrators during the protest event, and (8) the level of logistical control demonstration organizers have over the participants in the event.

The *negotiation* factor deals with the level of cooperation and communication between police and demonstration organizers in planning the event. The central issue in this factor is whether a permit was requested and the character of the negotiations over the permit. The *publicity* factor deals with the kinds of public statements made through the media, flyers, and public meetings about the militancy of the tactics to be used and the level of cooperation with the police. Did the organization make a public pledge of nonviolence, or did they advertise the use of illegal protest tactics such as sit-ins? The *transparency* factor concerns the openness of each group's planning process. Was there a general sense that the planning for the event was happening in an open manner or was there a perception that covert plans were being made that might result in unanticipated confrontational or illegal tactics? The *organization* factor measures the extent to which each organization had a strong infrastructure in place for the event. Were there adequate marshals and a system for communicating with police? The police generally prefer to work with organizations when they feel that the organizers have control over the crowd and can respond to changing circumstances and police demands as needed during the event. The final preevent factor is *history*, which measures the level of cooperation or confrontation in past interactions between the police and each organization. Has there been violence or arrests at this group's past events and is there a long-standing set of institutional relationships with the police?

The first "day of" factor is *permits*, which measures whether or not permits or other agreements with the police were reached and the degree to which they were followed. The *tactics/actions* factor concerns the degree to which there were actions during the demonstration that were illegal or significantly disruptive. The *logistics* factor deals with the level of organization among the protestors—especially their ability to communicate effectively with police and people participating in the demonstration. Were there adequate marshals, police liaisons, and a communication structure indicating that protest organizers had some control over the demonstration?

The police response to each of the six demonstrations was different as measured by seven factors that indicate the level of restrictiveness and aggressiveness of the actions taken by police: (1) flexibility of the police to changing circumstances, (2) use of barriers and large officer deployments, (3) mass arrests, (4) use of force, (5) special weapons and tactics, (6) negative advanced publicity about the event by the police, and (7) surveillance of demonstration organizers prior to the event.

The first factor, *flexibility*, measures the degree to which the police accommodated changes to the demonstration scenario in response to changing circumstances or organizers requests, such as allowing for a larger rally area, extending the time for a rally beyond that listed on the permit, or making space for a larger than expected crowd. *Use of force* involves the use of force by police. Did the police attempt to control the crowd or individuals within it through the use of force—whether reasonable or not, such as using baton charges, pepper spray, or horses or motorcycles to disperse crowds? The *aggressiveness* factor addresses the overall aggressiveness of the police posture. Did the police deploy very large numbers of officers relative to the size of the crowd, were large numbers of barricades used, and did police respond aggressively to minor violations of permits or minor legal violations by demonstrators? *Mass arrests* measure whether the police made mass and/or preemptive arrests, especially prior to the beginning of demonstrations. *Special weapons and tactics* deals with the degree to which the police relied on "less lethal" weaponry, special tactics, or specially equipped and trained riot units. The *publicity* factor measures the extent to which the police made positive or negative characterizations of the demonstration in the media. The final factor, *surveillance*, deals with whether or not there was police surveillance of the group in the form of infiltrating meetings or following organizers. I will now review each of the six demonstrations with an eye to the postures of both the police and demonstrators.

Critical Mass

The CM bicycle ride was held on Friday, August 27th.* This is a regular event held on the last Friday of the month in hundreds of cities around the world.† During the previous year, attendance had peaked at about 2,000 participants, who ride together in Manhattan without police permits for about 2 h on a route determined as the ride proceeds, through ad hoc decision-making processes at the front of the ride. In the previous year, there had been only a few citations issued to cyclists for traffic infractions. On the 27th, however, approximately 5,000 cyclists and several hundred police showed up for the event (Wald, 2004). The police initially made threats that they would try to prevent the ride from occurring; giving out leaflets stating that those violating traffic laws would be arrested and their bikes confiscated. So many cyclists showed up, however, that the police were not adequately equipped to stop the event from taking place. Therefore, the ride was allowed to commence. After about an hour of riding through midtown, and just as the ride neared the area of the convention, which would not begin until Monday, the police began to make arrests in three different ways. In some cases, large phalanxes of officers were used to stop the flow of the ride and encircle parts of it with orange mesh flexi-barriers and make mass arrests of all those enclosed. A smaller number of arrests were also made by undercover officers riding on unmarked Vespa scooters. These officers rode into cyclists forcing them to stop and then arresting them. Finally, some cyclists were pulled off their moving bikes by high-ranking officers, seemingly at random.

Altogether, over 250 people were arrested, several of whom were not participants in the event but merely running errands or commuting from work (Okie, 2004). Those who were arrested were transported to an unused bus depot on a nearby pier on the Hudson River, which had been converted into a temporary holding and processing facility. The conditions at the facility were a source of numerous complaints from both protestors and the police forced to work there (NYCLU, 2005, p. 36).‡ All of the participants were brought before a judge within 24 h after being arrested primarily for traffic infractions, which would normally result in a summons rather than processing. The bicycles of arrested protestors were held as evidence, meaning that most of them could not be retrieved until weeks after the convention ended, despite the fact that almost all of the charges were eventually dropped by the city, or resulted in acquittals.

---

* http://times-up.org/index.php?page=critical-mass
† www.critical-mass.org
‡ After the convention week ended, 40 police officers filed medical reports claiming that they had gotten ill while working there as a result of exposure to toxic chemicals embedded on the uncovered concrete floors (Dwyer, 2007a).

There were no negotiations prior to the event. The group has a history of not applying for permits or obeying all traffic laws and their web site and flyers indicate as such. However, there were no statements indicating a desire to foment a confrontation with the police and most past rides have occurred without arrests. The event is not highly organized and there is no formal organization or leadership in charge of the event making on-site communication with the police difficult. Overall the protest posture for this event was −5.

The police showed some flexibility in the beginning, but that came to a quick end as arrests were ordered without warning or negotiation for minor traffic violations (Dobnik, 2004; NYCLU, 2005, p. 28). The group was neither denied access to the gathering area nor subdivided. There were high levels of the use of force in the arrest process with officers pulling people off moving bicycles; scooters being used to knock over riders were mentioned by more than 10 participants in response to what were essentially minor traffic violations (NYCLU, 2005, p. 43). There was evidence of surveillance of event organizers prior to the event and there were police taking video during the event. There was no negative publicity in advance of the event. Special weapons in the form of mesh netting and undercover scooters were heavily used (Okie, 2004). The total of over 250 people arrested amounts to mass arrests. The overall police posture was 3.

United for Peace and Justice

The largest demonstration during the RNC was a march on Sunday, August 29th, organized by UFPJ.* After being denied a permit for a rally in Central Park, the group decided to have a march through midtown Manhattan on the day before the start of the convention, ending without a rally in Union Square.† Following that, they staged a small gathering in Central Park in defiance of the City's ban. Estimates by the media and organizers put the crowd at between 100,000 and 500,000 people (McFadden, 2004). Despite the large size and the heavy police presence there were very few incidents and only a handful of arrests.

There was an extensive period of negotiations with the police, but these did not result in a mutually satisfactory agreement. A permit, however, was issued and followed by the group. Despite statements of displeasure with the police in the negotiation process, the group said it would encourage lawful activity during the event. This group has a mixed history with the police. Most of their recent events have occurred without problems. In 2003, however, they held a major protest in Manhattan that ended in hundreds of arrests (NYCLU, 2003). UFPJ is a large well-organized group and had numerous marshals

---

* www.unitedforpeace.org
† The police initially offered a stationary rally on a highway on the west side of Manhattan, which was rejected by UFPJ (Cardwell, 2004a).

present during the event. There was one incident, however, when someone set a large paper and wood float on fire. The protest posture was 5.

The police were flexible in that they made no effort to stop the illegal gathering in Central Park, and did not interfere with the march except briefly following the float fire. The fire was quickly extinguished and the march was allowed to continue, although later the police waded into the crowd in an attempt to arrest those responsible, creating a significant disruption and some minor injuries (NYCLU, 2005, p. 45). Access to the march-gathering location was generally good. There were, however, minor problems at the southern extreme of the 7th Avenue march route, as crowds threatened to spill into 14th Street, which the police were trying to keep open. There was also a huge presence of police all along the march route along with heavy use of police barriers, making exiting and entering the march en route difficult. Since there was no stationary aspect to the event, there was no issue of subdividing the crowd. Finally, the only force used was limited to a few arrests related to the burned prop mentioned before. While there were legal grounds to make arrests, many departments would have avoided this in the middle of an otherwise calm and nonconfrontation crowd. There was a great deal of publicity prior to the event, but the police did not specifically suggest that there would be violent action at this specific event. There was some evidence of police surveillance, but it seemed to take the form of monitoring publicly posted information on web sites and possibly attending large public informational meetings (New York Times, 2004). The overall police posture was −5.

Still We Rise

This event took place at noon on Monday, August 30th, and was organized by a coalition of about 35 social service providers and social movement organizations representing the interests of the poor, homeless, and other at-risk populations.* The group had a permit to march from Union Square to the designated demonstration area adjacent to the convention on 8th Avenue. There were about 10,000 participants including a larger number of people of color than at other events (Della Piana, 2004). Overall the event went mostly smoothly, despite a heavy police presence. There were no arrests and limited complaints about the police.

Negotiations with the police were held prior to the event and a permit was secured. The group made no confrontational public statements and was well organized before and during the event with open organizing meetings. This was a new group, so there was no prior history. The group did not undertake any militant or illegal tactics and the event went off without incident, resulting in a posture rating of 7.

---

* www.champnetwork.org/index.php?name=swr

There were signs of flexibility in response to complaints about aggressive use of police scooters at the rear of the event.* There were no complaints about limited access, although the police presence was very high. The group was subdivided at their rally area. There were no incidents of police use of force; however, special undercover scooter units were utilized as a form of special weapons and tactics. There was some indication of surveillance of organizers prior to the event (New York Times, 2004; NYCLU, 2005, p. 17). There was no use of force, mass arrests, or negative publicity. The police posture was −2.

March for Our Lives

This event was organized primarily by the Kensington Welfare Rights Union, a militant grassroots poor people's organization based in Philadelphia.† In 2000, they had a very large unpermitted march in Philadelphia during that year's RNC, which occurred without incident. The organizers wanted to march from the United Nations to the RNC. The police refused to issue them a permit, and the group vowed to march anyway. There was a heavy police presence as the group gathered in Dag Hammarskjöld Plaza, across from the United Nations, but the police allowed the group to march with a heavy police escort. During the march there was extensive use of undercover police, who made a few arrests. There was also a report that an officer was injured during one of these arrests (Grace, 2004). Near the end of the march, as the group approached the designated rally area on 8th Avenue, the police charged into the line of march with metal barricades in an effort to break the demonstration up into smaller groups. The demonstrators, fearing arrest, and receiving no instructions or warning from the police, resisted the police. In response, the police charged the crowd with unmarked motor scooters and a phalanx of about a dozen officers with batons. This resulted in a few minor injuries to demonstrators and a serious injury to one of the plainclothes officers (Grace, 2004; NYCLU, 2005, p. 20).

The group did not negotiate with the police or obtain permits. The planning of the event was not very transparent and public statements indicated the willingness of participants to engage in civil disobedience. The group's actions at the 2000 RNC were indicative of a history of confrontation tactics. The group appeared to be well organized, but in the end had a limited number of marshals and was not able to fully direct the march. The overall posture was −3.

While the police appeared to be flexible in the beginning, their insistence on breaking up the crowd at the end of the march, without warning or

* According to New York Civil Liberties Union Associate Legal Director Christopher Dunn (personal communication August 31, 2004) march organizers complained of aggressive use of unmarked police motor scooters at the rear of the march. The police redeployed them after the NYCU raised objection to their use.
† www.kwru.org

consultation, showed some lack of flexibility. There were significant difficulties in obtaining a permit. Access was only partially limited at the gathering site, although there were large numbers of officers and barriers used both at the beginning and at the end point to subdivide the crowd. Force was used at the tail end of the event when marchers refused to be subdivided. The use of undercover scooters and undercover officers in the march were examples of the use of special weapons and tactics. There was no use of mass arrests, negative advanced publicity, or surveillance, giving the event a police posture of −2.

A31

This event was intended to be a large decentralized disruptive action with participants risking arrest using both traditional civil disobedience and more confrontation direct action tactics including blockading delegate's hotels and streets leading to the convention site. The event was organized by an *ad hoc* coalition of individuals and organizations—many oriented toward anarchist politics and direct action tactics. The group did not request any permits, and details of the exact nature, timing, and location of the actions were not made public. The goal of the event was to disrupt the convention and daily life in Manhattan as much as possible through a variety of "decentralized street actions targeting corporate fetes for delegates as well as the headquarters of 'war-profiteers' like the Carlyle Group and Hummer of Manhattan, followed by a mass convergence to 'reclaim the streets' outside Madison Square Garden with sound systems, marching bands and free food" (Ferguson, 2004). The police, however, had strong intelligence and were present in force wherever demonstrators gathered that day. There were over 1,100 arrests made including large groups near the World Trade Center site, Union Square, Herald Square, and the main Public Library (Cardwell, 2004b; NYCLU, 2005, p. 21). Orange mesh netting was used in many of these instances to corral large groups (NYCLU, 2005, p. 12). Arrestees were held for an average of 32.7 h before seeing a judge at arraignment (Dwyer, 2007a). This event scored negative in every category, resulting in a posture of −8.

Flexibility, access, and permits were not really relevant since there was no fixed demonstration area and no permits were requested. There were certainly large numbers of officers assigned to the demonstration, but its decentralized nature meant that they were rarely concentrated in one area. Instead, they were organized into mobile teams that were positioned as deemed necessary based on police intelligence. There were several reports of force being used, usually in connection with mass arrests. Overall, however, there were no reports of serious injuries (NYCLU, 2005, p. 44). There was extensive surveillance of groups and individuals planning to take part in the A31 day of action (Dwyer, 2007b; NYCLU, 2005, p. 16; New York Times, 2004). Surveillance was undertaken through infiltration of groups and open meetings in New York and around the country. In addition, the NYPD shared information and worked cooperatively with a number of other local and national law-enforcement agencies. Both named and unnamed police sources made reference to the possibility of violence at the demonstrations in the media on several occasions (Friedman, 2004; Meek, 2004; O'shaughnessy, 2004; Parascandola, 2004). There was also extensive use of orange mesh netting to effect mass arrests and undercover officers as forms of special weapons and tactics. All of the arrestees were held in excess of the legal maximum of 24 h at Pier 57 (NYCLU, 2005, p. 14). The police posture for the event was 7.

Central Labor Council

The CLC represents all of the major unions in New York City.* They called for a large rally near the convention to protest Republican antilabor policies. The event had a permit and was attended by several thousand union members from a wide variety of locals, mostly organized into identifiable contingents. The CLC has a history of organizing events with the police and, while a few locals have had confrontations with police in recent years, the council has not. Overall, the event was peaceful and there were no arrests or other incidents, resulting in a posture rating of 8.

While the event went smoothly, there were some problems assessing the event because of extensive use of barricades to subdivide the crowd and a large police presence (NYCLU, 2005, p. 17). Otherwise, there were no problems with flexibility, use of force, mass arrests, special weapons, negative publicity, or surveillance. The police posture was −6.

According to Earl, Soule, and McCarthy (2003), as the protest posture measure increased, the police posture measure should decrease. The higher the protest posture, the more open, prepared, and cooperative the protest was and the higher the police posture, the more flexible, relaxed, and cooperative the police were.

Overall the correlation between demonstrator posture and police action is rather high, as Figure 16.1 shows. This correlation, however, is not consistent as Table 16.1 illustrates. While the SWR and MFOL demonstrations had very different postures (7 and −3, respectively), the police posture was the same in both instances (−2), indicating that the demonstrator posture in at least one of these cases was not particularly relevant in explaining the police behavior. More importantly, there is a substantial grouping of the events at the two ends of the spectrum. Table 16.1 shows that two groups had strongly positive ratings, while the other groups all had negative ratings, with no groups landing in the middle. This suggests that rather than a continuum, the police response was tightly clustered around two different constellations of police practices. Just looking at the posture of the demonstrators—before and during the event—does not adequately explain the police response.

* www.nycclc.org

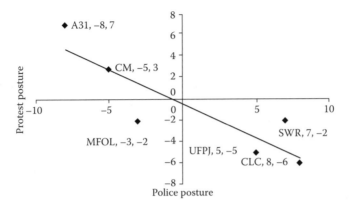

Figure 16.1 Relationship between police and protestor posture for six demonstrations.

Legal Frames

Since the actions of the demonstrators alone do not fully explain the differences in how the RNC demonstrations were handled, an examination of the role of the legal frames surrounding demonstration policing is needed.

Table 16.1   Protest Posture and Police Posture Scores for Six Demonstrations

	CM	UFPJ	SWR	MFOL	A31	CLC
		Protest Posture				
1. Negotiations	−1	0	1	−1	−1	1
2. Statements	0	1	1	−1	−1	1
3. Transparency	−1	1	1	−1	−1	1
4. Organization	−1	1	1	1	−1	1
5. History	0	0	0	0	−1	1
6. Permit	−1	1	1	−1	−1	1
7. Tactics/actions	0	0	1	0	−1	1
8. Organization	−1	1	1	0	−1	1
Score	−5	5	7	−3	−8	8
		Police Posture				
1. Inflexibility	0	−1	−1	−1	1	−1
2. Use of force	1	−1	−1	1	1	−1
3. Control measures	0	1	1	1	1	0
4. Mass arrests	1	−1	−1	−1	1	−1
5. Special weapons	1	−1	0	0	1	−1
6. Negative publicity	−1	−1	−1	−1	1	−1
7. Surveillance	1	−1	1	−1	1	−1
Score	3	−5	−2	−2	7	−6

The law plays a central role in police discretion. As an enabling force, it provides the police with legal backing to take enforcement action. From the point of view of the police, the law is a tool that is available to them for taking actions to restore order in a broad sense. As part of this dynamics, the police regularly make decisions about whether or not to "invoke" the law when presented with an opportunity to do so (Goldstein, 1977). As a restrictive force, the law sets constraints on the actions police can take. Legal restrictions on the use of force, grounds for making an arrest, and searches and seizures limit unfettered police discretion.

The basic framework for the policing of demonstrations by the NYPD prior to the RNC was the *command and control* approach (Vitale, 2005). There have been several legal challenges to this approach, which have helped to establish the legal framework in operation just prior to the RNC. Overall, the courts have not directly prohibited the methods used by the NYPD in previous demonstrations. In *Gutman v. City of New York; Stauber v. City of New York; Conrad v. City of New York* 2004—[S.D.N.Y., Index Nos. 03 Civ. 9162, 9163, and 9164 (RWS)], the federal courts ruled that some of the restrictive use of barricades at previous demonstrations was unconstitutional, but, that with minor adjustments, would be acceptable. In general, those adjustments were made during the RNC. In addition, there were several legal challenges to the denial of permits to protest groups under this approach including *UFPJ v. City of New York*—[S.D.N.Y., Index No. 03 Civ. 810 (BSJ)] (U.S. Court of Appeals, 2nd Cir., 03-7301) and *UFPJ v. Bloomberg*—(Supreme Court, New York County, Index No. 111893/04), both of which were denied by the federal courts. In essence, the basic strategy of micromanaging demonstrations has been held up to legal scrutiny.

There are several areas, however, where the courts have created clear restrictions concerning police actions at demonstrations, creating the outer boundary of the legal framework within which the police are expected to operate. In *Roundtree* et al. *v. Brown* the state court ruled that according to the New York State Constitution, people who have been arrested must be arraigned or released within 24 h, preventing police from holding large groups of protestors for long periods of time on the basis of backups in processing. The courts have also ruled that the police cannot make mass arrests unless a law has been violated and an opportunity to disperse has been provided. Finally, there is a clear standard that demonstration permits are not required for political activity taking place on public sidewalks as long as there is no use of amplified sound, and pedestrian traffic is not impeded.

This analysis should provide a clear set of legal boundaries for police actions during the RNC. In most cases this was true. While restrictions were present in the granting of permits and in access to demonstration areas, most events were policed in a manner consistent with this framework. On several occasions, however, the NYPD operated well outside this framework. At the

A31 event, they engaged in pre-emptive arrests, and held demonstrators well beyond the 24 h arraignment time limit. In fact, 90% of all arrests during the RNC have either been dismissed by the prosecutor or ended in acquittals, suggesting that the police routinely made arrests without sufficient legal basis. In one case, a top police commander was found guilty of "abuse of authority" by the city's Civilian Complaints Review Board, for ordering the arrest of a large group on August 31 without providing warnings or the opportunity to disperse (Dwyer, 2006). In addition, numerous claims of action against the city for false arrest are under way. What then could explain the decision to operate outside a legal framework in so many cases? The next part of the puzzle comes from looking at the ways in which the flexible assortment of police tactics are patterned.

Policing Style

The way police departments respond to a wide variety of circumstances is not happenstance or at the full discretion of individual officers or their commanders. James Q. Wilson (1968) in his pioneering study of police practices showed that departments tend to be grouped into broad categories based on their underlying philosophy of policing. He describes the fundamental differences in approach within three styles of policing: service, law enforcement, and order maintenance. Similarly, the policing of demonstrations is influenced by broad philosophies about what tactics to use to balance the demands of free expression and public order.

Over the last 10 years the NYPD has dealt with demonstrations primarily through the utilization of a *command and control* style of policing, characterized by a zero tolerance attitude toward disorder (Vitale, 2005). This approach is based on the NYPD's broad commitment to the "broken windows" theory (Kelling & Coles, 1996; Wilson & Kelling, 1982), and its emphasis on controlling serious crime through aggressive enforcement of even minor disorderly behaviors. This style of protest policing relies on the micro management of protest activities through restrictions on granting permits, deployment of large numbers of officers, aggressive response to even minor illegal activity, and tight control of the movement of demonstrators before, during, and after demonstrations in order to ensure that more serious disorderly or riotous behavior does not develop (NYCLU, 2003; Vitale, 2005).

This style of policing contrasts with two other predominant styles of policing associated with large national demonstrations. The first is the *negotiated management* approach in which the police attempt to facilitate demonstrations while protecting public safety. This approach relies on police flexibility in dealing with illegal behavior, by permitting them to avoid enforcement action if it is in the interest of avoiding an escalated confrontation. The second style is the *Miami Model*, which is characterized by aggressive policing—including heavy use of less lethal weaponry, infiltration of protest organizations, negative advanced publicity by city officials of protest groups, and extensive restrictions on protest timing and locations.

In the case of the RNC, the NYPD's tactics were tightly grouped around either the *command and control* style or the *Miami Model*. As mentioned before, the *command and control* style relies on large numbers of officers, extensive use of barricades, and a willingness to use force and arrests in response to even minor violations of the law. The *Miami Model* utilizes these measures as well as negative advanced publicity, surveillance of organizers, pre-emptive mass arrests, and the use of special weapons and tactics. The CM and A31 events both had significantly more aggressive police posture scores—3 and 7, respectively—and saw the use of special weapons and tactics and, in the case of A31, extensive surveillance and negative publicity. The other four demonstrations were all grouped between –3 and –6, and did not see much use of surveillance, negative advanced publicity, or special weapons and tactics.

This indicates that the police had two basic strategic orientations during the RNC protests. For groups that were reasonably cooperative with the police and not viewed as a major threat to public order, the *command and control* style was used. While this is a more restrictive model of policing than used by most other large American and European police departments (NYCLU, 2003), it allowed for four major demonstrations to take place without significant incident. The other two events, however, were met by the much more restrictive *Miami Model* style, which effectively disrupted these protests and together resulted in about 1,000 arrests. The question remains, however, as to why the NYPD chose to use one strategy rather than another in each case.

Political Context

The NYPD is led by a civilian Commissioner, who serves at the pleasure of the mayor. In addition, the City Council plays an important role in overseeing the department's budget and policies through its Public Safety Committee. Therefore, the police department must take some cues from the mayor and other political leaders—especially the chair of the Public Safety Committee, who at the time was Peter Vallone Jr., an outspoken supporter of the police. These two leaders played an important role in setting a political climate of permissiveness through public statements and legislative action.

The decision to host the RNC was strongly supported by New York's Republican mayor, Michael Bloomberg, who argued that the city would benefit financially from the business associated with the convention. He also pledged that he would not allow the city to be substantially disrupted by the convention despite the extensive security measures that would be required and the threat of large and possibly militant demonstrations.

Bloomberg stated that he supported the right to protest in the abstract, but that in concrete terms there would be significant limitations in people's ability to do so. Because of concerns about recent constraints on large demonstrations, the New York branch of the American Civil Liberties Union (NYCLU) undertook a political campaign to try to force the mayor to agree to secure a variety of basic First Amendment rights. They circulated a memorandum of understanding that called on the police to allow people free access to and from demonstrations, to refrain from spying on protest organizations, and to avoid the use of unnecessary force by police. The NYCLU got seven local members of congress to sign the memorandum and then present it to the mayor, who did not sign the memorandum or even respond to repeated requests to do so.

The NYCLU also attempted to work with the New York City Council to ensure that the police respected existing First Amendment protections. Following the large antiwar demonstration of February 2003, the NYCLU attempted to hold hearings in the Public Safety Committee to begin a public discourse over the crowd control policies of the NYPD. The chair of the committee, however, refused to hold any hearings about the NYPD's handling of the 2003 event. In addition, he refused to hold hearings in advance of the RNC to explore the policies that would be used. This sent a strong message to the police that City Council oversight of their past and future practices would be limited. The NYCLU and other advocates managed to go around the Public Safety Committee and have hearings in a different committee with a more sympathetic Council member, Bill Perkins from Harlem. Because these hearings were not held in Public Safety, however, there was little possibility of any specific legislative action to occur. In addition, the police refused to cooperate in these hearings by either not appearing or sending low-level officials who provided only minimal information to the committee. In the end, a very generally worded nonbinding resolution was passed (389-A) that called for timely issuing of permits, reduced use of restrictive protest pens, and placement of demonstrations near relevant RNC venues. All but the last of these were ignored by the NYPD, and the Public Safety Committee chair again refused to hold hearings on these and other failures following the RNC.

In another example of the mayor's support for restrictions on protest activity, different city agencies made the securing of protest permits very difficult. The largest protest group, UFPJ, was denied a permit for a rally in Central Park by the Parks Department and after losing an appeal in federal court decided not to hold a rally rather than do so in a remote location chosen by the police. Mr. Bloomberg's press secretary, Edward Skyler, said that "if U.P.J. [sic.] feels that marching past Madison Square Garden and having a rally off the Hudson River is such a tragic abuse of the First Amendment, then they have the option of not taking the city up on its offer" (Steinhauser & Cardwell, 2004). Most other groups did receive permits from the NYPD, but not until about a month before the convention, reducing the time available for planning and outreach.

Bloomberg also made two comments that indicated a disregard for some of the protestors and their right to demonstrate. Just prior to the beginning of the convention, the mayor, when asked about reports that some protests might be disruptive, said that if some people "start to abuse our privileges, then we lose them" (Steinhauser & Cardwell, 2004). This created a lot of concern among civil liberties advocates who pointed out that people do not lose constitutional rights at the whim of the mayor. In another press conference the mayor equated the more militant demonstrators with terrorists:

> It is true that a handful of people have tried to destroy our city by going up and yelling at visitors here because they don't agree with their views. Think about what that says. This is America, New York, cradle of liberty, the city for free speech if there ever was one and some people think that we shouldn't allow people to express themselves. That's exactly what the terrorists did, if you think about it, on 9/11. Now this is not the same kind of terrorism but there's no question that these anarchists are afraid to let people speak out (Archibold, 2004).

These statements suggest that the mayor's tolerance for demonstrations was limited to those that adhered to the guidelines created by the city, and that any protest activity falling outside that framework was no longer viewed as legitimate or protected by the First Amendment. This sent a message to both the demonstrators and the police that the mayor was willing to accept some aggressive policing in order to prevent demonstrations from creating any significant disruption to either the convention or everyday life in the city.

Conclusion

Understanding police discretion at protest events requires a multifaceted approach that takes into consideration interactional dynamics before and during the event, institutional dynamics that shape police knowledge and tactics, and the political and legal context within which the police must function. In the case of the RNC, on-the-ground police decision making was influenced by larger political forces both inside and outside the department. Police commanders made advanced decisions about how different demonstrations would be policed based at least in part on whether or not they believed these groups were likely to disrupt either the convention or daily life in the city. In those cases, the police utilized extralegal measures to disrupt the protests through pre-emptive mass arrests.

While one of the chief functions of the police is to maintain public order, they do not have a free hand in how they do this. The constitutional and other legal constraints placed on the police are essential not only for maintaining the rights of civil society to express its political views, but also for ensuring the legitimacy of the police in the eyes of the public. As Robert Peel understood almost 200 years ago, the success of a civil police force relies on its acceptance and support among the population being policed. The extensive use of illegal methods of crowd control threatens to undermine this legitimacy. Conversely, failure to maintain order can result in political pressures placed on the police by both elite and popular actors, which can also result in a reduction in legitimacy. The challenge is to construct methods of policing protest activity that maintain order within a legal framework. This means that the police need to be flexible in how they define order and when they take enforcement action. Either a zero tolerance attitude toward disorder on the one hand or a complete failure to ensure order on the other can result in substantial disruptions to police legitimacy and authority.

References

Archibold, R. (2004, September 3). Protesters try to get in last word before curtain falls. *The New York Times*.

Bittner, E. (1970). *The Functions of the Police in Modern Society*. Rockville, MD: National Institute of Mental Health.

Bjork, M. (2005). Between frustration and aggression: Legal framing and the policing of public disorder in Sweden and Denmark. *Policing and Society, 15*(3), 305–326.

Boghosian, H. (2007). *Punishing Protest: Government Tactics the Suppress Free Speech*. New York: National Lawyers Guild.

Cardwell, D. (2004a, July 15). Police offer convention protesters a site far from garden. *New York Times*, p. B1.

Cardwell, D. (2004b, September 1). At least 900 arrested in city as protesters clash with police. *New York Times*, p. 1.

Corsianos, M. (2003). Discretion in detectives' decision making in high profile cases. *Police Practices and Research, 4*, 301–315.

Das, D. K., & Jiao, A. Y. (2004). *Public Order: A Global Perspective*. Upper Saddle River, NJ: Prentice Hall.

Davis, K. (1975). *Police Discretion*. St. Paul, MN: West.

Della Piana, L. (2004). Protestors Demand Economic & Racial Justice at RNC. *Color Lines*, September. http://www.arc.org/racewire/040901l_piana.html.

della Porta, D. (1998). Police knowledge and protest policing: Some reflections on the Italian case. In D. della Porta & H. Reiter (Eds), *Policing Protest: The Control of Mass Demonstrations in Western Democracies*. Minneapolis, MN: Minnesota University Press.

della Porta, D., & Peterson, A. (2005). Special issue: Policing political protest after Seattle. *Policing and Society, 15*(3 September), 233–234.

della Porta, D., Peterson, A., & Reiter, H. (2006). *The Policing of Transnational Protest*. Burlington, VT: Ashgate.

della Porta, D., & Reiter, H. (1998). *Policing Protest: The Control of Mass Demonstrations in Western Democracies*. Minneapolis, MN: Minnesota University Press.

Dobnik, V. (2004, August 27). Police arrest 250 in mass bicycle protest. *Associated Press*.

Dwyer, J. (2006, March 9). Charges, but no penalty, for a chiefs role in a convention arrest. *The New York Times*, p. B1.

Dwyer, J. (2007a, February 8). Records show scrutiny of detainees in '04 protests. *New York Times*, p. B3.

Dwyer, J. (2007b, March 25). City police spied broadly before G.O.P. convention. *New York Times*, p. A1.

Earl, J., Soule, S. & McCarthy, J. D. (2003). Protest under fire? Explaining the policing of protest. *American Sociological Review, 68*, 581–606.

Ferguson, S. (2004, August 27). Dispatch from New York: Whose streets? *Mother Jones*.

Friedman, S. C. (2004, August 23). Radicals plot bad weather. *New York Post*.

Garland, D. (2001). *The Culture of Control: Crime and Social Order in Contemporary Society*. Chicago: University of Chicago Press.

Getzen, C. (2004, June 8). Infamous 'Miami Model' of protest clampdown, coming to a town near you. *New Standard*.

Goldstein, H. (1977). *Policing in a Free Society*. Cambridge, MA: Ballinger.

Grace, M. (2004, August 31). Protestors attack detective, kick him in head. *Daily News*, p. 7.

Kelling, G., & Coles, C. (1996). *Fixing Broken Windows: Restoring order and Reducing Crime in Our Communities*. New York: Touchstone.

Langan, P. A., Greenfield, L. A., Smith, S. K., Durose, M. R., & Levine, D. J. (2001). *Contacts Between Police and the Public: Finding from the 1999 Survey*. Washington DC: U.S. Department of Justice, Bureau of Justice Statistics.

McCarthy, J. D., & McPhail, C. (1998). The institutionalization of protest in the United States. In D. S. Meyer & S. Tarrow (Eds), *The Social Movement Society* (pp. 83–110). Boulder, CO: Rowman and Littlefield.

McFadden, R. (2004, August 30). Vast anti-Bush rally greets republicans in New York. *New York Times*, p. A1.

McPhail, C., Schweingruber, D., & McCarthy, J. D. (1998). Protest policing in the United States, 1960–1995. In D. della Porta, & H. Reiter (Eds), *Policing Protest: The Control of Mass Demonstrations in Western Democracies*. Minneapolis, MN: Minnesota University Press.

Meek, J. G. (2004, August 19). Violence at RNC feared: Protests may turn bloody, feds warn. *Daily News*, p. 8.

New York Civil Liberties Union. (2003). Arresting Protest. New York Civil Liberties Union.

New York Civil Liberties Union. (2005). Rights and Wrongs at the Republican National Convention. New York Civil Liberties Union.

New York Times. (2004). Police surveillance and the 2004 Republican National Convention. *New York Times*. Document File from www.nytimes.com/ref/nyregion/RNC_intel_digests.html.

Noakes, J., & Gillham, P. F. (2006). Aspects of the 'New Penology' in the Police Response to Major Political Protests in the United States, 1999–2000. In D. della Porta, & H. Reiter (Eds), *The Policing Transnational Protest*. Burlington, VT: Ashgate.

Okie, B. (2004). What's Scarier than 6000 Bicyclists? Portland Independent Media Center. http://portland.indymedia.org/en/2004/09/296942.shtml.

O'shaughnessy, P. (2004, August 26). Anarchists hot for Mayhem. *Daily News*.

Parascandola, R. (2004, August 13). What to Expect When You're ...; Expecting the Worst; Cops' Manual on dealing with Demonstrators at the GOP Convention Tells them to Watch Out for Dirty Tricks and Ignore Verbal Abuse. *Newsday*, p. A3.

Reiner, R. (2000). *The Politics of the Police*. New York: Oxford University Press.

Reiss, A. (1971). *The Police and the Public*. New Haven: Yale University Press.

Scahill, J. (2004, November 24). The Miami Model: Paramilitaries, Embedded Journalists and Illegal Protests. *Democracy Now*.

Schweingruber, D. (2000). Mob sociology and escalated force: Sociology's contribution to repressive police tactics. *Sociological Quarterly, 41*(3), 371–390.

Schafer, J. A., & Mastrofski, S. D. (2005). Police leniency in traffic encounters: Exploratory findings from observations and interviews. *Journal of Criminal Justice, 33*, 225–238.

Seron, C., Pereira, J., & Kovath, J. (2004). Judging police misconduct: 'Street-level' versus professional policing. *Law and Society Review, 38*, 665–710.

Skolnick, J. (1969). *The Politics of Protest: Violent Aspects of Protest and Confrontation*. Task Force on Demonstrations, Protests, and Group Violence, Washington, DC.

Skolnick, J., & Fyfe, J. (1993). *Above the Law: Police and Excessive Use of Force*. New York: The Free Press.

Steinhauser, J., & Cardwell, D. (2004, August 23). A week to go, and protesters wonder: Keep it legal, or go for the park? *The New York Times*, p. B1.

Vitale, A. S. (2005). From negotiated management to command and control: How the NYPD polices protests. *Policing and Society, 15*, 283–304.

Vitale, A. S. (2007). The Command and Control and Miami Models at the 2004 Republican National Convention: New forms of policing protests. *Mobilization, 12*(4), 403–415.

Waddington, P. A. J. (1993). Dying in a ditch: The use of police powers in Public Order. *International Journal of the Sociology of Law, 21*, 334–353.

Waddington, P. A. J. (1994). *Liberty and Order: Public Order Policing in a Capital City*. London: UCL Press.

Wald, J. (2004, August 28). 264 Arrested in NYC Bicycle Protest. *CNN*, CNN.com

Walker, S. (1977). *A Critical History of Police Reform: The Emergence of Professionalism*. Lexington, MA: Lexington Books.

Wilson, J. Q. (1968). *Varieties of Police Behavior*. Cambridge, MA: Harvard University Press.

Wilson, J. Q., & Kelling, G. (1982). Broken windows. *The Atlantic Monthly*, pp. 29–38.

Winter, M. (1998). Police philosophy and protest policing in the federal Republic of Germany, 1960-1990. In D. della Porta & H. Reiter (Eds), *Policing Protest: The Control of Mass Demonstrations in Western Democracies*. Minneapolis, MN: Minnesota University Press.

Urban Crime and Criminal Investigation in Slovenia* 17

GORAZD MEŠKO, DARKO MAVER,
and INES KLINKON

Contents

Slovenia is a country that has published official statistics for the last 60 years. In addition to official statistics on crime, the International Crime Victim Survey (ICVS) has been conducted since 1992 (three sweeps, 1992, 1996, 2000) along with several fear of crime studies (Meško, 2008; Mitar & Meško, 2008). Despite this, several changes in the Penal Code, Criminal Procedure Code, organization of police, and police practice as well as differences in gathering and dealing with police statistics make it very difficult for researchers to get an accurate picture of crime trends and the clearance rate situation in both

---

* Meško, G., Maver, D., & Klinkon, I. (2007). Applied criminological aspects of crime control in the capital of Slovenia: Good old statistics, police caseload and new challenges, *Nauka, Policija, Bezbednost*, 12(1), 25–44. With permission.

Slovenia and Ljubljana. Official statistics on recorded criminal offenses in Slovenia given by the General Police Directorate at the Ministry of the Interior are a collection of statistical data from 11 regional police directorates that represent the situation at their territory.

A general situation on crime and clear-up rates in Slovenia will be presented in the first section of this chapter. The second section will focus on property offenses, particularly on burglaries in Ljubljana, the capital of Slovenia. The third part is a reflection on a possible improvement of criminal investigation in the city.

General Trends of Reported Crime and Clear-Up Rates

Resolution on the national program of crime prevention and crime control (Official Gazette of the Republic of Slovenia, 43/2006, from here on "Resolution") gave an overview of trends of per year numbers of criminal offenses in the period from 1981 to 2005 (Figure 17.1). On the left-hand side of Figure 17.1 the scale depicts the number of recorded criminal offenses, while on the right-hand side the scale is meant to show clear-up rates in the corresponding period. Increases and decreases in volume are partly a consequence of changes in criminal activity, changes in penal law, and changes in criminal procedure, partly a consequence of peoples' perceptions of crime, and partly a consequence of the activities of political and law-enforcement agencies. This combination of factors, which together influence trends in annual numbers of criminal offenses, cannot be explained solely in terms of changes to the "objective reality of crime." It is also necessary to take account of the characteristics of suspects, victims, places, and interactions in which criminal offenses took place.

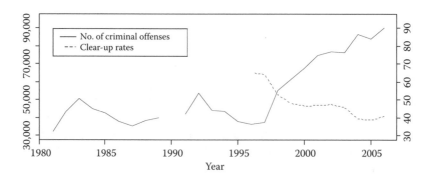

Figure 17.1 Number of recorded criminal offenses from 1981 to 2006 and clear-up rates in Slovenia from 1996 to 2006. (Adapted from Resolution of the national crime prevention and crime control programme 2006; Annual report of police work 2006, 2007.)

The overview of general trends (Figure 17.1) highlights that the number of criminal offenses increased after 1997. The greatest proportion of growth occurred in the category of criminal offenses against property. Since an important change in the penal law regarding the registration and prosecution of less serious property offenses was adopted in 1998 in Slovenia, the increase in recorded criminal offenses may be attributed to this fact (and not to the actual increase of offenses). From 1998 onward, the police had to investigate and press charges for all property offenses, irrespective of whether victims wanted the prosecution; hence many more offenses, which were previously abandoned because victims did not insist on pressing charges, were recorded.

While discussing efficient and effective criminal investigation, several performance criteria may be used. The most common measure, however, is the "clearance rate" (Cordner, 1989, p. 146), which means the percentage of known suspects in regard to all recorded offenses. Criminal investigation is therefore successful if it leads to a suspect and to criminal charges. The higher the rate, the better the work of the police. The clearance rate is different for different types of offenses; it differs across countries and through time. Decreases in clearance rates (on the right-hand-side scale of Figure 17.1) could be an indication of the diminishing effectiveness of police work. The other possible measure of investigative effectiveness is the number of convicted suspects. Not all suspects are convicted at the end of the trial; hence effective police investigation should only be done on the one that collects enough solid evidence for conviction. Since the end result of the trial depends on several agencies (law enforcement, investigating judge, and prosecution), the clearance rate will be used as the measure for investigative effectiveness.

In Slovenia, during the last decade, there has been a constant decrease in clearance rates, which dropped from the very solid 65% in the year 1996 to only 40% in the year 2006. At the same time, the number of recorded offenses increased (according to police statistics) from 36,587 criminal offenses in 1996 to 90,354 offenses in 2006 (Figure 17.1). The causes of such an increase in crime are difficult to identify without more detailed research (but was at least partly explained with the changes in the Penal Code), but it is a fact that police investigative work is not as effective as it used to be. The police used to boast of their good performance relative to other states, but it is quite a different story now. It is important to note, however, that another change in crime trends and clearance rates occurred in 2007 and there was again a decrease in recorded offenses (88,197) and an increase in clearance rates (43%). Such a trend was also evident in 2008. Again, it is difficult to say if these changes reflect an actual decrease in the number of criminal offenses and an increase police efficiency, or is in a result of rearranging statistics.

It is difficult to compare clearance rates among different countries for crimes in general, because there are differences in crime rates, crime patterns, systems of detection, investigation, and prosecution, and there are different court and trial procedures, organization of police and court systems, and criminal procedure and criminal law. Therefore, it is more appropriate to concentrate on specific criminal offenses such as burglary or larceny, which are typical and easily defined property offenses in all criminal codes.

Property Crime in Slovenia

Property crime and crime in general are generally a problem of urban environments. Three quarters of all criminal offenses in Slovenia were recorded in urban environments. Besides this, the fact that offenders are becoming increasingly violent in their acts is of mounting concern (Table 17.1).

By analyzing offense data provided by the general police administration, an increasing trend in the number and in the crime rates can be discovered. Not surprisingly, property crime constitutes the largest proportion of registered offenses. Annually, it accounts for more than 80% of all criminal offenses and about a half of all material loss inflicted by crime. Besides criminal offenses of sexual and/or violent nature, this group of offenses has strong sentimental repercussions and affects citizens' well-being with their unpredictability (Table 17.2).

Statistics for burglary offenses in Slovenia as a whole in the last decade show the same pattern as general statistics. In 1996 there were 7,729 burglaries, while in 2006 the number rose to 18,107. This kind of crime shows the highest jump in 1998 (twice the number of the year before), but that was at least partly due to new legislation in the field of prosecuting this kind of offense. Nevertheless, it is obvious that the clearance rate dropped from 30%

Table 17.1   Property Crime: Slovenia

Year	Number of Criminal Offenses Against Property
1996	23,645
1997	22,698
1998	37,441
1999	45,342
2000	48,157
2001	53,527
2002	54,835
2003	55,983
2004	65,250
2005	63,632
2006	65,278
2007	62,606

Source: Adapted from Resolution of the national crime prevention and crime control programme 2006; Annual report of police work 2006, 2007.

Table 17.2   Types of Property Crime: Slovenia

Year	Criminal Offense		
	Larceny	Burglary	Robbery
1996	9,885	7,729	507
1997	9,660	7,359	341
1998	14,659	13,492	379
1999	17,192	16,187	463
2000	18,597	15,962	474
2001	23,806	15,617	503
2002	23,803	16,431	449
2003	24,770	16,947	349
2004	28,176	22,460	398
2005	28,331	20,252	426
2006	31,639	18,107	521
2007	29,005	17,891	445

Source: Adapted from Resolution of the national crime prevention and crime control programme 2006; Annual report of police work 2006, 2007.

in 1996 to only 12% in 2005. In 2006, the clearance rate increased again to 14.7% and in 2007 to a solid 21.7% (Figure 17.2).

Crime and Clear-Up Rates in Ljubljana

Ljubljana, the capital of Slovenia, is a dynamic Central European city in a broad basin between the Alps and the Adriatic Sea. It covers a surface area of 275 km² and has a population of 276,000. Ljubljana's geographical position has governed its colorful past, since it is situated on a natural passage leading from Central Europe to the Mediterranean and toward the East called the "Ljubljana Gate." From its very beginning, Ljubljana's culture and lifestyle have been attuned to contemporary currents in Europe, while both the Central

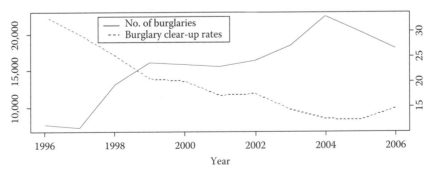

Figure 17.2 Burglary—clear-up rates. (Adapted from Resolution of the national crime prevention and crime control programme 2006; Annual report of police work 2006, 2007.)

European and the Mediterranean spirit have influenced the temperament of its residents. Ljubljana's economy has always been quite heterogeneous, enabling it to adapt rapidly to the ever-changing environment of the world economy. Ljubljana produces about 25% of Slovenia's gross domestic product and has maintained a constant orientation toward long-term international business cooperation. An increasingly comprehensive, high-quality tourist and catering sector has complemented this process on the one hand and well-developed commercial activities on the other. At present, the level of the active working population is 62%, and out of the total employed, 50% are women, 64% work in the economic sector, and 36% work in the public sector (according to the 2003 statistics). Industry is still the most important employer in the city (pharmaceuticals, petrochemicals, and food processing), and Ljubljana's industrial companies are among the major Slovene exporters. Retailing, financial and other business services, transport and communication, construction, skilled trades and services, and tourism and catering follow industry. In the public sector, employment is found in the fields of education and culture, followed by health care and social security, social organizations, and local administration. Ljubljana is certainly a city with a high quality of life.

Ljubljana Police Directorate and City of Ljubljana Police Stations

Ljubljana Police Directorate (LPD) (or Ljubljana Police Department) is by far the largest police department in Slovenia. It covers a territory of 3,807 km^2 (18.8% of the territory of Slovenia) with 565,000 inhabitants (28.2% of the population of Slovenia) and 34 communities divided into 1,378 settlements, where only Ljubljana has the status of a municipality. Within LPD there are 13 district police stations (five of them in the territory of the city of Ljubljana), four border police stations (toward Croatia), and nine so-called police offices. With the entery of Slovenia to the Schengen border system, new police departments were created for the control of international migration. Altogether, there are 1,228 uniformed and 265 plainclothes police officers in the directorate. Most of the uniformed police officers work at dislocated police stations, while the criminal investigation (detective) sector is centralized at the headquarters in Ljubljana. Ljubljana has five police stations, which are the most heavily burdened with crime within the authority of LPD. After reorganization of the police in 1992, the so-called "local criminal investigative units" were established at police stations and "mobile criminal investigative units" were set up in the four largest Police Directorates in Slovenia (Ljubljana, Maribor, Celje, and Koper). The formet units were responsible for investigation of less serious local criminal offenses, while the latter units were responsible for the control of criminal hot spots and for immediate response in critical situations. Members of both work in civil clothes.

It is important to emphasize that more than 50% of all recorded criminal offenses in Slovenia occur within the territory of LPD. Most of them

Table 17.3   Number of Police Officers (Uniformed and Plainclothes Members of Local Investigative Units) in the City of Ljubljana in 2007

	2007	
Police Station	Uniformed	Local Criminal Investigators (Plainclothes)
Bežigrad	87	16
Center	144	25
Moste	114	17
Vič	95	15
Šiška	81	17

Table 17.4   Number of Criminal Investigators at the LPD

CID Ljubljana	1994	1996	2000	2004	2007 (March 30)
Criminal Investigators	148	173	182	186	187

(around 80%) occur in Ljubljana and are property offenses, but there is also a significant concentration of other forms of more serious crime such as drug offenses, organized crime, economic crime, and contract killings. Nevertheless, it is important to stress that Ljubljana has been nominated as the safest capital city within the European Union even though crime rates continue to increase. About 80% of all recorded criminal offenses are dealt with by the uniformed police, while the criminal police concentrate only on the most serious crimes. Statistics presented in the following text are based on our analysis of data on reported crime and police in Ljubljana provided to us by the Ministry of the Interior for the purpose of this study (Table 17.3).

Local criminal investigators are formally uniformed police officers who do plainclothes criminal investigation at the local level (police station) and are employed at a local police station. Criminal investigators are police detectives who are employed at a regional CID and are plainclothes police officers (Table 17.4).

Applied Criminological Aspects: Crime in Ljubljana

Crime in most Slovenian urban environments is becoming increasingly worrying, as statistics on reported crime show that crime rates are highest in urban settings. Its main causes can be identified in the diminishing power of social control, social disorganization and low social capital, social exclusion, family breakup, identity crisis, and unsound urban planning as well as more opportunity for crime commission. In broader terms however, crime is influenced by some structural and political changes in recent years in Slovenia as well as in Europe more widely. Illegal trafficking of humans, arms, and

Table 17.5 All Criminal Offenses in the Municipality of Ljubljana

Year	Total Criminal Offenses	The Offender is Known
2000	23,308	6,533
2001	23,191	6,354
2002	24,674	6,737
2003	26,901	5,630
2004	31,633	5,560
2005	*	*
2006	35,822	10,211
2007	34,041	11,574

*Not available.

drugs is high on the European political agenda, more so for its outer borders where these problems are most present. The diminishing level of quality of life and well-being for certain social groups is in part a consequence of these processes. This is a measurable trend directly influenced by crime and, importantly, also affects fear of crime or more general feelings of (un)safety (Meško, 2003) (Table 17.5).

By spatially analyzing the evolution of crime over a five-year period in the Municipality of Ljubljana, this chapter will focus on the processes underlying criminal activity in Ljubljana and will demonstrate the advantages of spatial quantitative computer techniques used in this regard. It will particularly show the use of the methodology in the identification of crime hot spots as applied to the Ljubljana municipal area (Table 17.6).

Compared to foreign urban agglomerations, Ljubljana is a relatively small city. That is why indices of crime for local communities were calculated per 1,000 inhabitants (Figures 17.3 through 17.5). A problem with map displays of criminal activity is that they rely on official statistics on reported crime offenses. These statistics of course underestimate "real-life" crime rates and might be

Table 17.6 Property Crime in the Municipality of Ljubljana

Year	Property Criminal Offenses	Larceny	Burglary	Robbery
2000	22,655	9,059	8,841	237
2001	22,434	9,680	8,378	221
2002	24,002	10,157	8,748	190
2003	26,271	11,364	10,110	165
2004[a]	30,932	13,138	12,878	187

[a] Data for the years 2005, 2006, and 2007 are not available.

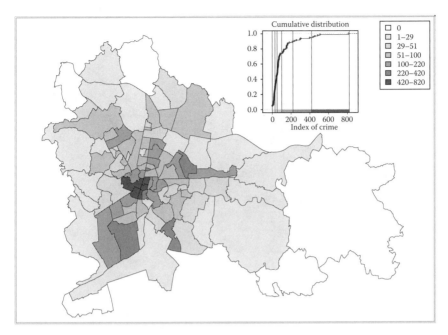

Figure 17.3 Crime index in the Municipality of Ljubljana (2003–2004)— larceny.

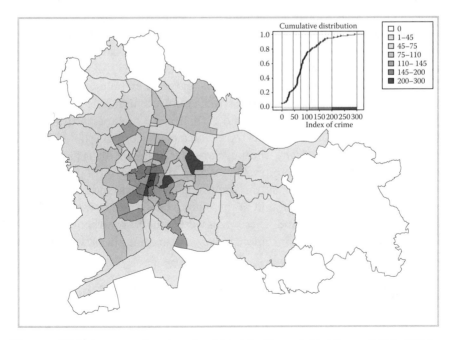

Figure 17.4 Crime index in the Municipality of Ljubljana (2003–2004)— burglary.

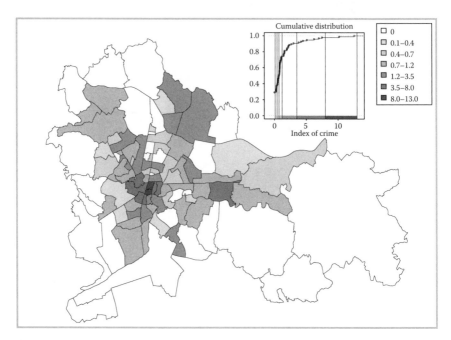

Figure 17.5 Crime index in the Municipality of Ljubljana (2003–2004)—robbery.

severely biased in particular areas due to nonreporting. Unavoidably, this involves qualitative or quantitative interaction with local residents.

Characteristic for most common types of property crime is a concentric decline from the center to the periphery of the city. Criminal activity is highest approximately within a circle of radius 1 km (Figures 17.3 through 17.5). This area is not particularly densely settled, but rather exhibits a marked business function. Besides that, larcenies stretch outward along the most important transport arteries (Figures 17.3 and 17.5). About 3 km and eastward from the center, an important hot spot is represented by the largest retail district in Slovenia called BTC. Larceny and burglary levels in this district attain the highest levels in the whole country. Offenses are not for the most part targeted on local residents but rather on the multitude of shops found there. Lowest levels of property crime are found at the outer edges of the city, especially its rural and semirural hinterland. These areas were "caught" by urbanization only a few decades ago. With urbanization, however, also came all sorts of deviance.

Geographic Information System: A System for Crime Follow-Up Research

A geographic information system (GIS) is a computer system that captures, manages, integrates, manipulates, analyzes, and displays data, which are spatially referenced to the Earth (McDonnell & Kemp, 1995, p. 42). GIS provides a forum within which crime data can be layered with base maps and other geographic data that represent the landscape of the area where the crime data are associated (Chainey & Ratcliffe, 2005, p. 38). There exist numerous overlapping definitions of GIS, but some emphasize more the analytic, others data storing, and others again its cartographic value. GIS is a science, a technology, and a useful methodology for solving spatial problems. This set of tools today enables us to abstractly measure, analyze, and map features from the real world (Longley, Goodchild, Maguire, & Rhind, 2005).

Technological advances, primarily in computer capabilities, are fundamental to recent analytical advances in the methods available for analyzing place-based crime data. The advent of computer mapping applications and accompanying GIS are crucial to being able to measure and represent the spatial relationships in data. Perhaps the most powerful analytical tools emerging from GIS technologies are (1) flexible spatial aggregation capabilities for facilitating the measurement of place-based crime and (2) simple contiguity matrices for representing neighbor relationships between different area units. In addition to these analytical advances, computerized police records management systems and computer-aided dispatch (CAD) systems of citizen calls to police make it possible to systematically quantify varying levels of criminal activity at different places within a city. Successful tackling of crime by means of GIS is only possible with accurate analyses coupled with police fieldwork and the perpetual search for causes in the social and physical environment, and with the application of models enabling us to predict the evolution of crime.

Crime mapping represents a discipline within the scientific field of cartography dealing with representational and analytical spatial aspects of crime activity in space and time. With the advent of GIS techniques, the discipline gradually increased its dynamic character and interaction. The analytical powers of mass data processing enabled spatial analysis not only to disclose hidden or semihidden aspects of criminal landscapes but also to understand the evolution of crime, its heterogeneous causes, the processes underlying it, and the actual effects exerted on the environment. The understanding of its causative forces is enabled through regular monitoring, early detection, and hence prevention (Harries, 1999). From this perspective, the current study presents information on the rather dynamic fluctuations in criminal activity in our largest urban settlement, Ljubljana, in relation to that city's spatial arrangement, and attempts to comment on them.

For spatial as well as more traditional statistical techniques, a toolset from open source software was employed. For spatial and tabular information retrieval and data mining PostgreSQL was used, while the R environment and GRASS represented the basis for spatial information analysis and cartographic output. Details on the interface between the relevant programs are more thoroughly described elsewhere (Bivand, 2000; Neteler & Mitasova, 2004).

Crime Hot Spot Methodology

A crime hot spot is a location or a small area within an identifiable boundary, with a concentration of criminal incidents. These chronic crime places, where crime is concentrated at high rates over extended periods of time, may be analogous to the small percentage of chronic offenders who are responsible for a large percentage of crime. To date, little is known about the actual life cycle of crime hot spots (Klinkon & Mesko, 2005).

Maps (Figures 17.6 through 17.8) representing crime hot spots were estimated by means of kernel density interpolation. They represent the distribution of the frequency of the respective offense in a particular area for the three most common property crime offenses summed between the years 2003 and 2004. The methodology of crime hot spots identification recognizes alternative techniques (e.g., spatial modus, hierarchical and nonhierarchical cluster algorithms, risk analysis, aggregation techniques, and mixed techniques) described in many spatial statistics textbooks (Bailey & Gatrell, 1995;

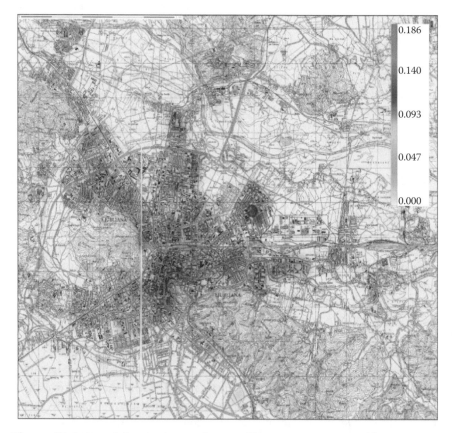

Figure 17.6 Kernel density interpolation of larceny events in Ljubljana.

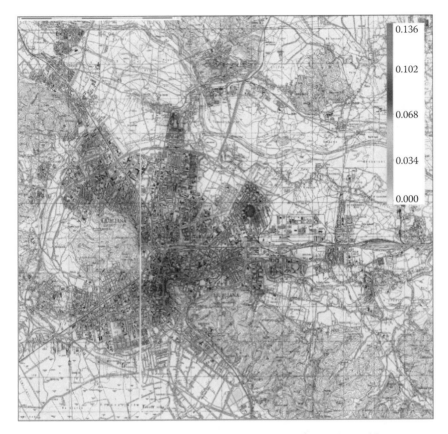

Figure 17.7 Kernel density interpolation of burglary events in Ljubljana.

Burrough & McDonnell, 1998; Levine, 2004; Unwin & O'sullivan, 2004). It is not the purpose of this chapter to venture into the undoubtedly interesting crime hot spots methodology.

Given the nature of the data, however, the most common two-dimensional (2D) Gaussian kernel was chosen for the interpolation. This type of kernel takes more into account events in the neighboring area rather than events that are more distant. It is the binned approximation to the 2D kernel density estimate. Linear binning is used to obtain bin counts and the fast Fourier transform is used to perform discrete convolutions. For each X, Y pair, the bivariate Gaussian kernel is centered on that location and the heights of the kernel, scaled by the bandwidths, at each data point are summed. This sum, after normalization, is the corresponding value in the output (Wand & Jones, 1995). Two input variables deserve particular attention. Gaussian kernels usually employ bandwidths equal to ±1 standard deviation. It should be chosen in order to reflect the actual distribution of the estimated phenomenon. Crime is often spatially distributed on neighborhood size. Getting the right

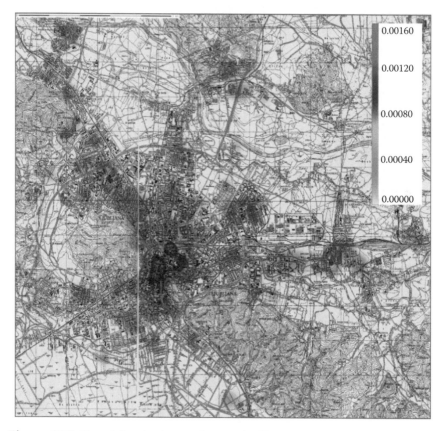

Figure 17.8 Kernel density interpolation of robbery events in Ljubljana.

bandwidth size to reflect the neighborhood character of crime is thus the task of bandwidth approximation. In all three maps, a bandwidth of 150 m was chosen. The second variable that strongly influences outcome values is the grid size over which the density is to be estimated. Since the sum of all cells in the grid corresponds to the number of events (criminal offenses in this case), the number of cells in the grid is decisive for the magnitude of the density values. Based on cell size, they could of course be transformed into events km^{-2} $year^{-1}$. In this way, Figure 17.6 representing the density of larcenies would reach a maximum of 5,784 events km^{-2} $year^{-1}$, Figure 17.7 representing the density of burglaries would reach a maximum of 4,229 events km^{-2} $year^{-1}$, and Figure 17.8 representing the density of robberies would reach a maximum of 50 events km^{-2} $year^{-1}$.

Figures 17.6 through 17.8, depicting kernel density estimations of larcenies (Figure 17.6), burglaries (Figure 17.7), and robberies (Figure 17.8), plotted under the network of streets (shown in black), have a palette going from yellow for lowest values through green and blue to red for largest values (i.e., densities of respective offense events). At first visual inspection, two hot spots can be quickly identified. The distribution of all three of the most common property crime offenses is very high in the center of the city and stretches along the main transport arteries outward. The kernel exhibits very high concentration in an area of the BTC (the largest retail district in Slovenia), which is by far the "highest ground" of the burglary landscape shown in Figure 17.8. This area of people daily attracts thousands who migrate, there for shopping or leisure time in the rapidly evolving entertainment parks such as cinema or wellness centers. Not surprisingly, property crimes are the most common in areas of large daily flows of people and goods, where the concentration of services is high, and less so in residential areas, where the concentration of people is highest. Large parking areas, proximity of a highway, and the anonymity guaranteed by large masses of people lure shoplifters, pickpockets, and burglars. Robberies (Figure 17.8) still persist in the center of the city and at specific amusement areas like around the railway station, Hala Tivoli (in the center of a park), or Tabor (neighborhood in the center of the city). Robberies are also relatively higher in residential parts of the city, especially blocks of houses and neighborhoods such as around Remiza, Trnovski pristan, and Nove Fužine.

GIS is a great tool for making crime maps, but one has to be aware that reliable and valid data are required in order to obtain a good picture of crime in a certain place at a certain time. Otherwise a GIGO problem is present, and maps are still attractive but totally unusable.

Criminal Investigative Aspects

Effectiveness of Crime Investigation in Slovenia: Results of a Research

Clearance rates for crime investigation are obviously still the best way of assessing police work, even though there are numerous methodological problems. Cordner (1989, p. 154) stated that "the use of 'clearance rate' as the indicator of investigative effectiveness can be challenged and may have introduced considerable measurement error." Therefore, it is not surprising that such research projects are rare and that the results are often contradictory. Many factors may influence the success of a particular criminal investigation; hence generalizations can be confusing and sometimes misleading. From the Rand study (Greenwood & Petersilia, 1975), the basis of the "circumstance-result" hypothesis and a rather extreme critique of effectiveness of detective work, through the opposite "effort-result" hypothesis stressing the "added value" of detective work (Rochester research, Bloch & Bell,

1976), to John Eck's (1992) "triage" hypothesis, there have been other studies that tried to determine the role of the various factors influencing investigative effectiveness of the police. For our purposes, research on the connection between agency size and investigative effectiveness can be of great significance. According to Cordner (1989), there are some natural advantages that are available to an agency in a rural area in comparison with an agency of the same size in a metropolitan area. Some statistical data confirm that clearance rates are higher in small, rural police departments than in bigger, metropolitan ones. However, there are many other factors that may influence investigative effectiveness, which have not yet been proven (Maver, 2006).

There have not been many studies on investigative effectiveness of the police in Slovenia. However, 2006 saw the completion of a research project "Analysis of effectiveness of police investigation of criminal offenses in regard to the development of criminal investigation and standards of proof in the criminal procedure" by Jager et al. (2006). Selected results from this study are presented in the subsequent section of this chapter. (The second author of this chapter was a member of the research group.)

The police statistical data of all criminal offenses in Slovenia between the years 2000 and 2002 were used (over 150,000 of them), and a sample of different criminal offenses was randomly selected for a detailed analysis. A questionnaire for detectives at all levels (state, regional, and local) was distributed, and another was prepared for state prosecutors. Two basic hypotheses were tested (Jager et al., 2006):

1. Effectiveness of investigation expressed through clearance rates depends on the use of investigative acts and police powers (intensiveness of investigation).
2. Impact of organizational factors on criminal investigation.

The research lasted for two years and was completed in June 2006. Despite some methodological and other problems, the results were interesting and informative. In general, Eck's (1992) triage hypothesis was confirmed. Yet, this research can mostly be seen as a starting point for further and more detailed research. For practical reasons, the results related to effectiveness of burglary investigation are presented.

In the documentation on burglaries in the years 2000–2002, there were 53,136 units: 41,959 (79%) burglaries were not cleared up and 11,177 (21%) were cleared. The documentation consisted of 166,079 documents, each representing one investigative act. A sample of cases was randomly selected for further detailed analysis—222 cases that were not cleared up and 122 cleared-up cases. The results below are based on this analysis.

The police successfully cleared about 20% of all cases. In 37% of all cleared cases (circumstance-result), suspects were known to the police from the beginning of the investigation. Two-thirds of the cases were low-intensity police investigations, and 75% of these remained uncleared. When high-intensity police investigative activities were applied in relevant police investigations, the clearance rates were significantly higher (effort versus result). The average time of an investigation was 37 days. For our purposes, it is significant that the clearance rate decreases in urban areas with police departments with heavier caseloads. The clearance rates at smaller police stations that dealt with <2,000 burglaries amounted to an average of 31%, those with 2,000–5,000 burglaries amounted to 18.8%, and those with more than 5,000 cases amounted to only 10%. In the city of Ljubljana, the clear-up rate for burglaries was below 10%.

Criminal Investigation within the LPD

Clear-up rates in the LPD have been consistently lower than the average of Slovenia as a whole. However, Maribor, the second largest city in Slovenia, has better clear-up rates. It is difficult to assume that bigger police departments have necessarily lower clear-up rates and are therefore less effective than the smaller ones.

With respect to crime in general and the clearance rates associated with certain police departments in Slovenia in the years 2004 and 2005, the situation is presented in Table 17.7 (the first section includes larger cities' police departments and the second the smaller ones).

It is evident that LPD shows the lowest clearance rates and the smallest, PD Slovenj Gradec, shows the highest. Still, from these data alone it cannot be argued that the size of the department or the investigation workload is crucial for the department's effectiveness. There are differences in the crime problems and structures of officially recorded criminal offenses as well as in

Table 17.7   Police Departments (Regions): Clear-Up Rates

PD	Number of Criminal Offenses				Clear-Up Rate (%)			
	2004	2005	2006	2007	2004	2005	2006	2007
Ljubljana	44,775	42,760	46,500	45,070	29.5	29.2	32.2	36.8
Maribor	10,629	11,575	12,806	14,208	44.6	42.8	42.4	44.8
Celje	8,745	7,935	8,422	8,005	46.8	47.1	48.8	50.5
Slovenj Gradec	1,280	1,192	1,329	1,287	65.0	63.2	67.6	66.3
Postojna	1,347	1,231	1,691	1,591	49.2	49.7	66.6	47.3
Koper	3,613	3,768	3,620	3,471	52.7	47.2	43.6	44.3
Total/average	86,568	84,379	90,354	88,197	39.5	39.0	40.9	43.3

other circumstances that influence "clearance rates" and, as a result, investigative effectiveness.

Characteristics of Criminal Investigation in Urban Areas

Demographic and other characteristics that may, one way or another, influence the investigation of crime in urban and rural areas are given below:

- Population density: More people at one place means less control and less possibility of detecting and investigating criminal offenses.
- Particular crime characteristics: In metropolitan areas, crime is much more sophisticated (organized crime, drugs, white-collar crime, economic crime, etc.), hidden, and more prone to proactive police work, but it takes a lot of time and work to process. Favorable results only show in the long run, thus not giving a clear picture in the relevant statistics on clearance rates.
- Way of life: There is anonymity in larger cities; people do not know each other, not even their neighbors; they are more reticent and unwilling to share any suspicious information with the police; they do not want to get involved in police or criminal procedures, not even to report all the crimes happening to them; sometimes they cannot even recognize people of different race or nationality living in their neighborhood.
- Lack of informal social control in larger cities: People do not care about each other, socialize, or have any influence on the lives of their neighbors.
- Daily migrations of people and tourists: One research study showed that most of the detected offenders of burglaries came from outside Ljubljana.
- Organization of police: Even in urban areas, there are different possibilities for organizing the police. In Ljubljana, there were two police departments until 1991: one for the city itself and the other for the outskirts. After the two merged, crime rates dropped significantly in the neighboring communities, but people complained about "losing" their police stations.
- Workload of detectives and the uniformed police: Police officers are overwhelmed by administrative work, spending much of their time in the office and not among the people. In addition, they are often assigned other administrative jobs and duties, that is, to file charges for petty offenses, which is very time consuming.
- Tactics of investigation: The tactics of detection, investigation, and prosecution of criminal offenses in urban areas differ from those in nonurban ones. Not much research has been done on this topic, but

some indications exist. In rural areas, the police and the population are more likely to know each other. This is important for two reasons: on the one hand, all possible suspects are already known to the police; on the other hand, all "outsiders" are soon recognized and suspected of any crime that happens in the area. However, there is another unfavorable implication not mentioned in the literature: police officers and people in the area are friends, relatives, and so on, and, therefore, many crimes are neither reported to the police nor investigated. Whatever the case, this might also be one reason why clearance rates in rural areas are higher than those in urban areas.

Toward a Better Strategy

Suggestions for better and more efficient criminal investigation work in Slovenia and in Ljubljana and for higher clear-up rates for volume crime as well as other forms of crime (organized, economic, ecological, and other sophisticated forms of crime) may include the following measures:

- Introduction of the "case screening" method for selection of burglary cases that would need more intensive follow-up investigation.
- Decriminalization of less serious property offenses.
- Use of more proactive investigative strategies, intelligence-based investigations, undercover methods, analytical methods, and so on.
- Improvement of standard investigative tactics, knowledge, and motivation, and use of modern technology [automated fingerprint identification system (AFIS) and DNA].
- Reorganization of crime scene investigation strategy, with more crime scene examiners conducting crime scene search and less administrative work.
- Reorganization of the LPD: The LPD has already undergone several reorganizations, one being that two departments were merged into one, which, in our opinion, resulted in less reported crime and lower clearance rates.
- Higher involvement of local investigative units at police stations to all forms of crime and better cooperation with CID within the LPD: Basic criminal investigative activities are done by detectives at the level of the regional Police Directorate Sector of criminal investigation at PD. (Police stations did not have their own detective department. We therefore introduced "local criminal investigative units" that were within police stations but were responsible only for criminal investigations and officers were in plainclothes.)
- Higher involvement of mobile investigative units: In larger cities we introduced the so-called mobile investigative units responsible for

covering the major meeting points of habitual criminals and for special operational tasks.

- Community-oriented policing: This has been a general police policy, but it brought no significant improvements in the detection and investigation of crime.
- Introduction of local safety/security councils: Local safety/security councils are the link between police and citizens, but it has not brought about any significant results in regard to crime investigation.
- Offender-oriented criminal investigation: Not many crimes are solved on the crime scene, but with proactive police action more crimes could be prevented and detected, especially in the field of organized crime, drugs, and so on.

Conclusion

Besides the analysis of spatial distribution of crime and its different kinds, geographical research on crime includes the spatial linking of crime with hypothesized driving forces—and in that way offers the possibility of revealing the influences that underlie the evolution of crime. In this process, a broad palette of very heterogeneous possibilities must be considered where collecting data in the field is of crucial importance. Computer-aided mapping and spatial information analysis in this respect are only a spatially enabling tool for identifying processes related to crime and related activity. Early detection based on the understanding of the underlying process can, however, lead to quick and effective prevention. Furthermore, such spatial models, after thorough testing in a particular environment, might even anticipate future events and be in that respect a planning tool for the forecasting of crime (over different timescales and over different geographic scales). Knowledge- and evidence-based crime control is crucial in urban settings. This chapter shows the importance of the use of new technologies in crime control strategies and tactics, as well as reconsideration about the efficiency and effectiveness of the police in the capital city of Slovenia.

References

Bailey, T. C., & Gatrell, A. C. (1995). *Interactive Spatial Data Analysis*. Harlow: Longman.

Bivand, R. (2000). Using the R statistical data analysis language on GRASS 5.0 GIS data base files. *Computers and Geosciences, 26*, 1043–1052.

Bloch, P. B., & Bell, J. (1976). *Managing Investigations: The Rochester System*. Washington, DC: Urban Institute.

Burrough, P., & McDonnell, R. (1998). *Principles of Geographical Information Systems*. Oxford: Oxford University Press.

Chainey, S., & Ratcliffe, J. (2005). *GIS and Crime Mapping*. New York: Wiley.

Cordner, G. W. (1989). Police agency size and investigative effectiveness. *Journal of Criminal Justice, 17*, 145–155.

Eck, J. E. (1992). Criminal investigation. In G. W. Cordner & D. C. Hale (Eds), *What Works in Policing? Operations and Administration Examined* (pp. 31–52). Cincinnati, OH: Anderson Publishing.

Greenwood, P. W., & Petersilia, J. (1975). *The Criminal Investigation Process Volume I: Summary and Policy Implications* (Report No. R-1776-DOJ). Santa Monica, CA: Rand.

Harries, K. (1999). *Mapping Crime: Principle and Practice*. Washington, DC: U.S. Department of Justice.

Jager, M., Gorkič, P., Mozetič, P., Čibej, Z., Brvar, B., & Šugman, K. (2006). *Analiza učinkovitosti policijskega preiskovanja kaznivih dejanj z upoštevanjem razvoja kriminalistične stroke ter dokaznih standardov kazenskega postopka (Analysis of effectiveness of police investigation from the perspectives of the development of criminal investigation profession and evidence standards in criminal procedure)*. Ljubljana, Inštitut za kriminologijo pri Pravni fakulteti.

Klinkon, I., & Meško, G. (2005). Uporaba geografskih informacijskih sistemov pri analizi kriminalitete [The use of GIS in crime analysis]. *Varstvoslovje, 2*, 133–149.

Levine, N. (2004). *CrimeStat III: A Spatial Statistics Program for the Analysis of Crime Incident Locations*. Washington, DC: The National Institute of Justice.

Longley, P. A., Goodchild, M. F., Maguire, D. J., & Rhind, D. W. (2005). *Geographic Information Systems and Science*. Chichester: Wiley.

Maver, D. (2006). Criminal investigation: Wishes, expectations and reality: In G. Meško & B. Dobovšek (Eds), *Past, Present and Futures: Policing in Central and Eastern Europe—Conference Proceedings*. Ljubljana, Faculty of Criminal Justice and Security, University of Maribor.

McDonnell, R., & Kemp, K. (1995). *International GIS Dictionary*. Cambridge: GeoInformation International.

Meško, G. (2003). *Analiza porazdelitve nekaterih odklonskih pojavov v Ljubljani* [Analysis of the distribution of deviance in Ljubljana, research report]. Raziskovalno poročilo. Ljubljana, Univerza v Mariboru, Fakulteta za policijsko-varnostne vede.

Meško, G. (2008). *Kriminologija*. Ljubljana, Univerza v Mariboru, Fakulteta za varnostne vede Univerza v Mariboru.

Mitar, M., & Meško, G. (2008). Reported crime, indications from crime victim surveys and fear of crime studies. In D. Košecka (Ed.), *Forecasting Crime Development and Control of Crime in Central and Eastern European Countries* (pp. 45–64). Bratislava: Bratislava School of Law.

Neteler, M., & Mitasova, H. (2004). *Open Source GIS: A GRASS GIS Approach* (2nd ed.). Amsterdam: Kluwer Academic Press.

Poročilo o delu policije za leto. (2005). (Annual report of police work in 2005). Found on 06th December 2008 at http://www.policija.si/portal/statistika/lp/pdf/lp2005.pdf

Poročilo o delu policije za leto. (2006). (Annual report of police work in 2006). Found on 06th December 2008 at http://www.policija.si/portal/statistika/lp/pdf/lp2006.pdf

Poročilo o delu policije za leto. (2007). (Annual report of police work in 2007). Found on 06th December 2008 at http://www.policija.si/portal/statistika/lp/pdf/LetnoPorocilo2007.pdf

Poročilo o delu policijske uprave Ljubljana za leto. (2007). (Annual report of Ljubljana's police directorate work in 2007). Found on 06th December 2008 at http://www.policija.si/portal/organiziranost/pu/lj/statistika/pdf/lp2007.pdf

Resolucija o nacionalnega programa preprečevanja in zatiranja kriminalitete (Resolution of the national crime prevention and crime control programme). (2006). Official Gazette of the Republic of Slovenia, 43/2006.

Unwin, D., & O'Sullivan, D. (2004). *Geographic Information Analysis*. New York: Wiley.

Wand, M. P., & Jones, M. C. (1995). *Kernel Smoothing*. London: Chapman and Hall.

Police Cooperation in International Drug Investigations in North America

18

CHANTAL PERRAS

Contents

The scope of drug trafficking has become one of the major national security concerns of Canada, the United States, and of Latin American countries due to their inability to control criminal organizations, despite the millions of dollars that were allocated to fight them. In the United States, several hundred million dollars have been allocated to governmental initiatives intended to encourage interagency cooperation and thereby reduce the isolationism of police agencies (Hayeslip & Russell-Einhorn, 2003).* International cooperation to address production and trafficking of drugs is a central component of American and Canadian foreign policies [U.S. Department of State, 1990; Royal Canadian Mounted Police (RCMP) Web site].

An important thing to be considered is that the fight against drug trafficking begins at the policy level. Means for cooperation exist but their mechanisms are very complex and result from a series of long and hard negotiations

---

* At the end of the 1980s, the U.S. Department of Justice established the Edward M. Byrne Foundation, whose mandate is to support and promote the implementation of multijurisdictional investigation teams by local (city), regional (county), and state (state) police agencies. This initiative has provided a funding of $200–$300 million in support of police partnerships.

(Anderson et al., 1995). International instruments have resulted from efforts of concerted states to establish mechanisms that serve their respective interests. There are formal structures (i.e., Europol, Eurojust, and Interpol), as well as secret agreements, informal networks, bilateral and multilateral arrangements, and conventions. Nevertheless, whatever the importance of a state's sovereignty or of its bilateral cooperation, there is increasing internationalization of police and justice cooperation at a supranational level. North American countries have some agreements with Latin American countries. Some studies have been done about the nature of the relationship between the USA and Mexico (Deflem, 2001). But they are few compared to those in the European Union.

Although there is still little coordination in terms of policy formulation between states, there is recognition that unilateral counternarcotics trafficking approaches have yielded little results. Some states persist in their pursuit of bilateral cooperation, while others seek channels for more comprehensive mechanisms to facilitate the exchange of information and the coordination of law-enforcement efforts. But significant obstacles to these initiatives are still present.

In fact, as the threats become increasingly globalized, police organizations must work together. This is not easy because they have to eliminate various barriers such as culture, religion, language, and tradition. There are different priorities and objectives depending on the country (Friedrichs, 2008). Some differences in culture can result in frictions. Resources are a key element, because the means given to police officers reflect the priorities of each government. Rivalry between forces is a constant obstacle. But generally, police forces help and support each other in major cases.

Furthermore, officers need to adapt the law to practice, since there are gaps between rule makers and concrete day-to-day issues. The basis of their collaboration is mutual understanding and common interests. Personal and most often informal contacts and goodwill are key elements for trust, speed, and cooperation.

This chapter focuses on how the Canadian and U.S. authorities deal with those obstacles in relation to Latin American authorities, particularly Mexican and Colombian ones. Numerous components of the coalition concept are suited to study police cooperation across borders. The focus is on the psychosocial perspective of the coalition concept, taking for granted that when people make alliances, they are relatively rational. They want to maximize their "profits" and furthermore minimize their losses. Finally, the primary thesis sustained in this chapter is that individual perceptions are essential for cooperation to be maintained. In fact, trust is indispensable. Furthermore, this is extremely restricting for officers expected to collaborate with other officers who come from so-called "corrupt" countries.

The following analysis is based on interviews about international cocaine investigations. These interviews were done with both RCMP and Drug Enforcement Agency (DEA) investigators involved in some of the most important international cocaine investigations in the last few years. They were produced thanks to the financial help of the Social Sciences and Humanities Research Council of Canada (SSHRC). The principal researcher is Professor Frédéric Lemieux, of George Washington University.

Coalitions: RCMP and DEA

In this section, we look at officers' perceptions in the creation of and upholding of police coalitions. We seek to know how important they are. This concern emerges from the observation that in the last few years, multijurisdictional investigations have multiplied (Dupont & Perez, 2006). In fact, in recent decades, ad hoc police structures, such as multijurisdictional investigative teams, have become widespread in the United States (Coldren, McGarrell, Sabath, Schlegel, & Stolzenberg, 1993; Jefferis, Frank, Smith, Novak, & Travis, 1998). But little work was done on the impact of the ideas and feelings of people who work daily in transnational investigations.

Precisely, we will focus on the working dynamics between officers during joint criminal investigations, which end with arrests and seizures at the national and international levels. Studies on coalitions offer a good conceptual framework to understand how and up to which level psychosocial factors have to be taken into account to comprehend the way in which international police cooperation is functioning in the field. The goal of the creation of coalitions is to obtain success in the process of being more prevailing than their actual or potential opponents, subsequently obtaining much more advantages than if the coalition does not exist, or if the coalition was imperfect (Lemieux, 1997).

The choice of coalition partners is primarily done on the basis of psychosocial variables. For example, Vinacke and Artkoff (1957) show that personality and friendship variables are fundamental. These variables have an influence upon the partners chosen, and then, on the creation and survival of the coalitions. Furthermore, the study of Komorita (1974) shows that the size of coalitions is important. A minimal coalition in the number of actors involved will be preferred, because it is easier to manage. Gamson (1961) studied both psychosocial and economic approaches together. He states that the most important factor in the creation of coalitions is the expected level of benefits, gains, and advantages. In fact, the psychosocial preferences have to be taken into account, but are less important since the officers should consider them only when they do not cause losses. Finally, Miller (1990) found that the establishment of coalitions depends more on the benefits, and on the way they are shared than on the initial resources possessed by the actors. This approach is similar to the one of economists. Miller thinks that the benefits are an explicative factor of the formation of coalitions.

We have chosen to study the point of view of some officers working in the international drug policing field from North American countries, that is, the RCMP for Canada and the DEA for the United States. Their way of reacting when they have to work with their Latin American counterparts will be the focus of the analysis. Few studies have been performed so far on the North American context. In fact, much more is known on the European part of the world, since they have the European Union, Europol, and Interpol. This choice has the direct consequence that the traffic of cocaine is the primary criminal enterprise to be studied here. Cocaine is the predominant drug on the American continent. Heroin is known to be easier to find in other continents, but things have slowly been evolving over the last few years.*

In fact, when it comes to cocaine, Colombia, Bolivia, and Peru have been the major producing countries since the 1970s. Until 1995, Peru and Bolivia constituted the raw material production countries of cocaine including coca leaves and coca paste, which are the base ingredients and the beginning of the supply chain. In turn, Colombian refiners produced cocaine. In the late 1990s, a shift occurred in interdiction practices led by the United States including the apprehension and dismantling of the Cali and Medellin Cartels (U.S. Department of State, 2002, 2003, 2004).

In practice, it is necessary to avoid the "displacement of criminality." An example of this is that the police intervened in Bolivia and Peru to prevent coca leaves from entering Columbia. The Columbian traffickers simply started producing their own coca leaves. This did not solve the problem and seem to actually make things worse. Colombia began to produce its own raw materials; a very large increase of production of coca plants was recorded since 1993. According to seizure data (UN Office on Drugs and Crime, 2003), cocaine trafficking is largely confined to the Americas (87% in 2002). The largest market, or consumer country, is the United States. Cocaine is most often shipped primarily through the Caribbean and/or Mexico by land or directly to the United States by air from Colombia. Since the end of the cartel era in Colombia in the early 1990s, cocaine trafficking has increasingly taken place in a decentralized fashion. Further, Mexican organized groups have taken over the smuggling of drugs to the United States and to Spain. The expanding UK market has been supplied by crime groups in the Caribbean, while West Africa has also served as a springboard for cocaine destined for the Western European market.

---

* Heroin is being grown in greater quantities in South American countries, such as Colombia. A market is emerging.

Before doing the analysis, we must mention one last point. Cocaine is produced and carried from Latin America to North America. Then, it should be usual that the countries implicated in the traffic are also involved in the police coalition fighting the displacement and selling of this drug. But as will see, it is not so simple, since the prevalence of corruption in the production countries causes the consumer countries to be mistrustful.

In fact, there is a polarization of the drug supply chains along the North–South divide which is explained by four factors including (1) favorable climatic conditions for the production of psychotropic substances; (2) prevalent economic conditions of the countries in the path of the chains; (3) political conditions that turn a blind eye to the production of drugs, particularly in countries with weak government institutions and limited capacity to eradicate and dismantle production installations (Labrousse, 1995); and (4) the intensity of police suppression—more important and systematic in developed countries.

Important Aspects in the Creation and Maintenance of International Police Cooperation

Exchanging information gathered during criminal investigations establishes networks and links between police professionals (Bigo, 1996), but it also goes a long way to build trust based on the principles of reciprocity and communication (Anderson, 2002). In addition, sharing information provides opportunities to develop strategies and set priorities to determine the resources necessary to conduct operations that often require the establishment of a team of interested foreign colleagues. International police cooperation allows investigators to organize more accurately their plan of attack since they have more knowledge of the activities of a group/perpetrator being investigated as a result of the big picture perspective that arises when bits of information are collected.

Like transnational drug supply chains, international police cooperation takes place under difficult environmental conditions. The national agency that participates in a system of police cooperation faces numerous obstacles due to the incompatible nature of various concerned structures, cultures, technologies, judicial procedures, policies, and politics, which limit the impact of the cooperative behavior. The cultural heterogeneity inherent in international cooperation introduces the potential to aggravate the lack of trust ever present in police subcultures. There are also a myriad of problems in the integration of information technology as incompatibilities in systems considerably complicate the establishment of informational bridges between police services.

We focus on the different ways utilized by the officers of the RCMP and of the DEA to do their "international" work. The axis "trust versus mistrust" (constraint/corruption) is the primary focus since it seems to be the most important aspect of international police cooperation.

Trust

Ward (1982) explains that social, cultural, and political similarities favor the formation of alliances.* Lalman and Neuman (1991) acknowledge that culture, ideology, and goals other than national security can be determinants in the creation of coalitions. Officers talk a lot about this subject and they agree entirely with the scientific literature. First, they explain that it is easier to cooperate with public police agencies rather than with other groups like Customs or with intelligence agencies. For them, a police officer is fundamentally a police officer, without any consideration of the color or shape of the badge or uniform.

The most important element in the maintenance of the coalition is the development of affinities and trust between police officers from different countries, in order to reduce the legal problems and to focus on some priorities. Furthermore, problems are often resolved thanks to previous informal meetings between them. But cooperation is still difficult, since real differences in legal systems, morals, and resources exist. For example, there are major differences between North and South America, particularly when it comes to resources.

International investigations that work well are the result of satisfying interpersonal relations. Intervening parties share mutual trust, since they already know each other. Most often, they have already worked together in another investigation or they have already met in some informal meeting. Those we interviewed emphasized that the easiest way to share information is to do it with friends. Doing it this way permits them to avoid problems, since trust and often reciprocity are already a fundamental part of the relationship.

Furthermore, the formal procedure is most often activated after those informal contacts. What is more important for them is not to follow the official process, rules, and treaties, but to have a direct conversation by phone or face to face with the future partner. In some cases, officers from the initiating country make a face-to-face visit to explain what they want from their future or actual partners. An interviewed officer emphasized that employing this method can actually increase the quality of the information exchange as well as the validity of it.

---

* "Alliance" is utilized as an equivalent word for "coalition." In French political sciences, they do not utilize "coalition" to talk about "alliance," since they consider the words to be two different notions. We do not.

Police officers explain and also show that to cooperate, they need common general goals and minimum legal agreements. If the police officers have differentiating opinions concerning the orientation or the result of their work, there can be political problems between authorities of the various implicated countries. Even when there are minimum agreements, it is necessary to make use of good relationship, in order to succeed in obtaining a special authorization.

In addition, it should be stressed that the police officers from North America often assume that others see the situations that worry them as problems, which is not always the case. It often happens that the visions diverge at least slightly and that in certain cases, organizations can withdraw because they do not see the situation as a "problem" for them. This context seems to be more relevant at the transnational level than when the implicated organizations come from the same country. It is necessary to consider these differences in opinions because they will have a major impact on the way in which collaboration or subsequent cooperation will be held or not.

In certain cases, cooperation is quite simply impossible or becomes possible, whereas it was not possible before, which shows that this is not a fixed process. It can become even more flexible if the political, economic, social, or moral conditions have changed.

Usually, in spite of different strategic objectives and a possibility of real conflict, the general objectives remain rather similar so that working together in this way is still advantageous. However, it is necessary to avoid a major pitfall, that is, corruption. This will play a fundamental role in the development of various forms of cooperation and also in the protection mechanisms in investigations.

Another constraint is the number of partners in an international investigation. Komorita (1974) thinks that the size of coalitions is important for their formation. A minimal coalition in terms of the number of actors will be favored. The police officers interviewed stressed that the greater the number of individuals and institutions involved, the more the work is difficult to manage. That creates frictions and tensions. That is why they generally seek to restrict the number of actors.

Mistrust: Constraints and Corruption

Laver and Schofield (1991) found that institutional constraints and governmental rules influence the formation process of coalitions. The police officers interviewed stressed that they sought to maintain the least complicated protocols possible because that enables them to preserve more discretion in their work. Constraining treaties are not welcome. They use them only when they are adapted to their needs or if they do not have the choice to use them.

In spite of the importance of treaties and official agreements in the scientific literature on international police cooperation, the remarks of the police officers interviewed revealed that they are not the most important elements in their daily work.

Different Types of Conflicts

In 1977, Manning underlined that regarding "the intensity of the conflicts of power which afflict in an endemic way the police organization, power is measured by the possession and the hoarding of information" (p. 110). Brodeur (1984, p. 31) commented on this argument by adding that "the existence of these conflicts generated police obsession to be covered, i.e. to have a legal or professional cover to justify their decisions."

In fact, cooperation coexists with conflicts in coalition partnerships. In general, alliances are used in international investigations because they promise more success than would be possible if a police organization is working alone. However, relations between police officers inevitably generate conflicts based on available resources, standards, bonds, supports, manpower, and information. When sharing of information is absent, it is clear that the power is concentrated in one police organization. If one agency carries out the arrests and/or seizures outside the agreement, it can possibly create conflict, or at least tensions and frictions.

There are several causes of conflicts. Firstly, conflicts are connected to politics and sharing of information. Indeed, it happens that some countries refuse to share their information for reasons that have nothing to do with police tasks. An example is the fear of the Cubans toward Americans, associated with their fear that the RCMP can be in complicity with Americans. In this case, political relations make the international police work very difficult to do.

A second type of conflict is caused by competition that exists between the various police organizations to finish the case, either by arresting the suspects or by seizing drugs. When a police organization finishes the case before what was planned by all, it causes frictions. An RCMP police officer interviewed told us that problems of this kind often happen with the DEA. This type of problem is exacerbated by political pressures. In other words, conflicts are connected to expected benefits.

Moreover, legal problems also emerge from these conflicts. In one case in which the DEA conducted a stop and seizure in international waters, it was done too quickly, and as a result Canada did not succeed in arresting all the people implicated in the possession chain and did not succeed in obtaining an informer since the agents could not question the suspects. In fact, it is forbidden in the United States. In another case, Colombian police did the same thing to the United States. The Colombian police arrested the main suspect before the DEA gave their consent. That shows that the American police officers, although they occupy an important place in the investigation, do not hold all the means, and thus have to share a little bit of their power with the Colombian police officers.

Another kind of problem relates to communications. Technological problems can cause problems in the exchange of information, in addition to the cultural differences on which we have already focused.

The police officers interviewed also emphasized that an investigation with international dimensions takes time. This can make exchange of information more difficult with international investigations, due to impatience or suspicion, and this is why they used the informal way and the liaison officer to increase the speed.

They also emphasized the fact that in spite of the incompatibility of some laws, they all go in the same direction. Really effective exchanges could be observed. They use the telephone and emails to communicate every day and are doing "PowerPoint" presentations for their colleagues to keep them mutually up to date and to agree on the important points to follow in the investigation.

Corruption is to be considered when working on police cooperation. The majority of the countries labeled as corrupted are countries of the South, but some interviewed stressed the importance of not of neglecting the corruption from the North, simply because it exists. But whether it comes from the South or from the North, corruption causes delays in the transmission of information. Indeed, as part of his work, the police officer must evaluate the level of potential corruption. In fact, if corruption is known to be rampant in a police organization, there is great probability that the information will not arrive in time to its recipient, therefore it will not be of any utility. On some occasions, the information simply cannot be shared for political reasons. But a solution to the problems connected with corruption is to provide the individuals or suspected countries the bare essentials so that they can do their work and obtain the required information.

Another solution to avoid the impacts of corruption is to utilize a liaison officer. Then, the countries, according to their style of cooperation, can apply the advice of the liaison officer in connection with the strategies to be adopted and the people to trust or not.

A Strategy to Screen Potentially Corrupted Agents

The strategy entailing the utilization of the liaison officers is important in order to prevent corruption from destroying an investigation. In fact, interviewed police officers think that a key ingredient is the liaison officer. For example, he is the intermediary between the police officers from different countries. It is he whom they contact when they need to work with members of a foreign organization. It is also he who evaluates the information transmitted by the police officers or its contacts in the country where he is working. He examines whom he can trust and why. The principal role of the liaison officers is thus to create contacts in the country and to establish confidence. A police officer interviewed qualified the liaison officers to be a "detector of corruption." Furthermore, legal and operational problems related to differences between the countries are often at least partially regulated by the liaison officer, who then uses his contacts or his knowledge of the various systems. Liaison officers are increasingly important and their chiefs understand that they have to be strategically positioned so that they can work on the most important actual problems.

Various Types of Cooperation for Various Contexts

Sabatier (2001) described five possible levels of cooperation. It is quite obvious that Europe is more advanced than America with regard to the levels reached until now. However, it seems that only the first two levels were clearly reached by the majority of the countries. The type of international police cooperation reached depends on the need and also on the level of sovereignty that the countries are ready to devote. Type 1 is the division of information and communication, while type 2 relates to dialogue and consultation. There is no real threat to sovereignty when they limit themselves to these two levels. Level 3 is to take action. Starting from this level the states must put their sovereignty on the back burner and stress their common safety. Then there is coordination, which is better represented by an organization like Europol. Finally, the Federation is the regrouping in a global police. This level does not exist yet. The model that approaches the Federation is the FBI. Sabatier explains that two eras of cooperation exist: the phase of construction and the phase of development of transnational cooperation.

The interviews reveal that the type of cooperation utilized depends on the various countries involved and on the contexts that connect them. In all cases, it is important to establish the roles of everyone and also the leadership. Normally, it is the organization of the police officer who initiated the first investigation and who asks for the assistance of another individual of another organization who assumes the leadership of it. This means that he possesses a certain form of control on the investigation because he has a more global perspective of the problems and holds the most amount of information on the case. This leader can decide the shape of his cooperation with the others. He can quite simply ask a country for a specific assistance or ask to start an investigation, which will make the link more permanent. He can also ask for information without reciprocating or rather establishing a real exchange, always in respect of boundaries imposed by rules, laws, and resources of each country.

Police cooperation is possible only between countries that have police bodies sufficiently free from corruption, that is, in which police officers can find at least some individuals in which they can really maintain confidence.

Deflem (2001) also raised the importance of police forces to be sufficiently autonomous from the political powers in their country. When there is not sufficient autonomy, a full cooperation with double-direction exchange of information cannot be found. At best, it is possible to see some collaboration, but not more cooperation.

Several elements can explain the type of "cooperation" chosen. Some organizations have a police philosophy more directed toward its own objectives whereas others have a vision directed toward common work. The number of financial and human resources available or allocated is also a factor to be taken into account. Indeed, the more the differences between the participating countries, the more chances that the leadership will be one-way. An example of that is the case of the DEA with countries of South America or Afghanistan. This choice is also based on confidence in the other countries involved in the investigation. For example, the DEA trusts Mexico very little, and this has the consequence of one-way exchange of information. This need to trust is largely connected to a phenomenon particularly spread in the countries that are low in resources. It is about corruption. The leaders thus will choose an approach based on an objective aiming at the cancellation of the possible impacts of corruption. These approaches are different according to the philosophy of the country. More precisely, there exist various types of leadership according to the initiating country (the receiver) and to the supporter country, according to their characteristics. Those are often connected to corruption. A notable difference in the method is observable when the United States are the leaders, which happens relatively often. This leadership is very strong and unilateral.

When the DEA leads the investigation, its leadership is strong. The others must limit themselves to fulfill the tasks that they were assigned. In general, the DEA does not have confidence in them and provides only information that is absolutely essential to the other country in order to do what they have to do. The DEA sometimes asks for a parallel investigation, when they want to establish a long-term cooperation. That is rare, but facilitates the investigation. When parallel investigations happen, the countries that carry out the parallel survey have a more active role in the exchange of information. The information is also more often multiway.

In the majority of the cases, the DEA is the only one to have access to all the information, that is, the sharing is done only in one way. Some police officers from the Netherlands also mentioned that the American police bodies, especially the DEA, take the control and do everything that has to be done when they carry out an investigation abroad. Moreover, a police officer from the DEA makes the same assertion. For him, it appears to be normal that when the DEA initiates the investigation, it is their agents who hold not only the leadership but also do all the work. In other words, it is mainly the DEA agents who deal with the field work connected with the investigation in the other countries. Besides, they have agents everywhere on the planet, which is not the case with many other countries. When they cannot really do something which they consider important to do and which is rather exceptional, they contact the liaison officers in the country concerned, which contacts the local police officers and uses them as subcontractors. In the majority of the cases, these other countries are never treated like equal partners, that is, they are not a partner of the team nor do they have access to the information piled up within the framework of the investigation.

It seems that Canada has a more egalitarian leadership. An RCMP police officer explains how he proceeds when contexts required him to cooperate with police officers from corrupted countries. Firstly, Canada offers and asks for assistance, contrary to the United States where information and assistance go mostly in one direction.

In light of the interviews, there are two ways of cooperating. The first can be described as unilateral and uses police officers from other countries as if they are subcontractors. From the point of view of the structure of power, this can be viewed as flexible hierarchy. The second way of cooperating would be bilateral or multilateral, and is formed of investigations evolving in parallel. The structure of power is more egalitarian. We can designate it as a quasi network, and ultimately it will be a network. The concept of the need to know (Brodeur, 1984), often used by police agencies to justify why they do not share their information, is important here. The way of seeing this "need to know" concept is of course different from one individual to another, according to the goals considered, but one sees well how this concept can be harmful for an effective cooperation.

The best way of exchanging information would be by parallel investigations, but only when there is enough confidence and when corruption is absent. In these cases, that facilitates, reduces, and accelerates the procedures to be followed. When this is relevant, there is a more formal agreement for the whole of the process.

Depending of the situation, bilateral exchange and parallel investigation could thus be the best way of exchanging information. However, when corruption is present, it is imperative to employ different methods to succeed in the exchange of information. Corruption has an impact on the structuring of the security network and on the sharing of power. For example, in an investigation initiated by the Netherlands, but carried out by the DEA, the police force of the Dominican Republic was not engaged, even in the interrogation of suspects. Because there were big risks of corruption, DEA agents went on the spot and directly conducted the interrogations.

In some cases, the two methods can be employed simultaneously. For example, a police officer talked about a case involving four countries. Italy and France carried out parallel surveys while Colombia and Venezuela carried assistance to them, because Italy and France did not trust them enough. Thus it is possible to collaborate without trust. In this case, mistrust is compulsory.

Conclusion

The following question has been asked: Why is an investigation with international dimension ever formed? The primary answer is because the police organization shares its human and financial resources, because they need to do it in order to be successful in the international investigation. Indeed, multiorganizational and international dimensions are added because the police officers recognize the need to call upon other organizations of other countries to solve problems that prove to be also present in these other territories. A police officer from the RCMP explained that the contribution of other police organizations largely helps in those types of investigations.

The goal of the analysis was to emphasize the important points in the creation and maintenance of police coalitions. The analysis can be summarized according to the three perspectives of the conceptual framework of coalitions. The economic logic is easy to see from the costs and benefit analysis remarks. The economic logic is an instrument that the transnational police officers use to make a decision. The psychosocial variables are also important. According to the perspective of Vinacke and Artkoff (1957), our analysis shows how much trust relationships are fundamental to establish a real cooperation. It was also shown that the domination of an actor on the others determines the form of the security networks. For example, when a member of the DEA initiates a work, the other implicated actors are necessarily subjected to its objectives, and the group is hierarchical. Sometimes, it happens that the investigations are more equal, when the implicated countries really mutually cooperate and share their information in the two directions. Another important component is the size and complexity of arrangements. The more restricted the number of individuals implicated, and the simpler the procedures, the less difficult the management. Our conclusion follows the remarks of Komorita (1974) since the coalitions that emerge are simple and small. Reasons for conflicts were also mentioned on several occasions. They primarily relate to perceived injustices (Lawler, 1975) concerning the sharing of benefit according to the initial input resources invested in the investigation.

It is also interesting to examine the remarks made by the police officers interviewed under the perspective of Gamson (1961) and Miller (1990), which proposed to combine the psychosocial perspective with the economic approach. For Gamson (1961), the importance of the expected benefit is dominating in the formation of the coalition process. Indeed, the initial distribution of resources and psychosocial preferences are important, but are secondary since the actors take account of them only when it does not involve losses of benefit, especially in relation to corruption. Miller (1990) finds that the formation of coalitions depends more on the expected benefit and sharing of them rather than on the initial resources. This approach is connected with economists, that is, profit is the most important explanatory factor in the formation of coalitions. Throughout the analysis, it was clear that profits and benefits incurred as part of a security network are important. Police officers of course mentioned differences in resources at the disposal of each country, but it was not the central point of their remarks.

Finally, Laver and Schofield (1991) added that institutional constraints and governmental rules influence the formation process of coalitions. This was mentioned on several occasions during the interviews and police officers agreed that the most effective work is done with a minimum of complexity, that is, if they must use the treaties and the agreements, they seek to do it most simply, and they often fulfill their obligations after having spoken with their colleagues abroad, with the result that the agreements and treaties seem more to be constraints than facilitators.

Following this synthesis, it seems obvious that the coalition framework is adequate, although it is difficult to say that the studied security networks truly materialize in coalitions. These are ideals to be followed. A coalition is temporary by definition, just like the security networks being studied. There is thus a precarious balance to maintain. But this balance is nevertheless well balanced in some teams, although certain countries have much more influence than others. The fact is that some countries may not want to take part in the war against drugs with the most powerful countries. But it is equally possible that they undergo often serious economic consequences if they refuse to cooperate. These countries do not really have the choice to cooperate. It is probably why the network is maintained. It is also possible that there is a true hidden resistance. It would be interesting to go further to understand the strategy adopted by the countries according to the stakes and possibilities of action (e.g., escape, avoidance, opposition, negotiation, support, or alliance with others). It should also be of interest to quantify each strategy, to see which of them are more prevalent.

References

Anderson, M. (2002). Trust and police cooperation. In M. Anderson & J. Apap (Eds), *Police and Justice Co-Operation and the New European Borders*. The Hague, The Netherlands: Kluwer Law International.

Anderson, M., Den Boer, M., Cullen, P., Gilmore, W., Raab, C., & Walker, N. (1995). *Policing the European Union*. Oxford: Clarendon Press.

Bigo, D. (1996). *Polices en Réseaux: L'xpérience Européenne*. Paris: Presse de science Po.

Brodeur, J.-P. (1984). La police: mythes et réalités. *Criminologie*, *17*(1), 9–41.

Coldren, J., McGarrell, E., Sabath, M., Schlegel, K., & Stolzenberg, L. (1993). *Multijurisdictional Drug Task Force Operations: Results of a Nationwide Survey of Task Force Commanders*. Washington, DC: Criminal Justice Statistics Association.

Deflem, M. (2001). International police cooperation in North America: A review of practices, strategies, and goals in the United States, Mexico, and Canada. In Koenig & D. Das (Eds), *International Police Cooperation: A World Perspective.* New York: Lexington Books.

Dupont, B., & Perez, É. (2006). Les polices au Québec, *Que sais-je?* Paris: Presses Universitaires de France.

Friedrichs, J. (2008). *Fighting Terrorism and Drugs: Europe and International Police Cooperation.* New York: Routledge.

Gamson, W. A. (1961). A theory of coalition formation. *American Sociological Review*, 26, 373–382.

Hayeslip, D., & Russell-Einhorn, M. (2003). Evaluating multijurisdictional drug enforcement task forces. *NIJ Journal*, November (250), 40–42.

Jefferis, E. S., Frank, J., Smith, B. W., Novak, K. J., & Travis, L. F. (1998). An examination of the productivity and perceived effectiveness of drug task forces. *Police Quarterly, 1,* 3.

Komorita, S. S. (1974). A weighted probability model of coalition formation. *Psychological Review, 81*(3), 242–256.

Labrousse, A. (1995). *The Geopolitics of Drugs.* Boston: North-Eastern University Press.

Lalman, D., & Neuman, D. (1991). Alliance formation and national security. *International Interactions, 16*(4), 239–253.

Laver, M., & Schofield, N. (1991). *Multiparty Government: The Politics of Coalition in Europe.* New York: Oxford University Press, collection Comparative European politics, 308p.

Lawler, E. J. (1975). An experimental study of factors affecting the mobilization of revolutionary coalitions. *Sociometry: A Journal of Research in Social Psychology, 38*(2), 163–179.

Lemieux, V. (1997). Réseaux et coalitions. *L'année sociologique, 47*(1), 351–370.

Miller, C. E. (1990). Effects of payoffs and resources on coalition formation: A test of three theories. *Social Psychology Quarterly, 43*(2), 154–164.

Sabatier, M. (2001). *La coopération policière européenne.* Paris: L'Harmattan.

ONUDC. (2007). *2007 World Drug Report.* Vienna: Office des Nations Unies contre la drogue et le Crime.

United Nations. (2003). *Global Illicit Drug Trends.* New York: Office on Drug and crime.

U.S. Department of State. (1990). "International Narcotics Control" Dispatch 1 (September 10): 83–86.

U.S. Department of State. (2002). *International Narcotics Control Strategy Report,* Washington, March 1.

U.S. Department of State. (2003). *International Narcotics Control Strategy Report,* Washington, March 1.

U.S. Department of State. (2004). *International Narcotics Control Strategy Report,* Washington, March 1.

Vinacke, W. E., & Artkoff, A. (1957). An experimental study of coalitions in the triad. *American Sociological Review, 22*(4), 406–414.

Ward, M. D. (1982). *Research Gaps in Alliance Dynamics.* Denver: Graduate School of International Studies of University of Denver, collection Monograph series in world affairs, pp. 3–26.

Information Sharing between Police and Intelligence Agencies

19

KATHLEEN M. SWEET

Contents

On September 24th U.S. Attorney General John Ashcroft told the House Judiciary Committee, "Law enforcement tools created decades ago were crafted for rotary telephones—not email, the internet, mobile communications and voice mail ... I regret to inform you that we are today sending our troops into the modern field of battle with antique weapons" (Riley, 2005).

The attacks on the World Trade Center on September 11, 2001, illustrated the immediate need to update U.S. intelligence processes. It has been argued that if a single unit had been able to assemble the pieces of this complicated and constantly expanding puzzle together, the current war on terrorism would be more successful. One of the biggest obstacles has been the different missions between intelligence officials and law enforcement. As a result, the Global Intelligence Working Group drafted the National Criminal Intelligence Sharing Plan. This plan was made to better foster intelligence sharing between local, state, and federal officials. The group made 28 recommendations and they appear to represent a good plan but can it be actually used as a useful tool that works? Several other pieces of legislation have also been passed and will be discussed. The major thesis of this chapter is that not nearly enough has been done and this raises the risks of another successful hostile attack.

Brief History of Intelligence in the United States

In order to understand the potential benefit of adding local law enforcement to the intelligence community, it is first necessary to look at a brief historical overview of how the community evolved. Intelligence in the United States has its earliest roots in the American Revolution. Benjamin Franklin could be considered the first intelligence officer operating on behalf of the United States. Franklin set up an office in Paris where "... he had a twofold mission: to get military and economic assistance from France, and to establish and run a network of agents in London following developments in the British government" (Holt, 1995). Nathan Hale is usually considered to be the first American spy and was hung by the British during the Revolutionary War. Thus, even though there were no laws or legislation regulating the intelligence community as a whole, intelligence functions have existed since the time before the independence of this nation.

Originally, the vast majority of the intelligence community remained within the armed forces. Each branch of the military has its own intelligence units and personnel, now also including the Coast Guard. This has always been necessary in order to serve the particular intelligence requirements of each branch of the military and they have continued to cling to the organizational structure. The need for a *central* intelligence source did not become apparent until World War II. The disastrous events at Pearl Harbor demonstrated to many top officials that there was indeed a requirement for some agency to be the central repository for all intelligence collected. The National Security Act of 1947 established the legal basis for the modern intelligence community (Berkowitz & Goodman, 1989).

However, for years, the intelligence and law-enforcement communities worked in two different worlds (Best, 2007). In fact, the National Security Act of 1947 specifically states that the CIA may collect intelligence through human sources and other appropriate means, but they do not possess any police, subpoena, law enforcement, or internal security powers (U.S. House of Representatives, 1996). The missions and goals of these two separate entities were complementary but not integrated. Intelligence is intended to shape policy maker decisions and the overall U.S. strategy (Best, 2007). Law enforcement, involving a more microview, seeks to curb crime and violence and to enforce laws. The attacks of September 11 showed the need for a more seamless transition of information and cooperation in general. Consequently, the Global Intelligence Working Group planned and drafted the National Criminal Intelligence Sharing Plan to foster and enhance improved communication between these agencies. The published mission was "to overcome the long-standing and substantial barriers that hinder intelligence" (U.S. Department of Justice, 2003).

Nonetheless, the Plan did not give the Director of National Intelligence (DNI) the authority or power to work with or direct the other intelligence units already in existence. The DNI did eventually become the lead agency for the collection, analysis, and dissemination of all-source intelligence and began producing National Intelligence Estimates. It soon became apparent that the spectrum of other intelligence agencies was intent on keeping their own secrets. Huge gaps of essential information were being withheld.

The United States initially expanded law enforcement and policing powers to fight against international terrorism centered on the pursuit of domestic terrorists, narco-traffickers, and organized crime. The extensive powers made it easier for police and intelligence agencies to share information, information that could be used for the possible prosecution of suspected terrorists. Changed policies and laws promoted efforts to collect personal information, religious and political affiliations, and records of finances and travel. Revisions of investigative rules expanded surveillance of oral and electronic communications and legalized a wide variety of undercover operations against suspected terrorist targets. The most controversial innovations allowed law-enforcement agencies to arrest suspected terrorists and detain them indefinitely without providing access to counsel or opportunities to seek judicial review. New criminal laws relaxed the definition of terrorism sufficiently enough to potentially reclassify drug trafficking and organized crime as threats to national security. Expansions of criminal involvement also made it possible to pursue fringe members of terrorist organizations without requiring individualized information about whether and how particular defendants promoted the aims of the organization with which they associated.

National Criminal Intelligence Sharing Plan

The expansion of law-enforcement powers was not simply a reaction to the 9/11 attacks. They were built upon initiatives under way well before 9/11 that targeted organized crime. Starting in the late 1980s and accelerating through the 1990s, many European nations had already established laws that, for the first time, tried to enhance law-enforcement powers. These controversial powers included covert policing methods, such as wiretaps, electronic bugs, and the strategic deployment of informants and undercover agents. Like the post-9/11 initiatives against terrorism, these developments arose from a perception that the targeted problem of organized crime transcended national borders; threatened the survival of the democratic state; and resisted more conventional modes of police inquiry. Like the post-9/11 antiterrorism campaigns, Europe's revamping of its covert policing apparatus was designed to facilitate international cooperation, particularly with U.S. law-enforcement agencies.

Problems that Remained

Although there were numerous examples of dismal failures on the part of the intelligence community throughout the time from the end of World War II up to September 11, 2001, internal bickering and narrow loyalty continued to plague the entire intelligence community. Whenever an intelligence failure was uncovered, the various entities within the intelligence community would often blame the fragmented system for the failure. Missed signals of an invasion into South Korea by North Korea, the Bay of Pigs incident in Cuba, the Phoenix program in Vietnam, and numerous other told and untold failures led to what became known as "The Year of Intelligence" in 1975 (Johnson, 1989). Congress, the media, and the public all demanded reform.

Reform and changes to legislation occurred during the 1970s and many within the community believed real change had been achieved. Unfortunately, the Iran–Contra affair in the early 1980s dealt yet another blow to the credibility of the intelligence community in the eyes of Congress, the media and the public at large regardless of the countless success stories that remain untold.

Post-9/11

The Bush administration, in reaction to the large-scale terrorist attacks in September 2001, made national security one of their most visible priorities and securing the country from additional terrorist attacks had become a huge part of the administration's foreign policy. The administration's first response was to establish the USA PATRIOT Act, which was modeled after the Foreign Intelligence Surveillance Act (1978). The USA PATRIOT Act stands for "Uniting and Strengthening America by Providing Appropriate Tools Required to Intercept and Obstruct Terrorism." Congress enacted it virtually without significant debate, without detailed committee reports, without a conference committee, and with little floor commentary. Submitted just days after the 9/11 attacks, it was rushed through Congress at lightning speed for a statute of its size and complexity. It passed the House on October 24, 2001 by a vote of 357 to 66, and passed the Senate the next day, October 25, 2001, by a vote of 98 to 1. It was signed into law by President Bush the following day, October 26, and is now, as amended, the law of the land.

Later, the first recommendation of the Global Intelligence Working Group was that all agencies regardless of size shall develop minimum standards for intelligence policing and utilization (U.S. Department of Justice, 2003). It also stated that management should be involved and that a position should be created to oversee the program (U.S. Department of Justice, 2003). Each manager was tasked with seeking ways to enhance intelligence sharing by participating in joint task forces at the state, regional, and federal levels.

One additional mandate required interface with the public and media (U.S. Department of Justice, 2003). The second recommendation required the creation of a Criminal Intelligence Coordination Council (CICC).

The purpose of this council would be to advise the Congress, the U.S. Attorney General, and the Secretary of the Department of Homeland Security on issues relating to utilizing intelligence more effectively through whatever agencies were most appropriate. It also stated that the council should be made up of representatives from local, state, and federal agencies (U.S. Department of Justice, 2003). Another recommendation authorized implementation of this plan and an annual report. The whole concept was to give an appearance of cooperation between federal, state, and local authorities, including an emphasis that all groups signing were to ensure that all citizens' privacy and constitutional rights were to be protected. This intricate plan of cooperation mixed with deception has stifled complete implementation of a workable solution to information sharing.

More Specifics on the PATRIOT Act

The PATRIOT Act contains more than 150 sections. It is divided into 10 separate Titles and is hundreds of pages long. The powers it grants to federal investigative agencies and law-enforcement agencies are unprecedented and reach everything from voice mail to consumer reports and banking records. The Act is among the most wide-ranging laws passed in recent memory, bringing new federal offices into being, creating new crimes, amending at least 12 federal statutes, mandating dozens of new reports, and directly appropriating $2.6 billion, with more funding to come from approval of various "authorizations" of unnamed amounts, scattered throughout the statute. Within the Justice Department, the Attorney General issued information-sharing protocols. These protocols make it clear that the Justice Department will use to the fullest extent the authorities granted to it by the Act. Among this information sharing is communication by Justice Department personnel to intelligence personnel within 30 days on whether a criminal investigation will be launched based on a given crime report and if the crime report indicates that foreign intelligence may be involved. Numerous federal investigative task forces have been created, and there are several ongoing cross-agency task forces to investigate terrorism or terrorist financing.

The PATRIOT Act has given not only new authority but also a new hubris to federal investigative agencies. Its emphasis on information collection, information sharing, expanded definitions, new regulations, cross-agency cooperation, wider authorities, enhanced surveillance techniques, swifter prosecutions, and more severe sentences have brought law enforcement and terrorism investigation to new levels. The entire PATRIOT Act is designed for increased surveillance, information gathering, and investigation of terrorism with a minimum of judicial review.

Under Title II, investigators can obtain information ranging from consumer reports, certain telephone data, certain details from Internet service providers, educational records, and banking transactions, all without a court order. All that is required is certification by a federal investigator that the information is necessary or required for a particular investigation, which does not even reach the standard of probable cause normally required with ordinary search and seizure warrants. There is no opportunity for judicial review of these information gathering activities since in general the information is obtained in secret and the Act provides that the person or entity providing the information is immune from civil liability. The Act's establishment of single jurisdiction search warrants and national service of search warrants effectively means that federal investigators only have to stop by one federal district court to obtain a search warrant for a particular investigation. Investigators will not be required to further justify their information request and continue to meet search warrant standards in any other federal court even if the investigation goes into other jurisdictions. This is "one-stop shopping" for federal search warrants and arguably takes the federal courts out of the loop.

The information sharing mandated chiefly by Titles II and IX is conducted by and large without any judicial review. In those limited instances where judicial review might be involved, such review is limited to specific challenges and those challenges can be delayed at the request of the government. "Special measures" that under Title III can be imposed by federal investigators upon domestic banks and other financial institutions are completely unprecedented in the history of federal banking regulation and represent a total rewrite of banking law. Yet these "special measures" can be submitted to banks by investigators once various required "certifications" are made by the Treasury Department, without any condition for a court order or court review.

Title IV of the Act identifies three types of terrorist organizations: (1) "Section 219" designations of terrorist groups borrowed from existing immigration law, (2) terrorist groups identified by the government under a similar procedure but with fewer requirements and no express judicial review, and (3) a wide-ranging category of any group of two persons or more "whether organized or not" which engages in any of the broadly defined list of "terrorist activities." The Act therefore gives federal investigators or agencies tremendously wide latitude in designating terrorist groups. It must be noted that the definitions of "terrorism" and "domestic terrorism" and "foreign intelligence" do not exclude the potential involvement of American citizens, so investigations, surveillance, and prosecution are not restricted to aliens.

The mandatory detention of aliens under Title IV allows for habeas corpus review. This allows an alien in indefinite detention a request for administrative review of the detention, every six months. This provision does not rely on judicial oversight to review the detention. There is limited judicial oversight of many other Act provisions such as forfeiture provisions, long-arm jurisdiction, and reduced or eliminated statutes of limitations. While these provisions may be seen as giving federal courts more power, in actuality the power is being given to federal prosecutors and investigators, who continue to drive federal criminal investigations and prosecutions.

The PATRIOT Act provisions for information sharing, grants and funding, and cross-agency training and cooperation, as well as the "fellow PATRIOT Acts" passed by State legislatures, have given state and local governmental law-enforcement units a new emphasis and a new influence. Now, the county Sheriff or local municipal law-enforcement unit may be involved in a terrorism investigation, can search for "foreign intelligence," and can take heed for "domestic terrorism." The professionalism of these organizations can sometimes be called into question, not to mention their lack of experience in these types of investigations.

No one can argue that the PATRIOT Act has not given federal agencies and law-enforcement agencies new powers, which can be used to gather and analyze information on a potential terrorist threat. But the real question is—have the provisions of the USA PATRIOT Act helped analysts and law-enforcement agencies uncover and prosecute that threat? In the first two years after 9/11, federal investigators and law-enforcement agencies recommended the prosecution of more than 6,400 individuals whom the government believed committed terrorist acts or who became targets on the grounds that charging them with some crime would "prevent or disrupt potential or actual terrorist threats." Based on these recommendations, as of September 30, 2003, the government had in one way or another processed 2,681 individuals who had been the subject of the recommended prosecutions. Analysis of the case-by-case data obtained by the Transactional Records Access Clearinghouse (TRAC) revealed the following data. Of the 6,400 individuals recommended for prosecution, 1,802 individual cases were closed without conviction and 879 were convicted of a terrorist-related offense. Of the 879 convictions, only five individuals were sentenced for more than 20 years; 23 were sentenced to 5 to 20 years; and 373 were sentenced to one day up to five years in prison. There were still 642 cases pending trial as of the time of the report on December 8, 2003 (TRAC, 2003).

Unfortunately, the Bush administration began withholding information that the government had previously released to TRAC. As a result, it is no longer possible to determine the exact number of individuals who the investigative agencies recommended be prosecuted. However, the two years of collected data are more than sufficient to show an overwhelming increase in the number of arrests and convictions by the federal agencies and law-enforcement agencies. Whatever the case, the absolute number of terrorism and antiterrorism situations that have been recorded by assistant U.S. attorneys around the country in the two years after the 9/11 attacks is sobering.

As a result of the 9/11 attacks, the Justice Department added a number of new crime categories to its internal record-keeping system tracking actions that in its view are in some way related to terrorism. Most prominent among the new groupings is what it now calls *anti-terrorism*. This area, according to the department's data manual, covers immigration, identity theft, drugs, and other such cases brought by prosecutors that were intended to prevent or disrupt potential or actual terrorist threats. Even if we were to set aside the antiterrorism matters referred to prosecutors by investigative agencies during the two-year period, more than half, approximately 3,500 were cases, were classified as involving actual acts of terrorism from one of the following categories: financial terrorism (added after 9/11), international terrorism, or domestic terrorism (TRAC, 2003).

Without question, the events of 9/11 resulted in a dramatic escalation in the government's enforcement activities in the terrorism area. Justice Department referrals for prosecution received during the two years prior to September 30, 2001, when compared with those received two years after 9/11, show the following. Both terrorism and antiterrorism experienced a sixfold increase in cases that were referred to prosecutors, from 594 such actions before to 3,555 after. There was an eightfold jump in convictions, 110–879. Some of this growth is naturally the result of the addition of "anti-terrorism" as a new category to be tracked under terrorism after 9/11. When antiterrorism was put aside, the increase in terrorism cases that were prosecuted or declined was less dramatic, from 544 to 1,778. The number of convictions grew by three and a half times: from 96 prior to 9/11 to 341 after. Surprisingly, despite the three-and-a-half-fold increase in terrorism convictions, the number of convicts who were sentenced to five years or more in prison has not grown at all from pre-9/11 levels. In fact, the number actually declined, dropping from 24 individuals whose cases began before the attacks to 16. What has jumped is the number of individuals convicted but sentenced to little or no prison time.

When looking at international terrorism only, investigative referrals that were either prosecuted or declined increased five times, jumping from 142 individuals before the 9/11 attacks to 748 after. The climb in convictions was even sharper, jumping over seven and a half times, from 24 to 184. Once again, despite the *increase* in convictions, the number of convicts who received sentences of five or more years declined from six individuals in the two years before 9/11 to only three in the two years after. Out of the 184 convictions under international terrorism, 80 received no prison time and 91 received sentences of less than a year. Although not all cases following the two years after 9/11 have been completed, current data suggest that terrorism investigations, prosecutions, and convictions were all sharply higher in the aftermath of 9/11, but the actual number of individuals who were sentenced to five or more years in prison years has fallen.

Increased Public Attention

This sudden thrust into the spotlight placed many activities and functions of the intelligence community in the public light that had conveniently gone unnoticed for years. The public and many in the media and Congress were becoming more involved. Eventually, the finger pointing gave way to more coherent discussions about how to really effect change in the intelligence community in order to prevent the next terrorist attack. After the events of 9/11, a relatively new significant player in national intelligence emerged: local law enforcement. From the morning of 9/11 forward, local law-enforcement agencies have been expected to perform functions for which very few at that level had been trained. Many local law-enforcement agencies were asked to check for contacts with vast lists of people and perform "threat assessments" on local groups or persons. While many in local law enforcement were happy and more than willing to help, many had no idea what it was that was being asked of them. For the first time in the intelligence community's history, they needed local law enforcement and their records in a new and vital way. After 9/11, the list of people that needed to be tracked—both from a historical perspective and in real time—was so massive that local law enforcement was necessary to assist in the searches.

The seventh recommendation of the Global Intelligence Working Group became one of the most important recommendations: that local, state, and federal law agencies partner with local and private sectors to "detect and prevent attacks to our nation's critical infrastructures" (U.S. Department of Justice, 2003). Recommendation 18 also provided that there should be a comprehensive training plan developed to mandate the use to all affected personnel (U.S. Department of Justice, 2003) and that the CICC establish a working relationship with the International Association of Directors of Law Enforcement Standards and Training organization and the International Association of Chiefs of Police (IACP) and State Provincial Police Academy Directors Section to coordinate training on these issues at all police academies and training centers (U.S. Department of Justice, 2003). Access to information was expanded via a web-based criminal information system that interfaces with existing databases such as that used by Federal Bureau of Investigation (FBI). They use the language of the Global Justice Extensible Markup Language Data Module (U.S. Department of Justice, 2003). All personnel who have access to this criminal intelligence information are to be subjected to a thorough FBI background check and then given access to a central site for the acquisition of sensitive information (U.S. Department of Justice, 2003).

Always a Problem

The plan, as recommended, would be a major milestone in the arena of intelligence sharing. Basically, the whole basis of the system was to develop a web-based system that allows law-enforcement officials to input and retrieve data in real time. Additionally, it will allow them to access other databases currently used by the FBI and other security agencies. It must be pointed out that for this program to be successful it must be well funded and fully accepted by all agencies. Unfortunately, the best laid plans sometimes fail and the intelligence community was not as willing to share as originally anticipated.

On the other hand, local enforcement can be a gigantic asset if only recognized as such. The first and foremost benefit they can offer is sheer mass of personnel. The number of FBI agents, CIA officers, and intelligence members of the military branches is very small in comparison to the number of police officers potentially available. This group of assets can effectively be used to search every corner of the United States for persons or things. It would be impossible for the FBI or CIA to even consider a nationwide search without the assistance of local law enforcement. The next benefit offered is extensive knowledge of a specific area and the people and groups that live and work within that area. Through day-to-day patrol and maintaining the peace of a city or county, police officers come to know who is doing what and where, unconsciously creating a huge intelligence database. In addition, local law enforcement can move throughout their community and perform certain actions much more seamlessly than federal entities. The lack of much bureaucratic red tape is perhaps another way local law enforcement can be of immediate service to the intelligence community.

Future of Local Law Enforcement and Intelligence

The first and foremost change that still needs to occur with respect to local law enforcement and the intelligence community is increased communication. There are obvious problems with security clearances that need to be addressed, but some personnel at each law-enforcement agency in today's environment should have some level of federal security clearance in order to expedite communication when the need arises. No one can predict which local law-enforcement agency will have jurisdiction over the next group of terrorists plotting an attack. It is vital to the intelligence process in the United States to take the time and effort to get security clearances in order to be able to adequately communicate within the intelligence community. To date, this has been slow in materializing.

Training presents another significant issue. A solid understanding of intelligence gathering will assist a patrol officer in daily functions by allowing him or her to use discretionary time for intelligence gathering. Intelligence gathering methods are essential to any detective in order to assist in completing their casework but many detectives do not even know that it is intelligence gathering that they are doing. By moving the police force as a whole into more of an intelligence mode rather than remaining reactionary will improve their ability to maintain the peace while offering up a mass of personnel ready, trained, and available at a moment's notice if needed by the intelligence community. Colleges and Universities around the world can assist in this training via Homeland Security and Criminal Justice Programs.

Conclusions and Recommendations: Accidents and Incidents

On January 25, 2007, Cathy L. Lanier, acting Chief of Police in Washington DC, proposed that law-enforcement officers should not only be considered "first responders" but "first preventers." She went on to point out that local police know neighborhoods best and are in the best position to detect criminal activity that may be connected with terrorism, given the right tools. She highlighted the need for the "right" intelligence, emphasizing that they are not asking to be privy to all information but only to intelligence that is relevant to their local jurisdiction. She suggests that if matched with the correct intelligence, local police will be more prepared to disrupt and prevent a terrorist plot (Lanier, 2007).

Local law enforcement should never be asked to take over the functions of the intelligence community. A rudimentary survey of 100 officers, including local, state, and federal agents, from Connecticut, New York, and Massachusetts revealed the following consensus.

A. Most of the day-to-day operations of the intelligence community can and should remain classified to law-enforcement personnel. But, by allowing this massive group of officers to develop some working knowledge of intelligence gathering prior to the next terrorist event, a resource will be ready and willing to assist the intelligence community in any way that it can.

B. Integrating information obtained by local law-enforcement officers with that of the several intelligence communities is a complex and cumbersome task. Each has a separate mission, a unique focus, and different rules for the collection and distribution of data. Further, if collected data were to be haphazardly combined, the result would be an unmanageable amount of data that would be less than useful. The attacks of September 11 proved that there was a desperate need for interagency sharing of information, provoking major changes that are still taking shape today and need to be continually monitored.

C. One pervasive issue against the use of intelligence is the basic legality of sharing information. The PATRIOT Act was designed to remove barriers in information sharing between law-enforcement and intelligence agencies by permitting the disclosure of intelligence information gathered as a result of criminal investigations (Bina & Nicolai, 2007). The problem is that by openly offering data gathered to any law-enforcement agency, the personal freedom and privacy of individuals could be compromised.

D. While it is evident that information sharing programs are necessary, they cannot simply allow unchecked access. There are three commonly cited reasons for not having an "open application" for security clearances. First, security clearance means having access to classified information. Second, the clearance process is labor intensive and expensive. Third, conducting an excess number of clearance investigations slows the system, thereby taking longer to process (Federal Law Enforcement Intelligence, 2004). Some methods that have been successful are labeling information "sensitive but unclassified (SBU)" or "for official use only (FOUO)." SBU information produces declassified reports by removing sources and methods. One method of declassifying is the use of a "tear line" that would separate classified from unclassified information and make it easily separated according to the intended purpose. Another is by writing intelligence reports in a way that relays all critical data but excludes data that should remain classified (Federal Law Enforcement Intelligence, 2004). The Department of Homeland Security commonly uses FOUO for information that is not classified but should only be distributed to persons who have a need to know (Federal Law Enforcement Intelligence, 2004).

E. Early attempts at sharing information uncovered some potential obstacles. Most law-enforcement agencies took a "shotgun approach" to prevention, trying to cover all possible issues and respond to all levels of threats. Defending everywhere, all the time is unaffordable, as evidenced by the overtime costs incurred by several cities after September 11 (Riley, 2005). Effective intelligence helps to recognize what is credible and deserving of follow through. It is also necessary to understand links between terrorism-related and nonterrorism-related information (flight training, drug trafficking, etc.) to be able to identify links as indicators of an emerging threat (Homeland Security Advisory Council, 2005).

F. The FBI has created an Office of Intelligence that publishes assessments, bulletins, and reports for local law enforcement use. Intelligence assessments are reports on intelligence issues or security threats within the territory of an FBI field office. The assessment may be classified, unclassified, or law enforcement sensitive. Intelligence bulletins are finished intelligence products, typically SBU and available to state, local, and tribal law enforcement. Intelligence information reports are time-lined raw data at various levels of classification (Federal Law Enforcement Intelligence, 2004).

Without doubt information sharing has its problems and benefits. But it is the conclusion of this investigation that in the five years since 2001, those responsible for quality intelligence and quality law enforcement have not come far enough. Better training and more support at the upper levels of management are needed to improve communication, commitment, and deterrence.

References

Berkowitz, B. D., & Goodman, A. E. (1989). *Strategic Intelligence for American National Security.* Princeton, NJ: Princeton University Press.

Best, R. (2001). *Intelligence and Law Enforcement: Countering Transnational Threats to the U.S.* Retrieved March 27, 2007, from http://www.fas.org/irp/crs/RL30252.pdf

Bina, R., & Nicolai, C. (n.d.) *Legal Framework in U.S. Law for Sharing Law Enforcement and Intelligence Information.* Retrieved March 30, 2007, from http://www.maxwell.syr.edu/campbell/Past%20Events/Papers/ISHS/BinaNicolai.pdf

Criminal Terrorism Enforcement Since the 9/11/01 Attacks. (2003, December). *A TRAC Special Report, Transactional Records Access Clearinghouse.* Retrieved March 26, 2007, from http://trac.syr.edu/tracreports/terrorism/report031208.html

Federal Law Enforcement Intelligence. (2004, November). *Guide for State, Local and Tribal Law Enforcement.* Retrieved March 30, 2007, from http://www.cops.usdoj.gov/mime/open.pdf?Item=1439

Holt, P. M. (1995). *Secret Intelligence and Public Policy: A Dilemma of Democracy.* Washington, DC: Congressional Quarterly Press.

Homeland Security Advisory Council. (2005). *Intelligence and Information Sharing and Initiative: Homeland Security Intelligence & Information Fusion.* Retrieved March 30, 2007, from http://www.iir.com/global/FusionCenter/HSIntel.pdf

The impact of terrorism on state law enforcement. (2005, April). University of Illinois College of Law Conference March 2005: Champaign, IL. Retrieved October 9, 2005.

Johnson, L. K. (1989). *America's Secret Power: The CIA in a Democratic Society.* New York: Oxford University Press.

Lanier, C. L. (2007). *Hearing on the State of Intelligence Reform, Transcript of a Speech from the Acting Chief of Police of Washington, DC.* Retrieved March 30, 2007, from http://newsroom.dc.gov/show.aspx/agency/mpdc/section/4/release/10459/year/2007

Riley, B. (2005). Information sharing in homeland security and homeland defense: How the U.S. Department of Defense is helping. *Crime and Justice, 20,* 11–14. Retrieved March 30, 2007, from http://www.cjcenter.org/documents/pdf/cji/Cji0501-02.pdf

U.S. House of Representatives. (1996, June). *The Intelligence Community in the 21st Century. Staff Study.* Retrieved March 26, 2007, from http://www.gpo.gov/congress/house/intel/ic21/ic21013.html

U.S. Department of Justice. (2003, October). *National Criminal Intelligence Sharing Plan.* Retrieved March 26, 2007, from http://www.iir.com/global/products/NCISP_Plan.pdf

Private Security Responses

Public–Private Partnerships in Los Angeles

20

MARGARET YORK

Contents

Los Angeles County, the largest and most populated county in the United States, has successfully developed an operational model that joins public law enforcement and private security resources to provide a safe environment for persons using and working in government facilities at a substantial savings to taxpayers. As will be documented, the cost of this same level of protection solely through the use of police officers would cost nearly $70 million more annually than the Los Angeles County Police model. The additional cost associated with a police officer-only force would negatively affect the county's ability to address the funding requirements of other priority programs.

The Los Angeles County Police model is the most efficient and economical way of providing essential protective services to county stakeholders. It can be replicated in any urban area where there are quality private security companies in operation who conduct their business ethically, using cost-effective business practices.

Professional, well-selected, and trained police officers are important to the success of any police organization, and Los Angeles County Police officers perform duties as required in any other police agency. Recruitment and selection of new police officers have become a difficult and critical endeavor as young men and women look for higher paying, lower-risk employment. Police officer pay and benefits are commensurate with the job requirements, education, and training that are required. Additionally, the candidate pool for potential police officers is limited, and police agencies across the United States are competing for the same individuals.

Public–private partnerships do not change or detract from that basic concept. In the protection of government facilities and properties there are security-related assignments; however, that do not call for the same level of training nor the same skill set that is required of sworn police officers. Security guards are a viable and less costly alternative in many assignments. This is not to say that security guards need not be selected and trained using high standards. The contrary is true. The California State Bureau of Security Investigative Services requires that certain standards be met for a person to qualify for a California-issued Security Guard Card.

Additionally, job-specific training, background checks, and careful selection of guards assigned to Los Angeles County facilities are necessary to ensure that Los Angeles County Police can continue to provide quality service to their customers. There must be strict standards for private companies providing security services, enforceable by required adherence to terms of a contract. A competitive process to determine the most qualified companies provides an opportunity to receive the best private security services possible. A safe environment and client satisfaction with services provided are the best ways to gauge whether this model of public–private partnership is successful. The safety of the environment will be determined by the reduction and deterrence of crime and disorder. The level of satisfaction must be determined by the stakeholders, who include

- Elected officials who represent the people of Los Angeles County.
- Patrons of the services provided by Los Angeles County.
- County entities that contract for the services of Los Angeles County Police.
- County employees who work at the facilities.
- Employees of Los Angeles County Police.
- Persons contracted to provide security services.

This chapter focuses primarily on the contracting aspect of this public–private partnership. Except for some comparison purposes, little information is provided concerning the challenges associated with recruitment of sworn police officers, training of those officers or their function and duties. There is ample literature concerning these issues. Instead, this chapter is intended to provide sufficient evidence to support the hypothesis that the use of private security guards to supplement a police force is efficient, economical, and safe. The contracting process and subsequent monitoring of the contracts are the tool by which those assumptions are quantified and measured.

Structure/Budget of the Los Angeles County Police

Los Angeles County Police is a specialized law-enforcement agency that provides law enforcement and security services for county hospitals, parks, and government facilities. With over 600 sworn police officers and 160 civilian employees, it is the fourth largest law-enforcement agency in the county. It consists of three operational bureaus and one administrative bureau. Additionally, Los Angeles County Police contract with private security companies for over 800 private security guards, both armed and unarmed.

Los Angeles County Police provide law enforcement and security services for other county departments who are its clients (Figure 20.1). The six major client departments are the Departments of Health Services (hospitals and clinics), Public Social Services (public assistance), Mental Health (clinics),

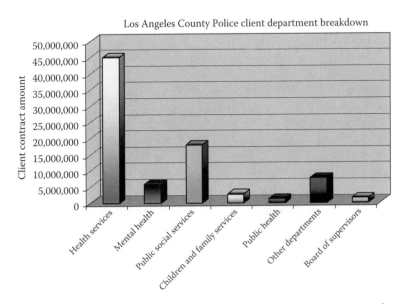

Figure 20.1 Annual contract value (USD) for each client department within the county.

Children and Family Services (protection of children and foster care), Public Health, and the Board of Supervisors (government facilities).

Health Services Bureau

The Los Angeles County health care system is the largest local system in the United States. There are five major general hospitals with a population of patients, visitors, and employees that is larger than most U.S. cities. Los Angeles County Police protect the interior and exterior of these hospitals in the core of urban Los Angeles with foot, vehicle, and bicycle patrols. Los Angeles County Police also provide protection to many medical clinics throughout the county. Private security guards are used extensively for fixed post positions inside the hospitals. There are 193 sworn police officers and 380 private security guards who provide this service and protection to nearly 19,000,000 people annually (FY 2005–2006) (Figure 20.2).

Parks Services Bureau

Los Angeles County has a beautiful and extensive park system that consists of 140 parks and recreational centers. Additionally, there are golf courses, regional parks, arboretum and botanical gardens, nature centers, lakes, horse riding trails, Raging Waters Theme Park, the world renowned Hollywood Bowl, and the John Anson Ford Amphitheatre. Officers patrol in black and white patrol vehicles, all terrain vehicles, bicycles, horses, and boats. There are 159 sworn police officers and no private security guards assigned to Parks Services Bureau (Figure 20.3).

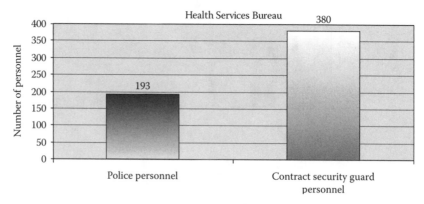

Figure 20.2 Ratio of police personnel to contract security guard personnel within Health Services Bureau. This ratio is approximately 1:2.

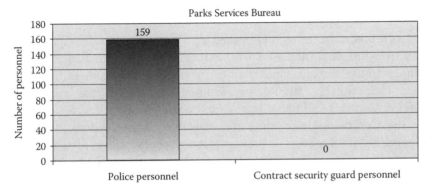

Figure 20.3 Ratio of police personnel to contract security guard personnel within Parks Services Bureau. There are no Security Guard Personnel in this Bureau because there are no positions suitable for security guard assignments.

Facilities Services Bureau

The Los Angeles County seat of government is protected by Los Angeles County Police. Additionally, the County Police contract with other County departments such as the Departments of Public Social Services, Children and Family Services, Mental Health, Probation, Libraries, and others to protect over 165 facilities throughout the county. Both armed and unarmed private security guards stand at fixed post positions in most of these buildings. Many of these facilities are in the toughest areas of urban Los Angeles. Sworn police officers provide roving foot, vehicle, and bicycle patrols. Many of the facilities have alarm systems that are monitored by County Police with a patrol response when required. There are 164 sworn police officers and 444 private security guards assigned to provide this service and protection to 5,000,000 people annually (FY 2005–2006) (Figure 20.4).

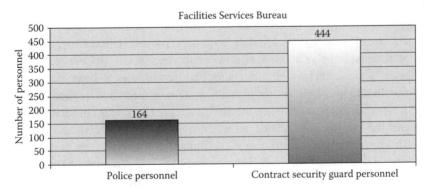

Figure 20.4 Ratio of police personnel to contract security guard personnel within Facilities Services Bureau. This ratio is approximately 1:3.

Administrative Services Bureau

The Administrative Bureau is headed by a civilian manager, equivalent in rank to a Bureau Chief, who works directly for the Chief of Police. The Administrative Bureau handles all of the support functions of the department, including Human Resources, Fiscal and Warehouse, Information Systems, Contract and Records, and Fleet Management.

The Contracts Unit, under the direction of the civilian manager, is responsible for all aspects of the contracting process within the Los Angeles County Police operation. Contracting with the County of Los Angeles is a complex and time-consuming process. It involves many steps and careful documentation.

Revenue Generation and Flow

Los Angeles County Police has a $100 million budget. Of that, 83.17% of its funding comes from client Los Angeles County departments who pay for law enforcement and security services. Only 16.29% of the overall funds come from the general county budget. Another 0.54% comes from citations and miscellaneous revenue.

Identification of Resource Requirements for Law Enforcement and Security Services

Law enforcement and security needs are determined through a consultation and assessment process between each facility manager and the law-enforcement manager responsible for the safety of the facility. ('Facility' is defined here as the building structure(s) and grounds, parking lots, etc. that encompass a campus.) Decisions must be made regarding if and how entry into the facility is controlled, the use of weapons-screening devices, closed circuit television cameras, specialty patrol vehicles, canine units, panic alarms, burglar alarms, and other strategies. Once the level and type of security are determined, a decision can be made as to how many sworn police officers and how many private security guards are needed. History, the potential for problems at the facility, and the crime situation in and around the facility are considered when making these decisions.

In coordination with the annual budget, a security assessment/survey is completed at least annually for each facility. The purpose of the security assessment/survey is to look at the *building* environment to ensure that the building itself is protected and to look at *control* of the environment to ensure that persons using or employed in the building will be safe. Issues such as lighting and landscape design, alarm systems (fire, burglar, and panic), closed circuit television surveillance of public areas, and perimeter control address the building environment. Entry control points, key issuance, photo identification/ badges, off-hour access authority, safety training, procedures for receiving mail and packages, and emergency evacuation plans are addressed.

Some facilities/properties have a higher potential for risk than others. The determination of whether any facility/property has that potential is, again, determined by the facility and law-enforcement managers in consultation. Examples of risk may include kidnapping, child abduction, or molestation, family violence, workplace violence, escape of mental patients, gang activity, and other situations that require a comprehensive approach to protect the public. Mitigation of potential risk factors is important to protect the persons visiting or employed within the facilities and also protects against liability for negligent conditions that could exist. Emergency preparedness is an important component, which includes evacuation plans, food and water storage, business continuity planning, notification procedures, and shelter.

In conjunction with the United States Department of Homeland Security, the State of California, and the City and County of Los Angeles, locations deemed to be critical public assets are identified and assessed. Critical assets under the jurisdiction of the Los Angeles County Police include the major county hospitals and public health clinics, the Los Angeles County seat of government, and other government facilities, water supply and delivery systems, emergency services facilities, and regional monuments and icons. Four integrated processes that include identification, assessments, management systems, and a Protective Security Task Force engender interagency cooperation and coordination to prevent, deter, respond to, and mitigate critical incidents, including terrorism.

Los Angeles County has adopted a regional service delivery model, known as Service Planning Areas, due to the size, population, and congestion in the county. This model divides the county, geographically, into eight Service Planning Areas. Private security companies bid to provide service to a specific subsection (Service Planning Area) of the larger county. This alignment provides better service delivery, management, and monitoring of the services and is more user and employee friendly.

Comparison of Sworn Police Officers/Private Security Guards

Los Angeles County Police officers enforce laws and investigate crimes pursuant to the authority granted to them in the California Penal Code §830.31. The officers perform patrol duties and site, arrest, transport, and book violators. They also perform specialized duties including dignitary protection, deployment of a mobile field force/mutual aid, and are trained to respond to attacks by weapons of mass destruction. A paramilitary chain of command provides a supervision, management, and reporting structure for the sworn officers consisting of Sergeants, Lieutenants, Captains, Bureau Chiefs, an Assistant Chief, and the Chief of Police.

Contracted security guards are responsible for covering fixed post positions and assigned areas to prevent and deter crime. They conduct screening and searches for weapons and contraband and intervene, as appropriate, to stop injurious acts toward persons and property. No police officer power or authority is granted to them under the California Penal Code; however, they have the same authority to arrest as a private person. They have the obligation, based upon the duties assigned to them, to be diligent in their observations, conspicuous in their presence, and interactive in their contact with the public.

The contracted private security company has the responsibility for selection, hiring, training, supervision, and compensation of the private security guards (Figure 20.5). Since they are not employees of the County of Los Angeles, no Civil Service employment rights attach. The chain of command structure for the private security guards consists of a supervisor and a post commander. The security companies' adherence to the provisions of their contract is monitored by the Contract Monitoring Unit and other police staff. Together, Los Angeles County Police and contracted security personnel form a partnership to provide a safe and secure environment for patrons, visitors, and employees of Los Angeles County facilities and protect property belonging to the County of Los Angeles.

Sworn police officers of Los Angeles County have employment protections provided by the Los Angeles County Civil Service Rules and by the California Peace Officers' Bill of Rights. If a police officer is not meeting the requirements of the job, a work performance process or a disciplinary process must ensue before the officer can be relieved from duty and/or terminated from employment. Private security officers, on the other hand, work for the private security company and are not employees of the County of Los Angeles. They have no Civil Service protections concerning their employment and can be removed from a county post at the discretion of their own or county managers.

The total cost package (pay, benefits, and administrative overhead rates) must be factored in when considering the difference between hiring police officers versus security guards for assignments that do not require police officer powers and authority. Although the County of Los Angeles recently adopted a Living Wage Ordinance that requires higher pay with an option for health benefits, it does not require other benefits or pension costs that contribute to the higher cost for police officers. Police officers cost about three times as much per hour as security guards (Figure 20.6).

Police Officer/Security Guard Comparison

County Police Officer	Armed Security Guard	Unarmed Security Guard
21 years old at the time of academy graduation	18 years old	18 years old
U.S. citizen OR	U.S. citizen OR	U.S. citizen OR
Permanent resident, alien, eligible and applied for citizenship	Legal right to work in the United States	Legal right to work in the United States
California driver's license	California driver's license— **only if required to drive on the job**	California driver's license— **only if required to drive on the job**
Submit to fingerprint search for criminal history	Submit to fingerprint search for criminal history	Submit to fingerprint search for criminal history
High school graduate or equivalent	—	—
Submit to background investigation	Submit to background investigation—**county requirement, not a state requirement**	Submit to background investigation—**county requirement, not a state requirement**
Be free of adverse physical, emotional, or mental conditions	Be free of communicable disease or adverse physical conditions	Be free of communicable disease or adverse physical conditions
Be of good moral character	—	—
No felony convictions	No felony convictions	No felony convictions
No high-grade misdemeanor convictions	No high-grade misdemeanor convictions	No high-grade misdemeanor convictions
Complete 18 weeks (720 h) of post academy training	Complete 40 h of BSIS training, 8 h prior to assignment	Complete 40 h of BSIS training, 8 h prior to assignment
Complete 12 week field training program	—	—
Complete 24 h of continuous professional training every 2 years, including 14 h of perishable skills training	Complete 16 h of continuous professional training every 2 years	Complete 16 h of continuous professional training every 2 years
Extensive lethal and less lethal force training during academy	Complete BSIS firearms class 14 h [every 2 years]	—
Firearms requalification 6 times/year	Firearms requalification 2 times/year	—

Figure 20.5 Differences in education and training, between Los Angeles County Police officers and armed and unarmed contract security personnel.

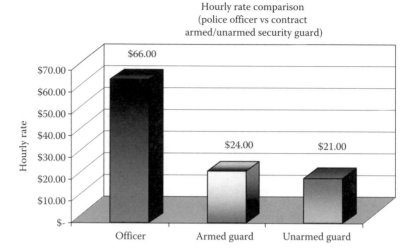

Figure 20.6 Hourly rate comparison between police officer and both armed and unarmed contract security guards. *Note*: The "Hourly Rate" used is the rate billed to client departments for service, not the hourly rate paid to the employee/contractor. The hourly rate paid to the security company post commander is $19.55, supervisor is $15.89, and security guard is $11.84 if they do not choose a health benefit option and $9.64 if they choose a health benefit option. The employer must pay at least $2.20 per hour toward a bona fide health care plan.

Contracting with the County of Los Angeles to Provide Security Services

Contracting with the County of Los Angeles is a complex process. The county is obligated, when contracting out services, to demonstrate that the contracted service results in monetary savings for the county. In other words, the contracted service must cost less if the county selected, trained, and employed its own workers to do the same job. The Los Angeles County Police estimates that it saves almost $69 million annually through contracting.

Additionally, the county must be assured that the companies with whom it contracts are financially stable and engage in good business practices. The bidders are required, therefore, to provide the county with financial statements audited by a Certified Public Accountant (must be for the three most recent years). The bidder must also provide a statement of their rates and budget sheet outlining direct and indirect costs.

Los Angeles County requires that the security companies have general liability, automobile liability, workers' compensation, and employee liability insurance when they contract with the county. The automobile insurance shall include coverage for all autos whether "owned," "hired," or "nonowned" and the limit of liability shall not be less than $1 million for each accident.

Workers' Compensation and Employers' Liability insurance provide workers' compensation benefits, and are required by the Labor Code of the State of California.

The process is competitive so that the best service at the most economical price can be selected. A requirement that the security companies strictly adhere to the terms of the contract ensures quality service throughout the term of the contract, which typically is three years, with two opportunities to extend for one year each. The companies, local, regional, and international, who currently hold contracts for security services with Los Angeles County Police are listed below:

- Akal (international).
- Securitas (international).
- Elite.
- Prudential.
- Top security.
- Perfect protective.
- Regional patrol.
- North American security.

Los Angeles County uses a contracting process that includes the stages listed below.

1. *Solicitation*
   - Request for proposal.
   - Scope of work/statements of work.
   - Draft agreement/contract documents.
   - Checklists.
2. *Bids and statements of qualifications review*
   - Prepared and submitted by proposer for evaluation.
3. *Proposal evaluations*
   - Minimum mandatory requirements.
   - Financial and labor-payroll review.
   - Consensus scoring.
4. *Notifications and proposer protest policy*
   - County police staff notifies proposer(s) of evaluation outcome.
   - Proposers provided an opportunity to protest decision.
5. *Negotiations*
   - Conducted with highest-ranked proposer.
   - Final agreement/contract documents.
6. *Award contract*
   - Submit to Board of Supervisors for approval.
   - Transition plan.

7. *Contract monitoring*
- Performance requirements summary.
- Contract discrepancy report.
- Contract monitoring system (electronic).
- Annual performance evaluation.

Requirements for contracting with the County of Los Angeles reflect the County Mission "To Enrich Lives Through Effective and Caring Service," and the County's Strategic Goals of Service Excellence, Children and Family Well-Being, Community Service, Health and Mental Health, and Public Safety. Therefore, contractors who wish to contract with the county must demonstrate their ability to successfully provide the required services and agree to abide by certain County Ordinances and solicitation-specific requirements, such as five years of similar service provision experience within the last seven years, providing employee health benefits as part of the Living Wage Program, having an office located in Los Angeles County, and agreeing to debarment and insurance provisions.

Monitoring/Discrepancies/Debarment Processes to Ensure Contract Compliance

Each contract has stipulations that require strict adherence to contract agreements on matters such as the scope of work, minimum staffing, bilingual staffing, background and security investigations of employees, training requirements, uniform and badge requirements, a complaint reporting procedure, record retention, and other requirements.

A Contract Monitoring Unit, which is staffed by civilian members of the Los Angeles County Police, regularly monitors the performance of the security companies and its employees for compliance with the contract agreements. There is a wide range of data requirements related to contract compliance; therefore, the Contract Monitoring Unit uses an automated business solution to manage information. The Contract Management System consists of an office application, a field application, and a data processing and storage server.

When services are not performed as required in the contract, a fine is generally imposed. These fines can run from $50 to $500 for a single occurrence. Some violations are considered much more serious than others. For example, failing to fill a post would result in a withholding of up to the full amount of any invoice otherwise due; liquidated damages of $1,000 per post per day upon a post being vacant three days in a row or three days within a month's time. Further violations could result in termination for default of the contract for failure to perform and debarment from county contracting.

Other serious violations of the contract that could lead to debarment include underpayment of employees, and failure to monitor and supervise the security company's own operation.

Debarment is a serious consequence considering the value of the contract and the loss of reputation of the business should they be debarred. The debarment process not only terminates the breached contract, but all existing contracts between the county and the security company. It is a necessary sanction considering the damage to the county should the security company fail to perform as required by the contract. The governing body, the Board of Supervisors, may debar if it finds, in its discretion, that the contractor has done any of the following: (1) violated a term of the contract, (2) committed an act or omission that negatively reflects on the Contractor's quality, fitness, or capacity to perform, or engaged in a pattern or practice that negatively reflects on the same, (3) committed an act or offense that indicates a lack of business integrity or business honesty, or (4) made or submitted a false claim against the county or any other public entity.

The security company is entitled to a hearing before a Contractor Hearing Board. The Hearing board is made up of county department heads including those from Internal Services, Public Works, the Chief Administrative Office, and the Office of Affirmative Action. Alternate board members include department heads from Health Services, Parks and Recreation, and Public Social Services. County Counsel serves as the legal advisor to the board.

During the hearing, evidence can be presented by both sides. After consideration of the evidence, the Contractor Hearing Board will prepare a tentative proposed decision and make a recommendation to the Board of Supervisors who make the final decision. The Board of Supervisors may modify, deny, or adopt the recommended decision.

If the security company has been debarred for a period longer than five years, and five years have passed, they may request that the debarment period be reduced or the debarment be terminated. The Contractor Hearing Board would again convene and propose a decision, making a recommendation to the Board of Supervisors who would make the final decision.

Performance Measures

Weapons Screening

Weapons screening is an important strategy for providing a safe environment for patrons and employees in county facilities and hospitals. Weapons screening is primarily handled by private security guards with oversight by sworn police officers. During weapons screening, weapons that are criminally illegal to possess and items that are legal to possess but can be used as weapons and are prohibited by policy from entering a county facility are confiscated. (Examples include knives, pepper spray, knitting needles, box cutters, etc.) Last year, over 24,000,000 people were screened in 64 locations, resulting in the confiscation of 1,553 illegal weapons and 44,354 prohibited items. The number of people screened and the number of weapons confiscated is a performance measure that is quantified and regularly reported.

Sixty-six of the 212 serviced locations have weapons screening equipment. Sixty-three percent of the security guards who work at the locations that have weapons screening capabilities are assigned that duty. When you consider the number of illegal weapons or prohibited items that are confiscated annually, it illustrates a very high productivity rate. An analysis of the number of items confiscated annually demonstrates the effectiveness of this strategy in averting the potential for criminal activity and, or an unsafe environment.

Service Assessment

Los Angeles County Police is critically judged by the quality of the service delivered. Sworn police officers receive training in the police academy and in-service regarding the importance of customer satisfaction and quality service delivery. Service Excellence is the county's number one Strategic Plan goal. Service-Oriented Policing is the foundation of Los Angeles County Police's Core Values. The importance of quality service delivery is constantly reinforced by supervision and management of the Los Angeles County Police.

Private security guards generally do a good job in providing quality service; however, the most frequent complaints heard from management of client departments are service delivery related. The complaints generally concern turnover in assignments, lack of proactive attention and behavior, and lack of diligence in performing tasks. The workforce that private security companies draw from are often young people lacking work and life experience, older people who sometimes seek the job after being retired from another career, persons who are not familiar with the customs and languages of the very diverse communities in Los Angeles, or people who have been unsuccessful at other employment. These factors make selection, training, and supervision of the security guards challenging. However, it is an important obligation of the security companies to ensure that their employees understand and adhere to a service excellence philosophy as this is a term of their contractual agreement.

The challenge for the Los Angeles County Police is to address service delivery issues quickly and responsively. This is accomplished through contract monitoring and establishment of regular meetings, which result in good business relationships with the security companies. The security companies must be held strictly accountable for the quality, training, and supervision of their employees. Los Angeles County Police, in partnership with its contract security companies, strives for continuous improvement in the manner in which services are provided to customers.

Incidents where the security officer or company has not performed satisfactorily are reported in a Contract discrepancy report. If the errant behavior is not corrected, the next step is to proceed to imposition of fines, liquidated damages, and ultimately, debarment if the failure to perform is egregious or not corrected within a reasonable amount of time.

Response Time

It is important that Los Angeles County Police respond quickly to emergency calls that require police intervention. Since private security guards are assigned to do the jobs that are more routine, more limited police resources are freed up to quickly react to incidents that may be more serious or life threatening, including alarm activations, assaults, patient/visitor disturbances, escapes, kidnappings, crimes against children, and domestic and workplace violence. Los Angeles County Police are able to routinely respond to these emergency calls within two minutes.

Conclusions

The strategic use of a combined police officer and contract security force provides a secure environment at county facilities at a substantial savings to taxpayers. As documented, the cost of this same level of protection solely through the use of police officers would cost nearly $70,000,000 more annually than the Los Angeles County Police model. The additional cost associated with a police officer-only force would negatively impact the county's ability to address the funding requirements of other priority programs. As proven, the Los Angeles County Police model effectively supports the County's Strategic Plan.

This model also appropriately uses the limited personnel resources of the Los Angeles County Police. Assignments of duties are made according to the training, experience, and skills set of a sworn officer or security guard. Personnel are aptly supervised and managed by a chain of command that efficiently determines operational needs.

The contracting process, while complex, protects the county's interest and ensures that the county's social policies are integrated into the policies of the security companies who do business with the County of Los Angeles. Contract monitoring, discrepancy, and debarment ensure accountability in the contracting process, guarantee consistently good service, and manage risk that could otherwise create liability for the county.

Although financial resources are always limited in public agencies, the Los Angeles County Police model provides a level of flexibility not achieved in a police officer-only model. As documented earlier, contract security guards are not afforded Civil Service protection. Therefore, during periods of budget shortfall, Los Angeles County Police and client departments can quickly reduce expenditures through the elimination of security guards. Additionally, as the requirements of the client departments change, the security force can be expanded or reallocated between facilities. Finally, performance issues can be quickly mitigated through the removal of contract security guards, whereas Civil Service procedures require a lengthy documentation process to discipline or terminate a police officer for performance issues.

An important measure of the quality of service that Los Angeles County Police provides is the level of satisfaction determined by our client departments. The level of service provided by the county police is consistently rated highly by clients.

Post-9/11 Port Security in Houston, Texas

21

GARY R. SCHEIBE and ELIZABETH H. McCONNELL

Contents

On September 11, 2001, over 3,000 people died in the terrorist attack on the World Trade Center (WTC) in New York. Since the attack, concern about terrorism resonates in the hearts and minds of everyone, especially emergency responders and security professionals. In fact, this catastrophic incident significantly changed the traditional roles of emergency responders and security professionals around the world, resulting in a paradigm shift in the security industry. The attack on the trade center made it apparent that any person, location, or work environment is a possible target of terrorists. Public and private security professionals scrambled to implement immediate changes in security measures, being sure to incorporate the latest technology. For example, as part of a global program to improve security and lessen workforce anxiety, New York-based Lehman Brothers provided personal safety emergency kits with every personal computer (PC) and workstation. The global head of security operations at Lehman Brothers reported that each kit contained a gas mask, safety goggles, and a whistle, which would be used to signal for assistance during an evacuation (Vernon, 2003).

Pre-9/11 Security Paradigm

Historically, and pre-9/11, the primary function of the security guard was similar to a Wal-Mart greeter—"good morning, good night, let me help you with the package," and the like. Approximately a year after the first terrorist attack on the WTC (in 1993), law-enforcement intelligence professional Jack Morris questioned why so many corporate security operations in the Western world were still performing their duties like antediluvian guards and not like a modern-day protector (Robinson, 1999). For example, some companies continued the "old school" practice of protecting company assets in a reactive manner that was mostly directed toward personnel safety, locking doors, and equipment theft. Morris emphasized the necessary shift from reactive to proactive in the management of security. Sennewald (2003) recognized that terrorist attacks have transformed security services into a professional occupation that is a vital and integral component of American business and industry. Further, the problems of terrorist attacks, coupled with corporate thefts, proprietary thefts, and personal safety have created an access-control matrix monster that presents enormous challenges for security managers.

The WTC attack on 9/11 propelled private/corporate security into a highly professional and technical domain. The security function has climbed out of the basement and into the executive offices. Prior to the events of 9/11, corporate executives were beginning to realize that proactive security management increased their profitability. American corporate executives viewed terrorism as an international problem; as such, profitability for effective security measures was their motivating force. Terrorism has now become a clear and genuine reality for corporate America. The professional security department's role of being a proactive protector of assets, proactive trainer, and proactive manager has become far more complex since *terrorism* has attacked the United States and *technology* has provided new attack methods (Sennewald, 2003).

For law enforcement and other emergency responders, terms like *secondary device, IED, suicide bomber,* and *Jihad* were problems that existed thousands of miles away and, thus, not really associated with the United States. However, the signs and problems associated with terrorism did exist in the United States prior to the WTC attack, for example, attacks by domestic terrorists such as Ted Kaczynski, Timothy McVeigh, and Eric Robert Rudolph had already drawn attention to the need for security in the workplace.

In May of 1998 Ted Kaczynski was sentenced to life in prison for being the "Unabomber," an antitechnology terrorist who in 1978 began a series of sporadic bombings across the United States. His first bomb was found in May 1978 at the University of Chicago: a package sent through the mail to a professor, it exploded and injured a university police officer. Over time the bombs became more sophisticated and fatal; however, little was known about the bomber's identity besides a widely circulated sketch of a man wearing sunglasses and a hood. In 1994, the Unabomber began demanding publication of his "Manifesto," a 35,000 word document railing against technology. The document's eventual publication by the mainstream media led David Kaczynski to suspect that his brother Ted was the Unabomber. Eventually, David contacted law-enforcement authorities about his brother Ted. Ted Kaczynski was arrested in April 1996, in a surprise raid by federal agents at his one-room shack outside of Lincoln, Montana, where he had been living as a recluse since 1971 (Ansers.com).

Timothy McVeigh placed the bomb that killed 168 people at the Murrah Federal Building in Oklahoma City, Oklahoma, on April 19, 1995. The bomb, made of fertilizer and oil packed into the rear of a rented van, destroyed the front half of the building and killed 149 adults and 19 children. McVeigh, who had served in the U.S. Army from 1988 to 1991, was an extreme conservative. He later told investigators that he was angry over the federal government's clashes with white separatist Randy Weaver at Ruby Ridge, Idaho, in 1992 and with religious zealot David Koresh and the Branch Davidians at Waco, Texas, in 1993 (Ansers.com).

Eric Robert Rudolph, also known as the Olympic Park Bomber, is an American domestic terrorist who committed a series of bombings that killed three people and injured at least 150 others. Rudolph stated that his bombings were part of a guerrilla campaign against abortion and gay rights. Rudolph's most notorious bombing was the Centennial Olympic Park bombing on July 27, 1996, in Atlanta. The blast killed spectator Alice Hawthorne and wounded 111 others (Ansers.com).

Changes Begin

On September 20, 2001, in response to the September 11 attacks, President Bush announced the establishment of an *Office of Homeland Security* (OHS) to coordinate "homeland security" efforts. The mission of the Office was to develop and coordinate the implementation of a comprehensive national strategy to secure the United States from terrorist threats or attacks. The *Department of Homeland Security* was established on November 25, 2002, by the Homeland Security Act of 2002.

The National Strategy for Homeland Security and the Homeland Security Act of 2002 served to mobilize and organize the nation to secure the homeland from terrorist attacks. One primary reason for the establishment of the Department of Homeland Security was to provide the unifying core for the vast national network of organizations and institutions involved in efforts to secure the United States. The major support columns for the National Strategy are to prevent and deter terrorist attacks, to protect against and respond to threats and hazards to the nation, ensure safe and secure borders, welcome lawful immigrants and visitors, and promote the free flow of commerce.

There are several companion documents and legislative acts that support the National Strategy: The National Response Plan, the National Incident Manage System/Incident Command System, the USA Patriot Act, the Maritime Transportation Safety Act, and new chemical industry legislation, to name a few.

Sun Tzu, an ancient Chinese military strategist, stated that you should attack where they are not prepared and go out to where they do not expect (Sawyer, 2003). In essence, Sun Tzu was implying that prepared *law-enforcement officers, security professionals,* or *emergency responders* should know their enemies in order to protect and defend themselves, personnel, property, equipment, and proprietary information. A foundational component of "knowing your enemy" is to be proactively learning terroristic strategies and incorporating technological advances to defeat the enemy.

To shed some light on this issue, and in line with five security recommendations from Stone (2000) and Ready (2003), we surveyed security professionals to explore pre- and post-9/11 security measures at critical infrastructure sites in the Houston, Texas, metropolitan area. More specifically, security managers assigned to critical infrastructure facilities in the Port of Houston were surveyed.

The View of Terrorism

Even after the terrorist attacks on the WTC in 1993, resulting in 12 deaths, and the Murrah Federal Building in Oklahoma City, resulting in 169 deaths, most security procedures for high-rise buildings did not change. Levy (2000) indicated that it was not uncharacteristic of human nature to allow the horrors of the past to quickly fade into memory and no longer be the center of attention. Levy's study addressed the issue of whether the earlier WTC and Murrah Federal Building bombings motivated building security managers to develop defensive plans against terrorist attacks. Seventy-seven percent of respondents from San Diego and Boston indicated that crime, not terrorism, was the motivating factor behind upgrading building security systems. Upgraded security measures included access controls, alarms, surveillance TV, patrols, staff awareness training, contingency plans, perimeter fortification, standoff distance, and window fortification. Only the most high-profile buildings used fortification measures and few facilities maintained or enforced vehicle parking restrictions in their parking garages (Levy, 2000).

According to Cavanagh (2004) most mid-market companies agreed that spending on security is a sound business investment, but the majority saw it as an expense that must be minimized. From his survey, Cavanagh determined that 61% of businesses indicated that security provides value for their firms and a positive return on investment, but 39% reported that security is simply a cost that must be tightly controlled. However, Cavanagh found strong support for security spending at "critical industries"—transportation, energy and utilities, financial services, media and telecommunications, information technology (IT), and health care.

Research conducted by Stone (2000) provided some insight regarding the apathetic stance of property owners. Stone found that terrorism was widely viewed as one of the principal security threats to *international* business, not U.S. business. Stone used a straightforward definition of terrorism, "kill one, frighten a thousand" in his examination of how one's level of fear shaped perceptions regarding terrorist threats. Stone recognized that the chances of business people or assets being involved in direct acts of terrorism are relatively low. However, business is often caught in the crossfire of political disputes and attacks on the economic infrastructure of a country inevitably involve business interests (Stone, 2000). Research completed by the Department of Homeland Security (2003) indicated that the private sector owns 85% of the critical infrastructure in the United States. As such, informed business owners and security managers recognize that terrorism is a significant and sustained threat.

Although the issue of terrorism in the United States was not proactively addressed by private/corporate security before the 9/11 attacks, this was not the case in England. For example, in December 1992 the city of Newcastle, through a cooperative initiative between private security and local police, installed a 16-camera monochrome CCTV system. According to Clarke (1997) this proactive approach to attacking crime and terrorism provided a level of public security that resulted in a reduction of crime in the targeted area.

Areas of Concern

Since 9/11, corporate security professionals have had to re-evaluate and reanalyze areas of significant risk and vulnerability. Four major vulnerability areas such as access control, mailrooms, corporate protection, and cyber/IT protection are a continuous security challenge. Security managers have to balance various levels of protection and limited access against the possibility of impeding efficient operations.

Access Control

Engebretson (2004) indicated that since 9/11 corporate security managers have rethought their need for security gates. Historically, security gates were simply a deterrence measure to deny access to the honest. Today, security gates and fencing are designed to prevent unwanted vehicle and/or pedestrian entries. Gates can cost thousands of dollars and, with a life expectancy of approximately five years, they present continuing costs. Engebretson pointed out the necessity for corporate security managers to automatically budget for the costs of replacement and maintenance.

The use of pass access cards, anti-pass-back access cards, and ground loops enhance the security of access gates. Pass cards are used to obtain entry into secured areas but are not required for exiting secured areas. Anti-pass-back access systems require that access cards be used for entering and exiting secured areas. Ground-loop systems are similar to sensors used at traffic control lights. Sensors are imbedded in driveways and as vehicles pass over them the sensors activate gate closing mechanisms to prevent piggybacking or vehicles entering through unprotected exit gates (Engebretson, 2004).

Some facilities are using turnstile access and exit gates for employees. Employees have to have access cards to activate turnstiles. Additionally, anti-piggy-backing controls are installed on turnstiles. Engebretson (2004) recommended that access systems have remote audio and opening capabilities that are monitored by CCTV. Also, some facilities are designing a multiple-use SMART card that allows employees to use a single card for all access requirements.

Mailroom Challenges

Giusti (2004) indicated that postal inspectors have experienced approximately 20,000 incidents of suspicious substances since the October 2001 anthrax incidents. To address this type of threat, Giusti recommended that risk assessments be conducted by qualified security professionals and that the assessments include account assets, vulnerabilities, threats, countermeasures, and consequence management for immediate and surrounding areas. The corporation must consider the ancillary legal effects of events that disrupt the operations of other businesses. Further, mail services should be separated from other facility areas as much as possible as this could significantly reduce the number of victims when there are terrorist attacks.

Giusti (2004) recommended that mailrooms have independent ventilation systems to prevent heating-ventilation-air conditioning (HVAC) cross contamination. Mailrooms must have high-level access control and CCTVs must monitor the area. Additionally, the security and life-safety systems should be integrated. To enhance employee safety, Giusti also suggested that employees' personal items should not be allowed into the mailroom. Additionally, one of the most important areas of concern is mail screening processes. Mailroom employees must be trained to identify suspicious packages and look for potential explosive devices and possible hazardous materials. The training must also include safety response protocols and isolation and decontamination procedures.

Corporate Protection

Simovich (2004) maintained that executive security is the responsibility of in-house security professionals. They must ensure that executives and others involved in travel understand the importance of addressing protection issues in the early stages of the travel planning process. This is especially important when traveling outside the United States. Security professionals should complete a travel risk assessment and develop mitigation strategies. The risk assessment should consider the history of the site, country, and region. Of particular interest are locations' political stability, crime, and violence issues. Security professionals were also encouraged to consult the State Department for risk assessment information.

Simovich (2004) further indicated that security professionals must develop logistical plans. These plans should be based upon the Secret Service's 11-point advanced planning technique. Some of the duties include points of contact, motorcades, arrival and departure points, the target's movement and schedule, and room/living quarters. Security professionals must also develop the executive's travel itinerary. Additionally, security professionals must keep abreast of new threats and maintain their protective skills through continuing education and training.

Cyber/Information Technology (IT) Protection

The theft of proprietary information costs corporations and businesses approximately $70 billion a year (Kanok, 2004). The losses often result from employees leaking confidential and sensitive information by way of CDs or emails. Surprisingly, IT departments focus more attention on the incoming information rather than the outflow of confidential materials. According to Kanok, there are three common methods of stealing or leaking confidential information: identity theft by temporary workers, loss of core intellectual property from outsourcing agreements, and posting confidential and sensitive information on electronic message boards.

If the corporation establishes and enforces information distribution policies, then proprietary information leaks can be prevented. A risk analysis has to be conducted, by the security and IT departments, to identify the communication platform(s) that are most vulnerable to information leaks. Additionally, all data and information have to be categorized and prioritized into levels of confidentiality—top secret to public access. The company also has to establish access authorization levels. Finally, monitoring and enforcement policies must be developed and implemented. The corporation has to invest in security monitoring and leak detection software (Kanok, 2004).

Target Hardening

To effectively guard a facility/corporation against a terrorist attack, security professionals have to change the facility from a soft target to a hard target. Terrorism is the weapon of the weak because it targets the defenseless and innocent. Terrorists want to cause the most death and destruction possible (Ready, 2003).

Security professionals need to complete a threat/vulnerability assessment of each facility and each operating component/section of the corporation. Ready (2003) stressed that a threat/risk/vulnerability team(s) has to be formed. Members of the team should include security managers, operations managers, IT managers, representatives of executive management, and safety personnel. Also, the designers and builders of the facility or IT systems should provide additional informational support and suggestions.

Ready (2003) identified three major areas to help create a more hardened facility:

- Information operations—convince terrorists that a facility is not a soft target by implementing observable enhanced security measures, conducting media press releases promoting the enhanced security measures, and maintaining a visible integration into the local police/security networks.
- Operational security—minimize the number of people who have access to sensitive information, create physical barriers to prevent terrorist from observing your operations, and develop counter-surveillance terrorism plans.
- Vulnerability improvements—integrate physical security measures and surveillance/intrusion detection technology, design and implement target-hardening measures, develop an effective command/control/communications/intelligence network, and have a *professional well-trained* security force that is coordinated with local law enforcement.

Stone (2000) provided similar recommendations regarding risk management. For example, he suggested that minimizing the risk of becoming a terrorism victim is not complicated; however, it is not possible to guarantee 100% immunity from a direct attack. Stone advocated that the most effective approach to ensure that proper risk/vulnerability assessments are completed is to have the support of top executives. Stone recommended a two-pronged approach toward risk management:

- Evaluation—assess the impact and likelihood of the risk of terrorism as part of the global risk management program, develop proactive intelligence to consider how, why, and when terrorist attacks are likely to occur, and have an integrated security force.
- Management and training—develop and implement full-scale and continuing education and training programs for all employees and secure all assets with various levels of access control.

Ready (2003) and Stone (2000) stressed the necessity for recognizing that risk profiles are constantly changing, and as such, security measures and countermeasures have to be continuously updated based upon the latest available intelligence information. Additionally, security measures must be flexible enough to meet the ever-changing terrorist threat. The responsibilities of security professionals are continuously evolving and changing to meet today's threats.

Port Security

The Maritime Transportation Security Act added additional security protections to every port in the United States. The Department of Homeland Security (2004) implemented the new security measures designed to create a layered security approach in the nation's ports. The Department of Homeland Security utilized the expertise of the U.S. Coast Guard, Customs and Border Protection, the private sector, and the state and local authorities to create a system of different security measures that ensures protective measures from the point of origin to final destination.

The Department of Homeland Security (2004) requires all port facilities to submit a security assessment and a security plan to the U.S. Coast Guard. The security assessments identified security vulnerabilities. The security plan outlines specific measures that will be taken to mitigate the identified vulnerabilities and utilizes a layered security approach. Local stakeholders developed security plans that are used to deter, prevent, and respond to terrorist threats.

The Coast Guard oversees the implementation of these security measures throughout the United States. Some of the specific security measures include

- Increased identification checks on crew members and visitors.
- Additional canine detection teams.
- Expanded baggage and passenger screening efforts.
- Strategically placed perimeter fencing equipped with newly installed surveillance cameras.
- Targeted restricted access to sensitive areas of the port.
- X-ray machines on all large cruise ships.
- Additional employee training procedures.
- Increased security patrols.
- Implementation of a certification program to ensure foreign flagged vessels docking in U.S. ports have met international security requirements.

The ability to secure ports requires a team effort that includes local governments and private citizens. The U.S. government does not have the resources to fully secure all of its ports and waterways. The Department of Homeland Security's goal is to find the appropriate balance between security and freedom that allows the maritime-trade industry to thrive.

Objective

The purpose of this study is to provide a descriptive analysis of the impact that terrorism and technology have had on security professionals working at facilities in and around the Port of Houston. This project is designed to compare specific security elements in various critical infrastructures or key asset facilities in the Port of Houston area with an emphasis on terrorism and technology with a pre- and post-9/11 time designation.

Research Method

The survey method was used to obtain information regarding specific security elements. Security managers were asked to respond to a questionnaire consisting of 50 multiple-choice questions: 25 questions pre-9/11 and the same 25 questions post-9/11. This survey investigated issues such as target hardening, use of media, access control, and use of technology and emergency operations plans (EOPs). The questionnaire also included questions addressing the security manager's size of organization, their position within the organization, and the type of facility.

Sample

The sample for this study included 40 security managers from different critical infrastructure facilities in the Port of Houston area. The Port of Houston is a 25-mile-long complex of diversified public and private facilities. The port is ranked first in the United States in foreign waterborne commerce, second in total tonnage, and sixth in the world. Most significantly, the Port of Houston has a large number of Department of Homeland Security designated critical infrastructure facilities. Questionnaires were distributed to security managers assigned to critical infrastructure facilities.

Data Analysis

Frequency distributions and univariate statistics were used in this study to describe the impact(s) that terrorism and technology have had on security professionals at critical infrastructure facilities in the Port of Houston area. The univariate statistic examines variables one at a time and provides information about how the variable varies.

Limitations

The survey is an appropriate method for descriptive research (Maxfield & Babbie, 2001). This project used the administration of a survey to a group of security professionals to collect data. However, this project has two major limitations. First, the data were collected from an opportunistic sample, thus nonprobability sampling was used. Therefore, the sample is not randomized. As a result, the study's findings may not truly present the parameters of this population. Secondly, the sample size of 40 may not be large enough to allow a meaningful statistical analysis or any generalizations from the findings. The findings of this project provide the basis for a more comprehensive research project in the future.

Findings

Levy's (2000) study clearly indicated that society allows the horrors of the past to quickly fade into memory and no longer be the center of attention. Levy found that the terroristic incidents at the WTC (1993) and Murrah Federal Building did not motivate security managers to develop defensive plans against terrorist attacks. The research revealed that crime, not terrorism, motivated security managers to upgrade building security systems.

The question that arises is whether the terrorist attack on September 11, 2001, has changed the crime prevention paradigm that had previously

Table 21.1   General Respondent Information (n = 40)

Average years of respondents security experience	12
Average years as security manager	6
Average number of employees at facility	332
Percentage of respondents working in petroleum facility	17%
Percentage of respondents working in chemical facility	56%
Percentage of respondents working in another type facility (fueling terminal, barge terminal, etc.)	27%

motivated security professionals. This project examines the effects of terrorism and technology on the security professional as it relates to a pre- and post-9/11 paradox. This survey considered upgraded security measures, access controls, alarms, surveillance TV, staff awareness training, contingency plans, perimeter fortifications, and management policies.

Table 21.1 depicts general information about the respondents and the facilities they manage.

The statistical analysis of the 50 multiple-choice survey questions are presented using five broad categories: access control, EOPs, information/technology, training, and target hardening.

Access Control

According to Engebretson (2004), corporate security managers have rethought their need for security gates and access controls since 9/11. This includes security gates, security fencing, pass access cards, anti-pass-back access cards, ground loops, and SMART cards. Limiting access also includes sensitive data, barriers, and parcel deliveries. Five survey questions addressed the issue of access controls. Analysis indicates significant changes in each type of access control since 9/11 (Table 21.2).

Emergency Operations Plan

To effectively manage any type of emergency incident, the security professional needs to ensure that an EOP is completed, updated, and exercised regularly. Ready (2003) and Stone (2000) strongly recommend that emergency plans, security measures, and countermeasures be continuously updated based upon reliable intelligence in order to address the paradigm changes in terrorist attacks. Because of the ever-changing terrorist threat, security measures must be flexible and it is the responsibility of the security professional to meet today's threats. Three questions focused on EOPs. Table 21.3 indicates that there is no significant difference in the annual review of EOP's in the Port of Houston area before and after 9/11 ($P = 0.064$),

Table 21.2 Access Control

Question	Pre Mean	Post Mean	t-Statistic	df	P
Our facility minimizes the number of people who have access to sensitive information	3.72	4.44	−2.38	34	0.010
Our facility has installed physical barriers to prevent terrorist attacks	3.00	4.22	−3.60	34	0.000
Our facility has installed physical barriers to prevent surveillance by terrorist	2.66	3.44	−2.08	34	0.022
Our facility has terrorism prevention measures for the mailroom and loading dock area	2.94	4.16	−3.17	34	0.001
Our facility uses access control for the prevention and detection of terrorism	3.22	4.44	−3.31	34	0.001

suggesting some lack of attention to ever-changing threats. However, facilities are more likely to have an EOP and to have completed a terrorism threat and risk analysis than pre-9/11.

Information/Technology

The integration of information and technology is a must in the prevention, detection, and recovery from an internal or an external attack against a facility. Kanok (2004) indicated that businesses lose approximately $70 billion a year related to misuse of information and/or technology. IT departments focus more attention on the incoming information versus the outflow of confidential materials. Ready (2003) recommended the integration of physical security measures and surveillance/intrusion detection technology.

Six questions focused on the integration and use of information and technology to prevent, detect, and respond to terrorism. Table 21.4 indicates that the integration of private security professionals with local law enforcement has not significantly changed ($P = 0.119$). However, significant changes have occurred in the other five categories of information and technology security.

Table 21.3 Emergency Operations Plan

Question	Pre Mean	Post Mean	t-Statistic	df	P
Our facility has an EOP for terroristic incidents	3.16	4.16	−3.04	34	0.002
Our facility reviews all EOPs annually	3.72	4.27	−1.55	34	0.064
Our facility has completed a terrorism threat and risk analysis	2.77	4.55	−5.72	34	0.000

Table 21.4 Information/Technology

Question	Pre Mean	Post Mean	t-Statistic	df	P
Our facility has used technology to develop integrated terrorism prevention, detection, and response measures	2.77	3.66	−2.48	34	0.008
Our facility proactively gathers and disseminates information regarding a possible terroristic attack	2.66	4.16	−4.02	34	0.000
Our facility proactively researches new security technology(ies) for the prevention, detection, and recovery from a terroristic incident	2.61	3.88	−3.72	34	0.000
Our facility has an integrated security force (i.e., private security services and law enforcement officers)	3.11	3.66	−1.19	34	0.119
Our facility uses CCTV systems for the prevention and detection of terrorism	2.72	3.61	−2.15	34	0.019
Our facility uses IT for the prevention and detection of cyber terrorism and/or the misuse of sensitive operational materials	3.33	4.11	−2.27	34	0.014

Training

To make training at all levels effective, senior executives have to support and participate in planning, reviewing, and testing security measures (Stone, 2000; Ready, 2003). The security force must be professionally trained and fully integrated into local law-enforcement response protocols. Six survey questions addressed training issues. Analysis indicated significant changes in each terrorism training category following the 9/11 attack (Table 21.5).

Target Hardening

Ready (2003) stated that security professionals have to change the facility from a soft target to a hard target. Terrorism targets the defenseless and innocent in an attempt to cause the most death and destruction possible. Five survey questions addressed target-hardening measures. Only one question, the use of the media to promote enhanced security measures, resulted in no significant change (Table 21.6).

Overall Summary of Survey Questions

As outlined above, three questions indicated no significant difference between the pre- and post-9/11 security measures at Port of Houston facilities: the annual review of EOPs, integration of security forces, and conducting media

Table 21.5   Training

Question	Pre Mean	Post Mean	*t*-Statistic	df	*P*
Our facilities security professionals are well trained regarding terroristic incidents	2.83	1.05	−3.05	34	0.002
Our facilities senior management staff has been trained in handling a terroristic incident	2.88	3.77	−2.71	34	0.005
Our facility conducts annual training exercises regarding terroristic incidents	2.55	4	−4.43	34	0.000
Our facility has all trained personnel regarding potential weapons of mass destruction (WMD)	2.5	3.77	−3.11	34	0.001
Our facility has all trained personnel regarding the reporting of suspicious persons, packages, or events	2.94	4.38	−4.25	34	0.000
Our facilities management and security staff is prepared to handle a terroristic incident	2.72	4.16	−4.09	34	0.000

Table 21.6   Target Hardening

Question	Pre Mean	Post Mean	*t*-Statistic	df	*P*
Our facility has taken target-hardening measures against terrorist attacks	2.72	4.55	−6.53	34	0.000
Our facility has implemented observable enhanced security measures	3	4.5	−4.91	34	0.000
Our facility has conducted media press releases promoting enhanced security measures	2.27	4.88	−1.11	34	0.135
Our facility is visibly integrated into the local police/security networks	3.05	3.72	−1.87	34	0.034
Our facility has developed countersurveillance terrorism plans	2.61	3.55	−2.41	34	0.010

releases promoting enhanced security measures. All of the other items indicated statistically significant changes from pre-9/11 to post-9/11.

Discussion and Conclusion

This project is specifically focused on critical infrastructures in the Port of Houston area and the effects that terrorism and technology have had on security strategies, procedures, and protocols since the September 11, 2001, terrorist attack on the WTC. The analysis from this project indicated that only three questions did not show significant changes. The first dealt with conducting media press releases related to enhanced security measures. Historically, critical infrastructure facilities in the Port of Houston area have dealt with national media incidents. Security managers have had to develop good working relationships with the media and have been proactive in sharing nonsensitive security measures. In other words, even during pre-9/11, these activities were likely to take place.

The second area covered the annual review of EOP. It was not unexpected to find that these facilities reviewed their EOPs annually even before 9/11. These facilities are inspected by many local, state, and federal agencies to ensure that safety measures are being implemented and followed. Additionally, the Maritime Transportation Safety Act requires these facilities to have security EOPs. The threat of being fined or, more significantly, of shutting down operations of motivates the security managers to keep EOPs updated.

The third area is related to the integration of private and governmental security forces. In a post-9/11 world, combined with today's economy, security managers have had to develop partnerships between their private security forces and local, state, and federal law-enforcement agencies. Security managers have realized that the integration of security resources will provide enhanced layers of security. Nevertheless, the change in this practice has not been as pronounced as in many other security measures and perhaps is an area that security managers and law-enforcement officials should look at more closely.

This project clearly indicates that security managers at critical infrastructure facilities in the Port of Houston area are motivated by the threat of terrorism and not merely traditional crime problems. Because of the small sample size, the findings cannot be operationalized to the hundreds of other critical infrastructures facilities found in all U.S. ports. However, the findings of this project do provide a basis to initiate a detailed research project to more fully determine the magnitude of the effects of terrorism and technology for the security professional.

The tragedy of 9/11 has forever changed the lives of all Americans and the world in general. The security professional will be required to be as cheerful as a Wal-Mart greeter and as tenacious as a suicide bomber. The paradigm for providing security will never be static again. The security professional must be well-trained, well-equipped, and well-supported by senior management to effectively and efficiently prevent, detect, and respond to terrorist incidents.

Although current security measures and strategies can be improved, this project clearly indicated that the security managers at critical infrastructure facilities in the Port of Houston area have taken significant measures to protect and defend against terrorist attacks. However, the actual degree and magnitude of those changes were not addressed in this project. A more detailed analysis should consider the effects on security policies, procedures, staffing, and budgets. Additionally, the questions of long-term commitment and sustainability for preventing, detecting, and responding to terrorism by senior leadership were not addressed.

References

Cavanagh, T. (2004, July). Security programs viewed as important to business success. *The Conference Board*. Retrieved November 30, 2005, from http://www.continuitycentral.com/news01393.htm

Clarke, R. (1997). *Situational Crime Prevention: Successful Case Studies*. Monsey, NY: Criminal Justice Press.

Department of Homeland Security. (2003). *Buffer Zone Protection Plan*. Washington, DC: U.S. Government Printing Office.

Department of Homeland Security. (2004). *Secure Seas, Open Ports: Keeping Our Waters Safe, Secure and Open for Business*. Washington, DC: U.S. Government Printing Office.

Engebretson, J. (2004, May). What customers want: Access gates with higher security. *Security Distribution and Marketing*, 77–78, April 24, 2004 from http://www.sdmmag.com

Giusti, C. (2004, October). The right mailroom milieu. *Security Management*, 91–96, from http://www.securitymanagment.com

Kanok, M. (2004, November). What they know can hurt you. *Security Management*, 71–75.

Levy, E. (2000, June 3). Survey finds building security managers strong on crime prevention not on anti-terrorism. *Insurance Advocate*, *111*, 23.

Maxfield, M., & Babbie, E. (2001). *Research Methods for Criminal Justice and Criminology* (3rd ed.). Belmont, CA: Wadsworth.

Ready, V. (2003, May). Effectively guard a complex against a terrorist assault: turn your facility assets from soft into harden targets. *Hydrocarbon Processing*, 100–103, from http://www.hydrocarbonprocessing.com

Robinson, R. (1999). *Issues in Security Management: Thinking Critically about Security*. Boston, MA: Butterworth Heinemann.

Sawyer, R. (2003). *The Art of War*. Philadelphia, PA: Westview Press.

Sennewald, C. (2003). *Effective Security Management* (4th ed.). Boston, MA: Butterworth Heinemann.

Simovich, J. (2004, October). To serve and protect. *Security Management*, 73–80, from http://www.sdmmag.com

Stone, M. (2000, June). Terrorism-threat assessment and counter-measures. *International Security Review*, 116 , from http://www.internationalsecurityreview.com

Vernon, D. (2003, May 19). Terror threats spark IT, physical security changes. *Computerworld*, *37*(20), 57.

Private Security in Bosnia and Herzegovina

22

DUŠKO VEJNOVIĆ, VELIBOR LALIĆ,
and MILE ŠIKMAN

Contents

The growth of the private security sector is a worldwide phenomenon. The reasons for this dramatic growth are mass private ownership in postindustrial as well as developing countries. Private owners' fear of crime grew faster than the government's interest in protecting them. Private security is one of the fastest developing industries; it has been expanding for over 30 years in the economic market of developed countries (Clede, 1993). Worldwide, the private sector security market is valued at US$85 billion and has an annual growth rate of 6–8% (Abrahamsen & Williams, 2005). Considering the fact that in the United States the private sector possesses and protects 85% of national infrastructure, private security plays an important role in its protection. In the United States, there are more than 10,000 private companies with 2 million employees (Morabito & Greenberg, 2005). It is estimated that in the European Union (EU) there are 20,000 private security companies with 1,100,000 employees (CoESS & UNI-Europa, 2003) after the latest EU enlargements in 2004 and 2007. In postsocialist countries, the development of private security is a natural outcome of a transitional economy, which resulted in the increase of private police. Social changes led to the change of police nature and its adjustment to the market economy (Mesko, Nalla, & Sotlar, 2004).

The private security sector in Bosnia and Herzegovina (BiH) is a new and the youngest sector in a security system, which is important not only in a security but also in a social and economic sense. The analysis of this problem is important for many reasons; some of them relate to BiH as a postconflict area and transitional society, where the whole security sector is going through a transformation from the authoritarian and war to the democratic model, and now it has a completely new role than it used to. However, the private security sector in BiH has not been sufficiently researched or discussed in the public sphere, although there are certain exceptions [Daničić, 2005; Muratbegović, 2004; Ahić, Masleša, & Muratbegović, 2005; Centre for Security Studies (CSS) (Bosnia and Herzegovina) & Saferworld (UK), 2006]. The EU has developed standards in the private security sector that constitute a fundamental condition to guarantee the necessary minimum of professionalism and quality in the private security sector. The necessity to harmonize the situation in the private security sector is not only important to EU member countries but to candidate countries as well in order to avoid possible political, economic, and social consequences, which it can encounter upon admission to EU due to different social and regulatory environments (CoESS, 1999). Moreover, the importance of this matter is that EU institutions are devoting their attention to it, considering the role it has in general security debate.

Using secondary literature and interviews, this chapter aims at identifying the main issues at stake and at providing a preliminary overview of the situation in the private security sector in BiH. The interviews were conducted only in one BiH city; therefore it represents a limited research sample. The findings presented here should therefore be understood as tendencies and will need validation by further studies. For analytical purposes we used the recommendations of the CoESS*

---

* In order to avoid misinterpretations and confusions of the term *European Model of Private Security Services*, it is necessary to clarify the status of CoESS and to explain the nature and status of *European Model of Private Security Services* itself. The CoESS is a professional association, not a regulatory and institutional body of the European Union. CoESS has been founded in 1989 by a joint initiative of several national associations of private security companies belonging to EU Member States. From its start, CoESS has therefore been a European umbrella organization for national private security associations. The purpose of CoESS is to ensure in Europe the protection of the interests of the organizations and national companies that provide security services in all their forms and to represent these joint interests, in particular, through involvement in the work aimed at the harmonization of national legislation concerning the activities of its members. Currently, CoESS has members in 22 out of 27 countries of the 27 EU Member States and in Norway, Switzerland, and Turkey. CoESS is continuing its efforts to look for membership also from other candidate countries. For more information, visit http://www.coess.org. The Code of Conduct and Ethics the Private Security Sector contains a series of standards that are jointly recommended by CoESS and UNI-Europa to all of the sector's companies and employees. Since CoESS and UNI-Europa are professional associations, that is, they represent an ideological view reflecting the interest of the profession, the Code of Conduct and Ethics for the Private Security Sector is not legally binding document. Its implementation solely depends on the commitment of each of the parties

and UNI-Europa*—formalized in the European model of private security—in order to discuss the situation in one part of BiH. This chapter also aims at serving as a catalyst for researchers and policymakers in improving collective efforts to respond effectively to challenges surrounding the private security sector in BiH.

Characteristics of the European Model of Private Security

The European model of the private security sector has been established by CoESS and UNI-Europa. The key standards that constitute the European model are described in the Code of Conduct and Ethics for the Private Security Sector adopted in July 2003. Respect these standards constitutes a fundamental condition to guarantee the necessary minimum of professionalism and quality in the private security sector. The European model implies that security companies must comply with regulations applicable to the sector and commit themselves to applying all of these regulatory provisions to the letter and in the spirit in which they were written. Additionally, the security companies must ensure that any internal organizational procedures implemented are made transparent and are applied without discrimination to all parties concerned. Besides, a company that is active in the sector, or that wishes to enter the sector, must satisfy the conditions imposed by national regulations in order to obtain the permits and authorizations needed by the company, its management, and its staff.

As far as worker selection and employment are concerned, they should be based on objective criteria. Moreover, in accordance with professional standards, employee training is important at all levels, especially basic training of new employees is crucial for retaining professional standards. The CoESS and UNI-Europa also emphasize the importance of a constructive dialog between labor unions and employers at all levels (European, national, and within the company). The "standards" imply good, safe, and humane working conditions and adequate salaries in the sector. Some jobs in this sector bear certain risks. But all the companies will try to keep minimum

---

in question—company managers, employees, trade union delegates, national trade union organizations, national professional associations, and European organizations. This Code of Conduct cannot be compared, for instance, with the Council of Europe Code of Police Ethics, which is an international code agreed by countries.

* In Europe, with 7 million members, UNI-Europa is a major trade union player in Brussels. Its aim is to be relevant to affiliates and members and effective at the heart of Europe—through social dialog in a range of industries, in contacts and lobbying with the European Commission, and, increasingly, taking our issues and campaigns to Members of the European Parliament. For more information, see http://www.union-network.org.

national health standards and safety at work. Also, companies will support the principles of equality and nondiscrimination. Companies should seek out a legal balance between two key areas: employees' security and the quality of their private life, on the one hand, and the satisfaction of clients' needs, on the other. Private security companies should conduct business in accordance with the rules of fair competition and morals. All employees in the sector should be guided by the Code of Conduct and Ethics. CoESS and UNI-Europa underline that employers' associations and unions should actively promote this Code of Conduct and Ethics.

Nature of the Security Sector in BiH

The security system, like any other system, is sensitive to social changes. Social changes that have been present in BiH for the last 15 years are a part of global social changes. Without providing here a detailed analysis of these changes, it is important to identify those changes that had a direct impact on the structure of the security system in BiH. In this regard, it is important to mention changes in economic, political, normative, and institutional spheres of social life. The security system is an organized social system through which society protects its vital values in order to facilitate progress and society development (Vejnović, 2002).

As far as BiH is concerned, one key component of the security system is the National Armed Forces. Aside from the Armed Forces, BiH has three police agencies at the national level (State Agency for Investigation and Protection, State Border Service, and National Bureau of Interpol) and one Intelligence Security Agency of Bosnia and Herzegovina. At the entity level,* each entity has its own police organization. In the Republika Srpska, there is a Ministry of the Interior, which has jurisdiction over security and safety, whereas in the Federation of Bosnia and Herzegovina there are 11 police agencies in charge of security and safety within the cantons.† In Brčko District, there is Brčko District Police in charge of security in the District. Aside from all of the mentioned security agencies established and organized by the state (or entity) in BiH, there is also a private security sector that is organized and functions in accordance with legal regulations formalized at

---

* The country is decentralized and is administratively divided into two entities, the Federation of Bosnia and Herzegovina and the Republika Srpska. The Brčko District has a special status. Additionally the Federation of Bosnia and Herzegovina is decentralized into 10 cantons.
† The Federation of Bosnia and Herzegovina consists of 10 cantons, which means that there are 10 Ministries of the Interior as well as the Federal Ministry of Internal Affairs of the Federation of Bosnia and Herzegovina.

the entity level. There is no national law on the private security sector and each entity has legislated in this area.*

Nature of the Private Security Sector in BiH

The private security sector in BiH was formally established in 2002 when entity parliaments passed the private security laws. The Brčko District passed a similar law only two years later, in 2004.[†] These laws regulate entirely the field of private security and contain dispositions relative to licensing of private security companies, legal powers of private security personnel, and supervision over the private security sector. It is important to say that the earlier law on self-protection of society of the Federal Republic of Bosnia and Herzegovina (FRBiH) of 1986 partially included the field of private security, but not sufficiently and precisely like the 2002 law (Ahić et al., 2005). The private security in BiH entails two main areas, namely the protection of persons and property both physically and technically (Vejnović & Šikman, 2004). The law of the Republika Srpska and Brčko District also allows private security companies to take over detective tasks or criminal investigation. Private security services can be provided in three different juridical forms: the first is private security companies, that is, contractual security services, the second is corporate security, and the third is a combination of contractual security services and corporate security (Mandić, 2004).

Existing legislation in BiH represents a good background for the development of the private security sector. This can be seen in the growth of the number of private security companies as well as in the number of employees working in the sector(s).[‡] However, the sector suffers from a number of limitations. The fact that there is no law at the state/national level brings a series of complications that affect the sector. The situation is complicated by the fact that regional police agencies (Center for Public Security in the Republika Srpska and Cantonal Ministries of the Interior in Federation of Bosnia and Herzegovina) are authorized for issuing licenses to private security companies and employees; this means that there is no centralized data system on the number of those companies, their capacities, business running, number

---

* Although the laws that govern the private security sector in BiH are different, those differences are not substantial in terms of licensing of private security companies, legal powers of private security personnel, and supervision over the private security sector. The key difference refers to private detective vocation. In accordance with the law of the Republika Srpska and Brčko District, detective vocation is a component of the private security sector, which is not the case in the Federation of Bosnia and Herzegovina.

† See Official Gazette Federation of Bosnia and Herzegovina, No. 50/02, Official Gazette Republika Srpska No. 50/02, Official Gazette Brčko District, 2004.

‡ Although there are no precise official figures about the number of the registered private security companies and its dynamics on the market, its permanent increase is quite visible.

of employees, and so on. In this context, it would be very important to collect the mentioned data and also other information, such as the impact of the private security sector on the economy, annual revenues, and their percentage in GDP. Additionally, it would be valuable to determine the ratio between the employees in the private security sector and the police. In Slovenia, for example, this ratio is 2:1, which is below the average ratio found in developed countries (Mesko et al., 2004) such as the United States where the ratio is 3:1.*

There are no official figures on the number of private security companies and employees in the sector. However, it is estimated that the private security sector comprises of 70 companies and employs at least 5,000 persons. It is further estimated that from the total number of registered agencies, about 5% are large companies employing between 500 and 1,000 employees, 35% are middle-size companies employing between 50 and 100 employees, and 60% are small companies employing up to 50 employees. Mostly, security companies provide security services in the banking sector, shopping malls, and foreign embassies. They also provide services of VIP security, residential security, installation of alarms, video surveillance systems, and so on. To a lesser extent, some companies offer services of security planning, risk analysis, and security consulting. The large companies and middle-size ones provide services throughout BiH, whereas the small ones provide their services locally. In BiH, there is not a single foreign security company in operation; similarly, there is no record of domestic companies in BiH providing services abroad. However, foreign security companies are known to recruit BiH citizens for deployment in crisis regions of the world—most likely due to the experience gained during the civil war in BiH.

Methodology

The analysis proposes a comparison of the European private security model and its 15 principles from the Code of Conduct and Ethics (CoESS & UNI-Europa, 2003) with the current state of affairs in the private security sector in BiH. The principles in the Code of Conduct and Ethics are arranged in three categories according to their nature: legal, professional, and socioeconomic aspects. As a method of data collection, open-ended interviews were conducted with target groups. The interviews were conducted with senior police officers (2), constables (2), private security company managers (2), private security officers (2), clients (2), and citizens (2). The interviews were conducted in Banja Luka, the second largest city in BiH. The purpose of the interviews was to obtain respondents' perceptions and attitudes on the situation and the

---

* In the United States, there are 677,933 police officers and 2 million employees in the private security sector (Morabito & Greenberg, 2005).

role of the private security sector. Given the fact that the interviews were conducted in one BiH city and included only a limited research sample, this methodology does not enable wider generalizations but certainly provides tendencies that allow identifying a number of problems in the private security sector in BiH.

Interpretation of Research Results

Legal Aspects

The opinion of the interviewees about the legislation that governs the private security has been only partly positive. The law is believed to have regulated the sector extensively. Besides, the law provided a unique opportunity to harmonize a situation inherited from the past. However, the interviewees are of the opinion that some legal provisions that regulate the private security sector have shortcomings at certain points and therefore should be changed in accordance with the needs of the practice. This is a general opinion of the majority of the interviewees, but ideas on what needed change varied depending on the respondent's category.

For example, interviewees from the police consider that the legal powers of the authorities are not sufficiently explicit, a situation that causes difficulties in practice. One interviewee, a senior police officer, stated:

> ... legal powers of private security officers are not stipulated well in law and are not entirely explicit. The sub-law regulation is needed in order to define authorities precisely. (Interview #5)

The same category of interviewees found that the licensing and authorizations system is ineffective. According to them, employment selection criteria for private security officers should be more rigid. One interviewee, a constable, in this regard gave the following statement:

> Acquisition of license and authorizations for private security companies and officers depends on personal influence and connections of the owners. These owners of private security companies with better social positions have no problems with acquiring the licenses for their staff. They get it easily, even without fulfilling all legal requirements. (Interview #8)

This opinion is not shared by private security officers. They consider that procedures are transparent and relatively fast, regulations are followed in practice, discrimination is not a problem, and so on. In order to substantiate that statement, they give examples of good practice regarding the implementation of legal provisions. One interviewee, a private security company manager, stated:

According to the law a person who is separated from the police force due to violation of disciplinary rules is not eligible to obtain license as a private security officer in the next five years. One ex police officer who left police force as a result of disciplinary action, wanted to join our company, but he did not get license from Ministry of Interior on the ground of failing to meet legal requirements. (Interview #1)

The interviewees from the police find that the essential problem with the law lies in the supervision and inspection of private security companies. They believe that the law should be more explicit with regard to the role of the Ministry of Interior. They believe that the problem lies both in the law and in the practice. As an example, one senior police officer emphasizes:

The police as supervising institution over the private security companies have not sufficient insight to the documents which companies are obliged to keep in accordance with the law. (Interview #6)

It appears, however, that the reason why the police have no sufficient insight into the documents that private security companies are obliged to keep in accordance with the law is simply that inspections are rare or do not exist. Moreover, according to the respondents from the police, it seems that irregularities found during inspections do not lead to consequences, sanctions for instance. Here again, private security officers do not share this opinion. As a matter of fact, they stated that their companies keep all necessary records, documents are available at any time, and moreover, inspections take place often. They stressed that there are indeed problems associated with the law, but are quite different in nature. One manager of a private security agency stated:

According to the law the private security companies are allowed to possess guns for only 50% of all officers employed in a company. It does meet the real needs of the field. In addition, there are some other confusing legal provisions, such as: in accordance with the law, the private security officer is allowed to use physical force and to arrest the person until the arrival of the police, but the law nowhere stipulates that private security officers can use handcuffs. It does not make sense! It should be definitely changed, powers of private security officers must be clear, private officers must exactly know what they are allowed to do and what they are not. (Interview #2)

One of the managers of a private security company identified another problem associated with the issue of training:

Namely, in accordance with law the fire range training of private security officers can be conducted by the Ministry of Interior only. It has been done once a year and it is definitely insufficient. The private security companies are not allowed to conduct that kind of training on their own. (Interview #3)

Based on the interviewees' statements, it appears that many problems do not come unilaterally from the law itself, but the lack of an appropriate implementation of the law is also seen as a problem.

Professional Aspects

Under "professional aspects" of the sector, we understand here issues associated with selection and recruitment, vocational training, relation with the police, relation with clients, and relation with other private security sector companies. The attitudes of the interviewees regarding these issues vary greatly depending on the interviewed categories. The police officers stressed that the selection and recruitment of private security personnel are absolutely inappropriate. Moreover, according to them, private security has been performed by untrained and unqualified personnel. Some police officers believe that some private security officers have criminal backgrounds, highlighting the fact that their employment in the private security sector might serve as a cover and shelter from criminal prosecution. As far as they are concerned, private security officers consider that selection and recruitment are quite adequate. They stated that usually a previous working experience with the police, military, or other security agencies is required. Those with experience have much more chance for employment than candidates without experience.

Respondents shared the opinion that there is an unregistered employment in the sector of private security. It is not a rare case that private security companies violate labor laws, that is, they fail to register their employees with employment authorities and fail to pay contributions for retirement funds and health insurance. That is how private security companies evade payments that they are obligated to pay in accordance with the law. Such illegal practices enable them to increase their profits. With regard to the issue of unregistered employment, it appears that the situation has recently improved as inspections by the Ministry of Interior have increased. Private security officers are required to obtain individual certificates in order to be authorized to work, a practice what narrows down the maneuvering space for illegal employment. However, this can still be bypassed by a known practice of security companies to register their employees only part time, although they work full time.

There are other practices that limit the full implementation of the rule of law. For example, the Ministry of Interior issues certificates to private security officers, but at the same time fails to check whether those people are employed in accordance with labor law or not. It opens the door for misuses and creates a huge communication gap between the labor authorities and the police. This gap is widely exploited by some private security agencies. One interviewee, a manager of a private security company, made the following statement about these issues:

> Estimations are that today 20% of personnel are illegally employed. Previously, the percentage was much higher, even up to 70%. (Interview #1)

Regarding vocational training, the interviewees agreed that the basic training, which is mandatory, is insufficient. There is no specialized training. The basic training for private security officers takes place in the Police Academy and lasts for only seven days. This training curriculum is mostly theoretical; it does not include practical and experience-based knowledge and skills. This training provides only basic knowledge on private security issues and can be considered only as a first step in professional development of private security officers. Some companies provide on-the-job training for their employees. One interviewee, a constable, made the following comments about that:

> The quality of the on-the-job training of private security officers is low. The trainers are apparently experienced private security officers, but I am very skeptical about their experience and ability to transfer knowledge and skills to others. (Interview #7)

The cooperation between police and private security companies is not satisfying. This is an opinion shared by all respondents. One manager of a security company gave us the following comment:

> In most cases contacts exist only when the police need to react ex officio i.e. in cases of committed criminal offenses. Beside that, when the companies initiate contacts with the police in connection with their work, usually the police is reluctant to respond. If that is not the case, then the quick reaction of police is based on personal acquaintance (friendship) of contacts from the police and security companies. (Interview #2)

There are no memoranda of understanding between the police and private security companies despite the fact that it is a good practice to define cooperation, communication, and exchange of information. There is room to improve the cooperation in the opinion of all respondents. As far as the relationship with other private security sector companies is concerned, the interviewees from the private companies emphasized that there is an intense competition in the market. However, some respondents said that the competitive price and quality of service are not necessarily essential for security companies to win a contract. Some respondents emphasized indeed that corruption is not rare in the sector. The manager of a security company stated the following:

> As an example, the security company with most lost (robbed) money transports still gets the best deals, but another highly professional company—one which once disabled an armed robbery—does not get a chance to win bids despite the fact that it might be the most adequate bidder in terms of price of services. (Interview #2)

Such situations generate an atmosphere of distrust between private security companies and ruin the business and professional relationships in the private security sector.

Socioeconomic Aspects

Socioeconomic aspects include issues associated with the working conditions of private security officers, salaries and awards, health and safety, equal opportunities, nondiscrimination, and social dialog. As far as the aspect of working conditions is concerned, respondents were only partially satisfied. They consider this issue as a mirror of the general situation in a postconflict society. Generally speaking, most private security companies make important efforts to provide appropriate equipments to their staff, that is, uniforms, guns, armored vehicles, guard booths, and so on. Investment in improvement of working conditions of private security personnel varies from company to company, depending on each company's financial abilities and position in the market. Although there is still a lot of room for improvement, significant achievements have been made in a relatively short period of time.

As far as salaries and benefits are concerned, the key finding is that salaries of private security officers are minimal and unsatisfactory. That salaries are not paid on time is not an exception; sometimes there is 2–3 months delay. Generally speaking, the average salary of a private security officer is exceptionally low and not enough to cover basic living costs. One interviewee—a security guard—stated the following:

> I used to work for one company for several months; for the last three months I have not got paid, although I know that company was doing well. I found job in another security company and I am being paid on time ever since. (Interview #4)

As far as health and safety conditions offered at the workplace are concerned, the key finding is that the private security companies do not undertake enough adequate measures to provide for the necessary safety and protection of their employees. Respondents stated that the level of protection of the security personnel should be raised due to frequent injuries originating from physical assaults and even armed assaults.

As far as equal opportunities and nondiscrimination are concerned, the respondents have not reported any serious case of discrimination on grounds of nationality, religion, sex, social origin, or sexual orientation. However, these statements do not necessarily imply that there is no discrimination in the sector. Certainly, a fact of concern is that today BiH is a highly segmented society, with ethnic lines corresponding to administrative and political territories, leaving little room for employment, for example, of non-Croats in parts of BiH populated with Croatian majority, or Serbs in the Federation of Bosnia and Herzegovina (BiH), or vice versa of Bosniaks and Croats in Republika Srpska.

Looking at the aspect of social dialog, we can state that there is no social dialog at all as there are no labor organizations in the private security sector that might protect workers' rights. The opinions of interviewees in all categories were that labor organizations could be a very good instrument for improving workers' rights, especially their basic rights and conditions in which they work. Respondents also concurred that the nonexistence of a social dialog in the industry is a handicap. However, some of the respondents were skeptical about the possibility to institute a dialog in the sector. One respondent—a citizen—made the following comment:

> Those people (private security officers) are deprived of their rights. There is no one to whom they can address and explain their problems. I think that the majority of private security companies' owners mostly care about their business and profit, but not about their people. Even if someone establishes the union in near future I am skeptical how it will work in a real life. The owners will formally encourage the union, but in fact they are ready to do everything to make it to fail. (Interview #12)

Conclusions

Bearing in mind the methodological limitations of this research as noted before, it might be concluded from this preliminary research that the private security sector in BiH is still in an early stage, and for this reason it is not yet entirely compatible with the principles that constitute the European Model of Private Security Services. The most important gaps can be found in the professional and socioeconomic aspects of the industry in BiH. The general opinion of the interviewees is that the private security sector has a constructive role and contributes to public security and safety. All interviewees observed that the private security sector will have a more important role in the future. But, on the basis of research results, it can be concluded that the current situation in the private security sector is not satisfying and that this sector can play a much more important role in public safety than what has been the case so far. Particularly, it is necessary to devote a lot of effort to building partnerships with the police—what has been largely ignored so far.

We can also observe that private security companies are driven mainly by profit making, whereas professional integrity is being neglected. The private security sector in BiH has now a legal basis, which is an important premise for its consolidation and development. However, currently, certain legal provisions should be critically reviewed in order to see whether they meet the needs of practice or not. It could be done through an encompassing scientific research of current legal solutions and needs in practice. Six years of implementation of the laws is a sufficient period to observe empirically these issues.

As emphasized earlier, the professional and socioeconomic aspects of the private security sector in BiH are not in line with the European model of private security. It is not sufficient to invest in material and technical operations of the private security companies, but investing in human resources is needed too. In this sense, private security companies should pay more attention to issues such as the recruitment and selection process, training of staff 'especially, specialized training, improving, of the working conditions, increase of salaries and contributions for allowances, safety at work, and so on. Additionally, it is necessary to organize labor organizations of the private security officers and support the establishment of professional associations of private security. It is urgent to build partnerships between private security companies and police, including partnerships with other law-enforcement agencies, and partnerships between private security companies themselves. This is possible to achieve in various ways, one of them being drafting a memorandum of understanding and developing an awareness of partnerships and joint activities with the overall goal of contributing to the security and safety of the society. It is also necessary to point out the possibility offered by the detective services in the private security sector, which is neglected in BiH.

The private security sector in BiH needs to be developed in accordance with best practices in the EU and elsewhere. The private security sector is an advantage to the society in general. Professionalism and integrity of the sector should be a crucial goal in order to develop the capacities to contribute effectively to crime control, public safety, safety of capital, and foreign investments, which are essential for European future of BiH.

References

Abrahamsen, R., & Williams, M. C. (2005). *The Globalization of Private Security, Country Report Kenya*. Aberystwyth: University of Wales.

Ahić, J., Masleša, R., & Muratbegović, E. (2005). Reformistički kurs u formalnom i faktičkom restrukturiranju sektora privatne sigurnosti u Bosni i Hercegovini. In Dobrivoje Radovanović (Ed.), *Kazneno zakonodavstvo: progresivna ili regresivna rješenja* (pp. 539–605). Beograd, Serbia: Institute of Criminology.

Centre for Security Studies (CSS) (Bosnia and Herzegovina) & Saferworld (UK). (2006). *The Sarajevo Code of Conduct for Private Security Companies.* Belgrade, Serbia: South Eastern and Eastern Europe Clearinghouse for the Control of Small Arms and Light Weapons (SEESAC) & UNDP.

Clede, B. (1993). *Security Officer's Manual.* Rhinelander, SAD: Lakeland Publishing.

CoESS & UNI-Europa. (2003). *Code of Conduct and Ethics for the Private Security Sector.* Retrieved from http://www. coess.org/documents/code_of_conduct.pdf.

Daničić, M. (2005). *Obezbjeđenje lica i imovine i preduzecá u Republici Srpskoj.* Banja Luka, BiH: Visoka škola unutrašnjih poslova.

Joint Declaration of CoESS and Euro-FIET on the Future Enlargement of the European Union to include the Central and Eastern European Countries. (1999), CoESS, Berlin, Retrieved from http://www.coess.org/documents/ conference_bx3_en.pdf.

Mandić, G. (2004). *Sistem obezbjeđenja i zaštite.* Beograd, Srbija: Fakultet civilne odbrane.

Mesko, G., Nalla, M., & Sotlar, A. (2004). Youth perception of private security in Slovenia: Preliminary findings. In G. Mesko, M. Pagon, & B. Dobovsek (Eds), *Policing in Central and Eastern Europe—Dilemmas of Contemporary Criminal Justice.* Ljubljana: Faculty of Criminal Justice, University of Maribor.

Morabito, A., & Greenberg, S. (2005). *Engaging the Private Sector To Promote Home- land Security: Law Enforcement—Private Security Partnerships.* Washington, DC: U.S. Department of Justice.

Muratbegović, E. (2004). Privatization of the security sector as a part of crime prevention strategy in Bosnia and Herzegovina. In G. Mesko, M. Pagon, & B. Dobovsek (Eds), *Policing in Central and Eastern Europe—Dilemmas of Contemporary Criminal Justice.* Ljubljana: Faculty of Criminal Justice, University of Maribor. Retrieved from http://www.fpvv.uni-mb.si/conf2004/ day1.aspx.

Pena, U., Šikman, M., & Amidžić, G. (2006). *Priručnik za pripadnike fizičkog obezbjeđenja.* Banja Luka, RS, BiH: Udruženje defendologa Republike Srpske.

Vejnović, D. (2002). *Defendologija—društveni aspekti bezbjednosti moderne države.* Banja Luka, RS, BiH: Viša škola unutrašnjih poslova.

Vejnović, D., & Šikman, M. (2004). Mjesto i uloga zakonskog i podzakonskog regulisanja oblasti o agencijama za obezbjeđenje lica i imovine i privatnoj detektivskoj djelatnosti. *Defendologija, 15 & 16,* 11–29.

Private Security in South Africa*

23

P. J. POTGIETER

Contents

The evolution of private security and its role in crime prevention have been recorded from ancient times, through the middle ages up to modern times. Europe, and especially the United States, contributed much in recording early histories of private security. Early forms to prevent and avert crime and danger confirm some sort of relationship between security measures and crime prevention. During Neolithic times "... security and crime prevention have been present in the earliest known forms of prehistoric civilizations" (Collins, Ricks, & Van Meter, 2000). Even in South Africa, some interesting and worthwhile research contributions about the role and significance of private security have been documented during the 1990s and the early beginning of the new millennium, and *inter alia* the statutory regulation and training of security officers, the relationship between private security and the South African Police Service (SAPS), its role in crime prevention, and so on (Berg, 2003; Minnaar, 1999; Minnaar, 2005; Minnaar & Ngoveni, 2003; Pillay, 2007; Ras, 2006).

Unlike the SAPS who are responsible for the "policing" of common law crimes and violations of statutory prescriptions, private security strives

---

* Potgieter, P. J. (2008). Can private security stand up to the challenges of crime and crime prevention in South Africa? A contemporary perspective. *Acta Criminologica, 21*(1). With permission.

toward loss prevention and assets protection in both private and business environments, thereby serving the interests of specific clients (Simonsen, 1998). It also has to honor a variety of functions that closely relate to crime prevention such as physical security, personnel security, alarm systems, disaster and risk management (Timm & Christian, 1991) and, *inter alia*, also body guarding (Ras, 2006).

Sophistication of private security functions over the past few decades became exceptionally important in the social well-being of ordinary South Africans. Constant outcries by communities, supported by calls from business enterprises for more efficient and effective public policing, sent clear messages to the government demanding the kind of safety and security contemplated in the Constitution of 1996. In this regard, the role of business against crime (BAC) in crime prevention has become more significant with the use of CCTV and metal detectors in larger shopping complexes, convenient stores, commercial banks, and fuel stations to curb the incidence of violent vehicle hijackings and other cases of armed robberies, while home alarm systems and body guarding fraternities are also mushrooming (Minnaar, 2005, pp. 89–90; Rapport, 2007b, p. 4).

Since the advent of democracy in South Africa almost 14 years ago, an irrevocable process of industrialization also took its course. However, social factors such as HIV/AIDS, unemployment, and a desire for better living conditions, primarily among previously disadvantaged people, directly contribute to the depopulation of traditional rural areas causing people to migrate to major cities. The World Watch Institute (WWI) recently hinted that urbanization is excelling quickest in Africa and Asia, where the "poorest of the poor" are battling to make a proper living and are therefore migrating from rural to urban informal settlements. The WWI estimates that during August 2008, the world's urban population is poised to surpass the rural total for the first time in the history of mankind. This estimation could rise to two-thirds by the year 2030 when more than half of all Africans will become city dwellers (Zulu, 2006, p. 13). Fast-growing neighborhoods may deteriorate into typical slum areas and could serve as the breeding ground for social contact as well as economic crimes and moral decay: perhaps the kind of living conditions so eloquently referred to in the Broken Windows concept developed by Kelling and Wilson (1982) (Schmalleger, 1999, p. 279) to depict the overwhelming presence of drug abuse, juvenile delinquency, alcoholism, prostitution, and most of the personal and economic crimes (Beeld, 2007b, p. 6).

Rationale and Aims of the Study

This study firstly aims to explore the assumption of whether or not private security would be capable of "standing up" to the challenges of crime and, more particularly, risk management and loss prevention in a crime-ridden South Africa. Data on selected private security functions and security measures obtained from a previous study (Steenkamp & Potgieter, 2004) have been consulted and re-evaluated in an attempt to either support or reject the foregoing assumption. Secondly, the current study is also set to assess contemporary perspectives about the nature and intensity of criminal victimization as well as crime prevention initiatives announced and debated in the printed media. Thirdly, factors negatively influencing sound police role fulfillment such as dwindling police resources, suboptimal police service delivery, an overloaded court system as well as overcrowded correctional facilities, and so on equally contribute to renewed interest in the role and services of the private security industry (Beeld, 2007a, p. 14; Pillay, 2007, p. 62). Prevailing levels of fear of crime and the general deterioration of South Africa's moral fabric are further proof that crimes, especially violent crimes, have spun out of control. Violent crimes that recently swept through the country are perceived to be associated with criminal terrorism reminiscent of guerrilla and terrorist warfare and it appears that cash-in-transit assets suffered the greatest and most brutal onslaught in this regard (The Mercury, 2007b, p. 2; The Mercury, 2007d, p. 1).

Research Design

The current study follows a typical quantitative research approach, that is, a positivistic inclination that paves the way for quantifiable statistical outcomes, while a qualitative orientation affords the opportunity to revert to valuable information forthcoming from printed media reporting on factors that may exert a negative influence on the capability of private security to honor its part in "handling" the crime problem.

Literature studies rest on the assumption that knowledge of social phenomena is accumulated and presented by other people in a variety of ways, ranging from scholarly journals, textbooks, theses, and government documents (laws), to documented reports by the mass media such as newspapers, television, the Internet, websites, and the like (Neuman & Wiegand, 2000, p. 87). Literature reviews are an important part of any research process, providing context, background, and a summary of what has already been documented about a subject. In a qualitative study of the consequences of bomb explosions suffered by 11 victims in Johannesburg, South Africa (Engelbrecht, 1991, pp. 147–149), *inter alia* documented information (newspaper clippings) was used to help in the reconstruction of crime scenes.

Literature reviews enabled the researcher to learn more about crime prevention and private security as social phenomena, facilitate common ground between past and present research, synthesize and verify what is known about a social problem (e.g., crime) in any given society, and build on what other people (e.g., journalists) have to offer about a specific social problem with the aim of constructing future research designs (Neuman & Wiegand, 2000, p. 87). Perceptions of opinion-forming people and the general reading public about the prevailing high crime rate, crime prevention, and the role of the police and private security, which have been captured in the printed media to better understand the functional operation of the latter entity, have been randomly but carefully selected for inclusion in the current debate.

Contemporary Perceptions of Crime and Crime Prevention

In recent times, South Africa has witnessed the creation of various kinds of crime prevention programs or strategies. The SAPS has, first and foremost, an obligation to constantly upgrade their crime prevention initiatives because they are being paid for a job they are expected to fulfill 24 hours per day. Recently, the National Prosecution Authority (NPA) also contributed its mite (halfpenny) when it announced a 15-year plan to tackle or prevent crime (The Mercury, 2007c, p. 5). However, more recently, President Thabo Mbeki announced a new crime prevention plan in which the private security industry would be involved with public police to speed up police response time in cases of criminal victimization. Less than 10 months later, President Mbeki announced another new "big crime plan" that promises a radical "... overhaul of the country's dysfunctional criminal justice system," improved salaries for public police officials, training of additional detectives, and allocating more money to "crime-busting equipment" (Sunday Tribune, 2007, p. 1). Apparently, this is not what is happening the at grass roots level. The mere improvement of existing crime prevention programs does not seem to be the solution to get the successful prevention of crime back on track. Other intervention techniques such as the use of security technology seem appropriate: "More sophisticated devices are capable of alerting the authorities without the aid of a human being" (Lab, 1988).

A quick glance at public perceptions about crime (and crime prevention) recently reflected in the printed media underscores the real problem of crime prevention in the country and the question of whether private security has indeed any role to play in the execution of their mission.

As recently as February 2007, Trade and Industry Minister Mandisi Mpahlwa warned against perceptions about crime in the country that will definitely exert a negative influence on prospective tourist behavior and their possible decision not to attend FIFA's 2010 Soccer World Cup event. According to Mpahlwa, the safety and security of tourists will receive top priority, in spite of overseas countries already issuing warnings on their respective websites to prospective visitors about the seriousness of crime in South Africa. Will the police alone be capable of handling the increasing demand for safety and security in the face of the intensity with which violent crimes (murder, brutal hijacking, abduction, rape, mugging, etc.) are being committed: in most cases of cold-blooded murder with military precision and execution style?

Finance Minister Trevor Manuel clearly indicated on March 28, 2007, that South Africa's economic growth is already negatively affected by the high crime rate that ravaged the country in the past few months or so. Meanwhile, a wage increase for police officers, prosecutors, and judges has been announced, as well as the erection of new prison facilities and police stations (Business Report, 2007, p. 4). The latter two initiatives would, retributively, prove superfluous unless crime prevention is correctly addressed and findings of previous and current scientific research reports on crime prevention (by tertiary and related institutions) meticulously studied and adapted for implementation. Hansgeorg Niefer, chairman of Daimler-Chrysler South Africa, also expressed concern about sustained growth in foreign investment in South Africa that could "very quickly drop to zero" if the crime problem is not timely solved. Without blaming the government for the high crime rate, he suggested that the solving of crime needed a concerted effort if it was expected to be successful: "[I]t is all about perceptions. We musn't wait until it is too late" (Business Report, 2007, p. 4).

In the same breath, speakers at a national symposium on crime and criminal victimization held in Cape Town by the National Democratic Convention (NDC) toward the end of March 2007 unanimously emphasized the poor condition in which the criminal justice system finds itself at present: "South Africa's criminal justice system is failing the community it is meant to protect" (The Independent on Saturday, 2007a, p. 6). Police services have been described as "undercapacitated" and functioning suboptimally; criminal courts are experiencing massive backlogs with outstanding cases of serious crimes and correctional facilities are overcrowded and are apparently not able to honor their commitment in terms of sound "rehabilitation" of offenders.

While certain categories of serious crimes seem to be on the increase, National Police Commissioner Jackie Selebi called for the legalization of prostitution and liquor consumption in public for the duration of FIFA's 2010 Soccer World Cup event. KwaZulu-Natal was the first province to react with dismay against such a kind of open sex trade and the violation of society's values by allowing people to consume liquor openly in public (The Mercury, 2007a, p. 1; Weekend Witness, 2007a, p. 1).

Architects of crime prevention programs do not necessarily represent all the role players in the public gallery. In most cases, crime prevention strategies are devised unilaterally without prior public input or consensus. The Members of the Executive Council (MEC) for Safety and Security in KwaZulu-Natal recently joined forces with architects of crime prevention programs by calling up "1,000 public crime prevention volunteers" who would be identified and trained to join hands with public police in the fight against crime. This "crime fighting project" has been "... met with great success in London and locally in Canada as well as in the Western Cape" (The Mercury, 2007c, p. 5) amidst police who are still not trusted in the "economic powerhouse" of the country (The Independent on Saturday, 2007b, p. 1). A further caveat seems appropriate: "shotgun attempts" calculated to instantly solve the crime problem in the South African context usually lack substance and are in most cases destined to be ineffective, especially if the proposed legitimization of prostitution and open consumption of liquor for the duration of the Soccer World Cup in 2010 is allowed. Admittedly, statutorily introduced Community Police Forums (CPFs) provide, on face value, the necessary avenues for public involvement in policing matters that concern them.

Can Private Security Stand Up to the Challenges of Crime and Crime Prevention in the New Millennium?

While the role of private security in crime prevention has been briefly highlighted so far, it should be appreciated that factors exerting a negative influence on its endeavors to play an even more significant role in the future safety and security of the country and its people are omnipresent. The CEO of South Africa's largest private security company (Gremick) predicts a criminal onslaught by violent gangs from some provinces' dilapidated neighborhoods. These gangs are expected to flock to the soccer stadiums to prey on nonsuspecting soccer enthusiasts (Beeld, 2006a, p. 32).

Crime prevention programs, campaigns, and strategies of the past 10 years or so (mostly in the postapartheid era) did not prove to be completely successful. Although serving the interests of their private clients, the private security industry does not necessarily subscribe to the same principles present in bureaucratic-type policing *per se* but rather "... provide protection for persons and property K" and are also involved in security activities like "... loss prevention, assets protection, security services, and many others ..." (Simonsen, 1998, p. 22). Private security functions often extend beyond their "private" call of duty, because much of their work overlap in functional purpose, mostly because their mere presence predicts a proactive inclination. The private security industry, through efficient body guarding as well as ordinary guarding services, is perhaps the only solution to preventing overseas visitors from falling prey to criminal victimization in 2010 (Ras, 2006).

Recently, the Constitutional Court of South Africa ruled that the private security industry should be reserved for South Africans only. Mindful of the influx of "illegal immigrants" from neighboring countries, too many people are dependent on the services rendered by this industry because of the apparent ineffectiveness of public police to successfully prevent crime. A high premium should therefore be placed on the selection of private security officers while no stone should be left unturned to guard against "illegal entrepreneurs" (Beeld, 2007a, p. 14). A vision of "Proudly South African" should be pursued at all costs.

On the other hand, there are indications that private security officers are also actively involved in the commission of crimes. The very same persons who are hired to provide personal safety and protection of assets are often vulnerable to crime syndicates as a result of the human element and the presence of crime precipitants (opportunities). According to vehicle detection companies (such as Tracker), the exchange of vehicle security information between employees and criminals is likely to cause security systems to be abused (Rapport, 2006a, p. 1).

Industrial Strikes

Recently, about 35,000 security guards went on strike in what is referred to as South Africa's biggest and bloodiest union-inspired 12-week national strike by members of the private security industry. During March and April 2006, security members of the South African Trade and Allied Workers' Union (SATAWU) went on strike for higher salaries. While SATAWU claimed victory in the interest of the well-being of security guards, about 60 were killed in the violence that ensued during the strike. Clearly, South Africa as a developing country cannot afford that kind of collective behavior in maintaining its democracy. All international airports, ports of entry, transport services, commercial banks, industries, and the like are being served and protected in one or the other way by that industry. Of the 306,000 registered private security officers, about 256,000 are employed as guards by 4,239 security companies (Daily News, 2006a, p. 1).

Criminal Onslaught

Toward the end of 2006, four security guards were burnt to death during an attack by heavily armed robbers near Lephalale in the Limpopo province of South Africa. Having transported money to a commercial bank, their cash-in-transit vehicle was ramped off the road by gunmen who came in a hijacked Mercedes-Benz and was fired at, causing it to overturn, and their vehicle was then set alight. All four security guards who were trapped inside the capsized van could not escape and were subsequently burnt to death (Beeld, 2006b, p. 2; Rapport, 2006b, p. 1). Following the spate of violent cash-in-transit robberies that plagued the country toward the end of 2006 and in 2007, the private security industry made an urgent call on the police and the army to assist and protect them in the execution of their duties. The government, however, bluntly refused to give way to such a request, urging the industry to get their "house" in order. "Ironically, some security companies used to guard police stations until the matter was exposed in the media" were now left on their own (The Star, 2006, p. 6). Even the National Minister of Safety and Security Charles Nqakula was adamant that private security companies that are contracted to transport cash on behalf of their clients should not expect any support from either the police or the army to protect them. The Minister insisted that firearm training of security guards be upgraded and the carrying of heavy-caliber weapons be considered. Heavy reinforced vehicles should also be given consideration for transporting cash by security companies (The Citizen, 2006, p. 3).

The Education MEC for KwaZulu-Natal province recently indicated that she considers employing security guards at school campuses because of an increase in serious and drug-related crimes (The Witness, 2007, p. 4). The foregoing aspects clearly reveal a significant role for private security in South Africa's crime landscape. While this industry is traditionally inclined to protecting the life and property of clients who are paying for their services, there are indications that it has been involved on various occasions in protecting police stations, tertiary campuses, patrol services, investigation of crime, and the like. This is especially evident from the fact that four private security companies—ADT, Enforce, Securelink, and Blue Security—have recently joined forces to protect the Hillcrest Highway area close to Durban in KwaZulu-Natal, following 19 murders within three months in that area (Weekend Witness, 2007b, p. 3).

In his State of the Nation Address in Parliament in February 2007, President Thabo Mbeki clearly indicated that, together, the SAPS and the private security industry can create a safe and secure environment with all the "ingredients" to satisfy the safety and security expectations of the nation. Discussions between various role players, namely the Deputy Minister of Safety and Security, various private security fraternities and senior members of the SAPS centered around issues such as the current status of security training, sharing of communication resources as well as crime information to enhance the reaction time to crimes, labor relations, and other related matters present in the private security industry calculated to prevent a repetition of the "2006-bloodiest strike" in the security industry. The only question that remains is whether the general approach to crime prevention should not be adapted to also include the maintenance of law and order (Rapport, 2007a, p. 16).

Current Private Security Training

For too long, private security has been rated an "inferior job." Early forms of private security in South Africa during the 1950s and 1960s had been observed in the form of African guards at shopping complexes who kept themselves warm during winter nighttimes with a drum containing fire. Those "guards" were usually low-skilled laborers with virtually no knowledge of private security work. Pillay (2007, pp. 61–72) correctly observes that modern private security gained momentum with the advent of ex-members of the British South African Police (BSAP) and the erstwhile Rhodesian Army (now Zimbabwe) to South Africa during the late 1970s and early 1980s to promote private security, based on their warfare skills and police training background. Ras (2006, p. 322), on the other hand, is adamant that "... many so-called unregistered ex-military and ex-police experts in the body guarding industry claim that they are [the] real professionals; the reality is that they are from a legal point of view illegal."

Regulation of the private security industry through the introduction of the Security Officers Board (SOB), promulgated in terms of Act 92 of 1987, to oversee and exercise control over the well-being private security industry, has become unavoidable. This piece of law was supplemented by the Security Officers Amendment Act (No. 104 of 1997) that paved the way for the introduction of the Security Officers Interim Board. The Private Security Industry Regulation Act (No. 56 of 2001) followed in January 2002 mainly to provide for a regulatory authority. Security officers' training comprises five distinctive grades (E–A). Skills development and black economic empowerment (BEE) among disadvantaged South Africans necessitated the introduction of the safety and Sector Education and Training Authorities (SASETAs), primarily to promote learning in the private security context through registration, accreditation, assessment, and moderation (Pillay, 2007, pp. 61–72).

Conclusion and Recommendations

Analysis of private security functions in crime prevention undeniably supports the notion of private security being an important part of the crime prevention equation in South Africa. Apart from the positive side, it also transpires that private security encountered turbulent moments in the recent past in terms of loss of life and property. This might be the case because (1) too many thugs still roam the streets and highways freely under the auspices of a human rights culture (The Independent on Saturday, 2007b, p. 1), (2) involvement of political activists and liberation movements during "... the first organized cash heists in South Africa in the early 1990s (Sunday Tribune, 2006, p. 4) created a serious problem in crime prevention, (3) vehicles transporting cash to and from commercial banks, especially in the Western Cape province, are believed not to be roadworthy (Rapport, 2006c, p. 14), (4) the South African Constitution does not allow for army support in the fight against armed robbery (Daily News, 2006b, p. 3), and so on.

Whether the private security industry will be able to cope with the criminal onslaught in the new millennium shall, to a large extent, depend on the sustainability of that industry. Residential burglary, theft and robbery, cash-in-transit heists, destruction of automated teller machines (ATMs) with commercial explosives, and the hijacking of large carriers on highways are only a few of the major risks facing both policing and private security in the new millennium. The accumulation of skills through focused practical training and education, competency in combatting crime with sophisticated security technology and intelligence gathering techniques, extended powers under the law, support by public policing, and the development of a climate that would be conducive to the maintenance of social order in close partnership with members of the community (witnessed during two armed robbery shooting incidents in the Gauteng province where 14 armed robbers in total were instantly killed (Daily News, 2007, p. 1) seem to be the real challenges facing the private security industry in their daily handling of crime.

References

Beeld. (2006a). Security industry SA's best chance. *Beeld*, November 20, p. 32.

Beeld. (2006b). Polisie moet daarna kyk nadat wagte sterf: Operasie verloor transitotande. *Beeld*, October 3, p. 2.

Beeld. (2007a). Security industry (trans.). *Beeld*, January 18, p. 14.

Beeld. (2007b). Helfte van wêreld gou stadsjapies. *Beeld*, January 22, p. 6.

Berg, J. (2003). The private security industry in South Africa: A review of applicable legislation. *South African Criminal Justice Journal, 16*(2), 178–196.

Business Report. (2007). Crime stunts growth, says DCSA boss. *Business Report*, March 29, 4.

Collins, P. A., Ricks, T. A., & Van Meter, C. W. (2000). *Principles of Security and Crime Prevention* (4th ed.). Cincinnati, Ohio: Anderson.

Daily News. (2006a). Guards to go back on duty. *Daily News*, June 22, p. 1.

Daily News. (2006b). Cash guards want firepower: They are sitting ducks, says union. *Daily News*, October 16, p. 3.

Daily News. (2007). Deadly force: Public backs cops' shoot-to-kill action. *Daily News*, December 13, p. 1.

Engelbrecht, E. (1991). *Slagoffers van bomaanvalle in Johannesburg: 'n Kriminologiese ondersoek.* Unpublished doctoral thesis. University of South Africa, Pretoria.

Kelling, G. L., & Wilson, J. Q. (1982). The police and neighborhood safety. *The Atlantic*, March, pp. 29–38.

Lab, S. P. (1988). *Crime Prevention: Approaches, Practices and Evaluations.* Cincinnati, Ohio: Anderson.

Minnaar, A. (1999). Partnership policing: A role for the private security industry to assist the SAPS in preventing crime? *African Security Review, 8*(2), from http://www.iss.co.za/pubs/ASR/8No2/Minnaar.html

Minnaar, A. (2005). Private-public partnerships: Private security, crime prevention and policing in South Africa. *Acta Criminologica, 18*(1), 85–114.

Minnaar, A., & Ngoveni, K. P. (2003, February 19–22). *The relationship between the South African Police Service and the Private Security Industry with specific reference to the outsourcing of certain operational functions in the police: Post-April 1994.* Paper presented at the International Conference on Policing and Security: In search of security. Quebec, Canada.

Neuman, W. L., & Wiegand, B. (2000). *Criminal Justice Research Methods: Qualitative & Quantitative Approaches*. Boston, MA: Allyn & Bacon.

Pillay, K. (2007). Introducing unit-standards-based education and training methodology for security practitioners—a South African perspective. *Acta Criminologica*, *20*(4), 61–72.

Potgieter, P. J. (2008). Can private security stand up to the challenges of crime and crime prevention in South Africa? A contemporary perspective. *Acta Criminologica*, *21*(1), 33–43.

Rapport. (2006a). Concern over guards' role in crime (trans.). *Rapport*, May 21, p. 1.

Rapport. (2006b). Wagte se doodsangs: "Ons brand!" *Rapport*, October 1, p. 1.

Rapport. (2006c). Geldwaens glo gedaan, draad hou deure toe, *Rapport*, October 15, p. 14.

Rapport. (2007a). Zuma "boul beleggers uit." *Rapport*, December 2, p. 16.

Rapport. (2007b). Metaalverklikkers ingespan by winkelsentrum: Talle veiligheidstelsels nodig sê kundige. *Rapport*, December 9, p. 4.

Ras, J. M. (2006). *Body guarding in a private security context. Volume 2*. Unpublished doctoral thesis. University of Zululand, KwaDlangezwa.

Schmalleger, F. (1999). *Criminology Today* (2nd ed.). Upper Saddle River, NJ: Prentice Hall.

Simonsen, C. E. (1998). *Private Security in America: An Introduction*. Upper Saddle River, NJ: Prentice Hall.

Steenkamp, D. G., & P. J. Potgieter. (2004). Private security and crime prevention: A factor analytic approach," *Acta Criminologica*, 17(2), 71–82.

Sunday Times. (2006). Inside SA's cash heist gangs. *Sunday Times*, October 1, p. 5.

Sunday Tribune. (2006). Skills honed during the struggle give heist crooks the edge. *Sunday Tribune*, October 8, p. 4.

Sunday Tribune. (2007). Mbeki's big crime plan. *Sunday Tribune*, November 11, p. 1.

The Citizen. (2006). Security firms can do better, says Nqakula. *The Citizen*, November 22, p. 3.

The Independent on Saturday. (2007a). R100 million for private security guards for police stations. *The Independent on Saturday*, March 10, p. 6.

The Independent on Saturday. (2007b). No trust in SA cops. *The Independent on Saturday*, March 10, p. 1.

The Mercury. (2007a). Selebi call to legalise 2010 sex trade. *The Mercury*, March 29, p. 1.

The Mercury. (2007b). Signs of criminal terrorism grip SA. *The Mercury*, April 2, p. 2.

The Mercury. (2007c). Initiative unveiled to tackle crime. *The Mercury*, March 29, p. 5.

The Mercury. (2007d). The changing face of crime in KZN, *The Mercury*, December 7, p. 1.

The Star. (2006). Security firms must protect themselves, state insists. *The Star*, November 17, p. 6.

The Witness. (2007). Cronjé considers employing guards at schools. *The Witness*, May 3, p. 4.

Timm, H. W., & Christian, K. E. (1991). *Introduction to Private Security*. Pacific Grove, California: Brooks/Cole.

Weekend Witness. (2007a). "NO" to 2010 sex deal. *Weekend Witness*, March 31, p. 1.

Weekend Witness. (2007b). Action to secure suburbs. *Weekend Witness*, December 1, p. 3.

Zulu, X. (2006). Urbanization on the rise, says study. *The Mercury*, 26 October, p. 13.

Body Guarding in South Africa

24

JOHAN RAS

Contents

Body guarding is all about people. It is about operating in an overt and clandestine manner to ensure the safety and security of clients—at all costs. In professional circles, it is all about people who believe that with every step they take and every move they make, there may be someone somewhere who knows (many of them believe "only God knows"), who may have them in the hair cross of a sniper's telescope, or who wants to draw them into an ambush where they have to shoot or fight it out to survive (Lonsdale, 1995; Pienaar, 1997; Ras, 2006, pp. 76–77).

From a bodyguard's perspective, body guarding is all about saving clients from all dangers, to prevent them from being "zipped into a jiffy bag" (i.e., a plastic bag with a zip) and stored in a cool room for another state autopsy, and to prevent a sensation-hunting journalist from scooping "their story of failure" for an annual reward. Qualitative research on body guarding in the private security context has analyzed how bodyguards operate and protect their clients in their functional environments and how they "plan, walk, talk, drive, shoot, fight and pray" in order "not to cross the river Jordan" (Ras, 2006, pp. 76–77). In the light of my past research, I believe that those working in this industry contribute directly to the safety and security of society. While policing has to do with the maintenance of social order, body guarding is focusing primarily on the protection of the client's life and ensuring that he/she can continue with his/her lifestyle without experiencing any form of danger or threats. More precisely, the purpose of a bodyguard is to proactively and reactively protect his client at all times.

Whether in an overt or covert manner, when bodyguards plan for the safety of their clients, and actively ensuring that safety by forming the first and last line of defense, they take over the task of the state or municipal law enforcers and, in an active sense, render a direct and personal protective service that is actually the task of the police force or service of any country or state. In other words, they directly assist the police in safeguarding the inhabitants or citizens of any country.

When highly trained private security bodyguards protect their clients, more police officers are available to perform other police duties. Wealthy and prominent business people, celebrities, and those with high status who normally can afford private security bodyguards are usually urban based—whether at home or at work, busy with their business transactions, holidays, or enjoying the high life. The presence of any professional bodyguard with his/her client in any situation that necessitates normally proactive or reactive policing will automatically assist state-appointed police officers who are supposed to respond, in terms of state legislation, to any form of danger of threats that may harm or endanger the life of any citizen, including the life of a bodyguard's VIP.

Through proper planning, the gathering of daily intelligence, liaison with other law-enforcement agencies, implementing preventative strategies, and executing professional tactics, bodyguards not only safeguard the lives of their VIPs, but they also ensure that no incidents occur in their presence. This simply means that the presence, visibility, *modus operandi*, and observational and tactical skills of bodyguards most of the time will simply prevent or reduce any form of crime, while they move around with their principals.

My past research has convinced me that the more the legally registered, professionally trained, and ethically committed private security bodyguards appear on the streets, especially in the South African urban areas, the less crime will occur. This, *elapso tempore*, will reduce the burdens that rest upon the shoulders of the police, and will result, in the long run, in a reduction of crime, which in return will create more opportunities for economic growth and expansion, which will further increase job creation and the generation of wealth (Ras, 2006).

Brief Historical Background

After the newly elected government under President Nelson Mandela came into power in 1994, replacing the former white apartheid government, South Africa did not experience large-scale political violence but a tremendous upsurge in crime, especially bloody and violent crime. In the 2004–2005 period, 449,352 police arrests were made in South Africa for serious and violent crimes; 681,128 arrests for less serious crimes; 23,813 firearms were confiscated, and 43,041 vehicles were recovered out of a reported 93,518 that were stolen (Burger, 2006: 115; Ras, 2007, p. 93).

Over the last 10 years, South Africa has also experienced a high number of murders of police officers. These annual killings reached a high of 280 in 1993 with the year 2000 being the first year on records in which less than 200 were killed in one year. During the first six months of 2006, 51 police officers were killed. The South African statistics are, per 100,000 population, according to Minnaar (2006, p. i), the highest rate in the world.

The South African Police Service (SAPS) comprises about 150,000 men and women. President Thabo Mbeki stated at the opening of the South African Parliament this year that this number is going to be expanded to 180,000 personnel within the next three years. The existing 150,000 is *in nomine* responsible for policing an estimated 44,187,637 people (https://www.cia.gov/cia/publications/factbook/geos/sf/html), that is, there is one police officer for every 295 persons.

At present, there are about 750,000 private security personnel on the database of the Private Security Industry Regulatory Authority (PSIRA) in South Africa. This means, if we take the existing figures (150,000 police personnel versus 750,000 security officers), there are about five private security officers for every police officer in South Africa. I think most countries will have an almost similar picture.

The visibility of private security officers, especially those who are armed, definitely acts as a deterrent in any place. If the police allow the expansion of these role players in the prevention of crime, then, logically speaking, the number of those with criminal or intimidating intentions has to come down. Although the police claim to prevent crime, the reality, however, especially in South Africa, is that they mostly only respond to crime. In other words, they are more reactive than proactive in the execution of their duties. Bodyguards, on the other hand, are exclusively proactive or preventative when rendering their services.

Police patrols, in which officers walk the beat, are definitely not prominent at all over South Africa. However, one frequently sees the movement of police vehicles now and then, or sometimes more often, up and down the roads, going somewhere to some unknown secret place, that the uninformed, believe, must be important. However, it is known to those who know what police patrols are all about that this has simply no effect on the reduction of crime (Ras, 2003).

Most of the time these police drivers have minimum contact with the public whom they are supposed to serve, or simply, no contact at all. No personal liaison takes place, no police–public relationships are built, and, most important, no intelligence gathering takes place (Ras, 2003). So ineffective is this typical everyday reality that if the criminals wave to the police, the police simply smile and wave back. The effectiveness of these vehicle movements remains in my opinion an unclassified South African government secret or mystery.

While many parts of South Africa are filled with poverty, unemployment, bad roads with huge potholes, and the country is experiencing an annual death rate of 370,000 for HIV/AIDS-related diseases, the high murder rate and other violent crimes such as car hijackings, taxi violence, rape, armed robberies, political murders, intimidations, economic strikes, and wild shootings or drive-by shootings at any random time all contribute to a high level of fear of crime or any threat or form of harm (Prinsloo, 2006, pp. 1–17; Ras, 2006, 2007, p. 95). Chronically, there are excessive and frequent violent crimes (including torturing) coming and going. Brutal and senseless killings occur almost on a daily basis. Execution-style murders in which people are shot behind the head are nothing strange. It has almost become a habit. Police statistics have become a joke and some believe that they are polished very smartly in order to ensure that the 2010 Soccer World Cup will take place in South Africa. Zululand, where I live, is considered the murder capital of South Africa (Ras, 2007, pp. 95–96).

In recent years, there were 22,000 murders that took place in South Africa according to police statistics, while the official opposition party in South Africa has claimed that the Department of Health had claimed that they had recorded that about 33,000 people have died in hospitals and clinics because of gunshot wounds. While the statistical difference of 11,000 deaths caused by bullet wounds is still a mystery, these figures indicate to me that the public's safety and security is seriously threatened if they have to rely on the police alone to protect them.

While the political leaders are frequently declaring war on crime and talk of criminals as animals and monsters, and police officials pleading for a moral regenerations (Ras, 2007, p. 96), the reality is that everyone's safety lies in his/her own hands. One can add that without the assistance of private security officers (like bodyguards), the hands of the police are simply tied up.

Personal Opinion

The safety and security of the general public, anywhere in South Africa, and in the world, are in my opinion directly linked to the presence of private security officers that must be utilized to support the state police, whether in a guarding (static) or patrolling capacity. The fact that private security officers outnumber the police services is something that must be effectively addressed in order to ensure peace and stability in any region.

This can be achieved by strict police control over private security officers in terms of their registration (via fingerprint screening), the setting of proper training standards, a code of conduct (Ras, 2006, pp. 375–377), and the implementation and execution of the administrative and quality control measures necessary to ensure that all members comply. Through competency-based training and an emphasis on quality service delivery, more professional security officers, including bodyguards, will operate in the field that will directly contribute to safety and security in any given area. This is now starting to happen in South Africa.

Legal Requirements for Becoming a Bodyguard in South Africa

It is necessary to understand what legal requirements were and are in place in order to operate as a bodyguard in South Africa. There is, in my opinion, a direct link between the training requirements expected from bodyguards, the quality of service, and levels of professionalism that clients can expect from their hired protectors, and the safety and security levels in society.

Requirements in the Past

The only legal requirement for becoming a bodyguard in South Africa in the past was that every aspirant bodyguard must have at least a minimum Grade E training certificate (i.e., one week of training), obtained from an accredited PSIRA (or SIRA) service provider, and he/she must also be registered with this Authority.

Although there was a PSIRA bodyguard course available that learners could do, the minimum legal requirement was only Grade E. All private security officers protect lives and property—whether you are a car guard (looking after vehicles), or a guard protecting assets, or in the case of bodyguards, protecting lives—the minimum requirement was Grade E. This is still valid today (Mhlongo, 2005). There was also no minimum educational standards for entry into the industry (Minnaar & Ngoveni, 2004, p. 59; Ras, 2006, p. 132). Anyone could and still can become a bodyguard.

Thirteen short modules constitute the Grade E training course. These are (i) personal hygiene and general appearance, (ii) public relations, (iii) the role and function of private security, (iv) bombs, firearms, and explosive devices (brief theory focusing on recognition), (v) discipline (marching orders),

(vi) self-defense, (vii) observation, (viii) guarding and patrolling, (ix) fire extinguishers, fire prevention, and fire fighting, (x) radio and telephone communications, (xi) basic legal aspects, (xii) industrial relations, and (xiii) symbolic safety signs (Mhlongo, 2005).

In practice, this means that a person has received one week of training—normally offered from 08:00 a.m. to 16:00 p.m. from Monday to Friday. This minimum training qualification enables the candidate to get access to the private security industry and to start operating as a security guard, a car guard, or someone who will look after other people or their assets. In other words, even body guarding duties can be performed.

After completion of Grade E, the applicant applies for registration at PSIRA, his/her fingerprints are scanned by the SAPS to see if the applicant has any criminal record, and only when they are satisfied, PSIRA will issue a registration certificate. Once the applicant has received his PSIRA registration certificate, he/she is legally entitled to start working as a private security officer, which includes, being or acting as a bodyguard.

Although the ideal situation would be that the student did further and additional Grades like Grade D (focusing on access control and searching), Grade C (focusing on threats and emergency planning), and Grade B (a supervisor course), as well as a bodyguard course, Grade E and registration were regarded as the bare minimum legal entry into the private security and body guarding field. However, this situation has changed drastically recently (Ras, 2006, pp. 175–189).

Future Requirements

In order to enhance the skills of the South African workforce, the Minister for Labor has introduced 25 different Sectorial Education Training Authorities, called SETAs. The SETA that is responsible for the training of those in the police, military, intelligence, courts, legal profession, correctional services, and the private security industry is the Safety and Security Sector Education Training Authority (SASSETA). This SETA will officially take over all the training activities and duties of PSIRA during 2008–2009.

In the future, the Grade E training, as well as all other training grades, will be replaced by different unit standards with specific outcomes (required evidence) that a learner must complete in order to be declared competent. There is also a specific unit standard that all aspirant bodyguards must complete to be allowed to work. In other words, they must be found competent in this particular unit standard before they may work in the industry. While PSIRA will continue to do the registration of all private security officers, including private security bodyguards, it is the SASSETA that must declare a learner fit to do body guarding in practice.

The SASSETA accredits and appoints service providers all over the country who will assist the SASSETA to assess learners in this regard. I myself am a SASSETA-accredited assessor and moderator (assessing the assessor) for the unit standard on body guarding. A transitional period is now in place while the SASSETA is taking over the PSIRA training functions (Ras, 2006, pp. 175–189).

In practice, a private security bodyguard who wants to work now for another private security company in South Africa only needs to have Grade E, a PSIRA registration number, and a SASSETA proficiency certificate in the use of a handgun. The security company must provide him with the firearm because PSIRA's regulations do not allow any private firearms to be used in the rendering of private security work, including body guarding (Ras, 2006, p. 177).

However, if the bodyguard wants to do solo and work on his own, he must meet all the requirements of someone who has his own private security registered company. One of the requirements for this is that he must have a minimum of Grade B (a supervisor qualification), that is, basically four weeks (20 working days) of training (Ras, 2006, p. 177).

When the SASSETA is fully in charge of all training matters, the only training qualification that will be accepted by them when someone wants to become a bodyguard is the successful completion of the South African Qualification Authority (SAQA) unit standard, entitled "Provide close protection for designated persons" (SAQA U/S id. 11510). This qualification is placed at NQF (New Qualifications Framework) level 5 and consists of 40 credits that represent 400 notional hours of training (Ras, 2006, pp. 178–179).

According to the bodyguard experts who have drawn up this particular unit standard, 400 notional hours is the average number of hours that a learner, who has no previous bodyguard experiences, will take to complete this national qualification (Ras, 2006, pp. 178–179). The purpose of this specific unit standard is to enable relevant personnel who are tasked with the protection of designated persons (VIPs) to provide protection to such persons against harmful threats while in transit, on foot, or at a venue.

The stated benefit for society is that a person who completes this unit standard will contribute to safety and security in society (Mhlongo, 2005). A person credited with this unit standard will be able to ascertain the principals' brief and risk profiles, plan the transit/foot/venue protection operation of a principal, protect a VIP during transit/foot/venue movement, and terminate and review the protection operation (http://reqs.saqa.org.za/view UnitStandard.php?id=11510; Ras, 2006, p. 179). *In praxis*, this means that urban and rural safety is also the responsibility and duty of private security officers like bodyguards. It is no longer the duty of the police alone to contribute to safety and security.

Before any aspiring bodyguard may complete SAQA's prescribed unit standard, he/she must be able to competently drive a motor vehicle, must be competent in the use and application of the law, all firearms as well as in the tactical application of all firearms. This means that the learner has also completed training in the use of other unit standards like use of a handgun, a shotgun, a rifle, and a hand machine carbine, and use of firearms in tactical duty-related situations (Ras, 2006, pp. 179–181).

This means practically that those learners who are going to render body guarding services in future in South Africa will be far better trained and will be competent to do this job. This will directly contribute to the safety and security of their clients, and society as a whole. There is no doubt in my mind that the higher levels of theoretical, practical, and skills training will put a member in the field who will be able to deal more effectively with any form of harm or threat in society. The great emphasis on different kinds of firearms as well as their tactical applicability means that competent individuals are now available and in place in society who can immediately act and respond to anything that may threaten the safety and security of any community. This, without doubt, will directly assist the police, by taking this burden off their own shoulders.

If a client needs assistance when threatened, for example by thugs, the bodyguard can immediately respond to that; if any person needs help when attacked by criminals, a competent bodyguard who knows that he/she must contribute to the safety and security of society, will certainly be morally obliged to act and to do wherever he/she can. What all this means is simply this: in terms of crime, the South African landscape is going to change. A new training system has been put in place where emphasis is now placed on a learner's competency and where it is expected that this person must contribute to the safety and security of society—whether he is in the rural areas of KwaZulu-Natal or in a city like Johannesburg or Durban.

While PSIRA was responsible for the training and registration of any bodyguard in the past, in future the training will be fully the responsibility of the SASSETA, while PSIRA will only do the registration and the enforcement of the law. The SAPS will do the screening of the candidate (like fingerprint checks) on behalf of PSIRA. Once a person is cleared by the SAPS, PSIRA will issue the person's registration certificate. The registration by PSIRA will only take place once the aspirant bodyguard or learner has successfully completed the SAQA unit standard in body guarding as required by the SASSETA (Ras, 2006, pp. 175–178).

The shift in the educational standards from a so-called knowledge-based training qualification to an outcomes-based education where everything has to do with competency (Ferreira, 2005) will ensure in future a more effective bodyguard operator at the grass roots level. The cutoff point is simply this: Unless a person is declared competent by the SASSETA and afterward issued with a registration certificate by PSIRA, no private security officer or private security bodyguard can legally operate as a security officer or bodyguard in South Africa (Mhlongo, 2005).

The tactical firearms competency training that members must undergo before they can enroll for the bodyguard unit standard course *inter alia* refers to armed response, cash-in-transit, and shooting skills such as dive, roll, and shoot, fast loading and reloading of firearms, different firing positions like prone, kneeling, and stand, the use of cover and concealment, movement with firearms, and the application of combat firearm techniques (Ferreira, 2005; K. Geldenhuys, 2005; L. H. Geldenhuys, 2005). Most firearm trainers and private security service providers believe that these techniques will equip bodyguards, and those carrying firearms, better to face a situation when one encounters an armed assault (K. Geldenhuys, 2005; Ras, 2006, p. 180). To be skilled in firearms, while wearing one, is a great advantage, and directly contributes to the safety and security of society (Butler, 2004; Le Roux, 2005; Ras, 2006, pp. 181, 600–602).

The new emphasis of the SASSETA on competency underlines also the beginning of a new level of professionalism in South Africa. The more professional a bodyguard wants to become, the more competent he must be. There is now a direct link between competency and professionalism. Gone are the days where a person would study, finish a course, and say he/she knows everything. Learning is now seen and implemented as a lifelong process (Tyers, 2003).

Different Categories of Bodyguards

In order to professionalize and fast-track the body guarding industry in South Africa, I have proposed different categories of bodyguards to be implemented (Ras, 2006, pp. 331–334, 347–357). This will lead to greater professionalism and will ensure that clients can expect excellent service. It will also directly contribute to a safer environment. Before these categories are mentioned, a few important remarks should be made.

I believe that the higher the levels of security training, competency, and professionalism a person reveals, the less the chance that attacks, crimes, and any form of threats will take place in the presence of the bodyguard and his/her VIP. I strongly believe that the low levels of training in the past and the incompetence of a majority of those who were supposed to assist in reducing crime, *inter alia*, had basically no major impact on crime reduction in South Africa.

Due to the compulsory military training and years of service that white South Africans had to do during especially the apartheid years, the majority of white bodyguards were regarded as real professionals (Ras, 2006, pp. 317–319). Bodyguards from the so-called historically disadvantaged groups (Africans) were not recognized in the past by their white counterparts. The reasons were lack of any military or previous policing experiences, indiscipline, illiteracy, the inability to communicate effectively in English and Afrikaans (the former official languages of the country), integrity, the question of trust, reliability, the absence of Westernized thinking, and the lack of professional close quarter fighting and shooting skills. Additional reason were lack of proper driving and planning skills, politics, racial divisions, and simply no proper contact and exposure to the Western way of doing things (Ras, 2006, p. 335).

The introduction of competency training to all aspirant private security officers and bodyguards is now opening the doors to any person to become a real professional. It all depends on the learner's commitment to training and his levels of competence. This means in practice that many more professional security officers are now active in the field and can also be generated through the accredited SASSETA service providers. This state of affairs directly influences the safety and security situation at the grass roots level—whether the bodyguard is operating in a rural, town or township setting, or inside the inner circles of a major city. The presence of bodyguards is felt at the grass roots level.

Development of Professional Bodyguards

The key to ensuring a more safe and secure society lies in training and putting in place competent private security bodyguards. This will occur when there is a commitment to academic excellence and the obtaining of body guarding skills in a private security environment. Exposure to thorough and proper academic training, directly related to security, develops a learner intellectually and sharpens his mind like a razor—something that is essential in body guarding, especially when split-second decisions need to be made.

I agree with Mark Lonsdale, who believes that the key to being a professional is personal integrity and bearing supported by rigorous training and years of experience (Lonsdale, 2005; Ras, 2006, p. 316). While shooting-, fitness-, and driver training are the main focus of basically all body guarding training in Germany and Europe (Thorpe, 2005), the emphasis in South Africa must rather be on competency skills training in observation, firearm handling, driving, fighting, planning, and first aid skills (Mhlongo, 2005; Ras, 2006, p. 344).

From an existential point of view, I believe that professionalism is not something that a person has or possesses; it is something that a person is and becomes. It is a process of becoming and being. It is a progressive and never-ending process where every individual bodyguard constantly improves himself and moves to higher levels of service of sharing, caring, and understanding. This is when a bodyguard discovers himself, develops one's capacity, and tries to improve himself. That is one reason why learning is seen as a lifelong process (Ras, 2006, pp. 336–338).

To draw a comparison, fighter pilots undergo many years of hard and enduring cognitive, psychological, and physical training under the most severe conditions. They are highly trained and are continuously preparing themselves to be fit to fight in any possible future air battles. Their objective is to take out the enemy, to survive, and to safeguard their country. Bodyguards are no exception (Ras, 2006, p. 344).

There is no doubt in my mind that the introduction of skills training in South Africa, especially when it comes to firearm handling and the training of bodyguards, has drastically upgraded the expertise and skills of all those who have enrolled for these unit standards. The confidence that members now have to deal with potential dangerous situations like armed attacks will greatly assist them to reveal superior survival, fighting, and shooting skills and to make a real difference by ensuring a safer society.

In short, if you want a safe and secure society, retrain all private security officers in terms of competency skills in a more professional manner and start experiencing the difference. Professional bodyguards know how to plan, to operate proactively, and to remove the VIP from any immediate and/or potential danger areas. The takeover of all PSIRA's training functions by the SASSETA in 2008/2009, before the 2010 Soccer World Cup, will in future definitely contribute to a more safe and secure South Africa. Those who are at present rendering private security service are now forced to comply and to upgrade their skills that will directly contribute to a safer South Africa.

The requirements that potential accredited SASSETA service providers have to meet in order to train learners as private security officers and bodyguards are today by far more difficult, but more competency based and certainly a huge improvement than what we had in the past. These strict requirements directly ensure that more professional and competent members are in charge of the training of those who, at the grass roots level, must go and do the job. The police will directly benefit through these members because they will in future attend to far less crime scenes than what they were experiencing in the past.

Due to the fact that assessor and moderator accreditations as well as firearm competency licenses are only valid for a maximum period of five years, the responsibility rests 100% upon the shoulders of every service provider and learner to perform and to upgrade his/her skills continuously to ensure future compliance. This whole developmental-skills process directly improves the safety situation on the ground—whether bodyguards operate in a rural setting or in a town or city. The more the bodyguards are trained and start to operate, the less the police will have to attend emergency calls.

I suggest that all those who want to become or are at present bodyguards must be classified into six different categories that are each progressively linked to higher levels of training and professionalism. The reason for this is to accommodate all those who are already in the field and/or those who do not have adequate opportunities in the past to study and to upgrade their skills. In order to provide enough time for everyone to upgrade their skills, there are interim categories running over a five-year period from 2007/2008 to 2011/2012 and permanent categories that will run from 2012 to 2017 and further. The different categories are followed by the training requirements for each category.

Interim Body Guarding Categories

Category one: Local bodyguards: Grade E and PSIRA registration. He only has to speak his mother tongue and can only work in the small local geographical area where he stays.

Category two: Area bodyguards: Grade D, PSIRA registration, and a driver's license. He must be fluent in his mother tongue and must be able to basically express himself in English. He can work in a wider geographical area.

Category three: Provincial bodyguards: Grade C, PSIRA registration, a driver's license, and fluent in English and in one other indigenous language. He can work anywhere in the specific province where he stays.

Category four: National bodyguards: He must have Grade C, PSIRA registration, a driver's license, and must have completed the prescribed future body guarding course of the SASSETA as published by SAQA, entitled: "Provide close protection of designated persons" (SAQA's U/S id. 11510). He can work anywhere in South Africa.

Category five: International bodyguards: He must meet all of the National bodyguard requirements and he must provide proof of having international bodyguard experiences.

Category six: Professional bodyguard councilors: He must meet all the previous requirements and must provide a portfolio of evidence that consists of proper academic qualifications (preferably university), all military, police, or private security and body guarding qualifications, convincing backgrounds and experiences, community involvement, recognition from PSIRA, the SASSETA, as well as any other established professional body with a proper code of conduct and sound ethics.

Permanent Body Guarding Categories

Category one: Local bodyguards: After 2011/2012, the bodyguard needs to have at least been declared competent in SAQA's unit standard on body guarding. This means in practice that every bodyguard in South Africa, even the existing illiterate ones, must have completed a K53-driver's license, all firearm-related training and must be competent in the use of handguns, shotguns, rifles, and hand machine carbines, the tactical use of firearms, as well as the prescribed SAQA bodyguard qualification. This will directly have a huge impact on the South African society and will ensure that more competent officers are spread all over the country to assist the police with safety and security issues.

Category two: Area bodyguards: The cutoff point is now that the bodyguards must have at least one three-year BA degree in private security or police studies, in addition to all the SASSETA's requirements like the SAQA bodyguard course.

Category three: Provincial bodyguards: Two university degrees are now required plus additional courses like rapelling, scuba diving, paragliding, or parachuting, after completion of all the previous requirements of the SASSETA.

Category four: National bodyguards: The bodyguards must now have a Master's degree, in addition to all the previous requirements. The students must also have completed their one-year internship. The Master's degree topic must be directly related to body guarding. The purpose is to have a bodyguard with an in-depth knowledge about private security, body guarding, and safety- and security-related issues.

Category five: International bodyguards: Everything that is expected from National bodyguards is also expected here, but in addition to this, the learners must also be able to add any foreign language qualification to their name, for example, Spanish, French, Dutch, or German. An internationally recognized driver's license is also required.

Category six: Professional bodyguard councilors: They must meet all previous requirements but must also have completed a doctorate on body guarding. All professional experts normally have doctorates in their specific fields. Professional bodyguard councilors are no exception. Their work is to constantly monitor and analyze the body guarding industry and to make recommendations to policy makers and those responsible for the safety and security of the country at the national level.

Future Trends

I have no doubt in my mind that the safety and security of any country, including South Africa, cannot be guaranteed by any police service or force alone (Ras, 2007, pp. 107–108). By implementing the principles of community and sector policing and letting private security officers, including bodyguards, work under certain conditions in certain areas, depending on their training recognition, skills, and competency levels, the workloads of the state police will definitely be reduced—especially when it comes to proactive and preventative policing. With the present threat of global terrorism (Rogers, 2007, pp. 111–116), any role player like private security officers cannot be excluded. All police operations in future must be intelligence-driven (Ras, 2006, pp. 221–228; Rogers, 2007, pp. 111–116; Rudolph & Miguel, 2007, pp. 17–29) in order to be successful and to ensure that objectives are met with limited resources.

By implementing skills training and by introducing quality control through a Sector Education Training Authority (like the SASSETA) and a body like the PSIRA, or a similar body that falls directly under the Ministry for Safety and Security, all private security officers are forced to comply and to contribute through their newly acquired training and competency skills to the safety of society (Ras, 2006, pp. 239–241).

Rapid urbanization, scarcity of natural resources, a huge influx of people streaming into cities to grab whatever opportunity they can get, the spreading of organized criminal syndicates (Standing, 2003), terrorism (Meek, 2006), and constant illegal business deals necessitate that the police of every country must be strengthened by private security officers if they want to remain in control. Well-trained professional bodyguards, who are committed to serve their country and not their own selfish interest, and who agree to operate according to a sound code of conduct not only are a great national asset, but they also have access to a lot of secrets in the world.

In fact, few people know more than professional bodyguards about the secrets of those whom they guard. They are constantly aware of what is taking place behind the scenes, because, in reality, they are the ones who send out the "recce" teams, to do sweeps, to plant listening devices, or to do debugging, when necessary (Ras, 2006, pp. 190–241). They are the first and last line of defense who prevent others to get close to the principal without his/her consent. To stay at arm's length away from the VIP also means that they pick up all the whispers and the soft talk that are sometimes essential to share with those intelligence operators who have national interests at heart (Ras, 2006, pp. 291–294).

While some governments attempt to work against private security operators (especially when they see them as mercenaries when these officers hired themselves out to do jobs outside their country—like in Iraq, Afghanistan, or the DRC—Ras, 2006, p. 293), they rather must strive to work together with them, but by reversing the process. The private security operators need to work together with the state police and not vice versa. This can happen only if the governments of today set the parameters and oversee the process and the context in which this collaboration must take place.

To ensure safety and security in every country, control these members through selection and screening processes, through training requirements in terms of competencies, and let them work together as informers. From a psychological point of view, these operators want to feel important and want to be recognized for the contributions they make to safeguard their clients. Acknowledge that and request them to assist with intelligence gathering.

Whether they are part- or full-time informants or intelligence operators, use them to gather valuable information that can assist the state police to have a holistic picture on the ground in terms of what is happening. Many bodyguards have first-hand knowledge of business people that may be involved in organized crimes; they perhaps have guarded persons who they later have discovered will easily allow smuggling of goods like nuclear materials that can set off World War III in order to satisfy their greed for money and power.

Sound cooperation between the police and private security officers is only possible when there is a close partnership between both law-enforcement agencies as spelled out by the Minister, the regulatory authorities, and those who are responsible for the training and those who must oversee the process and enforce the law. Proper recognition from the side of the government by allowing private security officers to operate, to have weapons, and to have freedom of movement, as long as they operate within the law of the state, can only benefit both parties.

There are today many ex-military and ex-police officers who are operating in the private security field, either as owners of companies, or highly skilled individuals who have the know-how to make a difference in terms of safety issues when necessary. However, in any state there are those, like in South Africa, who reveal antigovernment sentiments. It is the duty of the police to monitor those operating in the private security field and to ensure that they are not issued, for example with firearms, if they are not willing to comply with all government regulations and legislation and/or work together with the police.

Security operators must have the freedom to do their job, but that freedom comes with a responsibility, and it is, for example, not to commit high treason or sedition. I do not know of any bodyguard who will operate without firearms in South Africa—not only is it too dangerous to go unarmed, but the client also expects that the bodyguard must protect him/her with a firearm when necessary. Police are advised not to give permission to security operators who apply for firearms when they reveal antigovernment sentiments. In reality, bodyguards are "hired guns" that must assist their governments in safeguarding society—this is only possible if the private security officers know that they will only be allowed to carry weapons as long as they comply with the law and work together with the police (Mhlongo, 2005).

I have also recommended the establishment of the Professional Bodyguard Council of South Africa (PROBOCOSA), based on the work of the Health Professions Council of South Africa (Ras, 2006, pp. 454–455). This will be a professional overseeing body that will monitor the whole industry from a professional point of view and see that members are observing a code of conduct. This council will also set the standards for the body guarding industry and will make recommendations to the ministers, the directors of PSIRA, the CEO of the SASSETA, and to all those who must enforce the law to ensure compliance with sound ethical and responsible body guarding practices.

I have also recommended that bodyguards in South Africa start operating in the tourism industry in order to make a proper living. The monthly income of ordinary security officers today in South Africa is about US$200 or R 1,400.00. Private security companies who rent out armed guards, who basically protect lives, and in this sense also render body guarding services, knowing that they are not well trained, will ask anything from about US$400 (i.e., R 2,800.00) up to US $700 (i.e., R 4,900.00) per month for rendering this service. Unemployed Africans desperate for work are more than willing to render this service and are easily available to take the place of those bodyguards who want more money before they take the job. Professional bodyguards will find it very difficult to survive financially if they do not adjust their prices, by reducing it to that of an armed guard, or alternatively, to move into the tourism industry (Ras, 2006, pp. 388–427).

Very little research has been done in South Africa on the very strong and huge second economy that is operating in the country. All the so-called jobless people (some say up to 51% of those that can work are regarded as jobless) are still surviving on a daily basis. The reason is simple. They survive in the second economy. Although they live far under the government's breadline of R 1,500.00–R 2,000.00 per month, they still make it every day. How is that possible? Those who do not commit crime have simply learned to sell. They mostly sell small items and have learned to survive with less than US $200 (R 1,400.00) per month.

There are about 7,000 towns, townships, and cities in South Africa. The country was also divided into 80,000 small geographical sectors (enumeration areas) during the October 9–10, 2001 census period (Ras, 2006, pp. 461–462). I believe that if private security officers can be trained as township-, town-, and/or urban specialists, that is, they are people who know these areas very well, and they will operate as bodyguards, taking visitors through their areas, about 1,000,000 new jobs can be created in South Africa within the next few years. The presence of these members all over South Africa, where everyone operates in a small given area, responsible for the safety of his/her client, will have a huge impact on the safety of the country as a whole.

The so-called second economy will be tremendously boosted by the introduction of private security bodyguards who will now act as township-, city-, or rural area specialists. Unemployed persons who are part and parcel of the second economy will become financially more independent and, in the long run, will be able to create for themselves a sustainable income. Some of the more innovative and creative members will also be able to move from the second economy to the first one, and in the process create more jobs and wealth for others (Mhlongo, 2005; Ras, 2006, p. 462).

The reality is that people have a need to feel safe and secure. In South Africa, private security officers and bodyguards can address this need, as long as they quote cheap prices when they market themselves. In South

Africa, armed security officers are basically operating as bodyguards although professional bodyguards despise it because they do not get contracts and money because they quote too high prices. The more the bodyguards are employed by people, even on a short-term basis like a few hours, one day, or perhaps a week, the lesser burden rests upon the police to protect and secure these citizens who are utilizing the services of bodyguards.

However, it is vital that all bodyguards must adhere to a sound code of conduct. I have drawn up the following Code of Conduct for bodyguards, based upon the military code that we were using in the South African National Defense Force (SANDF) (Ras, 2006, pp. 375–377). I recommend that something similar can be used in other countries.

Code of Conduct

- I pledge to serve and defend my client in accordance with the Constitution and the law and with honor, dignity, courage, and integrity.
- I serve in the private security industry with loyalty and pride, registered with PSIRA and trained according to the requirements of the SASSETA.
- I respect the life and dignity of any client with whom I have an agreement as well as those who may cross my way.
- I will not advance or harm the interests of any political party or organization.
- I accept personal responsibility for all my actions.
- I will treat all clients and people fairly and respect their rights and dignity at all times, regardless of race, ethnicity, gender, culture, language, or sexual orientation.
- I will obey and execute all lawful commands when operating as part of a bodyguard team and respect my superiors.
- I will refuse to obey an obviously illegal order from any team member.
- I will carry out my duties with courage and protect my client, even at the risk of my own life.
- I will respect and support subordinates and treat them fairly.
- I will not abuse my authority, position, or public funds for personal gain, political motives, or any other reason.
- I will report any criminal activity, corruption, and misconduct to the appropriate authorities and will not get involved in any form of malpractice or corruption.
- I will strive to improve the capabilities of the body guarding industry by maintaining discipline, safeguarding my client, developing my skills and knowledge, and performing my duties diligently and professionally.

- I will treat all information as strictly confidential and will reveal nothing about my client except when it is of a criminal or corrupt nature or when requested by a court of law to do so.
- I will constantly upgrade my existing qualifications through professional studies of an academic and technical nature that directly relate to body guarding.
- I will always make use of the principle of minimum force whenever the situation necessitates any implementation of force.
- In situations of armed conflict I will abide by the rules of international humanitarian law as contained in the Geneva conventions.
- I will promote the interest of the Professional Bodyguard Council of South Africa (PROBOCOSA) and will adhere to this Code of Conduct.

Final Remarks

While doing my research, I discovered that South Africa is not behind other first-world and developing countries in terms of private security and body guarding issues. In fact, I have acquainted myself with the literature, mainly coming from America, Europe, and Australia. Although I have an in-depth knowledge of all the rotten apples in the South African private security and body guarding industry, I am bold enough to say that I think that the South African private security industry has now become one of the world leaders in terms of private security legislation and training.

The introduction of the SASSETA that forces all officers to do skills training has made us a world leader in this regard—notwithstanding the fact that we have taken only the first few steps in this right direction. I believe that the safety of our geographical areas, whether it is a country town or a busy city, is directly linked to the proactive actions of our private security officers and bodyguards, and I believe that the higher competency levels and professionalism that these personnel reveal will dramatically reduce any type of crime in their vicinity.

References

Burger, F. J. (2006). Crime combating in perspective. A strategic approach to policing and the prevention of crime. *Acta Criminologica. Southern African Journal of Criminology, 19*(2), 105–118.

Butler, O. S. (2004). Personal conversation, 7 August, Amanzimtoti. Firearms, private security and bodyguard expert. Former lecturer of Department of Safety and Security Risk Management: UNISA.

Ferreira, V. M. (2005). Personal conversation, 26 November, Pretoria. He is a private security and firearms expert. Former staff member of Department of Safety and

Security, UNISA; Accredited-SASSETA-Assessor and Moderator. Director of Training Dynamics Africa.

Geldenhuys, K. (2005). Personal conversation, 5 November, Durban. Bodyguard and private security expert. Owner of Marko Security.

Geldenhuys, L. H. (2005). Personal conversation, 11 March, Howick. Private security, bodyguard and firearms expert. Owner of Tactical Protection Services; Member of VIPPASA (VIP Protection Association of South Africa); Accredited SASSETA and SAPS firearms instructor of KZN Midlands Training Academy.

http://reqs.saqa.org.za/viewUnitStandard.php?id=11510. Accessed on March 15, 2007.

https://www.cia.gov/cia/publications/factbook/geos/sf/htm. Accessed on March 25, 2007.

Le Roux, J. T. (2005). Personal conversation, 11 February. KZN-representative for VIP Protection Association of South Africa (VIPPASA); accredited SASSETA-Assessor and Moderator; accredited SAPS-firearms instructor; Director of Umvoti Training Academy.

Lonsdale, M. (1995). *Bodyguard. A Practical Guide to VIP Protection.* Los Angeles, California: STTU.

Meek, S. (2006). *African Security Review* 15(3). [African perspectives on the international terrorism discourse]. Pretoria: Institute of Security Studies.

Mhlongo, Z. P. (2005). Personal interview, 26 July, Empangeni. She is an accredited SASSETA-Assessor and Moderator for all firearm-related and bodyguard courses. Manager of Human Resources and Private Security Industry. Regulatory Authority (PSIRA) Training Instructor of Facasa Security, Empangeni.

Minnaar, A. (2006). Let's help protect the protectors. *Acta Criminologica. Southern African Journal of Criminology,* 19(2), i–ii.

Minnaar, A., & Ngoveni, P. (2004). The relationship between the South African Police Service and the Private Security Industry: Any role for outsourcing in the prevention of crime? *Acta Criminologica. Southern African Journal of Criminology,* 17(1), 42–65.

Pienaar, A. H. (1997). *High Risk Executive Protection.* Durban: Marko Printing.

Prinsloo, J. (2006). The impact of victimization on fear of crime. *Acta Criminologica. Southern African Journal of Criminology,* 19(2), 1–17.

Ras, J. M. (2003). *Police Patrols in South Africa.* (February). KwaDlangezwa: University of Zululand.

Ras, J. M. (2006). *Body guarding in a private security context.* Doctoral thesis. KwaDlangezwa: University of Zululand.

Ras, J. M. (2007). Police Officer Safety: "Please God! Help Us to Dodge the Bullets and the Blood and Give Us More Dogs in Zululand!" *Law Enforcement Executive Forum,* 7(3), 93–110. [Illinois Law Enforcement Training and Standards Board Executive Institute, Western Illinois University].

Rogers, S. L. (2007). Police Officer Safety. *Law Enforcement Executive Forum,* 7(3), 111–116. [Illinois Law Enforcement Training and Standards Board Executive Institute, Western Illinois University].

Rudolph, B. A., & Miguel, C. S. (2007). Traffic stops: Opportunities and old and new threats to Police Officer Safety. *Law Enforcement Executive Forum,* 7(3), 17–29. [Illinois Law Enforcement Training and Standards Board Executive Institute, Western Illinois University].

Standing, A. (2003). *Rival Views of Organised Crime.* (February). ISS Monograph Series. Pretoria: Institute for Security Studies.

Thorpe, W. (2005). Telephonic conversation, 7 December. He is a bodyguard and firearms expert and author of the manual: *Close Protection Operations Course: Student Manual* (1995).

Tyers, J. (2003). *Assessing Workplace Learning: Making Skills Work.* Randburg: Learning Performance Link.

Urbanization and Security: Moving Forward, Key Themes, and Challenges

25

JULIA DAVIDSON and ELENA MARTELLOZZO

Contents

This chapter provides a concluding summary of the key themes arising from the 14th annual International Police Executive Symposium (IPES) held in Dubai on April 8–12, 2007. It is clear from the contributions in this book that ongoing urbanization will continue to present security challenges in much of the world, not least in engaging with disaffected communities and at the same time addressing global organized crime. This chapter begins with a short section describing the law-enforcement work of the host city Dubai: "a city that easily combines on the one hand both modernity and progress, and on the other hand, security and safety" (Abdulla, 2007, p. 5). This chapter is a tribute to the Dubai Police.

Dubai and the Dubai Police

Dubai has developed since 1990 into a global and financial business hub. There are currently 68 projects underway, including, for example, the World Islands and Palm Islands developments. Dubai's society consists of nearly 200 nationalities from different backgrounds, religions, and traditions; yet it still enjoys harmony and peace. Indeed, Dubai has an exceptionally low level of recorded crime. This success has been achieved through the creation of a robust relationship between a powerful economy and good security and the necessity of effective collaboration between international police forces (Beyat,

2003). The work of the Dubai Police force is underpinned by key values: honesty, impartiality, politeness, and respect. The senior management recognizes the importance of an educated police force, have striven to eradicate illiteracy, and have supported an increasing number of officers in undertaking postgraduate study to masters and PhD level.

The work of the Dubai Police is underpinned by good research; more than 1,000 publications have been produced by the Dubai Decision Support Centre. The degree of organization and development of human resources is exceptional, as is the employment of information technology. Conference participants were afforded an opportunity to view the deployment of information technology in action during visits to the Police Operations Room of the Dubai Police General Headquarters, one of the most prestigious and advanced security projects in the Middle East. As commented by Colonel Eng. Kamel Buti Al Suwaidi (Barco, 2008), Deputy Director, General Department of Operation Dubai Police, the reason why they wanted to build a sophisticated command and control center was to enable a fast response and best management and control of their resources in order to contribute to a secure Dubai.

Conference Themes and Law-Enforcement Challenges

Engaging Communities

Developing a better understanding of communities has recently emerged as an aim in policing (Jones & Newburn, 2002). A clear theme emerged regarding the importance of understanding local communities, and particularly in attempting to "build bridges" with minority, vulnerable, and disaffected groups. The necessity of actively engaging with these communities was emphasized in many presentations via the training of police officers, outreach work, and good quality research that explore the perceptions of community groups regarding policing practice. This approach should serve to educate practitioners and to foster trust with community groups. The conference heard, for example, about the importance of working with Arab-Muslim communities in the United States to dispel media myths following 9/11, and the government has made funds available to the police and local authorities in the United Kingdom to stimulate better engagement with Muslim communities in order to foster greater tolerance and understanding and ultimately to combat violent extremism.

The concept of this form of community policing may have developed in the United States. According to Albrecht (2006), the continued trend in crime reduction (New York offers a particularly good example of this) is thought to be due to community policing strategies in the United States. This has led to the introduction of similar strategies in Europe in an effort to address rising crime rates and to assuage public unease about increased criminality. However, as Demir, Davidson, and Das (2009, p. 3) suggest, community policing policies can prove to be too idealistic and difficult to transplant into countries where urbanization takes a different form:

> It is crucial to analyze the success of this strategy in the United States and its latest evolution in order to infer what might happen globally in other countries where this strategy is employed, being mindful of the fact that the success of such initiatives when adopted by other countries, is partly dependent upon factors such as: the social structure; the prevailing culture and the specific policing culture.

Albrecht (2006) argues that despite the perceived success of community policing in Europe, it is being replaced by more effective computer analysis and proactive strategic deployment in the United States. It could however be argued that at a basic level, and given the particular challenges posed by urbanization, developing an understanding of local communities and their concerns in an effort to better engage is the cornerstone of good local policing in any geographical context. Speakers pointed to the importance of actively engaging with minority communities, of training police officers to incorporate community understanding and sensitivity into practice, and of opening a dialogue in the United States with Arab-Muslim communities in the wake of the 9/11 bombings in order to address negative media representations. The first stage in the dialog was identified as developing a better understanding of community perceptions and fears.

The importance of engaging with the local community was stressed by participants in diverse contexts. For example, the role of community policing in Nigeria as a response to rising criminality and lack of public confidence, and the challenges of policing in multiethnic countries such as Bosnia and Herzegovina were presented. Furthermore, scholars from South Africa discussed the dramatic changes that have occurred in their country in the past few years and stressed that part of the transformation of their society is the metamorphosis of the police: "the whole philosophy of policing, structure and culture has been affected. Probably the most significant change is the creation of community policing" (Moolman, 2007, p. V). The importance of effective community engagement has been raised by speakers at previous IPES meetings. Chang (2006), for example, suggested that through strategic engagement the police should mobilize the community and use it as a resource.

Global and National Problems: Shared Solutions

Conference presentations pointed to the importance of international police collaboration in addressing issues of urbanization and security. Many problems are shared and the responsibility of finding effective strategies and solutions is also a shared one. Speakers described, for example, the illegal trafficking of human beings, emphasizing the victimization of women and children who often suffer abuse and exploitation; drugs trafficking across geographical borders; and international fraud and cyber crime. These offenses are without geographical boundary and require an international, strategic police response that goes beyond the national. As Demir, Davidson, and Das (2009, p. 5) suggest:

> All nations, peoples, areas, and resources of the globe are getting closer, increasingly connecting together and becoming interlocked due to the effect of the process of globalization, which made the national borders more porous and vulnerable to infiltration and manipulation. Transnational crime in the various forms of drug trafficking, small and light arms smuggling, piracy, cyber crime, people smuggling, human trafficking, money-laundering, fraud, and terrorism, is clearly expanding and growing. There has always been a border crossing, spill over aspect of crime; however crimes have never before than in the last decades been a big transnational problem requiring effective cooperation.

Presenters also addressed the importance of situational factors and urban environmental design in crime prevention. Situational crime prevention originates from mainstream criminology and focuses on the fact that crime may be opportunistic and that preventing the occurrence of crime is paramount (Clarke, 1997). The positioning of street lighting and furniture, for example, can influence the location and extent of crime in an area, as can the general physical appearance of the physical environment. Some organizations provide advice on *designing out crime* such as the Designing Out Crime Association in the UK, a group of practitioners from a range of professions providing advice on making the physical environment safer (http://www. doca.org.uk/intro.asp). Colquhoun (2004) suggests that there is an interplay between offending behavior and the physical environment; this is seen as particularly relevant in opportunistic offending where the environment may support the commission of offending via poor street lighting or concealed public spaces, for example.

Many of these problems are global and demand international collaboration and international solutions, or at least the systematic sharing of *good practice* between law-enforcement agencies at the practice and policy level. However, presenters reminded participants that there are also significant differences in experience that reflect the context in which policing is conducted. Participants learned about the difficulty of practicing law enforcement in countries characterized by political instability such as Bosnia and Nigeria, where poverty is extreme and survival is difficult for much of the population. These countries often experience population displacement that can lead to high rates of crime. This is often accompanied by public mistrust of police regimes.

Presenters reminded participants that crime has many victims; the poor are more likely to be victims, and repeat victims, of crime for example. The fear of crime, and perhaps the reality of facing crime on a regular basis, has led to an increased demand for and a resulting growth in the private security sector in many countries such as South Africa. There is a limit to the amount of protection a police force can provide for individuals within a community, and the wealthier seek protection for their property and their families in an increasingly insecure world. As a consequence, there has been a considerable expansion in the private security market in many countries such as Bosnia and South Africa. The presenters suggested that there is an urgent need to review and consider the role of private security alongside that of traditional policing.

Relationship between Policing Practice and Research: Effective Sharing of Information

The role of effective intelligence-led and proactive policing based on good quality "scientific" research was a recurring theme in Dubai. Speakers suggested that if the challenges presented by urbanization and threats to security are to be effectively addressed, researchers must work on projects of *real* concern and relevance to police practitioners and policy makers, producing findings that will inform the development of policy, practice, and training. Speakers presented good examples of such research. Knowledge transfer is however a two-way process and researchers must first understand practice and consult with practitioners regarding research need, in order to undertake useful and meaningful research that will inform practice. It is also important for police practitioners to work with academics and researchers in undertaking postgraduate degrees and qualifications, many of which include a research methods component. This will equip practitioners with the necessary skills to undertake basic research projects and to publish findings.

Police forces represented by conference participants have shared interests and experiences, despite the many different cultural, geographical, and social contexts in which the forces operate. Some presenters suggested that there is a need to develop a better means of sharing information about effective practice and short summaries of research findings to better inform training and practice, particularly in the face of increased urbanization and threats to global security. IPES has begun this process by bringing researchers and practitioners together.

References

Abdulla, M. M. (2007, April 8–12). Dubai: A nonviolent emirate. Paper presented to the International Police Executive Symposium, Dubai, UAE.

Albrecht, J. (2006, May 26–30). Community policing and problem solving: Facing extinction in the USA; Migratory Survival in Europe. Paper presented to the International Police Executive Symposium, Ayvalik, Turkey.

Barco. (2008). Dubai Police General Headquarters: A paragon of control room technology. Brochure available on-line at http://www.barco.com/projection_systems/downloads/SMD_apl_Dubai_police_l.pdf

Beyat, M. R. (2003, August 10–15). The efforts of U.A.E. police research centres in crime prevention. Paper presented to the World Congress of Criminology, Rio de Janeiro, Brasil.

Chang, C. Y. (2006, May 26–30). Taiwan's strategy in fighting transnational crime. Paper presented to the International Police Executive Symposium, Ayvalik, Turkey.

Clarke, R. V. (Ed.). (1997). *Situational Crime Prevention: Successful Case Studies* (2nd ed.). NY: Harrow and Heston.

Colquhoun, I. (2004). *Design Out Crime: Creating Safe & Sustainable Communities.* Oxford, UK: Architectural Press.

Demir, S., Davidson, J., & Das, D. (2009 forthcoming). Local linkages to global security and crime: Thinking locally and acting globally. In E. W. Plywaczewski (Ed.), *Current Problems of Criminal Law.* Bialystock, Poland: Temida 2 Publishing House, Faculty of Law.

Jones, T., & Newburn, T. (2002). The transformation of policing? Understanding current trends in policing systems. *The British Journal of Criminology, 42,* 129–146.

Moolman, C. J. (2007). "Foreword" in Roelofse, C. J., *The Challenges of Community Policing: A Management Perspective.* Cape Town, SA: LexisNexis.

Index

International Police
Executive
Symposium (IPES)
www.ipes.info

The International Police Executive Symposium (IPES) was founded in 1994. The aims and objectives of the IPES are to provide a forum to foster closer relationships among police researchers and practitioners globally, to facilitate cross-cultural, international, and interdisciplinary exchanges for the enrichment of the law-enforcement profession, and to encourage discussion and published research on challenging and contemporary topics related to the profession.

One of the most important activities of the IPES is the organization of an annual meeting under the auspices of a police or educational institution. To date, meetings have been hosted by the Canton Police of Geneva, Switzerland (Police Challenges and Strategies, 1994), the International Institute of the Sociology of Law in Onati, Spain (Challenges of Policing Democracies, 1995), Kanagawa University in Yokohama, Japan (Organized Crime, 1996), the Federal Police in Vienna, Austria (International Police Cooperation, 1997), the Dutch Police and Europol in The Hague, The Netherlands (Crime Prevention, 1998), and Andhra Pradesh Police in Hyderabad, India (Policing of Public Order, 1999), and the Center for Public Safety, Northwestern University, Evanston, Illinois, USA (Traffic Policing, 2000). A special meeting was cohosted by the Bavarian Police Academy of Continuing Education in Ainring, Germany, University of Passau, Germany, and State University of New York, Plattsburgh, USA, to discuss the issues endorsed by the IPES in April 2000. The Police in Poland hosted the next meeting in May 2001 (Corruption: A Threat to World Order), and thereafter the annual meeting was hosted by the Police of Turkey in May 2002 (Police Education and Training). The Kingdom of Bahrain hosted the annual meeting in October 2003 (Police and the Community).

The 2004 meeting in May of that year (Criminal Exploitation of Women and Children) took place in British Columbia in Canada, and it was cohosted by the University College of the Fraser Valley, Abbotsford Police Department, Royal Canadian Mounted Police, the Vancouver Police Department, the Justice Institute of British Columbia, Canadian Police College, and the International

Centre for Criminal Law Reform and Criminal Justice Policy. The next meeting (Challenges of Policing in the 21st Century) took place in September 2005 in Prague, The Czech Republic. The Turkish National Police hosted the meeting in 2006 (Local Linkages to Global Security and Crime). The 14th IPES was held in Dubai on April 8–12, 2007 (Urbanization and Security). The 15th annual meeting was hosted in Cincinnati, Ohio by the City of Cincinnati Police and the Ohio Association of Chiefs of Police in Cincinnati on the theme of "Police without Borders: The Fading Distinction between Local and Global." The 16th annual meeting was hosted by the Republic of Macedonia in Ohrid on June 9–14, 2009 on the theme of "Policing, the Private Sector, Economic Development, and Social Change."

The majority of participants of the annual meetings are usually directly involved in the police profession. In addition, scholars and researchers in the field also participate. The meetings comprise both structured and informal sessions to maximize dialog and exchange of views and information. The executive summary of each meeting is distributed to participants as well as to a wide range of other interested police professionals and scholars. In addition, a book of selected papers from each annual meeting is published through Prentice Hall, Lexington Books, the Taylor & Francis Group and other reputed publishers.

Closely associated with the IPES is *Police Practice and Research: An International Journal (PPR)*. The journal is committed to highlighting current, innovative police practices from all over the world; providing opportunities for exchanges between police practitioners and researchers; reporting the state of public safety internationally; focusing on successful practices that build partnerships between police practitioners and communities, as well as highlighting other successful police practices in relation to maintaining order, enforcing laws, and serving the community. For more information visit our website www.ipes.info.

The IPES is directed by a board of directors representing various countries of the world:

President
Dilip K. Das, 6030 Nott Road, Guilderland, NY 12084, USA; Tel: 318 274 2520, Fax: 318 274 3101, e-mail: dilipkd@aol.com.

Vice President
Tariq Hassan Al Hassan, P.O. Box 13, Manama, Kingdom of Bahrain; Tel: (973) 17 756777, Fax: (973) 17 754302, e-mail: Ropac@batelco.com.bh.

Treasurer/Director
Jim Lewis, 406 Quail Lane, Ruston, Louisiana 71720, USA; Tel: 318 413-0551

Directors

Rick Sarre, GPO Box 2471, Adelaide 5001, South Australia; Tel: 61 8 84314879 (h), 61 8 83020889, Fax: 61 8 83020512, e-mail: rick.sarre@unisa.edu.au.

Tonita Murray, 73 Murphy Street, Carleton Place, Ontario K7C 2B7, Canada; Tel: 613 998 0883 (w), e-mail: tmurray@ca.inter.net.

Mark Chen, Professor, Central Police University, Taiwan, e-mail: mark@mail.cpu.edu.tw.

Snezana (Ana) Mijovic-Das, 6030 Nott Road, Guilderland, NY 12084, USA; Tel: 518 452 7845, Fax: 518 456 6790, e-mail: anamijovic@yahoo.com.

Horace Judson, P.O. Drawer 607, Grambling, LA 71245 USA; Tel: 318 274 6117, Fax: 318 274 6172, e-mail: judsonha@gram.edu.

Paulo R. Lino, 111 Das Garcas St., Canoas, RS, 92320-830, Brazil; Tel: 55 51 8111 1357, Fax: 55 51 466 2425, e-mail: paulino2@terra.com.bv.

Rune Glomseth, Police Superintendent, Norway Police University, Slemdalsveien5, Oslo, 0369, Norway; e-mail: Rune.Glomseth@phs.no.

Mustafa Ozguler, Chief of Police, Ankara, Turkey; e-mail: Mustafaozg@hotmail.com.

Maximillian Edelbacher, Riemersgasse 16/E/3, A-1190 Vienna, Austria; Tel: 43-1-601 74/5710, Fax: 43-1-601 74/5727, e-mail: edelmax@magnet.at.

IPES operates through active support, cooperation, and subscriptions of Institutional Supporters:

1. Dubai Police Department (Dr. Mohammed Murad Abdulla, Director), Decision-Making Support Center, P.O. Box 1493, Dubai, United Arab Emirates; Tel: 971 4 269 3790, Fax: 971 4 262 3233, e-mail: dxbpolrs@emirates.net.ae.
2. Bahrain Police (Lt. General Shaikh Rashed Bin Abdulla Al Khalifa, Minister of the Interior), P.O. Box 13, Manama, Kingdom of Bahrain; Tel: 973 17 270800, Fax: 973 17 253 266, e-mail: Colonel Tariq Hassan AL Hassan, Ropac@batelco.com.bh.
3. Fayetteville State University (Dr. David E. Barlow, Professor and Dean), College of Basic and Applied Sciences, 130 Chick Building, 1200 Murchison Road, Fayetteville, North Carolina, 28301 USA; Tel: 910-672-1659, Fax: 910-672-1083, e-mail: dbarlow@uncfsu.edu.
4. University of Hull (Dr. Bankole Cole, Director of Undergraduate Programmes, Department of Criminology and Sociological Studies), Cottingham Road, Hull HU6 7RX, UK; Tel: 01482 465669, e-mail: B.Cole@hull.ac.uk.

5. National Institute of Criminology and Forensic Science (Mr. D. M. Mitra, Inspector General of Police) MHA, Outer Ring Road, Sector 3, Rohini, Delhi 110085, India; Tel: 91 996 826 2008, Fax: 91 11 275 10586, e-mail: Johndm_mitra@yahoo.co.in.

6. Birmingham City University (Mike King), Center for Criminal Justice Policy and Research, Perry Barr, Birmingham B42 2SU, UK; Tel: 0121 3315163, Fax: 0121 3316938, e-mail: Mike.King@bcu.ac.uk.

7. Defendology Center for Security, Sociology and Criminology Research (Velibor Lalic), Srpska Street 63,78000 Banja Luka, Bosnia and Herzegovina; Tel and Fax: 387 51 308 914, e-mail: lalicv@teol.net.

8. University of Maribor (Dr. Gorazd Mesko), The Faculty of Criminal Justice and Security, University of Maribor, Kotnikova 8, 1000 Ljubljana, Slovenia; Tel: 386 1 300 83 39, Fax: 386 1 2302 687, e-mail: gorazd.mesko@fpvv.uni-mb.si.

9. Florida Gulf Coast University (Charlie Mesloh, PhD, Director), Weapons and Equipment Research Institute, 10501 FGCU Blvd S., Fort Myers, Fl 33965, USA; Tel: 239-590-7761 (office), Fax: 239-229-3462 (cellular), e-mail: cmesloh@fgcu.edu.

10. Ohio Association of Chiefs of Police (Chief Michael Laage), 6277 Riverside Drive, #2N, Dublin, Ohio 43017, USA; Tel: 614 761 0330, Fax: 614 718 3216, e-mail MLaage@springdale.org.

11. Kent State University Police Services (John A. Peach, Chief of Police), P.O. Box 5190, Stockdale Safety Building, Kent, Ohio, USA 44242-0001; Tel: 330 672 3111, e-mail: jpeach@kent.edu.

12. Abbotsford Police Department (Ian Mackenzie, Chief Constable), 2838 Justice Way, Abbotsford, British Columbia V2 T3 P5, Canada; Tel: 604-864-4809, Fax: 604-864-4725, e-mail: bobrich@abbypd.ca, swillms@abbypd.ca.

13. Department of Criminal Justice, North Carolina Central University, 301 Whiting Criminal Justice Bldg., Durham, NC 27707 USA (Dr. Harvey L. McMurray, Chair); Tel: 919-530-5204, 919 530 7909, Fax: 919-530-5195, e-mail: hmcmurray@nccu.edu.

14. University of the Fraser Valley (Dr. Darryl Plecas), Department of Criminology & Criminal Justice, 33844 King Road, Abbotsford, British Columbia V2 S7 M9, Canada; Tel: 604-853-7441, Fax: 604-853-9990, e-mail: Darryl.plecas@ucfv.ca.

15. National Police Academy, Japan, Koichi Kurokawa, Assistant Director, Police Policy Research Center, Zip 183-8558: 3-12-1 Asahi-cho Fuchu-city, Tokyo; Tel: 81 42 354 3550, Fax: 81 42 330 1308, e-mail: tcr01@npac.jp.

16. Canterbury Christ Church University (Claire Shrubsall), Department of Crime and Policing Studies, Northwood Road, Broadstairs,

Kent CT 10 2 WA, UK; Tel: 44 (0) 1843 609115, Fax: 44 (0) 1843 280700, e-mail: Claire.shrubsall@canterbury.ac.uk.

17. Police Standards Unit, Home Office (Stephen Cahill), 4th Floor Fry Building, 2 Marsham Street, London SW1P 4 DF, UK; Tel: 44 20 7035 0922, Fax: 44 870 336 9015, e-mail: Stephen.Cahill@homeoffice.gsi.gov.uk.

18. Royal Canadian Mounted Police (Gary Bass, Deputy Commissioner, Pacific Region) 657 West 37th Avenue, Vancouver, BC V5Z. 1K6, Canada; Tel: 604 264 2003, Fax: 604 264 3547, e-mail: gary.bass@rcmp-grc.gc.ca.

19. Eastern Kentucky University (Dr. Robin Haarr), Stratton Building 412A, Stratton Building, 521 Lancaster Avenue, Richmond, KY 40475 USA; Tel: 859-622-8152, e-mail: robin.haarr@eku.edu.

20. The Faculty of Law, University of Kragujevac, Serbia, (Prof. Branislav Simonovic), Str. Jovanba Cvijica 1, Kragujevac, Serbia 34000; Tel: 381 34 306 580, Fax: 381 34 306 546, e-mail: simonov@EUnet.yu.

21. Marc Dann, Attorney General, State of Ohio, (Jessica Utovich) State Office Tower, 30 E. Broad Street, 17th Floor, Columbus, OH 43215-3428; Tel: (614) 466-4320, e-mail: mdann@ag.state.oh.us, JUtovich@ag.state.oh.us.

22. The Ministry of Interior, P.O. Box 13320, Doha. Qatar (Contact Brigadier Al Kaabi Nasser Rashid); Tel: 250 552 6009. e-mail nasser55@windowslive.com.

23. The Cyber Defense & Research Initiatives, LLC, P.O. Box 86, Leslie, MI 49251 (Contact James Lewis); Tel: 517 242 6730, e-mail lewisja@cyberdefenseresearch.com.

24. Audiolex (Contact Kate J. Storey-Whyte, PhD), 9-10 Old Police Station, Kingston, Hereford, Herefordshire HR53DP, England; Fax: 44 154 423 1965, Mobile 44 7833 378 379.

25. The Department of Criminal Justice, Molloy College, 1000 Hempstead Avenue, P.O. Box 5002, Rockville Center, NY 11571-5002, USA (Contact Dr. John A. Eterno, NYPD Captain-Retired); Tel: 516 678 5000, Ext. 6135, Fax: 516 256 2289, e-mail: jeterno@molloy.edu.

26. The Senlis Council, Center of Excellence on Public Safety (George Howell) Rua Maria Queteria, 121/305, Ipanema, Rio de Janeiro, RJ 22410040, Brazil; Tel: 55 21 3903 9495, Cel: 55 21 8156 6485, e-mail: howell@senliscouncil.net.

27. The Department of Applied Social Studies, City University of Hong Kong (Li, Chi-mei, Jessica, PhD, Lecturer), Tat Chee Avenue, Kowloon Tong, Hong Kong; Tel: 2788 8839, Fax: 2788 8960, e-mail: jessica@cityu.edu.hk.

28. University of Maine at Augusta, College of Natural and Social Sciences (Professor Richard Mears), 46 University Drive. Augusta, ME 04330-9410, USA; e-mail: Rmears@maine.edu.